American Cinema of the 2010s

SCREEN
DECADES

AMERICAN CULTURE / AMERICAN CINEMA

Each volume in the Screen Decades: American Culture/American Cinema series presents a group of original essays analyzing the impact of cultural issues on the cinema and the impact of the cinema in American society. Because every chapter explores a spectrum of particularly significant motion pictures and the broad range of historical events in one year, readers will gain a continuing sense of the decade as it came to be depicted on movie screens across the continent. The integration of historical and cultural events with the sprawling progression of American cinema illuminates the pervasive themes and the essential movies that define an era. Our series represents one among many possible ways of confronting the past; we hope that these books will offer a better understanding of the connections between American culture and film history.

LESTER D. FRIEDMAN AND MURRAY POMERANCE
SERIES EDITORS

André Gaudreault, editor, *American Cinema 1890–1909: Themes and Variations*

Charlie Keil and Ben Singer, editors, *American Cinema of the 1910s: Themes and Variations*

Lucy Fischer, editor, *American Cinema of the 1920s: Themes and Variations*

Ina Rae Hark, editor, *American Cinema of the 1930s: Themes and Variations*

Wheeler Winston Dixon, editor, *American Cinema of the 1940s: Themes and Variations*

Murray Pomerance, editor, *American Cinema of the 1950s: Themes and Variations*

Barry Keith Grant, editor, *American Cinema of the 1960s: Themes and Variations*

Lester D. Friedman, editor, *American Cinema of the 1970s: Themes and Variations*

Stephen Prince, editor, *American Cinema of the 1980s: Themes and Variations*

Chris Holmlund, editor, *American Cinema of the 1990s: Themes and Variations*

Timothy Corrigan, editor, *American Cinema of the 2000s: Themes and Variations*

Dennis Bingham, editor, *American Cinema of the 2010s: Themes and Variations*

American Cinema of the

2010s

Themes and Variations

EDITED BY

DENNIS BINGHAM

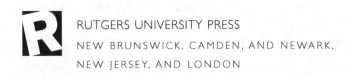

RUTGERS UNIVERSITY PRESS

NEW BRUNSWICK, CAMDEN, AND NEWARK,

NEW JERSEY, AND LONDON

LIBRARY OF CONGRESS CATALOGING-IN-PUBLICATION DATA

Names: Bingham, Dennis, 1954– editor.
Title: American cinema of the 2010s : themes and variations / edited by
    Dennis Bingham.
Description: New Brunswick : Rutgers University Press, [2022] | Series:
    Screen decades : American culture/American cinema | Includes
    bibliographical references and index.
Identifiers: LCCN 2021009097 | ISBN 9781978814837 (cloth) |
    ISBN 9781978814820 (paperback) | ISBN 9781978814844 (epub) |
    ISBN 9781978814851 (mobi) | ISBN 9781978814868 (pdf)
Subjects: LCSH: Motion pictures—United States—History—21st century. | Motion
    pictures—United States—Plots, themes, etc.
Classification: LCC PN1993.5.U6 A857955 2022 | DDC 791.430973/09051—dc23
LC record available at https://lccn.loc.gov/2021009097

A British Cataloging-in-Publication record for this book is available from the British Library.

www.rutgersuniversitypress.org

Manufactured in the United States of America

CONTENTS

CONTENTS

TIMELINE

2010s

2010

7 MARCH Kathryn Bigelow (*The Hurt Locker*, 2009) becomes the first woman to win the Academy Award for Best Director.

23 MARCH The Affordable Care Act (ACA, aka Obamacare) is signed into law by President Barack Obama, without any Republican votes in either house of Congress.

20 APRIL The Deepwater Horizon, a BP-leased oil well in the Gulf of Mexico, explodes, killing eleven workers. The spill is the worst in petroleum history, leaking oil at an estimated rate of 60,000 barrels a day and taking nearly five months to contain.

2 NOVEMBER In the U.S. midterm elections, Democrats lose sixty-three seats in the House of Representatives, throwing control to the Republicans. The new GOP class is known as the Tea Party.

17 DECEMBER Mohamed Bouazizi, a Tunisian street vendor, lights himself on fire to protest the arbitrary seizure of his vegetable stand by government authorities. This act, captured by the media, begins the Arab Spring, a series of uprisings leading to revolution or civil war in numerous Middle Eastern nations, including Tunisia, Egypt, Syria, and Libya.

22 DECEMBER "Don't Ask, Don't Tell," the 1993 legislation compromise that allowed gays to serve in the military as long as they kept their sexual orientation secret, is repealed. Now gays, lesbians, and bisexuals may openly serve in the U.S. Armed Forces.

2011

8 JANUARY U.S. Representative Gabrielle Giffords (D-Ariz.) is shot in the head, and six others are killed, at a meet and greet for constituents outside a supermarket in her district in Tucson, Arizona.

2 MAY Osama bin Laden, the terrorist mastermind behind the 9/11 attacks, is discovered hiding in a compound in Islamabad, Pakistan, and is killed in a raid by U.S. Special Forces.

25 MAY The final segment of *The Oprah Winfrey Show* airs, after twenty-five years and 4,561 episodes.

17 SEPTEMBER   Occupy Wall Street, a mass demonstration protesting income inequality, begins in Zuccotti Park in lower Manhattan and continues for two months.

5 OCTOBER   Steve Jobs, founder of Apple, dies at age fifty-six of a rare form of pancreatic cancer.

2012

4 MAY   *The Avengers*, the culminating film of Phase One of the Marvel Cinematic Universe, opens. It establishes the concept of the crossover narrative, interconnecting multiple characters and storylines from one film to the next.

30 AUGUST   Clint Eastwood, a speaker on the final night of the Republican National Convention in Tampa, Florida, creates one of the most talked about events of the campaign season. The actor-director turns a pro forma endorsement speech into a bizarre act of comedy improv, a dialogue with a chair, occupied by an imaginary President Obama.

22 OCTOBER   Hurricane Sandy forms in the Caribbean Sea. It affects twenty-four states, takes at least 233 lives, and causes $65 billion in damage in the United States alone.

30 OCTOBER   Disney announces its $4 billion purchase of Lucasfilm and its *Star Wars* and *Indiana Jones* franchises.

6 NOVEMBER   Barack Obama is reelected president of the United States, defeating former Massachusetts governor Mitt Romney.

14 DECEMBER   A twenty-year-old shooter enters Sandy Hook Elementary School in Newtown, Connecticut, killing twenty children and six adults before taking his own life.

2013

1 FEBRUARY   *House of Cards*, executive produced by David Fincher and starring Kevin Spacey and Robin Wright, premieres online as the first original series on Netflix.

13 MARCH   Jorge Mario Bergoglio, archbishop of Buenos Aires, is elected pope and takes the name Francis. He becomes the first Holy Father from the Americas.

15 APRIL   Two homemade bombs explode at the finish line of the Boston Marathon, killing three people and injuring several hundred others. The perpetrators, two Kyrgyz American brothers, are tracked down in four days in a manhunt involving federal, state, and local law enforcement.

6 JUNE   The *Guardian* and the *Washington Post* publish stories drawn from documents showing that the National Security Agency (NSA) spies on American citizens. The whistleblower, NSA employee Edward Snowden, reveals himself three days later in Hong Kong.

13 JULY   Black Lives Matter, an activist movement that fights institutionalized violence against African Americans, is founded in response to the acquittal of George Zimmerman in the fatal shooting of unarmed African American teenager Trayvon Martin in 2012.

25 DECEMBER   *The Wolf of Wall Street*, directed by Martin Scorsese, becomes the first major film delivered to exhibitors in digital form only.

2014

9 AUGUST   Michael Brown, an unarmed eighteen-year-old, is shot and killed by a police officer, Darren Wilson, on a street in Ferguson, Missouri, a St. Louis suburb. Days and nights of protests and violent confrontations follow. Ferguson is among the first of numerous incidents spotlighting the treatment of African Americans at the hands of police.

11 AUGUST   Beloved comedian and Academy Award–winning actor Robin Williams takes his life at age sixty-three.

19 AUGUST   A video posted on YouTube shows the beheading of U.S. journalist James Foley. It is the first of several similar atrocities by ISIS radicals posted to social media.

18 SEPTEMBER   In a referendum, the people of Scotland vote against declaring independence from the United Kingdom, 55 to 45 percent.

17 DECEMBER   President Obama announces the opening of normalization of relations with Cuba after fifty-five years.

2015

2 MARCH   The *New York Times* first reports that when Hillary Clinton was secretary of state (2009–2013), she used a personal email account for official business.

26 JUNE   Gay marriage becomes legal in the United States when the Supreme Court, in *Obergefell v. Hodges*, strikes down bans on same-sex marriage. The 5–4 opinion is written by Justice Anthony Kennedy, a Reagan appointee.

6 AUGUST   *Hamilton*, Lin-Manuel Miranda's sung- and rapped-through musical that tells the story of Alexander Hamilton with a multiracial cast, opens on Broadway.

12 DECEMBER   The Paris Agreement, reached at the end of the 21st Conference of the Parties, or COP 21, unites nearly 200 nations behind common goals: to adopt green energy sources, cut down on greenhouse gas emissions, and limit the rise of global temperatures.

2016

10 JANUARY   David Bowie dies of liver cancer two days after the release of his twenty-fifth studio album, *Blackstar*, which had been timed to coincide with the singer-songwriter's sixty-ninth birthday.

21 APRIL   Singer-songwriter Prince dies at fifty-seven of an accidental overdose of the opioid fentanyl.

23 JUNE   In a referendum, the electorate of the United Kingdom and Gibraltar vote, 52 to 48 percent, in favor of Brexit, the departure of the United Kingdom from the European Union.

27 AUGUST   Before the start of a preseason game, San Francisco 49ers quarterback Colin Kaepernick kneels during the singing of the National Anthem as a protest of police brutality against African Americans. Supportive at first, the NFL later buckles to financial pressure from fans. After Kaepernick becomes a free agent the following year, no team hires him, and he is effectively blacklisted.

7 OCTOBER   The Obama administration formally accuses Russia of cyberhacking intended to interfere with the U.S. elections of 2016.

7 OCTOBER   A 2005 backstage tape from the show *Access Hollywood* is released by NBC and posted on the *Washington Post*'s website. It reveals Republican presidential nominee Donald Trump making lewd remarks about women, which some say describe sexual assault. Despite calls by some Republicans for him to drop out, Trump remains the nominee.

13 OCTOBER   Bob Dylan wins the Nobel Prize in Literature.

28 OCTOBER   FBI director James Comey, who in June made an unusual public declaration of the bureau's decision not to prosecute Democratic presidential nominee Hillary Clinton after a probe of her emails, announces that he is reopening the investigation eleven days before the election.

1 NOVEMBER   The Chicago Cubs win the World Series in ten-inning Game 7 against the Cleveland Indians, breaking a 108-year drought, the longest in Major League Baseball.

8 NOVEMBER   Donald Trump, populist insurgent who won the Republican nomination, is elected president of the United States, defeating Hillary Clinton. The tally for the Electoral College is Trump 306, Clinton 232. Clinton wins the popular vote by more than 2.8 million.

2017

21 JANUARY   The Women's March, a worldwide series of protests against the inauguration of Trump the previous day, draws as many as 5 million people in cities across the United States and 7 million in other countries.

27 JANUARY   Trump signs an executive order banning travel into the United States from a handful of predominantly Muslim countries. The order, almost universally referred to as "the Muslim Ban," creates chaos in airports around the world and legal proceedings that continue for the next seventeen months.

24 FEBRUARY   Universal Pictures releases *Get Out*, a satirical horror film that flips the genre's script, placing a black male (Daniel Kaluuya) as the character in jeopardy. The writing-directing debut of comedian Jordan Peele, *Get Out*, made by Blumhouse Productions for $4.5 million, becomes a critical and commercial milestone, grossing approximately forty times its cost and launching a Black filmmaking renaissance in Hollywood.

9 MAY   Trump fires FBI director James Comey. The stated rationale concerns the handling of Hillary Clinton's emails, but the more compelling reason seems to be the bureau's investigation of Russian interference in the 2016 elections.

17 MAY   Deputy Attorney General Rod Rosenstein, in charge of the Russia probe after the self-recusal of Attorney General Jeff Sessions, appoints Robert Mueller, former FBI director (2001–2013), as special counsel to investigate Russian meddling in the election and possible links to the Trump campaign.

12 AUGUST   A rally in Charlottesville, Virginia, by far-right groups protesting the planned removal of a statue honoring Robert E. Lee quickly flares into violence. The melee culminates in the death of Heather Heyer, a counterprotester, when a neo-Nazi demonstrator drives his car into a crowd. Trump, asked for comment, replies that there were "very fine people on both sides."

5 OCTOBER   "Harvey Weinstein Paid Off Sexual Harassment Accusers for Decades," states a front-page story in the *New York Times* by Jodi Kantor and Megan Twohey. Ten days later, Alyssa Milano tweets: "If you've been sexually harassed or assaulted write 'me too' as a reply to this tweet." The more than 19 million replies to #MeToo over the next year signal a cultural sea change.

2018

16 FEBRUARY   *Black Panther*, the first movie based on the 1966 Marvel comic series set in Wakanda, a fictional African country that was never colonized, opens to blockbuster box office earnings and nearly universal acclaim.

26 APRIL   Bill Cosby is convicted of the 2004 drugging and sexual assault of a Philadelphia woman. He is later sentenced to three to ten years in prison.

15 JUNE   The U.S. Department of Homeland Security confirms that nearly 2,000 children have been separated from their parents since Attorney General Jeff Sessions announced a "zero tolerance" policy on illegal border crossings.

25 AUGUST   John McCain, six-term senator from Arizona and 2008 Republican presidential nominee, dies of cancer at eighty-one. McCain's family does not invite President Trump, who instigated a feud with McCain during his own presidential campaign in 2016, to the funeral.

6 NOVEMBER   In the U.S. midterm elections, Democrats win forty-one Republican-held seats, taking the majority in the House of Representatives. Of the new members of the House, over 60 percent are women.

2019

3 JANUARY   Nancy Pelosi (D-Calif.), the only female speaker of the house in U.S. history, retakes the gavel after eight years in the minority, as the 116th Congress opens session.

12 MARCH   The U.S. Department of Justice announces the arrest of some fifty wealthy parents, including actresses Lori Loughlin and Felicity Huffman, in a college admissions cheating and bribery scandal involving numerous elite universities, including Yale, Stanford, Georgetown, and the University of Southern California.

20 MARCH   The Walt Disney Company completes its acquisition of 21st Century Fox, including the film and television production

divisions but excluding Fox News, Fox Sports, and the Fox Television Network.

18 APRIL The report of Special Counsel Robert Mueller's two-year investigation into Russian meddling reaches Congress and the public in a version heavily redacted by the office of Attorney General William Barr.

20 SEPTEMBER A whistleblower in the U.S. intelligence community files a complaint about a phone call on 25 July between President Trump and President Volodymyr Zelensky of Ukraine. In the conversation, Trump asks Zelensky to find information about business dealings that Hunter Biden, son of former vice president Joseph Biden, had in Ukraine. At the same time, $400 million of U.S. military aid to Ukraine is frozen, creating the appearance of a quid pro quo. Four days later, Speaker of the House Pelosi announces the opening of a formal impeachment inquiry.

23 SEPTEMBER Greta Thunberg, a sixteen-year-old climate activist from Sweden, speaks at the United Nations Climate Action Summit. "How dare you?," she asks the representatives of world powers, "you have stolen my childhood." Thunberg appears on the cover of *Time* as the magazine's Person of the Year.

19 DECEMBER The U.S. House votes, mostly along party lines, to impeach Donald Trump for abuse of power and obstruction of Congress. A trial in the Senate is set to begin in January.

31 DECEMBER The Municipal Health Commission in Wuhan, China, reports an outbreak of a pneumonia of unknown origin. Within two weeks, the World Health Organization (WHO) issues guidance on the novel coronavirus, COVID-19.

American Cinema of the 2010s

INTRODUCTION

Movies and the 2010s

DENNIS BINGHAM

Although the 2010s were perhaps the most tumultuous decade since the 1960s, I predict that, over time, the 2010s will be seen as a decade without a strong identity of its own. The effects of the Great Recession of 2007–2009 lingered in many parts of the country for much of the following decade. Mass shootings, school murders, and apparently racially motivated killings of Blacks by police officers split the nation apart. Unabated global climate change continued, but with 17 percent of the American population, the most in the Western world according to a 2019 poll, continuing to deny and even rebuff international attempts to address it (Brackett).

In contrast, the 2000s evoke memories of the long-anticipated turn of the millennium. These were overtaken by the 9/11 attacks, the War on Terror, and the ongoing conflicts in Iraq and Afghanistan. Waiting at the end was the Great Recession, the worst economic downturn since the Great Depression, beginning in December 2007 and ending, according to economists, in July 2009. The 2008 election of Barack Obama, the first African American president of the United States, remained enormously consequential throughout the 2010s. Obama was re-elected in 2012, and presided over the Recession and recovery, directed the successful attack on Osama bin Laden (the architect of the 9/11 attacks), and governed amid painful schisms that rocked the country.

Through much of the 2010s, the person on the street would tell you that the Recession hadn't ended at all. Walking through average middle-class neighborhoods in many American cities until midway through the decade, one passed abandoned or foreclosed houses. Collateral evidence, such as pets gone astray or let loose by their owners, was everywhere in these years. Such experiential evidence, borne out in statistics, shows unemployment not shrinking to pre-Recession levels until 2015; real median household income did not surpass the pre-2007 mark until 2016 (Chappelow). Property values in many parts of the country—especially the Northeast and Midwest—took until past the middle of the decade to recover.

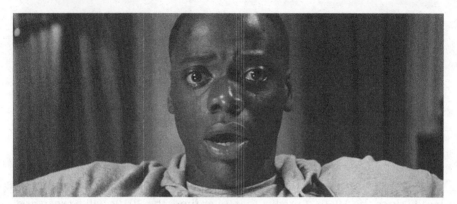

Get Out (Jordan Peele, Blumhouse, Universal, 2017). A month after Donald Trump's inauguration, comedian Peele's writing-directing debut opens. A horror satire reminiscent of earlier eras of cinephilia, it establishes twin waves of new Black American film and horror art cinema. Digital frame enlargement.

For example, in February 2006, my wife and I took out a new mortgage on our house in the neighborhood where we had lived since 1993 and where we expected 6 percent growth in property value annually. We were stunned, therefore, to learn in May 2009 that our home value had collapsed and our mortgage was underwater. It took years for a reappraisal to show that we finally owed less on the house than what it was worth. And we were not alone. The month of that positive reappraisal—November 2016—was more than coincidental. The election of Donald Trump was unquestionably the cataclysmic event of the second half of the 2010s, and, like the Great Recession, it set countless mini-effects rumbling in its wake. Many of these, years overdue, came about as a result of the decline of many sectors of society and the failure of millions to feel the recovery that economists, politicians, and other experts kept saying was underway.

The enactment of the American Recovery and Reinvestment Act by the new Obama Administration and Congress in February 2009 reversed the failure of the economy in the Recession (Chappelow). A 2019 report by the Center on Budget and Policy Priorities (CBPP) explains that the "Recession put the economy in a deep hole." This is because "the Great Recession created an unusually large and long-lasting gap between actual and potential GDP [Gross Domestic Product]." This "output gap" "was manifested in substantial excess unemployment and underemployment and idle productive capacity among businesses" (*Chart Book*). Huge numbers of jobs were lost in the Recession; the economy took until mid-2014 to recreate the 8.7 million jobs lost between 2007 and 2010 (*Chart Book*). As late as the end of 2017, more people were unemployed than there were job openings. The impacts of the Recession, together with the longer-lasting effects of globalization, beginning with the passage of the North American Free Trade Agreement (NAFTA) in 1993 and the normalization of trade with China, resulted in millions of manufacturing jobs being lost and blue-collar union voters feeling bereft and betrayed (Stockman SR 4). Few facets of the culture were not shaken and changed—perhaps permanently—by the Great Recession, although it feels too early to pronounce such historical insight; indeed, the aftershocks of the Great Recession may ultimately seem like nothing compared to the devastating economic avalanche generated by the novel coronavirus.

The Great Recession significantly affected, perhaps permanently, two industries relevant to this book: higher education, specifically the liberal arts, and the entertainment business. The change from film to digital, the most significant event of the first half of the decade, was on its way regardless. However, home video sales, which had Hollywood riding high since the introduction of video cassette recorders and tapes in the early 1980s, followed by DVDs in the late 1990s, had begun its irreversible descent by the start of the 2010s. The foreseeable end of the video disc is found in *Guardian* reporter Adam Sherwin's comparison of DVDs and Blu-rays in 2010 to the long-dead LP record—and this in a story about a mere 12.6 percent sales decline in 2009 and 2010 combined. Flash forward to a CNBC story nine years later pronouncing the demise of the physical video format, with an 86 percent fall in sales since 2008. Pictures tell the story. Sherwin's report is accompanied by a shot of video store shelves stocked with product. Sarah Whitten's 2019 story, devastatingly, has a photo of DVDs dumped into a Walmart cut-out bin, selling for the low, low price of $3.74. Streaming, like digital cinema, had been on its way and probably would have surged anyway, as all new technologies do when it's their time. But the section of the entertainment economy that mourned the loss of revenue from DVDs desperately needed replacement income, and streaming, it seems, was that new entertainment form.

Much more worrying was the downturn in higher education in the 2010s. Again, figures tell the story. Total undergraduate enrollment in the United States increased by 37 percent (from 13.2 million to 18.1 million students) between 2000 and 2010, but fell by 8 percent (from 18.1 million to 16.6 million students) between 2010 and 2018 ("Condition of Education"). Part of the decline was due, paradoxically, to the revived employment economy after 2010. This is a familiar pattern: lower employment sends people back to school to work on degrees to make themselves more employable. However, declines in enrollment in the liberal arts, especially the humanities, persisted throughout the decade, even after other disciplines, especially the vaunted STEM fields, rebounded. Small liberal arts colleges around the country merged or closed. While state colleges and universities may have taken up the slack, the unrelenting fall in allotments of state budgets to public colleges, the inability of students and families to pay tuition without going into levels of debt unimagined by their professors a few decades before, and the increasingly essential nature of a college education created a multifaceted bind from which there must be some release—but what?

The Politics of the 2010s

A decade that began with the second year of the administration of Barack Obama, the first African American president, ended with the third year of the presidential term of Donald Trump, a billionaire real estate developer and reality TV celebrity, the first president lacking any governmental or military experience. That Obama was succeeded by Trump, an authoritarian wannabe and admirer of autocrats, who spouted—or more precisely, tweeted—racial bigotry, sexism, misstatements (the *New York Times*, the nation's "newspaper of record," resolved to call them "lies"), and xenophobia, demonstrated divisions beyond what many Americans had been willing to admit. The country split along lines of race, gender and sexual identity, economic inequality, and educational background. How one felt about the nation, moreover, probably depended on whether one was a city dweller or a rural resident and whether one lived in the vast American heartland, from Pennsylvania to Nevada, of whose electoral votes Trump in 2016 won all but fifty, or in one of the northern states on or near the two coasts, of whose 178 electoral votes Hillary Clinton, the Democratic nominee, took all but one (the last being in Maine, which apportions its electoral votes by Congressional district).

Politically, the decade saw the polarization that had been increasing since the "Reagan Revolution" of the 1980s widen to a chasm that many felt threatened America's constitutional democracy in fundamental ways. The coalition that supported Barack Obama in the election of 2008 evaporated in the midterm Congressional election of 2010, returned in force to re-elect Obama in 2012, and then vanished again in 2014, while conservatives poured out. The result was an obstinate Republican "Tea Party" majority in the House of Representatives in 2011 and a matching Senate GOP majority in 2015. Obama's inability to legislate with an uncooperative Congress that was uninterested in democratic compromise (and uninterested, many thought, in government itself) resulted in events such as the 2011 "cliff-hanger," breathlessly covered by the political media, over whether or not the Congress would vote to lift the debt ceiling, enabling Congress to fund the government.

From Obama to Trump

The election of Barack Obama to the presidency seemed destined since his breakout on the national stage as the keynote speaker at the Democratic National Convention in 2004. "There is not a liberal America and a conservative America," the then state senator running for U.S. senator proclaimed, "there is the United States of America." From that time on, Obama represented unity, and by the time he was the Democratic presidential nominee four years later, the War on Terror–fatigued country embraced the "hope and change" of a "postpartisan," "postracial" era. But it was not to be. While Obama hoped for bipartisan cooperation, "the strategy of the Republicans," said Obama advisor Valerie Jarrett, was "to make him a polarizing figure, to try to separate him from the American people who elected him, to try to make him the problem as opposed to the solution" (Breslow).

The victory of Donald Trump in the presidential election of November 2016 was unexpected—and that is an understatement. It echoed, however, that June's "Brexit" vote in favor of the United Kingdom's withdrawal from the European Union; it also crystallized the cultural divisions in America that grew more obvious as the decade wore on. Trump, a fixture of reality TV, first entered the political arena in 2011 with the "birther" conspiracy theory, a media campaign alleging that the first African American president was born not in the United States but in Kenya. Trump "did not create the ugliness," Matt Bai of the *Washington Post* said to *Frontline*. "He did not create the Twitter social media universe. He did not create the xenophobia, the nationalism, the backlash against globalism and global crusades. He did not create entertainment politics, politics as a form of reality show television. He created none of this. He is its pure manifestation. The absolute, logical endpoint of a bunch of trends in American life." (Breslow).

The election of Trump, who was alleged to have abused women, and whose victory itself was aided by Russian hackers, drew furious reactions. "Trump won only by a fluke," wrote David Frum, the most prolific of the "Never Trump" Republicans. "He won without a popular mandate. He won with clandestine assistance from the Russian intelligence services. He won only after a six-year effort to block African Americans from voting. But win he did—and Republicans for a long time to come will have to reckon with the odium of his presidency" (*Trumpocalypse* 182).

Trump's election, furthermore, launched social activism, such as the Women's Marches on the day after Trump's inauguration and on its anniversary each subsequent year in the decade. These demonstrations led to an influx of women, minorities, and millennials (those born between 1980 and 1996) into politics. The upsurge made itself felt in the "Blue Wave" of 2018, the strong showing of Democrats in that year's midterm Congressional and state elections. Voter turnout rose dramatically in that year, from 39 percent in the 2010 midterms and 36.4 percent in the midterms of 2014 (the lowest since 1942) to 49.3 percent in 2018. Forty-one House seats flipped from the Republicans to the Democrats, putting Democrats in control of the House of Representatives for the first time in eight years. Nancy Pelosi, who had served from 2007 to 2011 as the first female speaker of the house, was once again elected to take up the gavel.

Media: Falling off an Analog

The 2010s may be remembered as the decade in which the change from analog to digital—from a culture of physical media to an entirely virtual, streaming one—was realized and nearly completed in ways that touched most people's lives. Many magazines, including *Newsweek*, *Redbook*, *Jet*, and *Glamour*, ceased print publication and came out only in digital form. *Entertainment Weekly* cut back from a weekly to a monthly (but kept its name). Time Inc, founded by Henry Luce in 1924, spun off from Time Warner, a merger that broke apart in 2014 after twenty-three uneasy years. The *Time* magazines, including *Sports Illustrated*, *People*, *Fortune*, and *Money*, were bought by Meredith in 2017. Time Warner, including Warner Bros., DC Comics, CNN, TNT, and TBS, was purchased by AT&T in a sale concluded in June 2018. Also in 2018, Marc Benioff, owner and CEO of Salesforce, a cloud-based software firm, bought, with his wife Lynne, *Time* magazine, stating a year later that he had hoped to address "a crisis of trust" (Duffy, Stetler). Five years before, in 2013, Jeff Bezos, owner of Amazon, purchased the *Washington Post* from the Graham family, its longtime owners. By the end of the decade, Bezos had turned the *Post*, its Watergate glory days far behind it, "from a local print-focused publication to a globally recognized digital brand" (Giuliani-Hoffman).

In technology, the most influential innovation was the Apple iPad, introduced in 2010, the year before the death of Apple founder Steve Jobs at age fifty-six. The iPad combined the portability of a cell phone with the storage and speed of a personal computer, but was lighter and less cumbersome than a laptop. In 2014, Amazon brought out the Alexa, the science fiction–like personal assistant that brought all our desires a voice command away (and is parodied as "Olivia" in Jordan Peele's *Us*, in which "she" mishears "Call the police" as "F*** tha Police" by N.W.A. and proceeds to play the song). Other new tech of the decade included the photo apps Instagram and Snapchat, the ultrapopular game Minecraft, the e-sports platform Twitch, the ride-hailing apps and services Uber and Lyft, the company chat platform Slack, the electric car Tesla Model S, the Apple Watch, the Oculus VR headset, the streaming services Chromecast, Roku, and Apple Firestick (any one of which allows former cable TV subscribers to "cut the cord" and stream channels individually instead of paying for costly cable packages), and the Xbox Adaptive Controller for players with disabilities (Marvin; Turakhia).

The quickening decline of newspapers, which began in the 2000s amid the popularity of the internet and was hastened by the Great Recession, continued throughout the 2010s as advertising and subscriptions slumped. Americans consumed their news mostly from politically and culturally inclined websites, such as *Politico*, *Salon*, *Slate*, *The Huffington Post*, and *Vox*, and traditional newspaper websites, such as those for the *New York Times*, the *Wall Street Journal*, and the aforementioned *Post*, as well as social media and television. The *Village Voice*, the nation's first alternative newspaper, ceased publication in 2017. For decades, the *Voice* functioned as a crucial source for investigative journalism and, significantly, cutting-edge film criticism—the pulpit from which Andrew Sarris propounded auteurism. J. Hoberman's reviews of less heralded avant-garde and experimental films also emanated from a perch at the *Voice*. The internet completed its takeover of centuries of traditions in other ways too. Except in a few fortunate locations, the bookstore ceased to be a place where a reader could browse through books, no matter how obscure, with the closure in 2011 of the Borders bookstore chain in the United States, the United Kingdom, and Australia. Scenes from *Wonderstruck* (2017) and *Can You Ever Forgive Me?* (2018) of bookstores packed from ceiling to floor with books, which would have been unremarkable even a decade earlier, were achingly nostalgic toward the end of the 2010s. (But New York City's Strand Book Store still survives and, we hope, prospers!)

Broadway: The *Hamilton* Decade

Without question, the most significant theatrical event of the decade—perhaps even of the past few decades—was *Hamilton*, the entirely rapped- and sung-through musicalization of Ron Chernow's 2003 biography of founding father Alexander Hamilton. "The show bleeds the spirit of the Obama era in terms of its tolerance and multiculturalism," said Chernow in 2017, pronouncing himself "flabbergasted" at what Lin-Manuel Miranda made of his book (Butter). Multihyphenate Miranda, who wrote the book, music, and lyrics and starred as Hamilton, conceived of the play as a showcase for actors of color, who play the founding fathers. The only white performers play King George III and his courtiers. Opening first at the Public Theater in Greenwich Village in February 2015, and moving six months later to the Richard Rodgers Theatre, *Hamilton* became a phenomenon, an instant sold-out smash, with the Broadway production commanding $500 (for the "cheap seats") to $3,000 a ticket. Nick Hanson in 2018 attributed the high price to the need to counteract "resellers/scalpers" who "charge five times the face value of the tickets." For *Hamilton*'s creators, reported Amanda Harding in 2019, "the last thing they want is for their show to only be attended by the rich and elite." Thus they invented Ham-4Ham, a daily lottery for ten-dollar tickets.

The show was credited with bringing young people to live theater, with spillover effects that benefited the theater world in general. The two-CD Original Broadway Cast (OBC) album was certified eight times Multi-Platinum, having sold over eight million copies as of May 2021 (Recording Industry Association). This makes the *Hamilton* OBC by far the highest-selling Broadway cast album of all time, having more than doubled the sales of decades-old albums like *My Fair Lady* (its second OBC, in stereo, 1959), *The Phantom of the Opera*, and *Les Misérables* (both 1987) in a matter of a few years. As of the end of 2019, the Angelica, Philip, and Peggy tours, named after characters in the show, played concurrently across the United States, in addition to a production in Chicago that ran from October 2016 to January 2020 and the continuing Broadway run. A production toured in Canada, and one debuted on the West End in London in December 2017, which continues to run. The show's director, Thomas Kail, made a film of the Broadway production in June 2016, months after Miranda was announced the winner of the year's Pulitzer Prize for Drama (only the seventh time the prize went to a musical), weeks after the show won eleven Tonys, and before the original cast, including Leslie Odom Jr., Renée Elise Goldsberry, and Phillipa Soo, began to depart. The film was sold to Disney and was scheduled for theatrical release in October 2021. Instead, it premiered on the Disney+ streaming service on the Fourth of July weekend in 2020 and became a rare pandemic blockbuster, with 37 percent of all streaming video downloads in the month of July attributed to *Hamilton* (the second place–holder had 13 percent) (Tran).

Other significant Broadway shows of the decade included: *The Addams Family* (2010); *An American in Paris* (2015); *Anastasia* (2017); *Beetlejuice* (2019); *Be More Chill* (2019); *The Book of Mormon* (2011); *Come from Away* (2017); *Dear Evan Hansen* (2016); *Fun Home* (2015); *Hadestown* (2019); *Violet* (2014); *Matilda the Musical* (2013); *Mean Girls* (2018); *Moulin Rouge! The Musical* (2019); *Natasha, Pierre & the Great Comet of 1812* (2016); *The Prom* (2018); *Something Rotten!* (2015); *Waitress* (2016); *American Idiot* (2010); *The Scottsboro Boys* (2010); *A Gentleman's Guide to Love & Murder* (2013); and *The Band's Visit* (2017).

Sports in the Decade

Lance Armstrong, once the most celebrated cyclist of all time, who came back from Stage III testicular cancer in 1997 to win seven Tours de France, was found guilty in a 2012 investigation by the U.S. Anti-Doping Agency of having used illegal substances. The *Union Cycliste Internationale* stripped him of all his post–August 1998 titles. Armstrong confessed publicly in January 2013 in a two-part, prime-time ABC interview with Oprah Winfrey. Other star athletes who fell into disgrace in the 2010s were Aaron Hernandez of the New England Patriots, who was convicted of murder in 2015 and hanged himself in his prison cell in 2017, and South African sprinter Oscar Pistorius, who was convicted in 2015 of murdering his girlfriend. Legendary Major League Baseball players Manny Ramirez and Roger Clemens ended their careers in doping scandals. A notorious Olympic athlete, figure skater Tonya Harding, became the subject of a biopic, *I, Tonya* (see the chapter on 2017).

In the National Basketball Association, Kobe Bryant won the last of his five championships with the Los Angeles Lakers in 2010, when the Lakers defeated their most iconic rival, the Boston Celtics, four games to three. The Miami Heat, with its newly assembled "Big Three" of LeBron James, Dwyane Wade, and Chris Bosh, went to the finals in four straight years, 2011–2014. It won two of those, against the Oklahoma City Thunder in five games in 2012, and against the San Antonio Spurs in seven games in 2013. After the Heat's six-game loss to the Spurs in 2014, James returned to the Cleveland Cavaliers. In 2015, the Golden State Warriors, led by Stephen Curry and Klay Thompson, commenced a dynastic run, progressing to the finals every year for the rest of the decade. From 2015 to 2018, they met James's Cavs, who managed to defeat the Warriors just once, in 2016, when the Cavs became the first team in the then sixty-nine-year history of the finals to win after trailing one game to three. They became the first team in thirty-eight years to win Game Seven on the road, and the first professional team in fifty-two years from Cleveland to win a championship. This story becomes even more outlandish when paired with the performance of the Chicago Cubs later the same year, who became only the sixth team and the first since 1985 to overcome a 1–3 deficit in the World Series. And it was against a Cleveland team, the Indians, which last won a World Series in 1948, that the Cubs captured their first pennant since 1908, dousing the longest drought in American professional sports.

In the National Football League, the New England Patriots, led by coach Bill Belichick and quarterback Tom Brady, added three Super Bowl championships, in 2015, 2017, and 2019, and two losses, in 2012 and 2018, to the three championships and one loss they had racked up in the 2000s. For the first time, the American (AFC) and National (NFC) Conferences achieved parity, each winning five Super Bowls in the decade. The United States Women's Soccer Team (USWST) won the Olympic Gold Medal in London in 2012, and the FIFA Women's World Cup in 2015 and 2019. Of the twelve teams in the Women's National Basketball Association (WNBA), the Minnesota Lynx were the most dominant during the decade, advancing to the finals six times and winning four, in 2011, 2013, 2015, and 2017.

In Memoriam

The 2010s saw the deaths of some of the most important contemporary film critics, including Andrew Sarris, Roger Ebert, Stanley Kauffmann, Richard Corliss, and Richard Schickel, increasing the sense that the age of cinephilia, which each of them had represented in significant ways, had itself passed away. Filmmakers who died in the decade make up a virtual who's who of the cinema of the 1960s, 1970s, 1980s, and beyond: Blake Edwards, Arthur Penn, Ken Russell, Sidney Lumet, Dede Allen, Paul Mazursky, Milos Forman, John G. Avildsen, Gordon Willis, Michael Cimino, Peter Yates, Mike Nichols, Richard Attenborough, Bernardo Bertolucci, Alain Resnais, Jonathan Demme, Věra Chytilová, William A. Fraker, Tony Scott, Garry Marshall, Penny Marshall, Lorenzo Semple Jr., and John Singleton. Actors lost included Peter O'Toole, Jean Simmons, Tony Curtis, Leslie Nielsen, Dennis Hopper, Jill Clayburgh, Patricia Neal, Lynn Redgrave, Lena Horne, Kathryn Grayson, Doris Day, Shirley Temple Black, Burt Reynolds, Mary Tyler Moore, Debbie Reynolds, Carrie Fisher, Gene Wilder, Robin Williams, Roger Moore, Mickey Rooney, James Gandolfini, Andy Griffith, Elizabeth Taylor, Luke Perry, Bill Paxton, Lauren Bacall, Anton Yelchin, Alan Rickman, and James Garner. Marvel Comics founder Stan Lee, who made a cameo appearance in all movies of the Marvel Cinematic Universe, ending with *Avengers: Endgame* (2019), died in 2018. Among musicians who passed away were Prince, David Bowie, Amy Winehouse, Aretha Franklin, Tom Petty, B. B. King, George Michael, Whitney Houston, Natalie Cole, and Chuck Berry.

Movies: Uniters, not Dividers?

Against what in a Hollywood historical drama would be termed a backdrop, the film industry made movies seemingly without regard for whether they would be seen by those in red (Republican) states or blue (Democratic) states. Even a Rorschach test like *American Sniper*, Clint Eastwood's surprise blockbuster biopic and Iraq War film from the end of 2014, drew sellout crowds in coastal cities such as New York and Los Angeles as well as red state centers like Dallas and Atlanta. It seemed that tentpole franchises, especially the *Star Wars* reboots that began appearing in 2015 following the 2012 sale of Lucasfilm to Disney, attracted audiences regardless of where they stood along socioeconomic political divides. Films like Jordan Peele's *Get Out* (2017) and *Us* (2019), each of which grossed $185 million in the United States, encouraged the whites in their audiences to experience their horrors from the critical point of view of an African American satirist.

One could say that movies continued to be uniters rather than dividers, except to the extent that the independent film sector, weakened since the 2008 financial crash, continued to offer niche audiences alternatives to the broad tentpole franchises. Auteurs like Todd Haynes (*Carol*, 2015), Wes Anderson (*Moonrise Kingdom*, 2012; *The Grand Budapest Hotel*, 2014; *Isle of Dogs*, 2018), Paul Thomas Anderson (*The Master*, 2012; *Inherent Vice*, 2014; *Phantom Thread*, 2017), and Joel and Ethan Coen (*Inside Llewyn Davis*, 2013; *Hail, Caesar!*, 2016), releasing mostly through the semi-indies, attracted audiences to their films. Long-standing auteurs working on bigger canvases for the major studios continued through the 2010s. Martin Scorsese released five very divergent films—*Shutter Island* (2010), a psychological thriller; *Hugo* (2011), a children's film in 3D hinging upon Georges Méliès as well as Scorsese's longtime film preservation project; *The Wolf of Wall Street* (2013), the outlandish biopic of criminal trader Jordan Belfort, and Scorsese's fifth collaboration with Leonardo DiCaprio; *Silence* (2016), a long-planned religious epic about Portuguese missionary priests in Japan in the 17th century who are forced to recant; and *The Irishman*, an elaborate gangster saga, made for Netflix (see the chapter on 2019).

Clint Eastwood, who turned eighty in 2010, directed eight films in the decade—his average amount—with a tendency for biopics: *J. Edgar* (2011), *Jersey Boys* (2014), *Sully* (2016), and *Richard Jewell* (2019). Besides the afore-mentioned *American Sniper*, Eastwood's most outstanding film of the decade was the only one in which he starred as well as directed, *The Mule* (2018). Based on a 2014 *New York Times Magazine* story, it features Eastwood as a kindly ninety-year-old, a solipsistic Santa blithely enjoying a second youth while spreading heroin and cocaine across the opiate-addicted Heartland. The film plays, like much of late Eastwood, as a generation's confession of guilt, according the rare satisfaction of watching a culpable patriarch actually go to prison for his crimes and our sins. You can blame Mexicans and other "foreigners" all you want, Clint the off-screen Trump-supporter (at least in 2016) says with his art, but Anglos are the ones who rake in the profits from the nation's decline.

Marvels of the Universe

The Marvel Cinematic Universe spanned twenty-three films, all but the first two of which were released in the 2010s (see the chapters on 2011, 2014, and 2018). The main planets of this cinematic universe were the four *Avengers* films, directed by Joss Whedon (2012, 2015) and Anthony and Joe Russo (2018, 2019), conglomerations of CGI-action set pieces and ensemble chamber scenes featuring accomplished actors (Robert Downey Jr., Scarlett Johansson, and Mark Ruffalo, among others) as well as actors such as Chris Evans and Chris Hemsworth, who were little known before being cast as Captain America and Thor, respectively. The films are interconnected, with the six or seven main heroes spinning off into their own individual films (e.g., *Iron Man II*, 2010; *Captain America: Civil War*, 2014; *Thor: Ragnarok*, 2017). As worldwide fans know, Phase One began with the first Marvel film, *Iron Man*, in 2008, culminating in *The Avengers* (2012). Phase Two opened with *Iron Man 3* (2013), picked up through *Guardians of the Galaxy* (2014), and concluded in 2015 with *Avengers: Age of Ultron* and *Ant Man*. Phase Three included new character films, *Doctor Strange* (2016) and *Black Panther* (2018), the latter being perhaps the most important film—and certainly the most popular—in a decade of milestones for African American films and filmmakers.

After twenty films centered mostly around male protagonists, the first female-oriented Marvel film, *Captain Marvel* (2019), premiered just seven weeks ahead of the conclusion of the two-part epic of *Avengers: Infinity War* (2018) and *Avengers: Endgame* (2019). Marvel, which was purchased by

Disney early in Phase One of the MCU in 2009, was the closest thing the 2010s had to one of the Golden Age Hollywood studios. Kevin Feige, CEO of Marvel Studios, developed characters and assembled movies around them the way that Irving Thalberg or Darryl F. Zanuck produced movies that showed off his roster of stars to best advantage. The key to the studio system, "house style," which transcended the work of individual directors and screenwriters, is also the best way of understanding the success of Marvel Studios. "Within ten years," writes Feige, who has produced every MCU film, "Marvel went from bankruptcy in the late 1990s to a $4.4 billion acquisition by Disney at the end of 2009. It's rare when a company goes through such remarkable change" (149). Moreover, as YouTuber Looper demonstrates in a 2019 video, the overarching films and their many characters can be summarized in a cogent, breathless chronology that fits into a twenty-two-minute video (that's about a minute per film). The fact that a series of movies whose combined running times add up to over fifty hours can be so easily bottled in a breezy video hints at how much heroic preening, villainous threatening, and empty CGI spectacle many of the individual films contain.

Superhero movies before Marvel tended to be subdivided by director. DC, the comic book line owned by WarnerMedia, made Richard Donner's Superman movies, followed by the Batman cycle of Tim Burton and that of Joel Schumacher. Years later, a reboot by Christopher Nolan found a new path for Batman. The same was even more true with the stand-alone *Wonder Woman* (2017)—Patty Jenkins's movie became the all-time highest-grossing film directed by a woman—and Todd Phillips's concept for the medium-budget, R-rated *Joker* (2019). Phillips became the first to receive an Academy Award nomination for best director for a superhero-related film, despite or because of the fact that *Joker* looks much more like a social problem psychological melodrama than a comic book or superhero movie.

With the MCU, on the other hand, audiences and even reviewers have some difficulty thinking of the twenty-three movies as separate entities. Only the most avid fan would be able to tell the directorial style of, say, *Guardians of the Galaxy* (James Gunn) from that of *Ant Man* (Peyton Reed), or *Captain America: The First Avenger* (Joe Johnston) from *Captain America: The Winter Soldier* (Joe Russo, Anthony Russo) or *Captain Marvel* (Anna Boden and Ryan Fleck). The choice of directors is also telling. The closest to an auteur ever hired for a Marvel film was Joss Whedon, director of the first two blockbuster *Avengers* films, who was best known for several television series. After Whedon is probably Kenneth Branagh, who directed the first *Thor* (2011). The film career of the Shakespearean actor-director

Branagh (*Much Ado about Nothing*, 1993; *Hamlet*, 1996) began with his frequently being compared to Laurence Olivier, though he generally fell short with any film whose source was not the Bard of Stratford-upon-Avon. With *Thor*, Branagh proved he could deliver a major effects-laden action film. In a delectable irony, however, the same year as *Thor*, Branagh was nominated for the Best Supporting Actor Oscar for playing Olivier, flawlessly, in *My Week with Marilyn*, a British independent film that recounts the production of *The Prince and the Showgirl* (1957), for which Marilyn Monroe went to London to be directed by Olivier. However, aside from Branagh's early nomination for *Henry V* (1989), no director ever nominated for an Academy Award for directing has made a Marvel film; the directorial names are not really on the A-list, either before their Marvel films or, so far, afterward. Taika Waititi, who won a 2019 Oscar for Adapted Screenplay for *Jojo Rabbit*, the independent black comedy he made following *Thor Ragnarok* (2017), has come the closest.

The most triumphant Marvel film overall has been *Black Panther*, which is, as of this writing, not only the only MCU film to receive an Oscar nomination for Best Picture and to win Oscars—for Best Costume Design, Best Production Design, and Best Music Score—but holds a number of other records: the most commercially successful film by an African American director, and the most successful film with a (nearly) all-Black cast. As Mikal J. Gaines writes in his chapter on 2018, Ryan Coogler, who was not quite thirty years old when he was hired to direct, was clearly given his head to make the film his way, on Marvel's huge canvas. For what was only his third movie, Coogler brought with him members of a team who had worked with him on one or both of his first two films, *Fruitvale Station* (2013) and *Creed* (2015), including Rachel Morrison, who had become the first woman nominated for Best Cinematography (*Mudbound*, 2017), production designer Hannah Beachler, and composer Ludwig Göransson, as well as the young star of those films, Michael B. Jordan.

Coming out late in Phase Three and opening in the "off month" of February, *Black Panther* became the top-grossing film of 2018, the decade's third top-grossing film domestically and its tenth top-grossing film worldwide. In addition to Jordan, the standout cast included, as King T'Challa of Wakanda, American actor Chadwick Boseman, who had starred in biopics of Jackie Robinson (*42*, 2013), James Brown (*Get on Up*, 2014), and Thurgood Marshall (*Marshall*, 2017). It also starred Academy Award–winner for *12 Years a Slave* Lupita Nyong'o, the American Kenyan Mexican actress who has been very choosy about her roles; Daniel Kaluuya, the British actor who enjoyed his breakout role in *Get Out* (2017) (which opened while *Black Panther* was in production); Angela Bassett, the long-underused star of *What's Love Got to Do with It* (1993) whose career had become emblematic of the small number of roles for African American actresses; Forest Whitaker, the veteran actor who produced *Fruitvale Station* (2013); and two young breakout actresses, Zimbabwean American Danai Gurira and Guyanese British Letitia Wright as T'Challa's younger sister Shuri.

It has become a familiar trajectory for a young director to start with a low-budget festival favorite, move onto a major studio film, and ultimately, film a blockbuster. Coogler knocked each phase of the trajectory out of the park. His breakout feature, *Fruitvale Station*, which Alexandra Keller discusses in the chapter on 2013, was released when he was twenty-six. The film, whose initial title was to be *Fruitvale*, takes place in Coogler's hometown, Oakland, California, and follows the last day in the life of Oscar Grant, a twenty-two-year-old Black man killed in a police shooting in a commuter train station on New Year's Eve of 2009. The film was a showcase for Michael B. Jordan, who went on to star in Coogler's unorthodox Rocky sequel, *Creed*, in which Jordan played the illegitimate son of the boxer Apollo Creed. The film, an unofficial reboot set in Philadelphia, is like a tribute to the original 1976 film, with Sylvester Stallone returning as the iconic character Rocky Balboa. Tessa Thompson, an inventive actress who makes her own breakout in the MCU in Waititi's *Thor Ragnarok*, and is also in *Sorry to Bother You* (see 2018), is the love interest. Once again, Coogler, with the highly versatile Jordan, aces a difficult test, showing that he could make original, even personal work within an established commercial framework (even if the conventions came creaking in whenever Stallone was on camera).

The two-track film industry that had existed since the 1990s—independent films that have their first exposure at festivals (Sundance, Venice, Telluride, Toronto) and major studio tentpole movies—continued, but with significant changes. The MCU pushed the studios toward ramped-up emphasis on superheroes, sequels, remakes, reboots, and animation. It has become increasingly difficult—though not impossible—to get even a moderate-budget "stand-alone" film made by the studios. The recourse of such film-makers as Noah Baumbach, Alfonso Cuarón, Joel and Ethan Coen, Martin Scorsese, Scott Alexander and Larry Karaszewski, and, into 2020, Spike Lee and David Fincher, to Netflix to finance major films that the studios turn down seems the definitive statement on streamers vs. studios as the decade closes. The 2010s saw the steady erosion of the studio-owned semi-indies, with only Sony Pictures Classics and Focus Features (Universal) remaining. Fox Searchlight was arguably the most successful "boutique studio" of the decade, with three Best Pictures (*12 Years a Slave*, 2013; *Birdman*, 2014; and *The Shape of Water*, 2017)—more than any other company—and at least one nominee nearly each year. The sale of the Fox movie companies to Disney in 2019, and the announcement that Twentieth Century and Searchlight would go on, with the Fox name associated in the present only with News Corp's TV networks and channels, appeared to promise that those companies would continue.

New indies appeared on the horizon. A24, founded in 2012, made films based upon provocative best sellers (*Room*, 2015, won the Best Actress Oscar for Brie Larson) and projects by up-and-coming directors: *Moonlight*, 2016, won Best Picture and established the African American writer-director Barry Jenkins; *The Witch* and *The Lighthouse*, both Robert Eggers; *The Florida Project*, Sean Baker; *A Ghost Story*, David Lowrey; *Lady Bird*, Greta Gerwig; *Eighth Grade*, Bo Burnham; *Hereditary* and *Midsommar*, both Ari Aster; and *The Farewell*, Lulu Wang. It also produced new works by veteran filmmakers such as Sofia Coppola (*The Bling Ring*), Yorgos Lanthimos (*The Lobster*), Paul Schrader (*First Reformed*), and Claire Denis (*High Life*). *Uncut Gems*, an audacious neo-noir by the New York–based Safdie brothers, Josh and Benny, and starring Adam Sandler, became the company's highest-grossing film in the United States soon after its release at Christmas 2019.

▬▬▬ Time's Up: Sexual Harassment and Racial Bias in the Entertainment World

Behind the scenes in the industry, however, outrage had long been simmering, and the presence of Trump in the White House evidently brought it to a boil. The #MeToo movement, founded by Tarana Burke in 2006, exploded in October 2017. The fuse was lit by investigative reports in the *New York Times* and the *New Yorker* exposing multiple accounts of sexual harassment and assault by producer Harvey Weinstein going back over twenty years. Accusations ensued against men at the top of the entertainment industry, from dozens more against Weinstein to damning accounts of intimidation and violation by Kevin Spacey, Bryan Singer, John Lasseter, Louis C. K., Charlie Rose, Matt Lauer, and others. One of the many criminal charges of sexual assault against Bill Cosby, an entertainment powerhouse and signifier of racial integration since the 1960s, finally resulted in a conviction in April 2018. Another social media hashtag, #TimesUp, expressed the demand that sexual misconduct by powerful men no longer be kept quiet within the industry or the culture. In February 2020, Weinstein was convicted of criminal sexual act in the first degree and third-degree rape. He was acquitted of three more serious counts of predatory sexual assault. The following month he was sentenced to twenty-three years in prison. Just days after the *Times* story ran, the Academy of Motion Picture Arts and Sciences (AMPAS) revoked Weinstein's membership, as it did in 2018 the memberships of Bill Cosby and Roman Polanski.

The Césars, the French equivalent of the Oscars, brought embarrassment and calumny upon themselves when Polanski won the César for Best Director in February 2020 for *An Officer and a Spy* (2019). Céline Sciamma and Adèle Haenel walked out of the ceremony in disgust. Woody Allen has been charged by Ronan Farrow, son of Allen and Mia Farrow, of abusing Allen's daughter, Ronan Farrow's sister, when she was seven. No charges have ever been brought, but damage has been done to Allen's career. As the decade began, Woody Allen won his first Oscar in twenty-five years; he was honored for his original screenplay for *Midnight in Paris* (2011). By the end of the decade, however, his reputation was so tarnished that actress Scarlett Johansson was said to be hurting her own Oscar chances for 2019 by saying that she was glad she worked with Allen on three films in the mid-2000s.

On another front of the Hollywood film industry, minutes after the Academy Award nominations for 2014 were announced, all-white slates in the four acting categories prompted April Reign, a Washington, D.C., writer and activist, to tweet, "#OscarsSoWhite they asked to touch my hair." The instantly immortal hashtag brought widespread embarrassment for AMPAS and the film industry it represents. The furor intensified when #OscarsSo-White applied to the acting categories in the 2015 nominations as well. Cheryl Boone Isaacs, who served from 2013 to 2017 as the first African American president of AMPAS, launched the A2020 initiative, a drive to double the number of female and minority members by the end of 2020. The new classes of members for the years 2016 to 2020 were 46 percent female and 31 percent people of color.

Subsequently, *Moonlight* (2016) won Best Picture; and African American actors won Oscars for Supporting Actor (Mahershala Ali, 2016, 2018) and Supporting Actress (Viola Davis, 2016; Regina King, 2018), as well as nominations for Director (Jenkins, 2016; Jordan Peele, 2017), the first Original Screenplay Oscar to an African American (Peele), and Oscars for Costume Design (Ruth Carter, 2018) and Production Design (Hannah Beachler, 2018), the latter for *Black Panther*, plus the first Best Director nomination for Spike Lee (*BlackKkKlansman*, 2018), who won for Adapted Screenplay. By the time of the Oscar ceremony in 2019, over 900 new members had been admitted. However, chagrin greeted the announcement of the nominations for 2019 when only one of the twenty acting nominations went to a performer of color. Four years into this drive, Rebecca Keegan and Ben Zauzmer reported days before the Oscars in 2020 that "the organization began from a place of such whiteness (92 percent in 2015) and maleness (75 percent) that the overall composition of the Academy—and in many ways its tastes and choices—are evolving much more slowly."

The Academy Award for Best Picture went to Bong Joon Ho South Korean *Parasite* (2019), the first time in the ninety-two years of the Academy Awards that the top award went to a non–English language film. "Another effect of the rapid expansion," wrote Nate Jones, "is that the Academy is much more global than it used to be: By many accounts, nearly one-fifth of the membership is now international. For them, proving the Academy would no longer shrink in fear of what Bong called the 'one-inch barrier of subtitles' was a chance to strike a major blow for global cinema." Like many, Reign was disappointed by the failure of the Actors Branch to nominate Lupita Nyong'o's intricate dual performance in *Us*, even though Nyong'o had won Best Actress from the New York Film Critics Circle, one of the most important precursors. Nyong'o's role was contemporary; she played a wife and mother. The role in Jordan Peele's film could easily have been written as male or even white. There are white "Tethered," a concept that for every "individual" aboveground, there is an underground double, Peele's metaphor for privilege and the underclass. (See the 2019 chapter.)

The one nonwhite performer nominated in 2019 was Cynthia Erivo, who played Harriet Tubman in *Harriet*. While voters may have been impressed with Broadway's Erivo, who co-wrote and sang the piece nominated for Best Song, Reign pointed out that "the majority of the roles that have been awarded by the Academy for black women have been them experiencing significant trauma, playing an enslaved woman or a woman living in abject poverty" (Keegan, Zauzmer). Peele's film, in which his lead characters' Blackness is significant but not defining, is key to Racquel Gates's call for "Black narratives that decenter whiteness or ignore it altogether, films that connect audiences with the pathos, joy, and even treachery of the Black characters and the lives they depict, the films that recognize their complex humanity" (AR 3).

Moreover, while America's deepening political polarization had little apparent effect on film spectatorship, film production was another matter, especially when Hollywood picked states that happened to be politically red as locations for movies and television shows. Because of its generous tax incentives, Georgia became the leading location inside the United States for runaway production in the 2010s, with a number of Marvel's films, including *Black Panther* (2018), *Guardians of the Galaxy Vol. 2* (2017), and *Spider-Man: Homecoming* (2017), being filmed there, as well as television series such as *Sharp Objects* (HBO, 2018), *The Walking Dead* (AMC, 2010–), and *Stranger Things* (Netflix, 2016–). The May 2019 passage in Georgia of the so-called Heartbeat Bill, signed by Governor Brian Kemp, which outlaws abortions past the term of six weeks—before most expectant mothers even know they're pregnant—caused many productions to consider leaving the state. The Georgia controversy provided rare common ground for archadversaries Netflix and Disney, with each company's CEO, Ted Sarandos and Robert Iger, respectively, saying that they would "rethink our entire investment in Georgia," as Sarandos put it, if the Heartbeat Bill stood as law. Cara Buckley wrote in the *New York Times*, "An estimated 92,000 jobs are connected to the industry in Georgia. . . . Any boycott would cause untold economic damage to [film companies'] workers in the state, and to their own bottom line. And it could easily alienate the huge swaths of the country where many people oppose abortion."

The 2010s brought a sea change to American life, with discontent blowing across the outward optimism of the Obama Era. The financial collapse prompted bitter portrayals of the dark sides of American success, such as *The Social Network* (2010), the documentary *Inside Job* (2010), *Margin Call* (2011), *The Wolf of Wall Street* (2013), and *The Big Short* (2015). Nonetheless, the presence of a harmonious African American first family for eight years seemed to bring forth trenchant yet cleansing depictions of America's past and the ways we might find to resolve its ramifications, in such films as *Lincoln* (2012), *Django Unchained* (2012), *Zero Dark Thirty* (2012), and *12 Years a Slave* (2013). These were called out toward the end of the decade by visions of America as a maelstrom from which there is no exit, as seen in *Detroit* (2017), *Get Out* (2017, more so with the ending writer-director Jordan Peele discarded—but kept for the DVD—than the one he used for the theatrical release), *Three Billboards Outside Ebbing, Missouri* (2017), *BlacKkKlansman* (2018), *First Reformed* (2018) (a nightmarish Paul Schrader vision that could have been retitled *Travis Bickle Lives!*), and *Us* (2019). Quentin Tarantino praised Jordan Peele for making theatrical films matter again with *Get Out*, which itself was sometimes disparaged as just "an indie horror movie," and the film's star, Daniel Kaluuya (also in *Black Panther*) marveled in 2018 that he was nominated for Best Actor in such prestigious company as Denzel Washington, Gary Oldman, and Daniel Day-Lewis (Hainey, Ritman).

By the end of the decade, movies appeared to have provided a perch from which one could look back at the early years for signs and signals of impending gloom. In a Vox.com piece published on the last day of 2018,

Emily VanDerWerff recalled Tarantino's 2015 *The Hateful Eight*, a movie that "is just *mean*, and . . . feels like the work of someone who looked around at America and concluded that it was a land full of angry, spiteful people who would be more willing to burn their own lives to the ground than admit either their own sins or the sins of their country." Tarantino, wrote VanDer-Werff, "understood better than most that the precipice we all stood on in 2015 was very different from the one we *thought* we were on. And yet," she continued, "few critics looked at the pop culture of the early 2010s and said, 'Yep, a culture war's brewing,' even if it seems blindingly obvious in hindsight."

In 2019, public radio host Krista Tippett referred to 2014 as a year that "feels like 25 years ago. It feels like a different world, although in my mind one of the characteristics of the world of 2014 as opposed to now is that it was easier to pretend that we had made more progress than we had," quickly adding, "for *some* of us," specifically the white and privileged. "So there were realities and there were realities," Tippett continued, "and it was possible to not know." On the other hand, issues such as gay equality, like others following the #MeToo and #TimesUp campaigns, marched trium-phantly toward the end of the 2010s in defiance of Donald Trump's "fan service" to his far-right admirers. Pete Buttigieg, mayor of South Bend, Indiana, and a married gay man and military veteran whose campaign for president picked up considerable traction throughout 2019, recalled that "it was unsafe for Democrats to support same-sex marriage at the beginning of this same decade that we're living in now" (Bruni 4).

One of the most significant films of the decade turned out in retrospect to be *Contagion*. The 2011 thriller, written by Scott Z. Burns and directed by Steven Soderbergh, and with an all-star cast including Matt Damon, Law-rence Fishburne, Gwyneth Paltrow, Kate Winslet, Marion Cotillard, Jude Law, and Jennifer Ehle, was largely forgotten after its release on the tenth anniversary weekend of 9/11. This is ironic, given that the film, based on research and interviews with health experts, is now seen as predictive of the most life-altering crisis since 9/11. After the COVID-19 pandemic deci-mated everyday life in early 2020, the film became a go-to title for many viewers under lockdown. Warner Bros. reported that in December 2019, *Contagion* was its 270th most-rented title. That was to be expected for an eight-year-old film that received no Oscar nominations or other awards, and that ranked forty-fourth among top-grossing films domestically in its year of release and sixtieth worldwide. Three months later, it was War-ner Bros.' second most-rented movie. Google Trends, a site which rates topics in terms of the number of times they are Googled and an even more accurate gauge of urgency, reported that the pandemic thriller had gone from 4 to 8 on a scale of 1 to 100 throughout most of 2019 to the chart-busting 100 in March 2020, the month that COVID-19 shut down the world.

Seen during the coronavirus, the Soderbergh-Burns movie appears astonishingly prescient. The narrative is structured as a mystery, documentary-style, during an outbreak that begins as a woman (Gwyneth Paltrow) becomes violently ill on her way home to Minneapolis from a business trip to Hong Kong. Acting as his own cinematographer under the nom de caméra Peter Andrews and shooting in the style of his drug trade thriller *Traffic* (2000), Soderbergh cuts among these locations, as well as Chicago, Washington, and Atlanta, where the deputy director of the Centers for Disease Control and Prevention (Fishburne) leads the search for a cure while fighting myriad political battles. None of these was with the president of the United States, as in the actual 2020 pandemic. Burns and Soderbergh had done their research, as the film's references to the ability of contagious diseases to travel on doorknobs, surfaces, and one's own hands rang amazingly true in the all too real pandemic nine years later. The film's mystery is solved through contact tracing, as Soderbergh, taking the point of view of public surveillance cameras, traces the virus from bats to pigs to humans—almost precisely the causes believed to have originated the coronavirus at the very end of 2019.

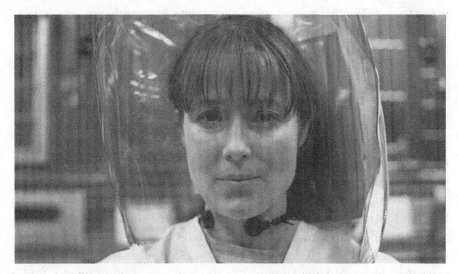

In *Contagion* (Steven Soderbergh, Warner Bros., Participant Media, 2011), the saintly Dr. Ally Hextall (Jennifer Ehle), just before she tests the vaccine on herself. Digital frame enlargement.

The key difference was that the actual bat-pig-fish-human connection was made at a wet market—in Wuhan, not Hong Kong. Even Dr. Sanjay Gupta, chief neurosurgeon at Emory University Medical Center and a member of the faculty at Emory's medical school, plays himself as a TV medical expert in *Contagion*, just as he became a CNN fixture during the actual pandemic in 2020. The movie depicts empty grocery shelves (although it fails to foresee the runs on toilet paper, hand sanitizer, and disinfectant wipes that characterized the actual contagion). The frequent comparisons to the 1918 Spanish Flu pandemic that killed, as the CDC deputy explains, "one percent of the world's population," heard frequently in 2020, are also heard here. References are also made to "novel viruses" and contact tracing, terms with which people became extremely familiar in 2020. Burns and Soderbergh orchestrated conventions common to the decade's dystopian science fiction, such as panicked crowds rushing pharmacies for promoted cure-alls and deserted streets piled with trashed cars and trashed trash.

Moreover, a demagogic blogger (Jude Law) who combatively promotes a miracle cure was outmatched in actuality by a demagogic tweeter who happened to be president of the United States. Donald Trump, in televised White House briefings, hawked hydroxychloroquine, a drug approved only for lupus and malaria, despite repeated warnings by the FDA that the drug was known to bring daunting side effects and had little or no efficacy against the coronavirus. In Trump's hands, the medication became, naturally, snake oil. And the idea of a president during a horrific public health crisis suggesting that his fellow Americans inject themselves with antiseptics could not have been imagined except perhaps by Stanley Kubrick and Terry Southern for a pandemic satire: *How I Learned to Stop Worrying and Ignore COVID*.

Of Theaters and Streamers

Amid all the cultural tumult, it was perhaps possible to disregard the transformative changes taking place in the film industry. On the final page of the last chapter of *American Cinema of the 2000s*, Dana Polan concluded his coverage of movies in 2009 with something of a prophecy: "What might have been the most consequential event of the year for the business future of the movies might not have seemed at first glance to have anything to do with film at all: namely, the FCC-mandated switchover of commercial television to digital standards" (236). Polan was right in more ways than he could have known. The absolute end of film came in 2011, the most massive year of conversion from celluloid projection to digital in theaters around the world. In 2017, the Motion Picture Association (the "of America" was dropped in 2019) THEME Report stated that "98 percent of the world's cinema screens are digital." In the first half of the decade, independent movie theaters around the world conducted fundraising campaigns so that they could purchase the new projectors that would allow them to stay in business. Most films were shot with digital cameras as well. The documentary *Side by Side* (2012) plays out the debate between the defenders of digital filmmaking, such as David Fincher and even Martin Scorsese, and celluloid's last passionate stalwarts, notably Quentin Tarantino and Christopher Nolan. 4K, a horizontal display resolution of 4,000 pixels, became the standard for both theatrical digital projection and HD television. After nearly seventy years in which television and cinema were profoundly different media, the home screen and the cinema screen now presented similar technologies for the first time.

Polan also wrote that "digital television sets facilitated the streaming of demanded video, and studios began pushing for ways to reduce the window (the amount of time) between theatrical release of a film and its video-on-demand distribution" (236). But the relative leveling of the home screen as compared to that of the cinema hastened the changes forced by the entry of the streaming video services into production. Such dates as 1 February 2013, when the first season of *House of Cards*, Netflix's first original television series, was posted online, or 16 October 2015, the premiere of *Beasts of No Nation*, Netflix's first original feature film, may be as well remembered by future media historians as the debuts of *The Jazz Singer* and *The Robe*, or *I Love Lucy* and *Saturday Night Live*. The same goes for Amazon with its first series, *Bosch* (13 February 2015), and its first feature film, *Chi-raq* (4 December 2015). The entry of Apple and Disney to the streaming parade as the decade ended brought the sense that still more changes to the status quo of the entertainment business, and film and television mediums themselves, lay just around the corner.

Netflix and Amazon adopted contrasting business models for their film releases. Netflix, more interested in mass audience appeal, released certain big-name films to theaters just long enough to distinguish them from television movies and qualify them for Oscars. Amazon, which began as a bookseller, appealed to a more literate audience; it took the art house route, starting by picking up films for distribution at Sundance and other festivals (one of its milestones was its release of *Manchester by the Sea* [2016], which won two Oscars). Amazon agreed to respect the customary window, allowing the films developed by Amazon Studios and those it had acquired for distribution to play the usual three months in theaters before releasing them for streaming. Netflix's more aggressive model attracted the enmity of exhibitors, especially as it released major works by Oscar-winning directors: Alfonso Cuarón with *Roma* (2018), Joel and Ethan Coen with *The Ballad of Buster Scruggs* (2018), and Martin Scorsese with *The Irishman* (2019). After *Roma* won ten Academy Award nominations, including Best Picture, AMC, Regal, and Cinemark, the three largest U.S. cinema chains, announced that the highly acclaimed film would not be screening in their annual Best Picture showcases because "it was never licensed . . . to play in our theaters," as AMC's press release put it. (In this particular instance, it might be the chains that suffer if patrons decline to buy pricey tickets to a nominee showcase that doesn't show all the nominees.)

This kerfuffle shows the fear that Netflix in particular struck in conventional film industry players. This dustup was followed in 2019 by protracted negotiations, covered intently in the entertainment news media, over *The Irishman*, a three-and-a-half-hour drama about the mob and Jimmy Hoffa, which Netflix financed at $170 million after the major studios passed. The exhibitors' refusal to back down from their insistence upon the standard three-month window between a film's opening in theaters and its appearance on home video meant that a major awards contender would not be available for showing at most of the nation's theaters.

Steven Spielberg led a drive in the AMPAS Board of Governors in 2019 to restrict films that play on streaming services without the usual three-month window prior to television showing from being eligible for the Oscars. "Once you commit to a television format, you're a TV movie," Spielberg said, in language that itself sounded outdated. "You certainly, if it's a good show, deserve an Emmy, but not an Oscar" (Nyren). Spielberg lost his campaign in June 2019 when AMPAS decided that the traditional week in theaters was all a film needed to qualify for Academy Awards. Following *Roma*'s ten nominations and three Oscars, the centrality of the streaming services, especially Netflix, to the industry became obvious. This transformation of the business by the streamers, which Owen Gleiberman in a *Variety* column in March 2019 called "potentially the biggest paradigm shift in movies since the introduction of VHS, and maybe bigger," was not even imagined earlier in the decade. Tino Balio's book, *Hollywood in the New Millennium*, published in 2013, mentions Netflix as only a movie rental company (150). This is an indication of how swiftly the film industry was transformed in the second half of the 2010s. One must look back to the introduction of sound film in the late 1920s to find a comparably rapid metamorphosis of the film medium and industry.

The entry of the streamers into series television altered the nature of TV viewing as well. Streamers deliver the entirety of a series' season all at once. Just as "I couldn't put it down" long described a response to reading, "binge-watching" now applied to the difficulty of turning away from the set without watching the next episode, and the next, and the one after that. "Appointment TV" soon applied to the increasingly archaic custom of waiting a week for the next episode to air at its scheduled day and hour. The Hollywood studios attempted to raise the drawbridge against the streaming filmmakers. The *New York Times* reported that in 2019, Netflix "will pump out about 90 movies, . . . To compare, the five conventional studios left standing—Paramount, Universal, Sony, Disney, and Warner Bros.—will make about that many *combined*" (Chozick and Barnes 6). The studios beefed up the fortifications: Warner Bros. in its purchase by AT & T in 2018; Twentieth Century-Fox by selling to Disney in 2017 (finalized in 2019); and Disney by reaping the bounteous rewards of its purchases of Pixar (2006), Marvel (2009), and Lucasfilm (2012), the latter sale allowing it to produce *Star Wars* reboots and sequels, five of which appeared between 2015 and 2019. The "Mouse House" lived high, for a time at least, off live-action remakes and sequels of its classic films (*Alice in Wonderland*, 2010; *The Jungle Book*, 2015; *Beauty and the Beast*, 2017; *Mary Poppins Returns*, 2018; and *Dumbo, Aladdin*, and *The Lion King*, all 2019).

None of these are without interest. The best is probably *Mary Poppins Returns*, directed by Rob Marshall (who also made a successful film version of Stephen Sondheim's *Into the Woods* for Disney in 2014) and starring Emily Blunt as Mary Poppins and *Hamilton* phenom Lin-Manuel Miranda as Jack. Marshall's movie seems equal parts sequel and remake. Nearly every song in the 1964 original has a corresponding slot in the new film, with a full song score by Marc Shaiman and Scott Wittman (*Hairspray*). The "Jolly Holiday" animated sequence in the original has a drawn animation analogue here, in which Mary Poppins, Jack (the Bert replacement), and the children pop into a decorative bowl rather than a chalk painting. The music hall number, "The Cover Is Not the Book," offers Miranda's breathtaking patter song–style rap done on a drawn staircase, in which each step materializes as he walks on it. Thus, the film contributes handsomely to the decade's burst of original musicals, which included Damien Chazelle's *La La Land* (2016), an innovative indie musical with Oscar-winning score by Justin Hurwitz and lyrics by Justin Paul and Benj Pasek; the Hugh Jackman vehicle *The Greatest Showman* (2017); and Bradley Cooper's remake of *A Star Is Born* (2018) with Lady Gaga in the female lead and an Oscar-winning song, "Shallow."

Disney's dominating 38 percent market share in 2019 bespeaks the success of its strategy. During the decade, and with Disney at 20.2 percent of the market share, Warner Bros. (16.3 percent), Universal (13.3 percent), Sony (11.3 percent), Paramount (9.2 percent), and mini-major Lionsgate (6.4) all attempted to hold on using conventional Hollywood business practices. For the record, Marvel, even though a part of Disney, accounted for 7.4 percent of the North American box office with just twenty-one films in the decade (uchanma 50).

Netflix's films, on the other hand, were just as capable as those of the studios of disappearing without a trace, with their potentially perpetual presence on the streamer's menus like video boxes that lingered on shelves during the video store era. Netflix's power to lasso audiences, on the other hand, can be seen in the phenomenon of *Bird Box* (2018), a poorly reviewed dystopian science fiction movie with big-name stars (Sandra Bullock, Sarah Paulson) and directed by Susanne Bier, whose Danish film, *In a Better World* (2010), won the Oscar for Best Foreign Film. *Bird Box*, released just before the Christmas holidays, was watched by 26 million accounts in its first week, according to Netflix, and 80 million member households four weeks after its release (Roettgers).

Of the top twenty-five grossing films of the 2010s domestically, ten were comic book movies: eight movies of the interrelated Marvel Cinematic Universe, and two from DC Comics (*The Dark Knight Rises*, 2012; *Wonder Woman*, 2017). Four were *Star Wars* reboots. Of these, most were sequels, as were the four animated features—the most popular single genre of the twenty-first century thus far. The exceptions are Disney's live-action CGI remakes of its own animated features, *Beauty and the Beast* (2017) and *The Lion King* (2019). The sole original, hanging on at twenty-five, is the film adaptation of Suzanne Collins's YA novel *The Hunger Games* (2012), which of course spawned sequels, one of which is on the list. Even the most successful movies of the decade by the wondrous Pixar were sequels (*Incredibles 2*, 2018; *Finding Dory*, 2016; *Toy Story 3* and *4*, 2010, 2019). Pixar still turned out successful originals in the decade, including three films that won the Academy Award for Best Animated Feature, *Brave* (2012), *Inside Out* (2015), and *Coco* (2017). DreamWorks produced the *How to Train Your Dragon* trilogy (2010, 2014, 2019), based on the books by Cressida Cowell. Looked at another way, in the top 100 domestic grossers, one finds only seven live-action originals, with the highest of these, *American Sniper*, the top-grossing film released in 2014, at thirty-nine ("Domestic Box Office").

▬▬▬▬▬▬ Black Widow Divorces Kylo Ren, or How the Franchises Vivify the Indies

Throughout the decade, inventive or socially conscious films were made by casting actors from the franchises, who seemed happy to flex their clout in order to get worthwhile independent projects made. Thus Scarlett Johansson, when not playing Black Widow in Marvel movies, won her first two Oscar nominations in 2019. One was for Best Actress in Noah Baumbach's *Marriage Story* for Netflix opposite Adam Driver (Kylo Ren in the *Star Wars* reboots). Johansson's Supporting Actress nod came for *Jojo Rabbit*, a black comedy set in Nazi Germany in the waning days of World War II, told from a child's point of view. Meanwhile, Driver, who was nominated for Best Actor for *Marriage Story*, also starred in writer-director Scott Z. Burns's post–Iraq War CIA torture exposé *The Report* for Amazon, with Annette Bening as Senator Dianne Feinstein. While Todd Haynes directed Mark Ruffalo (the Hulk) in the environmental legal procedural *Dark Waters*, Michael B. Jordan (*Black Panther*) and Brie Larson (*Captain Marvel*) starred in *Just Mercy*, based on the memoir by lawyer Bryan Stephenson. Thus, interesting low-budget work was often made on the merits of the name recognition of actors who had proved themselves in the franchises; this despite the fact that in general the major studios had not been interested for years in making medium-budget naturalistic dramas. However, between the streamers and occasional films by the studios (*Just Mercy* was from Warner Bros.), such films, too often stigmatized as "Oscar bait," did manage to get made and sometimes find audiences. Again, this is not new. The Oscar bait tag, moreover, is unfair, and often misleading. Mark Harris, in a 2016 tweet, called "Oscar bait" "a terrible term that takes our sideline fixation and tries to recast it as a defining motive for artists." Even blockbusters like *Black Panther* and *Joker* were not made with Oscars in mind, but won multiple nominations and gold statuettes all the same.

As the decade ended, a feeling closed in that those who disparaged superhero movies may be on the wrong side of film history and criticism. Those who looked condescendingly on superhero movies and the mass audiences that flocked to them may before long begin to resemble the reviewers of decades past who wrote patronizingly of any number of now canonized genres—Westerns, musicals, and "weepies" (aka women's pictures), among others. Some have wondered if there may well be art in a culminating film such as *Avengers: Endgame*, whose length (181 minutes) approaches that of *The Irishman* and whose first hour, for a blockbuster anticipated by millions, is as slowly paced, grim, quiet, and seemingly uneventful as an Ozu film. The Russo brothers, who directed the film, assumed a patience and also an involvement on the part of the film's enormous, eagerly anticipatory audiences willing to absorb a stately, immersive experience. Could it also be a sign that the binge-watching of streaming shows has acculturated audiences to longer sits? Are we missing something? Will the film's reviewers decades hence look as clueless as those critics in the 1940s and 1950s who dismissed the melodramas of Douglas Sirk or the suspense films of Hitchcock as slick and formulaic genre pieces? Regardless, major studies of the Marvel cycle appeared toward the end of the decade (Chambliss, et al.; Mc Sweeney), and it seems certain that the monumental popularity and diversity of the MCU will kindle scholarly interest into the future.

Similarly, on the spikier DC front, *Joker* engendered outrage as well as enthusiasm that might remind cinephiles of the reception of *Bonnie and Clyde* some fifty years earlier. Reviewers such as *Time*'s Stephanie Zacharek and the *New York Times*'s A. O. Scott appeared to trot out their crankiest, Bosley Crowther–like, socially conscious disgruntlement. On the other hand, it took film scholar Sean Redmond five days after the release of *Joker* to hit Film Studies listservs with a call for papers on a book about the film, citing its arrival "at a time of arguably unprecedented social malaise: it speaks to the culture of loneliness, toxic masculinity, the crisis in whiteness, the breakdown in social networks, the expanding gap between rich and poor, and to the anger and rage that has entered discourse more broadly." If this seems a lot of freight to load onto what some reviewers have insisted is just "a comic book origin story," the film still cannot be ignored, an impression verified in January 2020 when *Joker* led all films with eleven Oscar nominations—all for a "comic book movie," a genre famous for being ignored by the Academy.

The gradual decline of the mid-budget film for adults—a development that gave the streamers their opening to the film market in the first place—may continue to be held off by the Oscars, which stubbornly honor just such films, usually by the mini-majors and the studio-backed semi-indies. Fox Searchlight had three Best Pictures in the decade. Of the rest, two at the start of the 2010s went to films by the Weinstein Company, which became defunct almost as soon as Harvey Weinstein's rampant sexual victimization of women went public. Another mini-major, A24, scored a Best Picture with *Moonlight*. So did the mini-majors Open Road (*Spotlight*, 2015) and Neon (*Parasite*, 2019). The decade's only Best Pictures from the major "legacy" studios—the companies that existed in the Golden Age Studio era—were

Arthur Fleck (Joaquin Phoenix), backstage, in makeup and awaiting his cue. *Joker* (Todd Phillips, Warner Bros., 2019). Digital frame enlargement.

Argo (Warner Bros., 2012) and *Green Book* (Universal, 2018), movies that seemed throwbacks to the kinds of socially minded thrillers and race-relation dramedies that Hollywood made regularly in the 1960s and 1970s.

The number of Academy Award Best Picture nominees changed to ten for the first time since 1943; the Academy adjusted the number in 2011. Any film that received more than 5 percent of the overall vote would be nominated for Best Picture, with a minimum of five nominees and a maximum of ten. As a result, no year from 2011 on has seen fewer than eight Best Picture nominees and more than nine. So a happy medium was reached. However, the first two Best Picture slates after the expansion, as Michele Schreiber explains in the 2010 chapter, each included two films by female directors. That never happened again during the 2010s. Therefore, the lack of diversity in the nominees for 2019 (in 2020) sent the Academy back to its 2009 plan beginning with the Oscars for 2021.

The rise in the number of Best Picture nominees was pushed to the Board of Governors by 2010 Awards show producers Bill Condon and Lawrence Mark (Kilday). This settled the furor raised in 2009 when *The Dark Knight*, the second highest-grossing film of the 2000s, was not nominated for Best Picture, despite eight nominations and two eventual Oscars, including the first acting Oscar for a superhero movie (Best Supporting Actor to the late Heath Ledger). The wider net spread by the expanded field over the ensuing decade caught a number of popular films that probably would not have landed in a five-film field. However, it also pulled in numerous independent films that also would have eluded nomination in the earlier, narrower field. Kyle Buchanan speculated,

> If you cut the category back to the five movies that also received corresponding best-director nominations over the last decade, so many of the best-picture nominees that starred people of color would be lost: No *Black Panther*, *Selma*, *Hidden Figures* or *Fences*, to name just a few. Most of the female-fronted movies would go, too, including *Little Women*, *Brooklyn*, *Zero Dark Thirty* and *Winter's Bone*, not to mention nearly all the modern-day stories, films about queer people, and sci-fi and genre films that have recently been nominated: No *Call Me by Your Name*, *Her*, *Marriage Story* or *Inception*. ("10 Years Later . . .")

"And at a time when diversity is at the forefront of the Oscar conversation," Buchanan argued, "the expanded best-picture field may be one of the sole reasons this awards show hasn't completely collapsed under the weight of controversy" ("10 Years Later . . .").

Oscar mavens took note of other patterns. The preferential, or ranked-choice, ballot was devised in 2010 for the newly expanded Best Picture race so that a film could not squeak by with a sliver of the vote. This meant that the votes for the top prize were tabulated and its winner determined differently from the other categories. As an apparent result, no Best Picture in the decade won more than five Oscars, and only one film early on, *The Artist* (2011), got even that. The sweeps of between seven and eleven Oscars that were common for Best Pictures as recently as the 2000s seemed things of the past. Moreover, splits between Best Picture and Best Director, after a long stretch (from the late fifties to the late nineties and again in the late aughts) when they rarely happened, were back with a vengeance—half the Oscars in the 2010s went to different films for Best Picture and Best Director, the biggest ratio since the Academy's first decade. Interestingly, half the decade's Oscars for Best Director went to three directors from Mexico: Alfonso Cuarón (*Gravity*, 2013; *Roma*, 2018); Alejandro G. Iñárritu (*Birdman*, 2014; *The Revenant*, 2015—only the third director in Oscar history to win consecutively and the first in sixty-five years); and Guillermo del Toro (*The Shape of Water*, 2017). Add to this the fact that only one American won Best Director in the decade (and he, Damien Chazelle, seems an anomaly as the youngest winner ever at thirty-two); all this and two Best Pictures for films by Black directors (*12 Years a Slave*, 2013; *Moonlight*, 2016) whose directors themselves did not win. Oscars in the decade demonstrated the churning and convulsing characteristic of the 2010s.

A roundtable of industry artists and executives—people on the front lines of filmmaking—got together with the *New York Times* in June 2019 and debated the question, "Will the Movies Exist in 10 Years?" Even a book like the one you're reading now defines a movie as what director Joe Russo (*The Avengers: Endgame*) calls "the two-hour, closed-ended film" that plays in theaters, not a movie made for a streaming service (Buchanan, "Will the Movies Exist in 10 Years?"). However, I confess I allow a loose auteurist standard to guide the selections. If a film is made for Netflix—by Martin Scorsese, say—it qualifies as a movie. Who would exclude Scorsese, the Coen brothers, or Cuarón from a cinematic analysis?

Besides the "specialty market," however, for which each year's Oscar field is generally the main showcase, it needs to be said that on average, four or five "original," "stand-alone" films manage to find their way into each year's top twenty grossers; these are often also Oscar contenders. Writer-director Christopher Nolan has won unusual clout in that all three of the "personal" originals that his blockbuster *Batman* trilogy (2005, 2008, 2012) earned him the right to make in the 2010s were top-twenty grossers, and one, *Inception* (2010), was a genuine blockbuster, amassing over $250 million domestic and $800 million worldwide. This has given Nolan perhaps more power than any Hollywood filmmaker since Steven Spielberg. These original films are also where stars, often said to be fading in the franchise era, show their persistent drawing power. Six of Leonardo DiCaprio's seven films in the 2010s fall into this category, all by auteur directors: besides *Inception*, two each with Scorsese (*Shutter Island*, 2010; *The Wolf of Wall Street*, 2013) and Quentin Tarantino (*Django Unchained* and *Once Upon a Time . . . in Hollywood*, 2019); the others were for Baz Luhrmann (*The Great Gatsby*, 2013) and Iñárritu (*The Revenant*, 2015). Other top-twenty stand-alones were horror films (*Get Out* and *A Quiet Place*, 2018; *Us*, 2019); comedies (*Bridesmaids*, 2011; *Ted*, 2012; *We're the Millers*, 2013; *Crazy Rich Asians*, 2018); crossover films about African Americans (*Get Out*, *Us*; *Straight Outta Compton*, 2015; *Hidden Figures*, 2016); genre pastiches (*Django Unchained*; *Knives Out*, 2019); and musicals (*Les Misérables*, 2012; *La La Land*, *The Greatest Showman*, and *A Star Is Born*). The success of such films showed that Hollywood could still lure audiences to theaters for inventive flourishes to traditional movie fare. Thus as cinema looked at an uncertain and unpredictable future, the movies themselves held onto comforting formulas as the troubling 2010s drew to a close.

2010

Movies and Recessionary Gender Politics

MICHELE SCHREIBER

In 2010, the United States was still reeling from the after-math of the Great Recession, with millions out of work and many under-water in their mortgages. Though the Congressional Budget Office deemed that the recession had officially ended in June 2009, this supposed conclusion of the worst economic downturn since World War II did not provide much relief for those affected by the increase in unemployment and the destabilization of the stock market as well as the housing market. The Bureau of Labor Statistics showed that the unemployment rate doubled from 5 percent to 10 percent between December 2007 and October 2009, with a "higher proportion" of long-term unemployment (being unemployed for twenty-seven weeks or longer) than had been seen in previous recessions (bls.gov). Rates of unemployment among men were higher than those among women, with this gap widening significantly over a period of thirteen months. Specifically, in March of 2008, the unemployment rate among men was 5.2 percent and 5 percent among women (a .2 percent difference). By May of 2009, the male unemployment rate was 10.6 percent, 8 percent for women (a 2.6 percent difference), with male-dominated industries such as manufacturing and construction affected the most. Between December 2007 and June 2009, employment in construction saw a 13.7 percent drop, and manufacturing dropped 10 percent during that same period. Education and health services, female-dominated sectors, saw an increase in employment of 2.2 percent during the same period (BLS Spotlight). This difference prompted economists and the media to use gender-specific terms when discussing the recession, describing it as a "man-cession" or "he-cession" (Wall).

The ambitious agenda of Democratic President Barack Obama saw significant liberal legislative achievements. On 23 March, Obama signed into law the Patient Protection and Affordable Care Act (referred to in common parlance as Obamacare). The law was, according to the *New York Times*, "the most expansive social legislation enacted in decades," guaranteeing health insurance to every citizen in the country (Stolberg). As Vice President Joe Biden said to Obama during the bill-signing ceremony, "Mr. President, this is a big f***ing deal." The spontaneous comment caught on a "hot mic" went viral for its perfect encapsulation of the achievement, which Democrats had been attempting to pass in one form or another for decades. In fact, the Affordable Care Act was such a monumental accomplishment, that there were multiple and sustained efforts by Congressional Republicans to repeal the law for seven years.

The year saw two significant environmental disasters. First, on 12 January, Haiti was hit with a 7.0 magnitude earthquake, which killed 220,000 people, injured 300,000 and caused widespread destruction to the country's infrastructure. On 20 April, the British Petroleum–leased oil rig Deepwater Horizon exploded and then caught fire, causing eleven deaths and injuring seventeen other workers; it was the largest marine oil spill in history, with approximately 1,000 barrels of oil a day spreading into the Gulf of Mexico until the well was sealed five months later, on 19 September. The accident created a large-scale ecological tragedy, with the leaked petroleum moving across 57,500 square miles. A significant portion of the water in the Gulf was closed to fishing for three months, and tourism was down due to oil on the beaches, devastating multiple states' economies. BP established a compensation fund for those affected by the disaster, distributing $20 billion over three years.

The Affordable Care Act and other legislative accomplishments made possible by Democratic majorities in the Senate and House of Representatives sparked outrage among Republicans, allowing them to rally significant support for the midterm elections. On 2 November, the House of Representatives experienced the largest swing in party affiliation in over sixty years, with the Senate maintaining its Democratic control by a slim margin. Many of these new lawmakers identified as "Tea Party" Republicans and ran campaigns that were solely focused on disrupting the "business as usual" machinations of Capitol Hill. The gender implications of this election were also evident in the rallying cry among many Republican candidates to "fire Nancy [Pelosi]," the Speaker of the House, who was the embodiment of the liberal policies decried by conservatives, particularly because of her close affiliation with the Affordable Care Act victory. National Public Radio also reported that the 2010 midterm election saw the beginnings of a shift in female voters away from Democratic candidates toward Republican candidates, with scholar Kathleen Dolan quoted in the piece suggesting that there was "little reason to believe that women wouldn't be subject to the same forces and trends that men voters are" (Weeks).

On 22 December, Obama signed the repeal of the military's "Don't Ask, Don't Tell" policy, allowing LGBT members of the armed forces to serve the country without having to hide their sexual orientation. In his speech, Obama stated that "valor and sacrifice are no more limited by sexual orientation than they are by race or by gender or by religion or creed" (Lee).

The swine flu (also referred to as H1N1), the first influenza pandemic in over forty years, continued to spread throughout the United States during the first months of the year, affecting primarily children and young and middle-aged adults. The virus was a "unique combination of influenza virus genes never previously identified in either animals or people" (cdc.gov). The Centers for Disease Control and Prevention estimated that by 10 April, there were 60.8 million cases, 274,304 hospitalizations, and 12,469 deaths from the virus (cdc.gov). A vaccination targeted at priority groups managed to bring down the number of infections, and the formulation of the 2010–2011 seasonal flu shot included protection against the virus strain.

The year saw the launch of notable tech products and companies. On 27 January, Apple introduced the iPad, which was an addition to its already robust fleet of personal computers and its influencer-pleasing iPhone. The photo-editing and -sharing app, Instagram, appeared on 6 October, attracting nearly 500,000 users in its first month. The app gained such a significant following that their two full-time employees saw their infrastructure stretched to its limit. Eventually, the company grew into one of the most significant players in the social media landscape. To be sure, the growing prominence of social media was on everyone's minds, as evidenced by *Time* picking Facebook CEO Mark Zuckerberg as their Person of the Year, citing the 700,000 members a day that were joining the networking site and calling him "The Connector." In the article that accompanied the cover story, writer Lev Grossman remarked on the "open plan" style of the Facebook corporate offices with "no cubicles, no offices, no walls, just a rolling tundra of office furniture." Furthermore, he remarked that no one in a meeting he attended "looked over 30" (Grossman).

Notable celebrity deaths included writer J. D. Salinger, actors Dennis Hopper, Patricia Neal, Tony Curtis, and Jill Clayburgh, actress and singer Lena Horne, writer, director, and producer Blake Edwards, and producer Dino De Laurentiis. The best-selling books of the year were *The Help* by Kathryn Stockett and *The Girl Who Kicked the Hornet's Nest* by Stieg Larsson, with the latter topping the *New York Times* Best Seller list for eight weeks and the former for six weeks. Network television shows with the highest ratings included *American Idol, Dancing with the Stars,* and *Sunday Night Football,* along with *NCIS* and *NCIS: Los Angeles.* The top twenty-nine highest-rated shows occasionally overlapped with those that received the most critical acclaim, which included the hour-long dramas *Breaking Bad* (AMC), *Mad Men* (AMC), *The Good Wife* (CBS), *Friday Night Lights* (NBC), and the final season of ABC's *Lost*, and half-hour comedies such as *Community* (NBC), *Parks and Recreation* (NBC), *Louie* (FX), and *Modern Family* (ABC). The top five songs on the Billboard charts were "TiK ToK" by Ke$ha, "Need You Now" by Lady Antebellum, "Hey, Soul Sister" by Train, "California Gurls" by Katy Perry (featuring Snoop Dogg), and "OMG" by Usher (featuring will.i.am). In the theater world, the revivals of August Wilson's *Fences* and Arthur Miller's *A View from the Bridge* won numerous Tony Awards. *Fences* won the Best Revival of a Play award along with Best Performance by a Leading Actor and Actress for Denzel Washington and Viola Davis, respectively, and Scarlett Johansson won Best Performance by a Featured Actress in a Play for *A View from the Bridge*. The drama *Red* won for Best Play and *Memphis* won for Best Musical. Super Bowl XLIV on 7 February saw a matchup between the New Orleans Saints and the Indianapolis Colts, with the Saints beating the Colts 31–17, marking the team's first Super Bowl win. The game featured a halftime show by British rock band The Who, and was (at the time) the most watched Super Bowl ever, with 106.5 million viewers.

The 2010 box office was dominated by franchise films and animated features. Six of the top ten highest-grossing films of the year were sequels or part of existing franchises. The year's early releases included the Denzel Washington vehicle *The Book of Eli* which opened on 15 January and went on to become one of the year's top box-office draws. Romantic comedies *When in Rome*, *Dear John*, and *Valentine's Day* were released in late January through mid-February to capture the female audience with counterprogramming against the early February Super Bowl and capitalize on the Valentine's Day holiday. The Martin Scorsese–helmed psychological thriller *Shutter Island* was released on 19 February, performing well in its opening weekend and going on to be the director's highest-grossing film to date. Tim Burton's *Alice in Wonderland* opened on 5 March, dominating the family-friendly-film box office until the release of *Shrek Forever After* on 21 May. The early summer slate began with the female-driven *Sex and the City 2* on 27 May, which was a follow-up to the popular HBO television series and the very successful first film, but failed to draw the same enthusiasm as its predecessor.

June was dominated by two of the biggest box-office draws of the year with *Toy Story 3*'s release on 18 June and the third installment of the successful *Twilight* series (based on Stephenie Meyer's best-selling books), *The*

Twilight Saga: Eclipse, following on 30 June. *Toy Story 3* went on to be the first animated film in history to gross $1 billion at the box office (Finke). Early July saw the release of multiple family films, including *The Last Air-bender* on 1 July, a poorly-reviewed M. Night Shyamalan–directed adaptation of the popular Nickelodeon television show. The 3D computer-animated *Despicable Me* followed on 9 July, as well as Disney's Jerry Bruckheimer–produced *The Sorcerer's Apprentice* on 14 July. 16 July saw the release of *Inception*, Christopher Nolan's mind-bending suspense thriller about dreams and dream states. Released as an R-rated tentpole film in the middle of July, it offered adult-targeted, intellectually deep, high-concept entertainment, counterprogrammed against other, more family-friendly pictures and action films released in late summer and early fall, including the Angelina Jolie–fronted *Salt* (released on 23 July) and an action vehicle for aging male stars, *The Expendables* (released on 13 August).

The hotly anticipated film adaptation of Elizabeth Gilbert's best-selling *Eat Pray Love* starring Julia Roberts released on 13 August and was successful in its female-targeted counterprogramming, earning $250 million. Other fall romantic comedy releases, such as *The Switch* (20 August), *Going the Distance* (3 September), *You Again* (24 September), *Life as We Know It* (8 October), *Love & Other Drugs* (24 November), and *How Do You Know?* (17 December), signaled that the genre still had some legs, even as its ubiquity faded as the decade progressed. The strong reception of the Emma Stone–led teen comedy adaptation of *The Scarlet Letter*, *Easy A*, released on 17 September, also signaled that audiences were still amenable to the fading teen film genre.

While there was strong counterprogramming offered by a number of successful horror film releases, including *Let Me In* (1 October), *Paranormal Activity 2* (20 October), and *Saw 3D* (29 October), the fall was dominated by traditional, and some nontraditional, Oscar-bait films. There was a lot of buzz surrounding such studio releases as Joel and Ethan Coen's reimagining of the 1969 John Wayne film *True Grit* (22 December), indies *Black Swan* (3 December, directed by Darren Aronofsky) and *Blue Valentine* (29 December, directed by Derek Cianfrance), and the expected British-produced biopics *127 Hours* (5 November) and *The King's Speech* (26 November). The latter film eventually went on to win Best Picture.

A Tale of Two Genders

On 7 March, Kathryn Bigelow made history as the first woman to ever win the Best Director Oscar for her film *The Hurt Locker*

(2009), with the film also taking home the Best Picture award. To be sure, the 2009 Oscars (awarded in 2010) saw many historic shifts as it was the first time in over six decades that the Best Picture category had more than five nominees. The Academy enacted this change as a result of the growing sentiment among critics and moviegoers that the "Oscar voters had drifted too far from the moviegoing public" (Cieply). The increase to ten nominees, which was in effect for two years before the AMPAS changed it again in 2012, had the fortunate advantage of increasing the diversity of the nominees, at least in terms of gender. In addition to *The Hurt Locker*, Lone Scherfig's *An Education* was also nominated for the 2009 Best Picture, marking the first time in awards history that more than one film directed by a woman had been included in the race. This achievement was repeated in the 2010 race when two of the three female-directed films discussed below, *Winter's Bone* and *The Kids Are All Right*, were also nominated for that award. These shifts were worthy of celebration; however, when glimpsed within the context of the industry's long history of focusing on the work of Caucasian male directors, they signified only a modest step forward.

Bigelow's break through the glass ceiling of a largely male-dominated space provides a revealing foundation for understanding how broader gendered discourses operated in American cinema in 2010. Two types of films made in this year offer different glimpses into systems of power in transition. One, referenced above, saw independent women filmmakers breaking through to mainstream success. The widespread plaudits received by Debra Granik's *Winter's Bone*, Lisa Cholodenko's *The Kids Are All Right*, and Lena Dunham's *Tiny Furniture* showed that women-directed films were becoming central to conversations about the best of American cinema. The content of these films, which the directors also wrote or co-wrote, was personal and character-focused; it presaged a slow but steady increase in multifarious portrayals of social and cultural issues in the decade to come, with women, people of color, and the LGBTQ community seizing the reins of economic and industry power away from the dominant white male power structure.

The second group—David O. Russell's *The Fighter*, Charles Ferguson's *Inside Job*, David Fincher's *The Social Network*, Oliver Stone's *Wall Street: Money Never Sleeps*, and John Wells's *The Company Men*—are representative of that white male power structure, with all but one of these filmmakers (Ferguson) deeply entrenched in the Hollywood industry. These films, both in their context and content, reflect the anxieties surrounding the recessionary moment either through their explicit portrayal of the circumstances that led to the economic downturn or implicit engagement with a particular kind of masculine power in crisis, in which old and new ideals (which often correspond with old and new Caucasian bodies) are pitted against each other. Women are on the periphery of these narratives, and if they are present at all, are depicted as onlookers to the power brokering depicted therein.

Women on the Rise

Winter's Bone, Tiny Furniture, and *The Kids Are All Right* feature female characters in very different milieus, all of whom are dealing with significant shifts in their personal lives. Unlike the male-centered films on which I will focus later in the chapter that display intragender competitions based in the professional sphere, the changes in these films emanate from within private spaces. Characteristic of indie filmmaking, they focus on the small and the intimate, and are character- rather than plot-driven. They all present women-centric diegetic worlds in which men are at best a disappointment and at worst a hostile threat.

The first of these films to be released was Debra Granik's low-budget second feature film (after her 2004 release *Down to the Bone) Winter's Bone,* which won Best Picture and Best Screenplay (for Granik and Anne Rosellini) at the Sundance Film Festival. The film, adapted from Daniel Woodrell's novel of the same name, examines the toxicity of embedded patriarchal systems of power on a small scale through the perspective of seventeen-year-old Ree (played by the then unknown Jennifer Lawrence). Ree lives in a poor community in the Ozark Mountains that has been ravaged by the methamphetamine trade. She serves as the full-time primary caretaker for her two younger siblings and her mentally ill mother. At the beginning of the film, Ree discovers that Jessup, her meth-cooking father, has put up their house and land for collateral on a bail bond. Unless he turns up to his hearing the next day, the family is at risk of being evicted within a week's time. Ree embarks on a quest to track down her father and urge him to appear at the hearing. When it becomes clear to her that he has likely been murdered, she then pivots to trying to find his body so that she can prove his death to the police, thus nullifying the bond. This journey puts her into contact with many hostile members of her extended family. She is told at numerous times to stay away, stop asking questions, and back down, but she refuses, resulting in several violent confrontations, one of which ends with her being severely beaten and having her teeth knocked out.

Granik paints a vivid picture of this milieu with its wintry, barren landscape, houses falling to rubble and surrounded by detritus, and the dimly lit, unkempt interior spaces brimming with tired bric-a-brac and worn furniture. The few moments of fellowship presented in the film revolve around the playing of music, which is a central part of the film's soundscape (and performed by real locals) along with the rustling of trees and the sound of the numerous stray animals seen in the film (Badley 124). Linda Badley refers to the film as a "touchstone" for a neorealist turn in women's independent filmmaking, with its "insistence on scarcity, desperation, and women's daily grind." The film's consistent use of long shots depicting Ree walking amid a desolate rural backdrop just to keep the little she has, where the only signs of affluence are the ownership of an operable car or the promise of a stipend that comes with U.S. Army enlistment, demonstrates the film's reflection of the discouragement of day-to-day living in an economically depressed community.

Aside from the meticulously drawn setting, the film's power lies in Lawrence's rich, complex performance as a young woman who demonstrates a strength well beyond her years. She is unrelenting in her determination to discover the truth about her father and shield her young sister and brother from the dire reality of their predicament. American cinema doesn't often tell the stories of poor young women, and here Ree is depicted not unlike a superhero. She persists when she is told no and is unrelenting in her quest to find the truth. Yet there are limitations to how much she can accomplish as a woman in this world in which men still hold much of the power. With the exception of April (Sheryl Lee), her father's lover, all of the people she seeks out for information about her father's whereabouts are men, yet they all have women who serve as their gatekeepers. They are often sympathetic to Ree's predicament, yet ultimately yield to the decisions of the men. As Martha Nochimson puts it, "the relationship between men and women is cast in terms of pure subjugation, bearing no erotic connotations at all" (54). This subservience is seen in Ree's best friend, Gail (Lauren Sweetser), whom Ree chastises for asking permission from her husband to borrow his car and backing down when he says no. It also applies to Merab (Dale Dickey), matriarch of the Milton family, who throws hot liquid in Ree's face for confronting her husband, Thump, at a cattle sale after she implored her to stay away.

Granik, through both the script and her direction, reveals a certain strength in women's restricted roles in this milieu. For instance, Merab seems to take pride in the fact that she and other women beat Ree, saying that they wouldn't let a man do that to her. It is also Merab and other women who eventually take Ree to her father's body so that she can prove that he is dead, bringing back the precarious equilibrium that Ree has threatened

In *Winter's Bone* (Debra Granik, Roadside Attractions), Ree (Jennifer Lawrence) asks Merab (Dale Dickey) for help finding her father. Digital frame enlargement.

in the community. It is therefore significant that it is Merab who cuts off the dead Jessup's hands with a chainsaw when Ree is too overcome with emotion to do so. By all but admitting to being responsible for murdering Jessup and then chopping off his hands, Merab, with her steely gaze and weathered face, still does more for Ree than Ree's own mother can do. With Merab's brutal gesture, Ree is finally able to move out of her father's shadow and save her family's livelihood.

Later the same month, a different kind of family struggle was portrayed by *The Kids Are All Right*, the fourth feature directed by Lisa Cholodenko and the third which she wrote and directed. *The Kids Are All Right* centers on a same-sex married couple, Nic (Annette Bening) and Jules (Julianne Moore), who live an upper-middle-class life in their beautiful Los Angeles home with their two children, Joni (Mia Wasikowska) and Laser (Josh Hutcherson). Nic is a doctor and Jules is a landscape designer struggling to build her business. Their oldest child, Joni, is getting ready to leave for college, and Nic and Jules's relationship is growing a bit stale, with the couple struggling to find moments of connection in the midst of shifting family dynamics. The film is brightly lit, with few stylistic flourishes, presenting a meticulous production design where spaces are differentiated only by where their inhabitants fall on a spectrum of affluence. Paul's house and restaurant portray a minimalist, bohemian chic, with his home's hilltop setting, overgrown yard, and the predominance of natural wood striking a visual contrast with the cozy, understated, pink-beige-and-taupe interior of Nic and Jules's house.

At the beginning of the film, Joni has just celebrated her eighteenth birthday, and Laser urges her to seek out the name of the anonymous donor whose sperm their moms used to conceive them. Upon getting this information, they arrange a meeting with Paul (Mark Ruffalo), a successful, handsome, motorcycle-riding local restaurant owner. Laser is initially more invested than Joni, but their positions change after meeting Paul. Joni is intrigued by his lifestyle and his commitment to local agriculture, while Laser thinks Paul is "a little into himself." In an effort to be involved with this newly established relationship, Jules and Nic invite Paul over for a meal. While Nic remains cautious, Jules slowly warms to him when he hires her to landscape his backyard. As Jules and Paul work together, she finds herself attracted to his similar spirit of wanderlust and resemblance to her children. They begin to have an affair, which brings to light the difficult dynamics of her and Nic's relationship of many years and points to the challenges in keeping long-term relationships thriving. For Jules, sex with Paul is a symptom of a larger feeling of dissatisfaction with her marriage; though, as many critics (highlighted below) pointed out, the film mostly avoids a lengthy examination of introducing a straight male as the ultimate representation of sexual virility, with only a few short conversations about whether Jules is "straight now," which she vehemently denies. The conclusion of the film does not promise a happy ending for Nic and Jules after the former learns of the affair, but does signal a possible reconciliation when they drop off Joni for her first year of college.

Jules (Julianne Moore) and Nic (Annette Bening) chat with Paul (Mark Ruffalo), their children's sperm donor, in *The Kids Are All Right* (Lisa Cholodenko, Focus Features). Digital frame enlargement.

Cholodenko was a leading voice in women's independent cinema prior to the release of *The Kids Are All Right*, but this film received more widespread attention because it was one of the first films to not only foreground a lesbian married couple but also a same-sex couple raising children. As Jodi Brooks humorously points out, "Even if a lot of the talk was about how much the film was being talked about, *The Kids Are All Right* was still being talked about a lot" (Brooks 111). It was the target of both praise and criticism from film critics and cultural commentators. Its "normalization" of Nic and Jules's domestic situation was celebrated for bringing to light that the challenges involved in marriage are not restricted to heterosexual couples. In fact, the story was inspired by Cholodenko's own long-term partnership with musician Wendy Melvoin and their children.

Critics were almost uniformly positive about the film. The *New York Times*'s A. O. Scott writes, "its originality, the thrilling, vertiginous sense of never having seen anything quite like it before also arises from the particular circumstances of the family at its heart" ("Meet the Sperm Donor"). However, many cultural commentators found it offensive, albeit for different reasons. Conservative groups thought that it demonstrated the degradation of traditional marriage between a man and a woman. *Focus on the Family* wrote an extensive article on their website in response to the film, introducing research they claim refutes the premise that same-sex couples can raise healthy children, saying, "Nature and Nature's God has had us settle for these sub-par mother/family families all these millennia" (Stanton). Queer theorist Jack Halberstam criticized it for how it "sadly trades in stale stereotypes about lesbians." Another major source of critique was how it integrates a heterosexual male perspective into this family structure, even going so far as to suggest that because Mark Ruffalo's character is portrayed with such "sexual power," Jules harbors a secret desire for heteronormative sex as a salve for her dissatisfaction with her marriage to Nic. Or, as Halberstam states, "it becomes inevitable that Jules will sleep with Paul, that she will become dick-obsessed, that Nic will be cast as the sad, slightly butch partner who loses out to the dynamic, phallic dad." This film was also among those nominated for Best Picture in 2010, with Bening nominated for Best Actress, Ruffalo for Best Supporting Actor, and Cholodenko and Blumberg for Best Original Screenplay.

Setting the scene for another significant transmedia artist of the 2010s, writer, actor, and director Lena Dunham's debut feature, *Tiny Furniture*, received a limited release in theaters in November after playing in the South by Southwest Festival, the Los Angeles Film Festival, and BAMcinemaFest earlier in the year. Dunham plays Aura, a recent college graduate who moves back in with her mother (played by Dunham's real mother, Laurie Simmons) and sister Nadine (played by her real sister, Grace) in New York City while she is trying to figure out what professional path to pursue. The film chronicles Aura's difficulty in overcoming a recent breakup, finding a job, relating to new potential romantic partners, and reestablishing relationships with her sister, mother, and friends from childhood. Her postgraduation plan is to find a job so she can get an apartment with her college friend (played by Merritt Wever) when she joins her in New York at the end of the summer; but Aura becomes so entrenched in the social dynamics of her old life that she backs out of this commitment, choosing instead to continue living with her mother and sister.

The narrative is episodic in nature, borrowing the meandering conversational style of the mumblecore genre, a group of films made in the early 2000s that were character focused, dialogue centered, and featured interpersonal dynamics of early twentysomethings. *Tiny Furniture* offers a similar glimpse into the nonevents that make up Aura's day-to-day life, in which she attempts to exact some control over the trajectory of her future. When she does find a job as a day hostess, her primary preoccupation is her flirtatious interaction with the sous chef, Keith (David Call), who complains about his fellow kitchen workers and live-in girlfriend and tries to persuade Aura to bring him Vicodin. She is introduced by a mutual friend to Jed (Alex Karpovsky), a YouTube "artist" who makes comedic videos, a nod to Dunham's own history making short YouTube videos, one of which (where she strips down to her underwear in a fountain and then proceeds to brush her teeth) is featured in this film. Hoping to transform his online notoriety into mainstream success, he passively manipulates Aura into letting him stay in her apartment while her mother and sister are out of town.

Tiny Furniture is filled with a kind of ineffectual, slacker sensibility in which everyone, including Siri, Aura's mother, seems to be floating through one of the most expensive cities in the world without a deep concern for the origins of their next paycheck. Aura is not a conventionally likeable character, though Dunham's writing carefully avoids the overdone quirky and zany qualities that can sometimes accompany indie films' portrayals of women. She spends a good portion of the narrative complaining that she is having a difficult time (hence the marketing tagline "Aura would like you to know that she is having a very, very hard time"), and her bodily comportment remains slouchy and resigned throughout the film. More often than not, she appears small in relationship to her surroundings, with the camera's framing making her appear like the "tiny furniture" her mom so carefully arranges in her photographs. She is often captured in the corner of long or medium long shots, where the minimalist, white décor of her apartment makes her seem sloppy and unkempt by comparison.

Her difficulty in standing up for herself, particularly with men, culminates in a particularly painful scene (in a film filled with moments of abjection) where Aura has sex with Keith in a piece of pipe on the street. She is literally contained within a small space and seems to derive no pleasure from the interaction. As Maria San Filippo has aptly discussed, Aura's sexual humiliation in this scene is consistent with Dunham's approach to sexual provocation in her larger body of work that highlights her "defetishized, naturalistic self-representation" (36). The act of sharing the experience with her mother later that evening is played with subtlety, and as Corinn Columpar puts it, "offers a closure of sorts insofar as it provides Aura with the intimacy and reciprocity she seeks, at least provisionally" (282). In true indie fashion, the ending offers a fleeting moment of self-reflection on Aura's part through this interaction with Siri but offers no resolution to any of the problems she has faced throughout the film.

Tiny Furniture's unique style won Dunham the Narrative Feature prize at the South by Southwest festival in March of 2010, and a deal to develop a comedy pilot at HBO. The film wasn't particularly successful at the box office, though its originality and the high-profile media coverage Dunham received, including a profile in the *New Yorker* magazine four days prior to its release, earned Dunham a sort of indie "it girl" status.

Men in Crisis

The male-directed, male-centric films made in 2010 offer a completely different worldview from the female-centered, female-directed independent films discussed above. This group of movies focuses extensively on the professional sphere and is permeated with a sense of anxiety related to threats to existing embedded systems of power from new industries, new approaches, and a trend toward computer automatization. These are threats that are enacted and felt almost exclusively by and among men, as expressed in both implicit and explicit ways. In *The Fighter* and *The Social Network*, the battles waged between different types of men and the different types of masculinity they represent are symbolic of past versus present approaches to success. With *Inside Job*, *Wall Street: Money Never Sleeps*, and *The Company Men*, these issues are explicitly played out in relationship to the 2008 financial crisis and its aftermath. By nature of their fixation on white men in crisis and the rendering of women and people of color as bystanders or victims of power struggles (with a few notable exceptions), these films manage to conceal as much as they reveal about shifting hierarchies of inequity in a new economic and political climate that, according to Hanna Rosin, saw the economy becoming "more amenable to women than to men."

David O. Russell's *The Fighter* is an entry in the boxing film genre but deviates from its typical formula by centering its plot not on the conflicts between Micky Ward (Mark Wahlberg) and his opponents in the ring but on those between him and his brother, Dicky Eklund (Christian Bale), and the retrograde outlook he represents. The plot's framing device is a documentary shoot featuring Dicky, also a boxer, for the HBO series *American Undercover*. Dicky and his mother believe this attention will help reignite his welterweight boxing career, when in fact the documentary is profiling his deteriorating health and growing crack addiction (eventually released as *High on Crack Street: Lost Lives in Lowell* in 1995). Dicky is training Micky as the latter tries to elevate his status in the boxing world, but Dicky is irresponsible, frequently missing training sessions and spending most of his time at a local crack house. Micky is held back by his family's preoccupation with Dicky's former glory as the "Pride of Lowell" and their bygone approach that is out of touch with the changing landscape of the sport and ignores new opportunities to book matches outside of their usual networks.

The visceral performances by Wahlberg and Bale (with Bale taking home a Best Supporting Actor Oscar for his portrayal of Dicky) allow for the central tensions of the film to play out as a battle between two ends of a spectrum of working-class masculinity. Micky's muscular, powerful body is highlighted throughout the film as rippling with sweat and resilient even in the face of a serious hand injury that almost derails his career. Dicky's body, on the other hand, is diminutive, seeming to decrease in size in direct correspondence with the darkening of the circles underneath his eyes as his addiction takes over his life. Dicky's body is a body of the past which is holding on dearly to his lost fame and unable to come to terms with the present, whereas Micky's is yearning to break through the small-town mediocrity and move into a more successful future.

Their conflict is exacerbated by the women in their lives. Their overbearing mother-manager Alice (Melissa Leo in an Oscar-winning performance), whose aging, chain-smoking, expletive-filled antics are often comically supported by the bullying behavior of her seven daughters, is in denial about both Dicky's addiction and the need to evolve and innovate in her strategies to guide Micky's career. She too is stuck in the past and resistant to moving forward. On the flip side is Micky's young girlfriend, Charlene (Amy Adams), who is smart and headstrong and whose youth and sexuality are positioned in direct contrast to Alice's aging body. Charlene encourages Micky to move into the future and break free from his family's toxic influence. Her college-educated spunk and more worldly views are deemed more sensible than the trashy abrasiveness of the other local women. Eventually, the "old" and the "new" reconcile, with Dicky recovering from his addiction after a prison stint and Micky winning a pivotal fight—the world championship—with Charlene, Dicky, and Alice by his side. The film resolves with the HBO documentary team interviewing both Micky and Dicky, bringing its plot full circle to uphold the boxing genre's necessary triumphant victory as well as establishing a precarious harmony between the brothers. *The Fighter*'s forced resolution did not escape the attention of *Time* critic Mary Pols, who remarked, "the screenplay, credited to three writers, has that overdoctored feeling to it, and we're asked to take on a larger redemption tale that undermines the truth of Bale's wholly unsympathetic portrayal of a drug addict and a narcissist. *The Fighter*'s desire to show us what that awful combination looks like is overwhelmed by its urge to show us a Hollywood-style triumph."

The Social Network similarly focuses on the rise of a new guard and the death of an old one, while also capitalizing on the growing prominence of Facebook, the social networking site. However, in contrast to *The Fighter*, which, as Pols says, is overly allegiant to known Hollywood formulas, *The Social Network* feels innovative in gesturing toward but not adhering to the conventions of the biopic genre. The complementary strengths of veteran screenwriter Aaron Sorkin's precise command of dialogue (adapting Ben Mezrich's book *The Accidental Billionaires*) and director David Fincher's exacting visual style (with his usual low-key-lit, desaturated color scheme, as overseen by his regular collaborator, cinematographer Jeff Cronenweth) make the film pulse with a propulsive energy that tells what amounts to a David and Goliath story (if David were a socially inept, Harvard-educated computer genius and Goliath the old guard that has historically controlled social and economic power). Chronicling the early days of Facebook and its creator and founder Mark Zuckerberg (Jesse Eisenberg), the narrative moves back and forth between depositions in the present time wherein Zuckerberg faces legal challenges from both the Winklevoss twins (played by Armie Hammer with body double Josh Pence) and his former friend and business partner Eduardo Saverin (Andrew Garfield), and the past, which sees Mark as a Harvard student developing an idea for an online social network that connects people.

The great irony at the heart of the film is that Mark is terrible with people. Thus, his goal to build a social networking site is predicated not on establishing human connections but on his quest to prove two intertwined beliefs: first, that he is an innovative and brilliant thinker who is superior to those around him, and second, that there are alternatives to the old-money, high-society connections that are built in and around Ivy League schools. As I have argued elsewhere, coming on the heels of the man-cession, the film, both in its digital production and as a story *about* the rise of the digital, perfectly epitomizes the struggles of its historical and cultural moment. It shows how the global economy was in the process of shifting away from production and productivity that relied on a top-down model of physical and economic prowess toward a more automatized, computer-dominated one in which "control" was more diffuse. Many writers, like Hanna Rosin, have argued that this historical moment saw the economy moving toward more female-associated qualities and professions. *The Social Network* demonstrates how it also furthered the interests of a different brand of male power whose skills may have been more cerebral than physical but whose aims overlapped in significant ways with its predecessors.

For example, early in the film, Mark enacts a virtual form of revenge after being dumped by his girlfriend Erica (Rooney Mara) over a fight about Harvard's final clubs. He creates FaceMash in a matter of hours, an interactive website which prompts its users to decide which of two women is hotter. The scenes detailing Mark's programming process, done in the privacy of his small dorm room with his male friends cheering him on, are crosscut (using an intensified continuity style) with an exclusive final club party scene that is seemingly happening at the same time in a different part of campus. The party sees numerous young, attractive women waiting in line to enter the party so that they can drink and take ecstasy while being ogled by the male club members. The scene seems to come from a fantasy world, with the loud music and swiftly moving camera creating an aura of enticement and exclusivity. Meanwhile, Mark has staged a similar type of degradation for those who can't get into the club or its parties but have access to a computer and a mouse. The quick-paced sequence that moves back and forth between these locations encapsulates the film's primary themes. In one space there is a young, outsider, upstart white man exerting power through a website that reaches thousands of people quickly, whereas in the other space a group of established, well-connected young white men are using an already established power to exert a form of social control through the perception of popularity. One is virtual, the other in person, but both are at the expense of young women. The film chronicles this one-upmanship as representative of a seismic shift in the distinctions between the private and the public wherein the social media platform that Mark eventually creates begins to be the virtual stand-in for the final club social space. One of its most notable traits is the way it celebrates Mark's triumphant victory over his Goliath while simultaneously offering a critique of his achievement as nothing more than the exchange of one form of control for another. The fact that the film was released a few months prior to Zuckerberg being named *Time*'s Person of the Year is evidence of just how much he had already changed the social landscape.

Charles Ferguson's documentary *Inside Job* deals directly with the toxic masculinity surrounding the shifts brought on by the 2008 financial crisis. Its structure is broken up into four parts which chronicle the context in which the Great Recession arose, the series of events that led to big investment firms and banks failing, and the aftermath and repercussions of this downfall on the economy. Through a series of talking head interviews and easily digestible graphics explaining complicated economic concepts, Ferguson reveals the inequitable power structure that sees a handful of people who work in financial institutions prioritize their own short-term profitability over the interests of the individuals who have placed money in their hands. The film was positioned as offering an in-depth explanation and historically informed examination of how the crises came about, and as a rallying cry to change the system that allowed it to happen. As Kenneth Turan wrote in his *Los Angeles Times* review, "You have questions, *Inside Job* has answers. After watching Charles Ferguson's powerhouse documentary about the global economic crisis, you will more than understand what went down—you will be thunderstruck and boiling with rage" (Turan). Other reviews called it "a crime story like no other in history" (Germain), and "scarier than anything Wes Craven and John Carpenter have ever made" (Morris). Ferguson structures the film's narrative around the threatening, horrific force of the men in positions of control of wealth in the United States, revealing that the reality of the situation is considerably more terrifying than any fictional narrative.

Indeed, the director makes a point through his narration (voiced by actor Matt Damon) that this is a story that features mostly wealthy and powerful (and predominantly Caucasian) men in positions of power disenfranchising other segments of the population, even stating toward the end of the film that the "*men* and institutions who caused this crisis are still in power" (my italics). It is notable that Ferguson mirrors this male-centricity by only featuring five women in the forty-five interviewees who appear in the film. Only two of these five women are engaged as experts on the topic—Gillian Tett, the U.S. managing editor of the *Financial Times*, and Christine Lagarde, the French finance minister. Of the other three, two are victims of the financial crisis—one a Chinese worker and the other a woman who was given a subprime mortgage—and the other, Kristin Davis, is the owner of a high-end prostitution business who was forced to take a plea deal for serving as a madam to many high-profile Wall Street executives (though, as the film points out, none of the evidence she provided was used to crack down on the use of corporate credit cards to employ prostitutes).

There are a small number of powerful women who are identified as being intertwined with the financial malfeasance that the film highlights, and one—Brooksley Born, a former chair of the Commodity Futures Trading Commission—who is cited as making several unsuccessful attempts to enforce regulation of the financial markets. Certainly, there is a profound truth to the fact that this system is male dominated, and that women are still scarcely represented in the upper echelons of Wall Street power. However, the film gives the explanatory power to male experts, describing where men went wrong, and disproportionately emphasizes female victims, both those interviewed and the wives at home who don't realize their powerful husbands are sleeping with prostitutes. In this way, the film seems to mirror the very inequity it seeks to uncover.

Though *Inside Job*'s reviews compare the film to a fictional narrative because of the sheer audaciousness of the actions behind the crisis, it is difficult for Ferguson to provide a satisfying Hollywood upbeat ending. As the *Hollywood Reporter* puts it, "Ferguson exposes a level of greed that would make even Gordon Gekko cringe" (Byrge). Appropriately, Gordon Gekko resurfaced in Oliver Stone's sequel to his 1987 film *Wall Street*, *Wall Street: Money Never Sleeps*, that same fall. Stone's film tells the story of the financial crisis through a fictional lens, with Gekko (Michael Douglas) indeed cringing at the new financial terrain but also, expectedly, capitalizing on the moneymaking opportunities it presents. The original *Wall Street* was seen as a celebration of the economic boom of the 1980s, featuring Douglas as Gekko, a sleek billionaire financier who joins forces with, and is later betrayed by, young stockbroker Budd Fox (Charlie Sheen). Douglas's performance as Gekko earned him an Oscar, and his speech about how "greed is good" is iconic for its celebration of 1980s excess.

Money Never Sleeps takes place in 2008 and positions the story of a generational conflict between young trader Jake (Shia LeBeouf), who is trying to stake his claim in the competitive world of Wall Street, and the old guard represented by his future father-in-law, Gekko, who is released from prison at the beginning of the film. Jake is devastated when his mentor, Louis (Frank Langella), the head of a fictionalized Bear Stearns, commits suicide after the company goes bankrupt. Jake then joins forces with Gekko to avenge

Louis's death and strike back against the perceived opportunism of Bretton James (Josh Brolin), who, it is revealed, was also involved with Gekko's arrest in the 1980s. The sequel draws parallels between the corruption of the past and the present. It implies that, although credit default swaps might be the newest symptom of Wall Street malfeasance, the broader economic landscape has been and will always be a competitive game between men. As Gekko puts it, "It's not about the money, it's about the game between people and that's all it is."

Like its predecessor, *Wall Street: Money Never Sleeps* is also steeped in both narrative and aesthetic excess, or as A. O. Scott puts it, "An insomniac restlessness that is by turns thrilling and enervating" ("The Pride"). Stone's nonstop camera movement, random incorporation of visual effects, use of split screen, and staging of a mise-en-scène intent on communicating "wealth" create a sense of the emptiness at the heart of these characters as well as their persistent efforts to earn more and more money. The sequel does have more substantive roles for female characters, though they are so thinly drawn the effort comes off as window dressing. Jake has one female colleague, Audrey (Vanessa Ferlito), who disappears from the plot halfway through the film, and his mother's (Susan Sarandon) only function is to ask Jake to invest in her real estate business. The primary effort is put into developing the character of Winnie (Carey Mulligan), Gekko's daughter and Jake's fiancée. After her much-acclaimed starring role in the previous year's *An Education*, Mulligan is at the height of her career here, and elevates the film to the degree she can given that Winnie is written as a reactive, rather than active, character. As the publisher of a progressive news website who is openly hostile to her father, she acts as the moral conscience of the film; she takes a stand against Jake and Gordon's dealings. She is presented as considerably more emotionally intelligent than any other character in the film (and is certainly rendered a more three-dimensional character than Daryl Hannah's Darien in the first *Wall Street*); however, her rigid ethical stance relegates her to an irritant and hindrance to Jake and Gordon's ambitious financial revenge. Her role transitions to a kind of mother-savior when she learns of her pregnancy, offering Jake, as father, and Gordon, as grandfather, a chance to invest in family connections rather than monetary power. Similar to *The Fighter*, the film offers a pat ending in which personal tensions and professional calamities are resolved and all of the main characters gather happily at a birthday celebration for Jake and Winnie's son.

The conflict between new and old business practices, wherein handshakes, golf matches, and the literal or figurative act of men "building things" come up against a new workplace model, is most literally represented in John Wells's *The Company Men*. Similar to *Wall Street: Money Never Sleeps*, the film introduces the financial crisis in its opening sequence with a cacophony of voices from various news broadcasts detailing the country's economic woes. These visual and aural cues are juxtaposed with the next sequence's montage that shows the interiors and exteriors of the large and expensive houses owned by the film's three main characters, Gene McClary (Tommy Lee Jones), Phil Woodward (Chris Cooper), and Bobby Walker (Ben Affleck), all of whom are employed by GTX, Global Transportation Systems, a publicly owned transportation conglomerate. The sequence shows the objects that come with wealth, including luxury cars, golf equipment, appliances, bicycles, and motorcycles, using match cuts as the three men gaze into the mirror and put on a tie at the beginning of the workday.

The film is a multiprotagonist narrative, although the primary action is focused on Bobby, the youngest of the three characters. The day that begins the narrative shows Bobby arriving at work, gleefully walking into a meeting with news of a terrific golf game only to be met by his co-workers' grim faces. He finds out that GTX is downsizing due to the recession and that he is one of the casualties of these cuts. Phil and Gene, who have been employed at the company for most of their adult lives, survive this first round of layoffs, but both see the writing on the wall that the company culture with which their careers have been intertwined is shifting before their eyes. Gene in particular is incensed when he discovers that cuts have been made to the division that he heads while he was out of town, and he subsequently stages a confrontation with his friend and boss Salinger (Craig T. Nelson). Gene expresses his investment in keeping the company operating as usual, without such major cuts, whereas Salinger explains that "manufacturing is dead" and that the future is in health care infrastructure. "Our stock is in the toilet!" exclaims Salinger, to which Gene responds, "Everyone's stock is in the toilet!" This level of tension and insubordination eventually leads to his firing. He, along with Phil, is forced to start over with his career at an age when many would be on the verge of retirement.

Whether intentionally or not, *The Company Men* foregrounds masculine power as a performance that withers in the face of change. It is about how these men's egos, which are deeply involved with being perceived as sucessful, are forced to recalibrate as they face the upheaval that comes from a shifting economy in which their roles as solid, reliable "company men" are no longer valued. There are a number of scapegoats onto which this inner and outer rage is projected. The primary villains in the film are the "stockholders" whose interest is solely in the economic viability of the company.

Bobby (Ben Affleck) leaving GTX (Global Transportation Systems) on his last day in *The Company Men* (John Wells, the Weinstein Company). Digital frame enlargement.

The other villain is Sally Wilcox (Maria Bello), the executive in charge of the layoffs. Despite the fact, or perhaps because of it, that the film is focused entirely on men losing their jobs—save one tertiary character, Diane (Nancy Villone), a female co-worker of Bobby's—the film makes Sally, a woman, the embodiment of all that is unjust and impersonal about corporate culture. As if the destruction she wields in the workplace isn't enough, Sally is also portrayed as a home-wrecker, as she is having an affair with Gene. She is the young, ambitious, sleek contrast to Gene and Phil's staid, white-shoe mentality and Gene's traditional, homemaker wife. Sally is a powerful woman to be sure, but she is never portrayed by herself, for herself; she is only ever seen through the lens of the male characters. In fact, it is unclear what kind of connection is at the heart of her and Gene's relationship since, besides their one sexual encounter that involves them talking exclusively about work, their intimacy seems to consist entirely of resigned glances and shrugs.

This animosity toward women in the workplace is extended to tertiary characters throughout the film. When Bobby's secretary asks him if his termination means she lost her job too, he looks at her as if her self-interest is selfish and inappropriate. Karen (Kathy Harum), the counselor at the outplacement firm, is deemed ridiculous for her messages of positivity for the group and irritating for her straight talk about the challenges of the job market. (Phil later snaps at her for not respecting his authority by saying, "Do we know each other? You keep using my first name.") A human resources employee who is interviewing Bobby for a sales job receives the brunt of his anger for mentioning an open position that pays half his previous salary, and later in the film, Bobby leaves a voice mail for Sally, who won't return his phone calls, calling her a "fucking cowardly bitch," which is subsequently celebrated by the men (again, save Diane) around him.

The only primary female character treated with a degree of sympathy is Bobby's wife, Maggie (Rosemarie DeWitt). With a South Boston accent that is here one moment and gone the next, Maggie luxuriates in wealth that comes from Bobby's six-figure salary but hasn't gone too far away (figuratively and literally) from her working-class background. She is responsible, telling Bobby that his job loss means they will have to make sacrifices like dining out less, budgeting their dry cleaning, and skipping their yearly skiing trip. They also eventually sell his Porsche and their house and move in with her parents. It is when Bobby realizes that she has stopped paying the dues at the golf club that the reality of his situation hits home. He pleads to her, "I need to look successful, not like just another asshole with a resumé." She responds, "You are just another asshole with a resumé!"

Bobby's most profound sacrifice of dignity is when he finally accepts his brother-in-law Jack's (Kevin Costner) offer to employ him as a carpenter on a 4,000-square-foot home renovation. Whereas initially Bobby scoffs at the offer, saying, "I don't exactly see myself pounding nails," he ends up doing just that, requiring a complete orientation for a work environment based entirely on physical labor. It is an interesting plot development to portray carpentry and house renovation as the reliable industry in a film that introduces the circumstances that befell its main characters as a direct product of the recession, which hit construction particularly hard. Bobby initially struggles with this work, but eventually takes pleasure in it, the film romanticizing the calluses and muscles he develops as providing more of a sense of accomplishment than was achieved by spending the day typing on a keyboard and staring at a computer screen (the opposite message from that put forward by *The Social Network*). Even at the end of the film, after Phil has committed suicide and Bobby leaves Jack's employ and goes to work for Gene's new company, the film instills a sense that his economic struggles have brought him in touch with a more enlightened version of himself, one free of the superficiality of commodities and more in touch with the salt-of-the-earth authenticity of building something from the bottom up. *The Company Men*, even in its deep exploration of the crisis of masculinity brought on by the Great Recession, still manages to present a hopeful fantasy that older white men with an outdated sense of labor practices can reinvent themselves in the midst of a seismic shift in the economic landscape.

Overall, the turn of the decade of the 2010s saw a continuation of trends that were already deeply entrenched in American media industries: The disproportionate box-office revenues earned by children's films and sequels to existing franchises, women filmmakers making their mark and finding success almost exclusively in the independent film sphere and television, and straight, Caucasian, Hollywood male directors making films that focus predominantly on the power struggles of straight, Caucasian men. However, the year's films made small inroads into a subtle paradigm shift in which a certain kind of institutional male power was rendered ineffectual and corrupt, often leading to catastrophic economic circumstances, while new conceptions of strength, whether real or virtual, male or female, were introduced.

2011

Movies and Masculinity
at a Crossroads

DAVID GREVEN

2011 marked the third year of Barack Obama's presidency. Obama's first presidential term was associated with hopes for a more progressive and inclusive U.S. cultural atmosphere. Perhaps the most notable indication of social unrest that year was the Occupy Wall Street movement's inaugural protest on 17 September 2011 in New York City's financial district. 2011 films such as *Margin Call* (written and directed by J. C. Chandor) revisited the financial crisis of 2007–2008 while heralding the tensions fomenting Occupy.

One incident in early 2011 infected the period with a sense of impending danger. On 8 January in Tucson, Arizona, a gunman shot U.S. Rep. Gabrielle Giffords, killing six people and injuring fourteen. The image of shooter Jared Lee Loughner, with his bald pate, off-kilter smile, and smirking eyes, a harrowing snapshot of mental illness, hovers over one's memories of the year, especially in contrast to the vulnerability and resilience of Giffords, who survived and remains a gun law activist.

New York State signed the Marriage Equality Act into law, making same-sex marriage legal. This historic moment was the capstone of a year that was described on the 31 December episode of National Public Radio (NPR)'s *All Things Considered* as an "extraordinary" one for gay rights (NPR Staff). The "Don't Ask, Don't Tell" antigay military policy ended this year, and Secretary of State Hillary Clinton gave a notable speech to the United Nations in support of global LGBT rights. Perhaps the most significant indication of changing tides in favor of LGBT rights was the *New York Times* article by Sheryl Gay Stolberg on 18 June discussing President Obama's "evolving" views on gay marriage, a shift toward support for marriage equality.

2011 also signaled a retrenchment of conservative ideals in lockstep with the expansion of LGBT awareness and support. In her 2010 book *Save the Males: Why Men Matter, Why Women Should Care*, the center-right columnist Kathleen Parker lamented the decline in male authority and traditional gender roles, noting that in "the dangerous world in which we really live, it might be nice to have a few guys around who aren't trying to juggle pedicures and highlights."[1] Parker spoke from a position of xenophobic national pride as she lamented that American males were in danger of losing their phallic potency. "What we privileged Westerners refer to as the 'gender wars' would seem a holiday for women in countries that are incubating the next generation of Islamic jihadists. Yet here in America, we don't seem to get just how great our men really are (most of the time)."[2] However one responds to them, Parker's views articulated broader fears informing the representation of postmillennial masculinity. It is difficult not to read the effort to capture Osama bin Laden, the founder and leader of the militant group Al-Qaeda and the most-wanted fugitive on the U.S. list, in terms of this effort to reclaim American masculinity's integrity against a foreign threat. On 1 May, President Obama made it known that U.S. military forces had killed bin Laden in Pakistan.

In a remarkable blow to expectations that traditional forms of masculinity—in this case organized sports—would be immune to moral and gender role failings, Penn State reeled from the shock of seeing Jerry Sandusky, a former assistant coach for the Penn State University football team, arrested in November on nearly forty counts of molesting eight boys over a fifteen-year period. Perhaps even more startling to many, famous Penn State coach Joe Paterno—the beloved "Joe Pa"—and university president Graham Spanier were fired. Paterno's firing led to violent protests by those who claimed to be his supporters. Elsewhere in sports, the Dallas Mavericks, led by power forward Dirk Nowitzki, had long been known for stumbling in the playoffs after dominating in the regular season. Now, however, the Mavs won the NBA Finals, four games to two, upsetting the highly favored Miami Heat and its newly assembled "Big Three" of LeBron James, Dwyane Wade, and Chris Bosh. In Game Six of the World Series, another Texas team, the Rangers, twice came within a strike of winning their first pennant, but lost the game and, in Game Seven, the series, to the St. Louis Cardinals. On Broadway, the musical smash of the year, *The Book of Mormon* (music by Robert Lopez, book and lyrics by Trey Parker and Matt Stone of *South Park* fame), swept the Tonys, winning nine.

In pop culture, Wendy's introduced foie gras burgers in Japan. The integration of Siri into the iPhone 4S occurred in October 2011, one day before the death of Apple founder Steve Jobs of cancer at age fifty-six. Two-time Academy Award–winner Elizabeth Taylor, one of the most enduring of movie stars created by the Hollywood studio system, passed away at seventy-nine. Blues singer Amy Winehouse died of an overdose at twenty-seven. Among other notables the world lost were *Rope* and *Strangers on a Train* star Farley Granger, durable character actor Peter Falk, and New Hollywood–era producer Bert Schneider. To add a wedding to these funerals, Prince William and Catherine Middleton were married on 29 April 2011 in London at Westminster Abbey.

■ Films and the "Crisis in Masculinity"

If we can dismiss as hackneyed and alarmist the frequent reports of a "crisis in masculinity" at the time, 2011 American films conveyed a consistent sense that this crisis was genuine. Films as diverse as *The Descendants*, *X-Men: First Class*, *The Artist* (French but an Oscar-winner for Best Picture), *Shame*, *Fast Five*, *Limitless*, *Thor*, *Warrior*, *War Horse*, *The Adjustment Bureau*, *The Ides of March*, *Jeff, Who Lives at Home*, and *A Dangerous Method* focused on masculinity at a crossroads, the crossroads of gender, race, sexuality, class, and temporality itself. In each of these films, traditional masculinity verges on collapse, threatening to lose its coherence.

The comedy *Jeff, Who Lives at Home*, directed by Jay and Mark Duplass, offers an instructive example. The narrative focuses on the heartfelt but frustrating bond between brothers Pat (Ed Helms), lacking confidence and struggling to hold his marriage together, and the titular Jeff (Jason Segel), an enigmatic man still living at home with their mother and, by his own admission, adrift. ("I'm not doing well," he tells his brother. "Not. At. All.") In a significant shot, the brothers lament their wayward lives while sitting together in a hotel bathtub, a cinematic image of regression (the return to childhood, if not infancy, as the two brothers bathe together). Yet by film's end, Jeff has saved his brother's life (after he attempted to save someone who had fallen off of a bridge), gained competence with the household chores his frustrated mother chides him over, and verges on transformative change.

Jeff encapsulates a key pattern in films of this moment. 2011 films often subject masculinity to a series of destructive trials, a dynamic that I call "dismantling." At the same time, they always hold out the promise of reparative retrenchment. While genre cinema often literalizes transformation into new forms, most vividly in the comic book movie where bodies morph into superpowered entities, 2011 films transcend genre specificities in their shared larger themes. Chief among them is the shattering and reconstruction of male identity.

▬▬▬▬▬ Beleaguered Castle

Source Code, directed by Duncan Jones and written by Ben Ripley, shares something with another 2011 film, Captain America: The First Avenger, directed by Joe Johnston: a captain for a protagonist. Source Code's Captain Colter Stevens, played by Jake Gyllenhaal, is a U.S. Army pilot who last remembers action in Afghanistan. Gaining consciousness while asleep on a Chicago commuter train, he has no idea why he's there. A woman seated across from him—dark-haired, droll, sweetly smiling Christina Warren (Michelle Monaghan, perhaps best known for HBO's True Detective)—expresses her gratitude: "I took your advice. It was good advice. Thank you." Bewildered by this woman who speaks as if she knows him and keeps calling him "Sean," Stevens reels with astonishment when he catches his reflection in the train window. Briefly visible, this reflected visage is certainly not Stevens's own. "Did you see that?" he asks the increasingly befuddled Christina. He then lashes out at her as a stranger who inexplicably believes him to be Sean. Stevens heads into the restroom, shutting the shiny steel door behind him. Looking into the mirror, he sees a man who is quite different in appearance from himself, though also white. As Stevens learns, he is inhabiting the consciousness, and the body, of a schoolteacher named Sean Fentress, Christina's friend. After being on the train for eight minutes—enough time for a bustling lady to spill coffee on his shoe, an African American male passenger to ask the ticket officer if they will make up ten minutes of lost time, and a surly male comedian to insult the officer over the same issue—Stevens and his fellow passengers all seemingly die in a fiery explosion on their train. This explosion occurs when the commuter train is alongside a freight train, which, due to its proximity, also explodes. But Stevens does not die. He wakes up, strapped in a seat and garbed in his military gear in a kind of isolation booth, and hears a voice speaking to him. The person communicating with Stevens does so from outside of the booth and through a video screen. She is Air Force Captain Colleen Goodwin (Vera Farmiga), who explains that Stevens, stateside for two months now, has been enlisted to discover the identity of the terrorist who planted the bomb on the train. Stevens can investigate this past event because the titular source code technology, invented by Dr. Rutledge (Jeffrey Wright), allows him to live within the last eight minutes of Sean's life before the bomb on the train goes off. "Quantum mechanics, parabolic calculus, it's all very complicated," Rutledge responds when his agent asks about source code. Stevens's mission involves discovering the location of the bomb as well as the terrorist's identity, which demands that he eliminate a series of fellow passengers from his inquiries. As Goodwin identifies it, the call sign for the source code program is "Beleaguered Castle," which is also the name of a game of solitaire. Stevens will be playing such a game throughout the film.

The director Duncan Jones brings a sense of pathos and unpredictability to *Source Code*, one rooted in the male body. Jones finds a perfect embodiment for his themes in Gyllenhaal, whose sensitive screen presence deroutinizes action genre masculinity. The first shot of Stevens establishes his vulnerability. He is sleeping with his head resting against the train window, an image that figures him as defenseless and childlike. His bouts of panicked bewilderment and disorientation as he confronts his countenance, a face not his own, signal a narcissistic crisis with his own image, evoking Lacanian psychoanalytic theory. Given the emphasis on the mirror image as the key to male identity and the film's thematic focus on issues of temporality, Stevens is a prime example of the "ghost face" of 2000s cinematic masculinity. As I discuss, ghost faces thematize historical masculinity, recalling prior forms of male gender performance and foregrounding the citation of these prior forms. Stevens inhabits the role, identity, and the very body of a man from an earlier, if recent, time, indicating the film's awareness of masculine style as a phenomenon of temporality and male gender performance as a citation of such prior performances.[3] As we learn, what appears to be the "real" Stevens within the isolation booth is an illusion of masculine identity. Stevens is a war-torn lump of flesh, practically dead, kept alive so that he can be sent on the source code mission. In the movie's futuristic time, the Stevens we see exists as an illusion of his prior bodily coherence, a sharp contrast with what remains of his body. An armless torso, Stevens's body recalls Gaspard Marsy's sculpture of Enceladus—a giant of Greek mythology who used his body as a battering ram—the difference being that the small portion of Stevens's brain that remains active is the source of his intransigence.

The most disturbing aspect of *Source Code*, one that fully accords with 2011's representations of problematic masculinity, is the movie's obfuscation, not a successful one, of its racial anxieties. The movie performs a Barthesian inoculation against accusations of racism, ethnophobia, xenophobia, and the like by having Christina explicitly chastise Sean/Stevens for "racial profiling" when, attempting to use her as a resource, he asks her to point out which passengers look "suspicious." When Christina makes the accusation of racial profiling, it is during a giggly, flirtatious exchange with Stevens, genuine on her end but only playacting on his. He suspects a brown-skinned, bespectacled businessman—seemingly meant to be ethnically

In *Source Code* (Duncan Jones, Summit Entertainment), Captain Colter Stevens (Jake Gyllenhaal) finds his own face a bewildering mystery. Digital frame enlargement.

Arab—of being the terrorist. Breaking with the typical events of each repeated eight-minute-long source code mission, Stevens, Christina in tow, gets off the train to follow the possible terrorist, even into the men's room where he has retreated to collect himself. As it turns out, the businessman suffers from motion sickness, hence his having staggered off the train. In a deeply awkward moment, Stevens grabs the visibly ailing businessman's briefcase to inspect its contents and, to Christina's loudly voiced horror, even punches the queasy man in the face. From a distance now, we see the trains exploding up ahead. Still not believing that the businessman is innocent even after Stevens rifles through his contraband-free briefcase, Stevens throws him to the ground and aggressively searches his body. In the melee, the businessman manages to kick off Stevens, who tumbles onto the tracks where the oncoming train crushes his head.

The reason why this episode is problematic is that it visually and narratively represents an aggressive act of racial profiling that negates the narrative's seeming opposition to this profiling (Christina's concern that Stevens is being racist). Moreover, *Source Code*'s extended racial profiling sequence results in a brutal assault.

These racial anxieties intersect with homoerotic themes. *Source Code* foregrounds a surprising motif of cruising during Stevens's bathroom bouts with male identity. When he goes into the bathroom and locks the door in order to inspect his face, he sees what appears to be a different man altogether—Sean Fentress—in the mirror.[4] While the chief intended effect is to convey Stevens's shock at seeing someone not himself in the mirror, the visuals convey the impression that two distinct men warily but intently stare at one another in the enclosed, private space of a train restroom. When Stevens goes into the train station men's room to surveil the activities of the racially profiled bespectacled businessman, the two men exchange a pointed look, its intensity exceeding the encounter's ostensibly nondescript nature (nondescript since Stevens still keeps his suspicions hidden). Gyllenhaal's role in Ang Lee's plangent *Brokeback Mountain* (2005), an Oscar-nominated performance that cemented the actor's star persona, cannot be overlooked in considering the actor's subsequent films. His role in Lee's film, especially the sensitivity he brought to his performance, established queer potentialities in his star image. Thus *Source Code* capitalizes on Gyllenhaal's sensitivity and vulnerability at the same time that it strives to endow Gyllenhaal with aggressive male bona fides.

Stevens finally uncovers the villain, Derek Frost, aboard the train. Played with a wonderful, unhurried, sinister mildness by Michael Arden, Frost explains his motivations for the apocalyptic, grand-scale mayhem he's orchestrated: "The world is hell. We have a chance to start over in the rubble. But first, there has to be rubble." Jeffrey Wright's Rutledge, however, emerges as the secondary villain. Neither showy nor grandiosely malevolent, Rutledge nevertheless resembles Derek Frost in his general indifference to anything but the effectiveness of the technology he invented. Rutledge adds to the gallery of suspect nonwhite males in the movie. True, the villain of the film is a white man, but it's nevertheless inescapably disturbing that all the nonwhite men in the film range from odious to potentially terroristic. With his cerebral detachment and chilling disregard for Stevens's plight, as well as his unhesitating betrayal of his promise to terminate Stevens's life once the source code mission is completed, Rutledge reflects a phobic view of the science-bound rationalist. His bloodless—though, in its hygienic way, bloodthirsty—approach to life fails to *understand* life, in stark contrast to Stevens, Christina, and also Goodwin, who is touched by Stevens and willing to help him in defiance of Rutledge's dictates. Which is to say that none of the sympathetic characters in this film are nonwhite.

If the film's racial attitudes are suspect, *Source Code*'s treatment of the heterosexual couple, that cinematic cynosure, evinces a more radical edge. The film relishes opportunities to depict the heterosexual couple's annihilation. That these shots reflect Jones's cinematic brilliance adds to the disturbance. In one great shot, Stevens and Christina crouch on the ground floor of the train with the corridor beyond them. When Stevens asks, "What would you do if you only had a minute left to live?," fiery flames engulf the corridor and surge toward them in slow motion. Christina's face melts away in slow-motion flames, a hellish image repeated later. The painstaking use of practical effects indicates that the grotesque distortion of Christina's lovely face was significant for the filmmakers. In another sequence, Stevens confronts Frost in his white van loaded with bombs (in a case bearing the colors of the American flag). Christina, having followed Sean/Stevens, makes her way to the van and discovers Stevens, having been shot by Frost, lying on the ground. Frost then shoots Christina. In a striking shot, Stevens and Christina, both dying, lie on either side of the white van, a kind of Crucifixion image. *Source Code*'s Crucifixion imagery extends to the recurring fantasies of the heterosexual couple's annihilation. When Frost drives away, headed to the execution of his master plan, the bodies of the would-be lovers remain on the ground, like sacrificial objects of an abandoned, forgotten ritual.

It is worth noting that Stevens's major personal quest throughout the film is to speak with his father again. In his last source code mission, finally able to thwart Frost's plot—and, in defiance of Rutledge's science, change the past so that the commuter train bomb never goes off—Stevens contacts his father at last. (The voice-over of Stevens's father is done by Scott Bakula, whose TV series *Quantum Leap* was an inspiration for *Source Code*.) The conversation between Stevens (still playing Sean Fentress, since Stevens is in actuality dead) and his grieving father successfully solicits tears. Yet it also rather obviously foregrounds the most traditional Oedipal scheme. Stevens forges an identificatory alliance with the father and proceeds to claim the woman he now loves, an astonishingly neat summary of the Oedipal trajectory of the conventional Hollywood film's male protagonist. Indeed, the film's conclusion of its train-bound action crystallizes the symbolic meanings of the heterosexual couple's relationship within the genre film. In the end, *Source Code* is a loopy but consistent Cavellian comedy of remarriage. Stevens pays one passenger, an obnoxious comedian, to perform the routine he has been practicing throughout the journey. The performer accepts the payment readily. Redeemed by audience laughter, the comedian delights the passengers as we track forward through the aisle and land on a freeze-frame of Stevens and Christina kissing at last. Their kiss lasts beyond the time limit of the source code, signifying the future's continuation embodied by the couple and blessed by the comedian, whose raucous cheer and healing laughter establishes this future as a happy one.

■ **Bodies and Faces**

Captain America: The First Avenger, like *Source Code*, foregrounds a male crisis over body image. Scrawny, diminutive Steve Rogers (Chris Evans) is desperate to fight for the United States in World War II but, suffering from asthma and weighing only ninety pounds, he is consistently rejected for being physically inadequate. Rogers finds a champion in Dr. Abraham Erskine (Stanley Tucci). This German émigré, a scientist now aiding the U.S. fight against Hitler, develops a serum that transforms the noble but ill-suited Steve into a modern-day titan, the titular figure. Erskine's top secret project is funded by Howard Stark (Dominic Cooper), a billionaire tech guru and the father of the future Iron Man. Both Erskine's and America's foe is a would-be dark god who even considers Hitler expendable, Johann Schmidt (Hugo Weaving). He transforms into the monstrous, crimson-faced Red Skull—the Nazi equivalent to Captain America—making use of the same occult, futuristic technology of the Tesseract and the glowing blue orbs of unimaginable power pursued by the Avengers in Marvel's big-screen extravaganzas. Schmidt/Red Skull breaks off from the Nazis to create his own power-mad, world-domination-seeking evil faction known as HYDRA. Once again, male identity and masculine contest are rooted in the body, but the on-screen male bodies are either wildly incommensurate with those who inhabit them or undergo brutal transformations that render them inhuman.

As Karina Longworth puts it in her review of the film, "Created by Joe Simon and Jack Kirby for Marvel Comics in 1941, *Captain America* was among the first American comic books intended as an explicit work of patriotic, political propaganda: The cover of the first edition, available a year before Pearl Harbor, famously featured the titular costume hero punching out Adolf Hitler." She clinches her pan thusly: "Captain America assembles a ragtag multi-ethnic band of soldiers to help carry out his elite missions, but there's not so much as a single mention of the ideological divides that plagued the times—and, subsequently, spawned the original anti-Fascist *Captain America* comics." In this critic's persuasive view, this empty film suffers from and models a profound ahistoricism.

While there is much one could explore about the film's denatured version of WWII conflict and the history of the *Captain America* comic as context, for our purposes the chief fascination here is the predicament of a male body doubly transformed into a special effect. First, Chris Evans's face is CGI-grafted onto a different person's body in the first third of the movie featuring his scrawny, presuperhero attempts to join the war effort and be taken seriously as a soldier (these scenes, with Tommy Lee Jones playing an implacable general unimpressed with any version of Steve Rogers, play like a male version of the 1980 Goldie Hawn comedy *Private Benjamin*). Second, when the short and stymied Steve transforms into Captain America by being encased in a gleaming metal sarcophagus that pumps the serum from multiple canisters into his erupting body, we see, as the finished product, *Chris Evans's own glistening, sculptured body.*

Which is to say, Chris Evans the actor is the man who pretends to be himself, presenting his own body as the ultimate special effect. In the Lacanian scenario, the child of the mirror stage misapprehends his or her reflected image as an authentic image of bodily coherence and unity. The narcissist falls in love with a mirage. *Captain America*, in the hands of director Joe Johnston, performs a peculiar sleight-of-hand whereby an actor's own physical endowments transform into stupendous spectacle, convincing the audience that the revelation of this wondrous male form is the result of magical or alien technology rather than the implacable demands of contemporary Hollywood filmmaking organized almost entirely around comic book multiverses and metahuman bodies. In *Source Code*, Stevens comes to accept a body not his own, while Steve Rogers gapes in wonder at a body that is already his own. A secondary version of Lacan's concept of the primary mirror stage (which occurs in infancy), Rogers gains access to a coherent body image made spectacularly and resplendently literal.[5]

The emphasis on bodies, on men *as* bodies, finds a counterpoint in the male face. Something of a Cartesian split located in corporeality, a face-body dualism has emerged as one of the chief hallmarks of contemporary representations of masculinity, as I argue in my book *Ghost Faces*. Just as

Steve Rogers (Chris Evans) becomes Captain America, allowing Evans to gape in wonder at his own mythic body. *Captain America: The First Avenger* (Joe Johnson, Marvel-Disney). Digital frame enlargement.

Source Code does, Nicolas Winding Refn's 2011 film *Drive* lingers on faces, particularly male faces, as if they yield some secret knowledge of masculinity, or as if to brood obsessively on a face is to possess the man who wears it.

Drive stars Ryan Gosling as the unnamed "Driver." The Driver multitasks. Sometimes he acts as the getaway driver in the criminal underworld. At other times, he performs as a stunt double, a job for which his driving skills are also quite useful. Making an explicit metaphor of faces, the Driver dons an oversized, pasty-white mask that makes him look like a mass-produced muscleman. The mask signifies masculinity as a role one can put on and lose oneself within, while the diversity of Gosling's masculine styles—his alternating personae as getaway driver, stuntman, and slow-burning lover to a single mother (as she first appears to be)—further signify gender as, essentially, role-playing. *Drive* constantly contrasts the Driver with other kinds of men, defined by type: the violent but ultimately victimized Hispanic ex-husband (Oscar Isaac) of the woman (Carey Mulligan) the Driver loves and protects; the mob boss (Albert Brooks); his large, formidable, violent henchman (Ron Perlman); and the Driver's much-loved and perhaps only friend, Shannon (*Breaking Bad*'s Bryan Cranston), a wreck of a man who runs an auto repair shop and also works for the mob boss.

The film meditates on Gosling's impassive face with a focused intensity that exceeds the demands of the plot. Gosling specializes in being able to hold the camera's gaze with unflinching and resolute tenacity. The actor's capacity for stillness and coiled fury has never been put to more forceful use. His intense, blank stare is one of the major motifs of the film, suggesting reserves of banked desire and potential violence. The Driver, in his general impassivity and his fits of controlled rage and capacity for violence,

Ryan Gosling as the unnamed "Driver" in *Drive* (Nicolas Winding Refn, FilmDistrict) donning his stuntman mask. Digital frame enlargement.

evokes earlier screen masculinities—the stoicism of Humphrey Bogart in noir and Alan Ladd in *Shane* (George Stevens, 1953, an obvious inspiration for *Drive*)—but also the moments when the stoic hero leaves behind civility and avails himself of the tools of retributive violence. Refn deploys Gosling's star persona complexly. It indicates a new and pointed blankness that demands and refuses interpretation while also channeling the codes of classical Hollywood masculinity.

Caesar Is Home

Two more distinctly different films than the following could not be imagined: *Rise of the Planet of the Apes*, directed by Rupert Wyatt and the first installment of 20th Century Fox's reboot of the *Planet of the Apes* series, and *We Need to Talk about Kevin*, directed by Lynne Ramsay and adapted from Lionel Shriver's novel. Yet both films explore the rebellion against the strictures of the family by a son whose feelings of estrangement lead him to embrace violence as liberation. The chief distinction between the narratives is the gender dynamic in each intransigent son's war against a parent; in *Apes*, Caesar, the ape with a human mind, radically breaks with his surrogate father; in *Kevin*, the son masterminds a terrifying killing spree chiefly to appall the mother he has perpetually scorned—and who scorns him in return.

Apes is a far more successful attempt at a reboot of the franchise than Tim Burton's ill-fated 2001 version starring Mark Wahlberg, Helena Bonham Carter, Tim Roth, and Michael Clarke Duncan. 2011's *Apes* benefits immeasurably from the talents of Andy Serkis in the role of Caesar, the ape character who leads the rebellion against humans. Serkis's acting is a marvelous example of the technology of performance capture, wherein the actor wears a skintight bodysuit with sensors that capture his or her performance. The filmmakers manage to endow the digitally created simian characters, Caesar especially, with a remarkably believable and lifelike quality.

Caesar gains his extraordinary self-awareness and ability to think from ALZ-112, a drug developed by biologist Dr. William "Will" Rodman (James Franco) to cure Alzheimer's disease. Will first tests the drug on chimps, including Caesar's mother. She goes mad and is put down; her offspring is nearly killed in the process (she was trying to protect him). A kindly assistant saves Caesar and places him in Will's care. The apes given the drug develop telltale blue rings around their irises. Seeing the amazing effect the drug has on Caesar, Will gives it to his father (John Lithgow), who is suffering from Alzheimer's. Will's father responds to the drug powerfully, and it does indeed seem like a miracle cure—until, one day, it stops working. (Another 2011 film, *Limitless*, starring Bradley Cooper, has a similar premise of a drug's initially wondrous and eventually suspect effects, albeit on human subjects who go from dim to devilishly smart.)

Caesar enjoys a rollicking home life with the Rodmans, the house his jungle; his amazing abilities grow all the time as he swings from the attic to the ground floor. But when Will's father, mentally diminished once again, encounters a belligerent neighbor, Caesar swings into action, nearly killing the neighbor to protect the disoriented old man, the ape's "grandfather." As a result, Will is ordered by the courts to place Caesar in a primate shelter. The wrenching separation between Will and Caesar is heartrending enough, but then Caesar discovers that the shelter is anything but. Run by sadistic humans and teeming with sadistic apes, it is a hellish place. Nevertheless, Caesar eventually bonds with some of the gentler apes, and his consciousness is raised. Feeling rejected by Will, who keeps failing to rescue him from the shelter, Caesar eventually reaches a point where he feels closer to his fellow imprisoned apes than he does to his human parent. Finally able to bring Caesar home, Will and his girlfriend, Dr. Caroline Aranha, a primatologist played by Freida Pinto, go to retrieve him. Much to Will's shock, however, Caesar refuses to leave—he has much bigger plans. Caesar escapes the shelter and sneaks into Will's scientific facility in order to get a supply of ALZ-112. After dosing his fellow apes with the drug, Caesar leads them out of the shelter and into the world, where they quickly stage a large-scale insurrection that culminates in an epic battle between the rebel apes and their human enemies on the Golden Gate Bridge, the high point of which is a dramatic leap by a noble and courageous gorilla into the corporate villain's helicopter. The gorilla dies in Caesar's arms, an ingenious revision of a conventional Hollywood romantic moment.

Perhaps no one can compete with a center stage CGI ape, but Will Rodman is nevertheless a strangely blank, recessive figure. Franco brings little of his characteristic oddball vitality to this role. Will's romance with Pinto's primatologist also lacks conviction. That leaves Caesar with all the moments of poignancy and interest. In one scene, Will and Caroline take Caesar to the park, leading him by a leash. Caesar notices a family leading their dog on a leash. The ape is struck by the sight, the subsequent battle of growls and barks a clear indication of the primate's agitation. Walking back to the car, Caesar asks, "Is Caesar a pet?" Will answers, "No. *No.*" But Caesar is clearly troubled and in no way reassured.

The most notable moments of the film involve the apes' interactions, especially after Caesar has given them the drug and begins liberating them, unifying the disparate, once mutually aggressive apes. In a remarkable moment, the drug-enhanced apes exit their cages and exchange newly knowing, complicit, awakened glances. Of particular interest here, the ape world—save for Caesar's mother Bright Eyes, a maternal figure signifying origins—is entirely male and homosocial. If we recall Leslie Fiedler's argument that the men of nineteenth-century American literature, fleeing their homes, wives, and families, escape these constraints in the company of their male companions (usually of a different race), *Apes* extends Fiedler's thesis by depicting a male homosocial cadre of apes coming together in defiance of human civilization. This theme finds cinematic expression in highly charged images of male love, as when Caesar holds the gigantic, noble, dying gorilla martyr in his arms. But these Fiedlerian apes do not wish to leave home and light out for the territories, as Huck Finn would say. Rather, they want to *return* home. After the mayhem of their battle with the humans, the apes, led by Caesar, return to the natural world, the newfound jungle of California's trees and forests. Will makes his way into the apes' forest enclave, still hoping he can persuade Caesar to give up his rebellion and return to the Rodman home. But Caesar does the talking. Startling his former father with the ability to speak, the ape holds the human man close and whispers in his ear, "Caesar *is* home."

Postmillennial Hippolytus

Lionel Shriver's 2003 novel *We Need to Talk about Kevin* was rejected by several publishers before being published by Serpent's Tail. Not much hoopla greeted the novel at first, but word of mouth, particularly among female readers, made it a breakout hit. Perhaps its female fan base was drawn to the novel's unusual hook. Though about a fictional high school massacre in upstate New York, the novel's first-person narrator is the teenage killer Kevin's mother, Eva Khatchadourian, who writes a series of letters about their son to her husband (also murdered, along with their younger daughter, by Kevin).

The brilliant film version, adapted by Lynne Ramsay and Rory Stewart Kinnear, casts Tilda Swinton as Eva, John C. Reilly as her husband Franklin, and Ezra Miller as the teenage Kevin. The film's notably effective casting choices also include Rocky Duer as the toddler Kevin, the heartbreakingly touching Ashley Gerasimovich as Kevin's much younger sister Celia, and especially Jasper Newell as the six- to eight-year-old Kevin. The central trauma—the teenage Kevin's annihilation of family members and classmates—seeps into and tugs at every image of the film. Microtraumas, smaller-scale but acute assaults between mother and son, occur throughout the narrative, resulting in a film that plays like a splintered, fragmentary poem of loss and wounding. The first shot of the film establishes its simultaneously ominous and elliptical tone. In a darkened room at night, the camera tracks forward to an opened pair of patio doors over which ghostly white curtains blow. As the camera moves steadily forward, we hear a drumbeat, amplifying the sense of impending dread.

Before Kevin is born, Eva is a successful travel writer. The film proper opens with Eva in a state of orgiastic crimson abandon, losing herself in a festival of tomatoes in Spain. Held aloft by fellow revelers, eyes closed in ecstasy and drenched in the oozy red pulp, Eva looks like a high priestess at an ancient ritual. As I will discuss, the link to ancient rites is significant. Clearly, this opening sequence works on two levels—a statement about Eva's heady access to pleasure and career fulfillment before giving birth to Kevin on the one hand, and, on the other, a harbinger of the climactic bloodbath, with Eva swimming in what looks like blood and being pelted by what looks like torn flesh.

From the start, Eva struggles to bond with Kevin. Though a helpless infant, he cries so incessantly that Eva, it is strongly indicated, experiences his behavior as vindictive. Utterly zonked as she pushes his stroller, she stands stock-still before construction workers drilling into the pavement. It seems that, miraculously, the deafening noise has appeased the crying Kevin, but it has only momentarily muffled his continuous cries. Her attempts to bond with him continue to fail miserably. She rolls a ball toward Kevin as they sit opposite one another on the floor. He ignores the ball each time, despite her increasingly strained enthusiasm. Suddenly, success seems secured—he rolls the ball back to his mother. Elated, she rolls it to him again, and he once again ignores it.

Now six years old or so, Kevin becomes much more openly hostile to Eva. When she tries to speak lovingly—and we see it's a strain for her—he immediately mocks her, speaking in aggressive gibberish, conveying the sense that this is what her words sound like to *him*. All the while, Eva's husband Franklin, convinced his son is simply a sweet boy misunderstood by his tense mother, obstructs any of Eva's attempts to address Kevin's behavior as a problem, blaming her for being unmotherly. Her conflict with Kevin reaches an explosive standoff when, refusing to be potty trained, he deliberately, and more than once, poops in his diapers. Irate, Eva flings him to the ground, breaking his arm. Realizing how inappropriately she has acted, Eva apologizes to her son in their car ride back from the hospital. Indicative of her detachment and difficulty coping, Eva speaks in the third person as she apologizes, calling herself "Mommer": "Mommer is so sorry for what she did." The boy mocks her apology, his gibberish exposing her inauthentic reaching. When they get home and he sees his father, Kevin races up the stairs to the house, crying out "Dad!" and refusing to heed Eva's requests that he stay still. While we cannot know for sure, it is likely that Eva is hoping to coax Kevin into concealing the cause of his broken arm. Just when Eva believes that Kevin is about to divulge everything to his father, Kevin defies expectations and answers his father's questions about the accident with a skillful lie about falling off the bed when "Mommer" was changing him, leading Franklin to console Eva. The entire queasy incident confirms that Eva can barely parent this child and that Kevin thrives on exerting power over her, clearly a terrible situation. Indeed, when they are out driving the next day, Kevin insists that Eva take him home when she says she needs to make a stop. When she tries to reason with him, he massages the scab from his broken arm, blackmailing her. It's a realistic, contemporary version of the terrifying 1961 *Twilight Zone* episode "It's a Good Life," where a little boy named Anthony Fremont (Billy Mumy) controls things with his mind and holds all those around him in a perpetual state of subservient terror.

The relationship between mother and son is so fraught that the rare moments of bonding and tenderness simply clarify how awful relations are the rest of the time. Reading Howard Pyle's *The Merry Adventures of Robin Hood* (1883) to the young Kevin, Eva appears to reach her son for the first time. Normally hostile and icily distant toward her (as she is to him, only more so), Kevin now snuggles with his mother on the bed. And when his doting father comes by, Kevin surprisingly commands, "Go away." Eva's look of surprise at her newfound ability to bond with Kevin is one of the few moments of emotional release in the film. Whether or not the whole episode was yet another manipulative ruse on Kevin's part or simply an anomaly (he also has a fever at the time), Kevin reverts to his hostile ways with a vengeance. Asking him what he wants for breakfast the next day, Kevin cruelly responds, "I don't give a rat's ass." Later, when Eva tries to give Kevin a euphemistic talk on the birds and the bees, Kevin retorts, "Is this about fucking?" Frequently, Kevin speaks in a foulmouthed way (recalling another great horror film about a disturbed preadolescent, *The Exorcist*). We do not, however, see either of his parents doing so, perhaps an indication that he's picking up on their, or at least Eva's, carefully hidden habits.

As superbly cast as Swinton, with whom he shares a tense, angular, inward intensity and stark, dark-haired beauty, Ezra Miller creates a portrait of unsettling young masculinity that deserves comparison to Anthony Perkins's Norman Bates. Hitchcock's 1960 *Psycho* and the indelible character Norman Bates, obsessively devoted to a tyrannical mother—even if she exists only in his mind and as a corpse—haunt *We Need to Talk about Kevin*. Miller's Kevin comes across as Norman Bates 2.0, updated as a millennial whose affect is the antithesis of Norman's goofy sincerity (or so it seems) and unfailing courteousness. Foulmouthed and openly aggressive much of the time and especially to his mother, Kevin always verges on disturbing behavior. Yet—and this is the Norman part—he can put on the charm, fooling everyone around him except for the ever-suspicious, failing Eva. In a grisly "accident," his sweet, blonde, much younger sister Celia loses an eye to a bottle of Drano. That Kevin is the culprit is obvious to Eva and the audience, especially given the reason why Eva took the Drano out in the first place. When Celia's guinea pig had gone missing, Eva assured her that the pet went to live in the backyard. But Eva discovered the slain pet's guts clogging up the garbage disposal. She grabbed the Drano to solve the problem and hide the evidence. Why Eva conceals this gruesome discovery is not made explicit but can probably be explained as her attempt to manage relations with her husband, who blames her for thinking ill of their son and insistently disavows knowledge of Kevin's disturbance. As has been well documented, serial killers usually begin with pets and other animals. After killing Celia's guinea pig, Kevin's violence steadily intensifies, Celia's partial blinding another horrible warning sign. All the while, Ramsay's film proceeds from the basis of a numbed detachment that cannot endure.

Interspersed with scenes of quiet, mounting domestic horror are those depicting the shattered and largely expressionless Eva in the present. Scorned and repeatedly harassed by her community—slapped in the street, her shabby new abode and car spray-painted red and her eggs smashed in the supermarket (she buys them anyway, while the culprit, the seething mother of one of Kevin's victims, looks on)—Eva finally manages to find a job at a sketchy travel office. The scenes of Eva enduring and trying to find some regularity in her new job—a complete comedown from her high-powered media world, running her own publishing company—evince a surprising connection with other 2011 films such as *Jeff, Who Lives at Home*, a beta male comedy written and directed by Jay and Mark Duplass and starring Jason Segel and Ed Helms. Like the pariah Eva, Jeff (Segel), a thirty-year-old slacker still living with his mother, drifts through life, unmoored. (Fascinatingly, Jeff embarks on a series of adventures after he answers a wrong number from someone asking for "Kevin," which he takes as a sign.) Detached from the main Kevin plot, Eva's story in the present day plays out like a female-focused version of the beta male comedies of the day (often starring Segel, Seth Rogen, James Franco, and their ilk) featuring young men unable to find a job, romance, goals, or any of the above, haplessly adrift.

Though the Robin Hood tradition is explicitly evoked, providing a basis for Kevin's hobby of archery which he weaponizes as the means of annihilating his victims, another, much older work provides a fitting intertext for a film that evokes ancient ritual and foregrounds troubled young manhood. The titular figure of Euripides's tragedy *Hippolytus* is a beautiful young man, the son of the famous hero Theseus, desired by his young stepmother Phaedra. Spurned by Hippolytus, Phaedra takes her own life, but not before she writes a suicide note incriminating her stepson for the crime. When Theseus returns home and reads the letter, he effects his son's death, only later realizing that Hippolytus had been framed. Of particular relevance here, Hippolytus is notably misogynistic, railing against the very existence of women after Phaedra makes her desire for him clear. Moreover, Hippolytus rejects sexual desire itself. He spends his days with his favorite companion, the goddess Artemis, with whom he goes hunting. The image of the virginal but also steely, resolute young male archer in Euripides prefigures the murderous, ascetic Kevin.

Artemis's chief symbols are the bow and arrow. She was venerated as one of the main goddesses of young women, childbirth, midwifery, and chastity, the latter acutely important to Hippolytus. Is Kevin chaste? He is never shown to have a girlfriend (or a boyfriend, despite the queer possibilities of Miller's screen presence), nor any interest in sex. At the same time, however, Eva walks in on him masturbating in the bathroom. In a shockingly sustained moment, she watches him without shutting the door as he continues, furiously, to masturbate. Then she abruptly slams the door shut. The severity of Eva as wife and mother—her pared-down, ascetic presence in such stark contrast to her sensual abandon in the orgiastic tomato festival prelude—suggests a renunciation of sexuality that matches Kevin's. The masturbation scene, however, implies an underlying incestuous possibility, one that drives mother and son apart and locks them together.

The incest theme adds to the darkest, and most darkly funny, aspect of the film, which is that much of the interaction between Swinton/Eva and Miller/Kevin plays like a tortured romance. Eva's frustrations with Kevin's obstreperous and spiteful behavior are not altogether distinct from those women have with their boyfriends and husbands in beta male comedies. When Eva asks Kevin out, essentially, on a date—a game of miniature golf followed by dinner in an elegant restaurant—she comes downstairs to discover Kevin ravenously, or mock-ravenously, chawing on a huge piece of leftover roast, its meaty matter dribbling down his mouth. "But we're going out to dinner," the stunned Eva remarks. Eva, for her part, is dressed to the nines; she clearly wishes to impress, as if an evening out with Kevin is an opportunity for glamor and sophistication that will signify her commitment to her son, convincing him of her sincerity. At the restaurant, Eva eats alone. Kevin transforms the soft insides of a piece of bread into a row of tiny hard pellets, as if he were transforming the bread into a gun, its contents into bullets. His responses to Eva's attempts to reach out to him are as lacerating as possible; before he shoots arrows into his victims, his sneering words penetrate as weapons.

That Kevin kills everyone around him save Eva suggests that his killings are, in a horrifying way, a kind of tribute to, as well as the ultimate revenge against, her. When she sees her imprisoned son for the last time in the movie, before he is transferred to Sing Sing, she brings up the time she broke his arm. Tellingly, he describes that incident now as "the sincerest thing you've ever done." Therein lies the entire truth of his disposition to her, perhaps: he has never believed she cared. And for the first time, Kevin expresses vulnerability when, with novel trepidation, he speaks of being transferred to Sing Sing. In answer to Eva's question about why he committed the massacre, he responds that he once believed he knew the reason why but is no longer sure. In a moment both heartbreaking and spare, Eva hugs Kevin before she leaves. It has taken their near mutual annihilation to join this mother and son, however briefly.

The films of 2011 are encapsulated by this moment, the tentative, fleeting, deeply hard-won intimacy of mother and son. Wholly inscrutable, but then again not so enigmatic, Kevin resists every attempt to normalize him. Terrifying to contemplate but nevertheless inescapable, the truth is that he synthesizes 2011 screen masculinities. Steve Rogers in *Captain America* refuses to conform to society's relegation of him to the scrap heap of male gender norms. In his presuperhero state, Steve, played by Chris Evans with his head grafted on to a fragile body, looks not so very different from the strike-a-pose, angular Kevin. The intransigence of the Driver, and the simultaneous modes of utter inscrutability and emotional yearning in Gosling's persona, find a complement in Kevin as well. His mysterious aloofness dominates, yet on occasion moments of deep, barely stifled rage belie that aloofness, as in the restaurant scene when he pitilessly exposes his mother's attempts to reach out to him as rote, hollow, predictable gestures. Like Caesar, the leader of the enhanced apes, Kevin rebels against the family that nurtured him, eventually dispatching them or consigning them to a living death of social shame. Whether striving for connection or shattering its possibilities, the males of 2011 film refuse the trajectories determined for them and adamantly emulate the words of Private Robert E. Lee Prewitt (Montgomery Clift) in *From Here to Eternity* (Fred Zinnemann, 1953): "A man don't go his own way, he's nothing."

NOTES

1. Parker, *Save the Males*, x.

2. Parker, *Save the Males*, xii.

3. For an extended description of the ghost face, see Greven, *Ghost Faces: Hollywood and Postmillennial Masculinity*, 54–63.

4. Discussing the endurance of film noir tropes in contemporary Hollywood, John-Paul Trutnau writes, "Essentially, the mirror is used to reflect male activity, while women . . . usually are not placed in a position which 'reflects upon them,' i.e., through a mirror. The variety in which men, especially the protagonist, are given prominence in such reflection, also leads to the assumption that men are more important to the narrative than women." Trutnau, *A One-Man Show?*, 94.

5. As Jane Gallop elucidates in her incisive *Reading Lacan*, in the Lacanian mirror stage, the infant becomes captivated by its own image in the mirror and "assumes a mastery that" it will "actually learn only later" (78). What makes the mirror stage such a difficult concept is that it signifies both "anticipation and retroaction" (81). In "the generally understood notion of the mirror stage," it is a "turning point where 'the body in bits and pieces' becomes a totalized body-image, a proto-self" (79). Perhaps most relevant for our reading of *Captain America* is the status of the mirror stage as "a turning point. After it, the subject's relation to himself is always mediated through a totalizing image that has come from outside" (78). See Gallop, *Reading Lacan*, 81.

2012

Movies and Myths, Heroes, and History

RAYMOND HABERSKI JR.

By 2012, a battle-hardened Barack Obama campaigned for president of the United States. In 2008, he offered "Hope"; in 2012 his slogan was simply "Forward." He entered the White House in 2009 as the first African American president; he campaigned for reelection in 2012 as the guy who bailed out the country's largest banks and automakers and made the federal government an even larger holder of student debt (Stoler). He ramped up drone strikes on suspected terrorist suspects and ordered the raid that killed Osama bin Laden. He fought for the passage of universal health care, an act that became a rallying point for critics on both his political left as well as right. His party controlled both houses of Congress for only two of his first four years and watched as the nation's capital became deadlocked in an era of political polarization. David Fahrenthold remarked in the *Washington Post* the day after the 2012 election that, against John McCain, "Obama had run as a symbol of limitless hope. This year, he ran as a symbol of hope's limitations" (Fahrenthold).

True enough. Obama's presidential arc had gone from dream to reality, as must happen. He had to govern, and in governing, his 2012 presidential campaign transformed into a complicated set of strategies, tactics, ideas, and reactions. Like all historical actors, Obama proved Karl Marx's famous maxim in *The Eighteenth Brumaire of Louis Bonaparte*: "Man makes his own history, but he does not make it out of whole cloth; he does not make it out of conditions chosen by himself, but out of such as he finds close at hand" (Marx). In other words, Obama might have made history in 2008, but by 2012, history had shaped him.

Indeed, while the potential reelection of the nation's first Black president consumed a great deal of Americans' attention in 2012, Obama's campaign did not dominate headlines as it did in 2008. Many events that shaped trends and story lines emanated from the Middle East. The escalation of the Syrian civil war was punctuated by the deaths of journalist Marie Colvin and photographer Rémi Ochlik, two victims of Bashar al-Assad's targeting of those who tried to tell the story of his war on noncombatants. In the aftermath of the Arab Spring (beginning in 2010) that challenged governments throughout the Middle East, Egypt demonstrated the unintended consequences of removing dictators from power as Mohamed Morsi rode to leadership on the back of the Muslim Brotherhood, a force for Islamic fundamentalism, in the country's first election following the overthrow of Hosni Mubarak. Benghazi, Libya, became another symbol of the ironies of the Arab Spring when rebel fighters who had overthrown and killed dictator Muammar Qaddafi led an attack on the American consulate, killing U.S. ambassador Christopher Stevens. The Israeli-Palestinian war grew deadly after a period of relative peace when Israel assassinated Ahmed Jabari, the military commander of Hamas, setting off an exchange of violence that killed at least 160 Palestinians and five Israelis.

In China, the Communist Party consolidated its power around a new leader, Xi Jinping, who took over a huge, fast-growing economy plagued by corruption, pollution, and popular discontent. Italians grappled with a completely avoidable disaster caused by a massive cruise ship, the Costa Concordia, running aground and capsizing. At more than 900 feet in length, the ship was twice the size of the Titanic; thirty-two people died when the captain and crew failed to lead a safe evacuation—indeed, the captain left his post before all the passengers had made it off the ship. And as the American death toll in Afghanistan reached a grim new milestone of 2,000, Hurricane Sandy caused unprecedented damage along the northeast coast of the U.S., and a typhoon devastated the Philippines a few weeks later, killing over 1,000 people.

The unleashing of historical forces often resembles a hurricane—even though we know a storm is coming, we tremble as the world around us changes. President Obama clearly felt that way with events in Libya and especially Syria, as his administration seemed helpless when dealing with violence that claimed tens of thousands of lives. In other moments, Obama seemed to harness history, delivering a dramatic denouncement of American gun culture in his public eulogy for the children massacred at Sandy Hook Elementary School by a mentally ill young man who had apparently lived part of his life in a dark web of violent video games, bizarre chat rooms, and shooting ranges. The case of Trayvon Martin, a Black teenager in Florida who was shot and killed in February by George Zimmerman, a designated neighborhood watch coordinator, produced one of Obama's most remarkable speeches. Martin was killed walking home from a convenience store when his murderer, Zimmerman, confronted him because, as he told a police dispatcher, "he look[ed] like he [was] up to no good" and was "wearing a dark hoodie." The killing of Martin sparked nationwide protests and an outpouring of solidarity for Black families who lived in fear that their sons, like Trayvon, would be targeted for "walking while Black." In an address to the nation, President Obama empathized with Black Americans in a way that no other president had before:

> You know, when Trayvon Martin was first shot, I said that this could have been my son. Another way of saying that is Trayvon Martin could have been me thirty-five years ago. And when you think about why, in the African American community at least, there's a lot of pain around what happened here, I think it's important to recognize that the African American community is looking at this issue through a set of experiences and a history that doesn't go away. (Obama)

Listing events in any year often belies the historical fault lines that created them. For example, the chaos in Syria and Libya had its most immediate origins in the Arab Spring uprisings of 2010, but also had deeper roots in the historical oppression suffered by different groups throughout the Middle East. The death of Trayvon Martin hit many Americans, particularly African Americans, as yet another act of racist violence against Black men that has a long, tragic history in the United States. Even Hurricane Sandy, while a singular weather event, reflected how climate change has increased the frequency and ferocity of storms in the Atlantic. The trial of Jerry Sandusky, an assistant football coach at Penn State University who was arrested in 2011 following the revelation of horrific details of a child sex abuse scandal that happened under the nose of head coach Joe Paterno, caused the reverence for college sports to be scrutinized as much as Sandusky's actions. And a mass shooting in Aurora, Colorado, before a midnight preview showing of Christopher Nolan's *The Dark Knight Rises* provided pundits another opportunity to condemn the effects of violent media on the minds of young men.

There were other events that, while fleeting, generated a great deal of public interest. At the Summer Olympics in London, American swimmer Michael Phelps continued his dominance by becoming the most decorated Olympian in history. The 2012 Super Bowl between the underdog New York Giants and the New England Patriots, an efficient and dominant football dynasty led by quarterback Tom Brady and mercurial coach Bill Belichick, became the most-watched program in American history. While the game was played in Indianapolis, Indiana, it reached a staggering 111.3 million American households. The Pulitzer Prizes caused a stir when the committee overseeing the fiction category failed to agree on a recipient, explaining that while many authors were worthy of the prize, no one writer secured the votes required to win. That was not the case for prizes given to journalists who wrote about tornadoes that ripped through the South; the war in Afghanistan; the Penn State football program; and dirty cops and wealthy Americans who avoid taxes. Biographies of Malcolm X and George F. Kennan won the nonfiction and biography categories, respectively, illustrating the odd poles of American life between Black Power and Cold War containment. Finally, Wesley Morris, then of the *Boston Globe*, became only the fourth film critic and the first movie reviewer of color to win the Pulitzer Prize for Criticism.

Iconic names made news in 2012, as Facebook issued its first stock offering to the public and Instagram moved across OS platforms to accommodate Android devices. Musicians Taylor Swift, Adele, Rihanna, and Bruno Mars released massive hit records, and Americans watched *The Voice*, *NCIS*, and *Homeland*, on TV. The queen of England, Elizabeth II, celebrated her Diamond Jubilee in February, becoming only the second British monarch to do so. The American economy continued a gradual rebound from the recession of 2007–2009 as the unemployment rate dropped and inflation declined to under 2 percent. The average cost of a new home in the United States was over $250,000 and a gallon of gas was $3.91, while consumer spending powered an increase in the GDP throughout 2012. The year, though, was also the last for a number of notable Americans, including jazz singer Etta James, actor Ben Gazzara, pop singer Whitney Houston, Monkee Davy Jones, *American Bandstand* and *New Year's Rockin' Eve* host Dick Clark, *60 Minutes* reporter Mike Wallace, children's author Maurice Sendak, American auteur critic Andrew Sarris, American cultural historian Paul Fussell, *Fahrenheit 451* author Ray Bradbury, screenwriter-director Nora Ephron, actors Andy Griffith and Ernest Borgnine, author Gore Vidal, *A Chorus Line* composer Marvin Hamlisch, first man on the moon Neil Armstrong, and jazz musician Dave Brubeck.

According to surveys conducted by the Pew Research Center, global attitudes about the United States steadily improved from 2007 to 2012. High on the list for people around the world were views of American democracy and American technology. Popular culture was slightly lower than these two categories, though those between the ages of eighteen and twenty-five had very favorable feelings toward it. At the same time, the president's approval rating around the world fell; in Europe the decline was almost inevitable, as Obama had an 86 percent approval rating shortly after his first election, and by 2012 had dipped to 80 percent. Not so for the popularity of Hollywood movies.

■ Hollywood's Biggest Year!

Box-office receipts hit an all-time high in 2012, earning studios over $10.8 billion. Leading the way were huge, worldwide blockbusters: *The Avengers* with $1.5 billion, *The Dark Knight Rises* with $1.08 billion, and the latest James Bond movie *Skyfall* with over $1 billion. But perhaps the most startling development in 2012 for Hollywood was the transition to digital projection. The industry made history as "all theaters shifted from showing 35mm film to all-digital projection. . . . No more reels, no more sound-on-the-side, clicking projectors . . . but rather only bread-box size cartridges that managers click in and out easily" (Wood). While not quite as transformative as the introduction of sound films, Daniel Wood of the *Christian Science Monitor* noted that many small theaters in the United States closed, at least temporarily, as they found it difficult to upgrade their equipment because of the $50,000 it typically took for a digital setup (Wood). And yet, ticket sales increased for the first time in a few years, suggesting that streaming services like Netflix did not hold the attention of all generations of Americans; those over the age of fifty generated many of those ticket purchases (Wood).

Supporting this surge in the domestic box office were the usual suspects: *The Amazing Spider-Man* joined fellow superheroes in the *Avengers* series and *The Dark Knight Rises* to post a top-ten return. Animated films showed up big: *Brave* led the bunch, scoring at the box office, winning Best Animated Feature at the Academy Awards, and doing both with a female lead character. Other animated films followed close behind, including *Madagascar 3*, *The Lorax*, *Wreck-It Ralph*, *Ice Age: Continental Drift*, and *Hotel Transylvania* all in the top twenty highest-grossing films of the year. Films that were part of a series also demonstrated Hollywood's ability to hook viewers for multiple years. In addition to *The Avengers*, *The Dark Knight Rises*, and the latest James Bond film, the *Twilight* series continued with *The Twilight Saga: Breaking Dawn—Part 2*; *The Hobbit* began its three-film run with *An Unexpected Journey*; *Men in Black 3* did well at the box office, as did other well-known, actor-driven action movies, such as Liam Neeson's *Taken 2*, Matt Damon's *The Bourne Legacy*, and Tom Cruise's *Mission: Impossible—Ghost Protocol*. Finally, two of Hollywood's most highly regarded auteurs provided assured counterpoints to the high-octane, big-budget thrill rides of the top ticket sellers. Paul Thomas Anderson made many critics' top ten list with *The Master*, his character-driven drama about modernity, the self, and ego. Wes Anderson delivered another quirky but sensitive, intelligent, and deeply romantic feature in *Moonrise Kingdom*. The persistence of such filmmakers in a year of billionaire blockbusters illustrates the complex nature of Hollywood—often the same companies own and produce both kinds of films, suggesting there are different ways to be the country's projector of myths.

American movies have been a prime medium for creating and wrestling with American myths, and the best stories are often those with complicated heroes. By 2012, the film industry had had four years to consider the hero-election of 2008 and, like the president himself, the darker aspects of American mythology. Obama grappled with the reality of the presidency and the weight of history. By becoming a kind of antihero, he created a way for Americans to contend with myths that had faltered since 2008—chief among them the inability to become postracial. In 2012, the eighty-fifth Academy Awards provided a fair snapshot of these movies. And fittingly, the ceremony made the connection between politics and film more obvious, as First Lady Michelle Obama announced the winner for Best Picture from the Diplomatic Reception Room in the White House.

■ The Antihero

The conflicted hero, tempered by reality and made more accessible to the rest of us, has a particular history in Hollywood. An excellent essay about the emergence and popularity of the conflicted hero was written by Robert Brustein in 1959 entitled "The New Hollywood: Myth and Anti-Myth." Brustein is a celebrated and distinguished playwright and cultural critic who wrote for the *New Republic* (America's premier "little magazine" for most of the twentieth century). While there have been other Hollywood eras labeled "new," Brustein was the first critic to use this declaration, explaining specifically how Hollywood had turned toward realism in popular films. It was probably no surprise to Brustein that the label "New Hollywood" had been recycled by various generations of writers and observers of American movies. But what makes his insight particularly significant is not that he was first to use it but that he understood how well it described Hollywood's ability to absorb contemporary trends, repackage them, and produce a "new," marketable style. To Brustein, that new style was realism. "Is it possible," Brustein sarcastically asked, "that our celebrated dream factory has abandoned its artificial merchandise for the complex stuff of life? Is the industry undertaking to agitate the populace with harsh truths rather than lull them asleep with comforting fantasies? Is Hollywood, in short, now prepared to subsidize works of art?" (Brustein 23). Brustein channeled the prevailing high-culture critique of American movies—that movies made money for their makers and were artistic only by accident. But perhaps, Brustein mused, something had changed.

A killer combination emerged after World War II that forced broad, industry-wide changes in American movies: the rise of television; the forced divestment of theaters from studios; an influx of gritty, extraordinary foreign films; and the social and emotional effects of the war on American art and fiction. To stay relevant, Hollywood got real—or, more precisely, realistic. The settings, story lines, and especially main characters changed. "If the hero of the romantic film is accustomed to performing mighty deeds, usually in an open-air setting, the realistic hero is more often victimized by the confining world in which he lives," Brustein observed. "And he is trapped not only in the interior of his world but in the interior of his soul" (Brustein 28). But why did American audiences pay money to see darkness? On this point, Brustein mused: "Why, when America has the largest middle-class population in the world (when, in one sense, it sees itself as entirely middle class), are its predominant movie heroes dock workers, motorcyclists, juvenile delinquents, prostitutes, butchers, Southern farmers, seamen, and drifters, the economically and the emotionally dispossessed?" The answer reflected Hollywood's traditional role as a projection of America's emotional state: "For the adult audience . . . these heroes are interesting precisely because of their *distance* from everyday life. Americans can now afford to be indulgent toward grubbiness and poverty because they have been enjoying over the past ten years a prosperity unparalleled in their history" (Brustein 30). Hollywood realized that audiences would trade one formula for another, broadening the dimensions of the cinematic landscape while still embracing movies as mythmakers.

The myth of Americans conquering the West expanded to include the antimyth of the conquerors being damaged by their conquest. The myth of money buying happiness broadened to incorporate the antimyth of the quiet despair of the affluent. Neither twist on old themes made Hollywood especially revolutionary; rather, movies gave audiences a chance to do some hand-wringing while they went about their business. In other words, as Hollywood films grew more gritty, profane, violent, and, one could argue, realistic, they rarely engaged the reality of the topics they portrayed. Thus, we might get films about the Holocaust shot in black and white, but we don't see (perhaps because it is difficult to see) the ideas and politics behind the evil portrayed on screen. After all, Hollywood, like mainstream American politics, is conservative about change. That was Brustein's point: he suggested that Hollywood's turn toward realism showed an awareness of the market more than a commitment to art. And yet, the antihero of

antimyths also revealed an underlying social function of American movies—it demonstrated *what* Americans had questions and concerns about. It
was not pure escapism from reality but an escape into a space of unresolved
problems and issues.

New York Times columnist and critic Frank Rich found the movies of
2012 more than adequate for his typical blend of politics and the arts. In an
essay that appeared in *New York Magazine* two weeks before the Oscars, Rich
observed: "The movie industry has reconnected with the country. It has
produced no fewer than four movies that have provided animated, often
rancorous public debate: *Zero Dark Thirty, Argo, Lincoln,* and *Django
Unchained*" (Rich 16). Each of the four won awards in categories that
matched their political relevance: *Zero Dark Thirty* won for sound editing,
reflecting scenes in which the darkness of torture and killing were made
visceral. *Argo* won Best Picture as a story of qualified triumph in an era of
complicated politics. *Lincoln* won for Best Actor, the only category that
faithfully reflected the broad, popular interest in the sixteenth president.
And for *Django Unchained,* the Academy awarded Quentin Tarantino his
second Oscar for Best Original Screenplay, recognizing the extraordinary
intellectual challenge this story posed to American amnesia about race.

Movies are made by audiences in much the same way that popular
songs become the soundtracks of high school students—in both cases, we
make what we want out of what we see and hear. Frank Rich contended
that for the four movies he profiled, "the political context and climate of
[Obama's] presidency [were] present in them all. These movies may or may
not be for the ages, but future viewers looking back to see what our age was
like may find them invaluable" (Rich 18). There was not an instant classic
among the films released, but just as history complicated the image of President Obama, many of the films of 2012 played against the prevailing per-
ceptions of historical tropes. *Lincoln* showed a complex but ultimately
triumphant executive in the midst of extraordinary political battles; *Zero
Dark Thirty* asked questions about justice in an age of terror; *Django
Unchained* let audiences fantasize about racial retribution for the sins of
slavery; and *Argo* suggested that innocence persisted amid the dark history
of American operations in Iran. *The Dark Knight Rises, Les Misérables,* and *The
Hunger Games* asked questions about the truth and limits of popular revolution through strong female characters. And each of these films brought in
over $100 million in worldwide box-office receipts. Which leads to a ques-
tion: Even if the times shaped the context in which these movies were
made, did these movies help generate a culture for the times?

The Hero Is Black

Quentin Tarantino enjoys messing with his audiences. He makes them listen to long, winding monologues; he gets them to watch intricately composed scenes and shots with quick cuts and long takes and music that engulfs emotions; he makes us laugh at violence. In *Django Unchained*—an homage to blaxploitation films of the 1970s and a nod to the race films of the pre–World War II period—he made us suspend, yet again, our sense of history, our understanding of race, and, for many in a typical Tarantino audience, our comfort level with being white. "It's gutsy, and arguably arrogant, for a white man to attempt this," Frank Rich wrote, "and I feel strongly that Tarantino pulled it off" (Rich 21). Tarantino did two things: he made a film with the ultimate antihero—a freed slave killing white people—and he gave his antihero license to question American history. Indeed, Tarantino actively violates what we know about the history of slavery in order to produce a movie that speaks sharply and critically about American racism. "Doing history with a capital *H* keeps the movie at an arm's distance, puts it under glass a little," Tarantino explained. "The whole idea of doing a movie like this was to take a rock and throw it through the glass" (Rich 21). From the first scene in the movie, it is clear that Tarantino wasn't bothered by the historical record or circumstances. He introduces the first sequence with an intertitle that reads, "1858, two years before the Civil War." Of course, that is incorrect; the Civil War began in April 1861. The inauguration of Abraham Lincoln as the sixteenth president gave South Carolina its pretext to start the war. Likewise, Tarantino changes the historical reality of slave rebellions. One of the main characters in the film is a German bounty hunter named Dr. King Schultz (Christoph Waltz), who in the opening scene "unchains" a slave named Django (Jamie Foxx) from a chain gang. While this act allows Django to become the film's protagonist, a hunter of bad white guys, it also casts Schultz as the white savior of the slaves—something that rarely happened in such rebellions. When slaves won their freedom through violence it was largely through their own efforts at terrible costs to themselves. But such details do not matter to Tarantino's use of history. He created an antihero who exists outside of history, a character who forces white supremacists to answer for the racism that made the country a brutal, backward place.

It is Tarantino's departure from history that makes the film interesting. Because he has no pretense of being historically accurate, Tarantino uses his artistic freedom to make sharp historical and political points. The audience gets to watch an armed Black man confront the layers of racism, violence, and degradation of the American South. There is no shortage of academic histories about slavery to let us know how impossible such a scenario was, but that is often the point of making movies about history—filmmakers create worlds that critique our own.

In an essay about Tarantino's "subversion" of reality, cultural theorist Jack Black argues that *Django* suggests the historical implications of slavery legacy by creating a fantastical destruction of slavery's structure. Relying on the great Marxist theorist Slavoj Žižek and his reading of film through Lacanian theories on symbolism, Black suggests the greatest subversion of Tarantino's film (or any film about the past) is the way it uses a counterfactual narrative to bend the conditions of history to the will of the characters. Black explains: "Tarantino recharges the history of American slavery with a contemporary significance that does not shy away from failing to interpret this past in all its 'historical truth' (both factual and counterfactual). Instead, through his subversion of generic conventions, his counterfactual approach to history and his acknowledgement of the Real, Tarantino is able to draw a more fundamental connection between the significance of slavery, for both the past and the present" (Black 630).

The character of Django is hero and antihero at the same time, thus engaging and deconstructing the myth of agency in antebellum America. The audience gets to see Django confront white slaveholders and plantation owners, forcing them to reckon with the reality of a free, armed Black man. Most of the scenes are played for humor, as when a character such as "Big Daddy" (Don Johnson) stumbles to explain to his Black slaves what Django is; but in another sense, such fumbling for words resonates with audiences who know that their cultural lexicon cannot contain the power of an armed Black man. In addition to the satisfaction of watching Django whip, gun down, and blow up various despicable white characters, Tarantino clearly enjoys portraying white characters in a froth of indignation when confronted by this antihero as hero.

Yet the most effective scene comes near the end of the film, when Django wreaks vengeance on the one Black character who Tarantino lets speak the awful truth. An older house slave named Stephen (Samuel L. Jackson) is the confidant and right-hand man of Calvin Candie, an odd character with a Francophone fetish played by Leonardo DiCaprio. Candie owns a plantation called Candyland, and Stephen has become the ultimate product of that historically heinous system—he is a Black slave with just enough power to prove his allegiance to his white master through violence and degradation against other African Americans. Just before Django ignites

Stephen (Samuel L. Jackson), the house slave in *Django Unchained* (Quentin Tarantino, the Weinstein Company, Columbia), delivers memorable lines about the fate of the hero, Django (Jamie Foxx). Digital frame enlargement.

a long fuse that will destroy the "Big House" of Candyland, he shoots Stephen in both legs, making sure he can't flee before the explosion. Django gets the ultimate revenge, right? No. As Django walks slowly away from the house, Stephen—and history and reality—have the last word: "You can run, n*****, but they gonna find yo' ass," Stephen shouts after him. "And when they do, oh I love what they gonna do to yo' ass. They ain't gonna just kill you, n*****. You done fucked up. This Candyland, n*****! You can't destroy Candyland! We been here—they's always gonna be a Candyland!" (Black 625).

For all of Tarantino's fantastical scenes, this moment hits so hard because it is so true, real, and antimythical. No matter how great his hero's courage and power, there is no escaping the system of racism that sustained slavery and has ensnared every generation of Americans. Tarantino's characters exist within an ahistorical world until Stephen's monologue; but his incendiary final statement momentarily breaks the spell of the film, destroying the satisfaction the audience felt watching justice served in a way that, to a considerable extent, they will never see outside the movie.

The Hero as Myth

Historians of the United States constantly combat mythical heroes: Columbus, the Founding Fathers, the Greatest Generation, John F. Kennedy. But there is really only one who sits atop this list—Abraham Lincoln. The election of the sixteenth president precipitated the Civil War—the country's most brutal and costly war—and led to the end of slavery in the

United States after that institution's nearly 300 years of existence. As president, Lincoln followed a string of predecessors who were politically inept and nearly incapable of providing moral leadership in the face of the nation's original sin. His successors for the next thirty years were not much better, as they proved equally inept in building on the significance of the Civil War. And so, even though Lincoln was a victim of history (he did not escape Marx's maxim), he had a remarkable ability to put into language intelligible for generations of Americans what was significant about this war for their nation. How we understand and use Lincoln matters because he not only wrestled with enormous historical issues but did so in ways that remain politically relevant and morally instructive.

The historical Lincoln might be a singular character; but his legacy has many versions. Historian Andrew Ferguson writes: "It never stops, this appropriation of our greatest president for dubious purposes. He evolves in the public mind to conform more closely to the self-image of each generation's verbal class" (Ferguson 64). Barack Obama claimed the mantle of Lincoln—they were both elected president from Illinois and, it is not too much of a stretch to say, Obama shared considerable rhetorical skills with Lincoln. Not surprisingly, Hollywood released a film about the sixteenth president at an auspicious moment—when Americans deliberated the presidency of the first African American to hold that office. *Lincoln* is touted as perhaps the greatest example of the Lincoln genre; its director Steven Spielberg and writer Tony Kushner use the pretext of the debate over the Thirteenth Amendment to abolish slavery to reimagine a Lincoln for their contemporary moment.

Ferguson praises the Spielberg-Kushner version of the president as "the most plausible rendering of Lincoln in the history of movies," but also points out that the language of the film, crafted by playwright Tony Kushner, echoes twenty-first-century politics (especially liberal politics, according to Ferguson) more than those of the nineteenth century (Ferguson 65). Arguing in a similar vein, sociologist Barry Schwartz notes that while Spielberg and Kushner "give their audiences an authentic representation of the *physical* setting of the Thirteenth Amendment debate, [the filmmakers] never come close to capturing the thought world of the time" (Schwartz 503). David Zarefsky suggests that, like all films, this one has problems with historical accuracy and interpretation, but thinks it aligns with the way "mainstream scholarship has moved toward a more nuanced portrayal of Lincoln . . . appreciating his genius while also acknowledging his faults and limitations" (Zarefsky 156). Zarefsky also believes the reception of the film reflected the particular historical mood of the audience—it is "a message

to our current president about the need to use all means of power to cir-
cumvent a recalcitrant Congress on important matters of principle" (Zarefsky 157). Like almost any movie, Spielberg's *Lincoln* is, if not for the ages,
for us.

Unlike *Django Unchained*, which created an alternative history to demonstrate deep problems in contemporary America, *Lincoln* borrows from
history to suggest that a more magnanimous America might yet exist. Taken
from a small section of historian Doris Kearns Goodwin's book *Team of
Rivals*, the film depicts how Lincoln secured the necessary votes in the U.S.
House of Representatives to move the Thirteenth Amendment out of Congress and into the states for ratification. The book was a popular success,
even influencing how President Obama constructed his cabinet to include,
like Lincoln, a few of his political rivals. Daniel Day-Lewis plays Lincoln as
well as anyone probably ever will, embodying a man many Americans
assume they know but who the actor and director introduce to us in a way
that is as stunningly realistic as it is relevant to our time. The time and care
that Day-Lewis and Spielberg devoted to constructing the character of Lincoln infused the pivotal scenes with a visceral power. To take just one
example, in a climactic scene, Day-Lewis's Lincoln makes clear to his cabinet (his "team of rivals") the meaning of the fight: "A constitutional provi-
sion settles the fate for all coming time, not only for the millions now in
bondage but for unborn millions yet to come." The scene emphatically
declares not merely why the story portrayed in the film matters but why
Lincoln's evolution regarding slavery has such historical significance.

The film focuses on a few months in early 1865, a period so short that it
allows for scenes to develop into quiet character pieces and moments of
remarkable revelation. If Spielberg had gone with the original script that covered much more history—including Lincoln's views on slavery and his man-
agement of the war—he would have had to include many more characters,
turning points, and potted histories just to keep audiences informed enough
to follow the narrative. Instead, the film is tighter but historically narrow; the
narrative is easier to follow because it leaves out much of the history of the
actual end of slavery. Spielberg was able to fill the movie with Lincoln telling
stories, engaging in fiery debates with his cabinet, and, in one memorable
scene, grappling with Euclid. And even though Lincoln the historical actor
actually did all of this (more or less), he did not act alone when it came to
ending slavery: he was one part—a very important part—of a historical process that included slaves and free African Americans who forced Americans
to reckon with the institution that held millions in bondage for generations.
What the movie provides, then, is a revealing portrait of Lincoln the man and

Lincoln the myth; he is the kind of person I think we would want in the White House—thoughtful, decisive, heroic—with the ability to manage history in ways that are highly unlikely, almost impossible.

Among the many moments that do justice to Lincoln as both man and myth is the Euclid scene. The president is draped in a shawl, walking the White House halls in the middle of the night, deep in contemplation. The death toll of the war weighs on him, and he owes General Ulysses Grant a message regarding Confederate delegates who have traveled to northern Virginia in anticipation of speaking to the president about ending the war. Lincoln sits in a quiet room filled with telegraph machines and dictates a message to one of the two lonely soldiers who serve as their operators, played by Adam Driver. Before he gives the command to send the message, Lincoln pauses and asks the two young men if they think "we choose to be born or are we fitted to the times we are born into?" The point being that someone born with dark skin before 1865 would very likely be a slave in the United States, a fate sealed by historical chance. The meaning of the war, he preached in speeches such as the Gettysburg Address, had to be shaped by moral will rather than the accident of historical time. Lincoln viewed ending slavery as the only true way to reckon with the moral rationale of the war and the hundreds of thousands of deaths. To make this point, Kushner has his Lincoln speak about Euclid's first common notion: that things that are equal to the same thing are equal to each other. "That's a rule of mathematical reasoning," Lincoln says, "it's true because it works." This, he sighs, is a self-evident truth. "There it is in a two-thousand-year-old book of mechanical engineering, that things that are equal to the same thing are equal to each other." Harkening back to the Declaration of Independence, Lincoln believed the Founding Fathers had stated clearly what the origin story of the United States was: that all people are equal under God and are therefore, ultimately, equal to each other. Giving new instructions to the telegraph operator, Lincoln asks Grant to keep the Confederate delegates in Virginia and await further instructions from him, thus perhaps buying a bit more time for the Thirteenth Amendment to pass and for justice to be done (Wilentz 28).

Any film that seeks to be historically accurate invites scrutiny from those who study history. At the same time, though, historians who chastise filmmakers and pick apart their films for historical inaccuracies must contend with the inevitable defense that films don't come with footnotes; they are works of art, made by an industry. In *Lincoln*, historians took particular issue with the lack of almost any major Black character, which, in turn, left audiences with the impression that slavery ended solely because of

Lincoln's persistence with the Thirteenth Amendment. Eric Foner and Kate Masur both suggested alternative movies that Hollywood could have made if interested in the story of abolition. Jim Grossman, executive director of the American Historical Association, summarized many of the other complaints:

> Historians will disagree over whether this was Lincoln indeed. My friend and colleague Lerone Bennett will wonder what happened to the evidence that Lincoln never believed in racial equality. David Blight will no doubt scratch his head over the absence of Frederick Douglass. Others will question the accuracy of this Lincoln's approach to the presidency and presidential power, or the portrayal of family dynamics in the White House; or the implications of a film about emancipation that elides the agency of slaves and ex-slaves (except for the role of black soldiers). Others will note that Spielberg seems to get the importance of manhood, but doesn't really know how to use gender as a category of political analysis. This is what a film like this should do: stimulate discussion about history (Harvard University Press Blog).

Grossman's conclusion that films get us to talk about history rather than settle on new interpretations sounded quite similar to what the director said about his movie. Spielberg delivered a keynote at the ceremony commemorating the 149th anniversary of the Gettysburg Address, in which he offered that while it is "a betrayal of the job of the historian to promise perfect and complete recall of the past . . . one of the jobs of art is to go to the impossible places that other disciplines like history must avoid" (Spielberg). Not unlike his other movies with fantastical journeys and encounters, Spielberg saw this film as a way to return to 1865 and spend time with the sixteenth president. Seen in those terms, it is not surprising that Spielberg's film more accurately captured the wallpaper in Lincoln's office than the social history of slavery's abolition. What he gave us was the perfect president, the mythical Lincoln, the politics of hope, rather than, as Barack Obama found out, the politics of limitations.

Spielberg gave audiences a Lincoln artistically rendered but historically simplified. Of course, historians do not wait for movies to make their cases about the past; yet as essayist and critic Jelani Cobb argues, by focusing on the heroic aspects of Lincoln, we miss the human failings of a president and the presidency—we get the myth without having to think too much about the man. "By lionizing Lincoln," Cobb explains, "we are able to concentrate on the death of an evil institution rather than on its ongoing legacy. The paradox is that Lincoln's death enabled later generations to impatiently wonder when black people would cease fixating on slavery and just get over it" (Cobb 62). For Lincoln, the war and slavery's abolition did not spell the end of racism—just as Obama's election in 2008 failed to affirm a postracial America. Both events gave rise to hope that Americans might overcome their own history, and both crashed into another apparently self-evident truth, that myths do not replace reality. Cobb points out that "the recalcitrant racism of the Obama era will be as vexing to the story of American virtue as Lincoln's failings were to those of his era. Lincoln was not as flawless as we've been told, and we are not as virtuous as we've begun to tell ourselves" (Cobb 62).

In one sense, the ahistorical *Django Unchained* is a scathing rebuttal to the historically aspirational *Lincoln*, especially if we imagine the character of Stephen screaming not at Django but at the mythical Lincoln and those who believe the myth of a postracial America. However, there is also something powerful about *Lincoln* wrestling with the historical Lincoln. The United States did have a politician whose ambivalence about slavery's abolition changed so much that as president he was willing to fight a war to decide slavery's fate. In the end, though, Spielberg and Kushner created a realistic Lincoln but chose to show him in a mythical America. No wonder *Lincoln* seemed a movie appropriate for the era in which America's first Black president demonstrated the realities of racism in the United States.

The Naive Hero

U.S. historians have long written about the paradox of American enemies. From the beginning of European settlement, Americans have projected their worst fears onto "the other"—groups such as Native Americans, African slaves, immigrants, communists, and Muslims. These groups are products of a popular need to explain, at least in part, struggles over national identity, morality, and economic stability. At bottom, when Americans have pursued their national enemies, they have done so ultimately to answer one question: Who are we? The desire to answer that question is wrapped up in the heroes Americans have: the Indian killer, the great white man, the self-made man, the Cold Warrior, and, most recently, the counterterrorist agent. This last hero is an avenger, understood almost solely as a reaction to the terrible acts of violence perpetuated on innocent civilians. The 9/11 terrorist attacks had an exponential effect on counterterrorism, providing justification for an almost unlimited expansion of power, from police departments to the president of the United States. In the years since 9/11, Americans accepted almost any use of power and violence if it was in the name of tracking and hunting down terrorists. No president since George W. Bush has turned away from this power.

Two movies in 2012 used Islam and Muslims as the antagonistic "other," and both spoke to an era popularly known as an age of Islamic extremism. *Zero Dark Thirty*, directed by Kathryn Bigelow and written by Mark Boal, tells the story of the CIA's deadly manhunt for Osama bin Laden through female CIA agent Maya, while also showing, in an almost clinical way, how the use of torture achieved what many Americans considered a worthy end. Mark Harris declares that the movie "confirms Bigelow and Boal's position as probably our most prominent and least sentimental cultural custodians of the post-9/11 war era" (Harris 114). The other is *Argo*, a true story of American embassy personnel and some of their family members who escaped from Tehran following the fall of the Shah in 1979 by following an ingenious plan cooked up by CIA agent Tony Mendez. Played by Ben Affleck, who also directed the film, Mendez manufactured new transit documents for the Americans under the guise that they were part of a filmmaking crew he was using to scout locations. Both films are based on specific historical accounts and use elaborate appeals to history to sell themselves to audiences—far more than did Spielberg's *Lincoln* and, of course, Tarantino's *Django Unchained*.

However, such commitment demonstrates an inherent danger in claiming that a particular movie is "based on a true story" or "actual events." Such films open themselves to relentless scrutiny by those with access to the historical record, and can become political footballs in partisan assessments of the recent past. If *Django Unchained* requires an ahistorical hero to make a political point, and *Lincoln* creates a mythical hero to inspire contemporary Americans to hope for a better politics, *Zero Dark Thirty* and, to a lesser extent, *Argo* give us naive heroes who help audiences rationalize, if not glory in, the War on Terror. The problem with being naive about history is that, at some point, we fail to be self-aware enough to recognize that whatever it is we fear has been overwhelmed by the tactics we used to combat that fear. For *Zero Dark Thirty*, that is a central problem; for *Argo*, apart from an opening sequence that relates a history of U.S. involvement in the Shah's authoritarian regime, there is little recognition among the Americans about why Iranians might want them dead. In both movies, though, history is played straight, and because of that the audience gets a sense of how unaware Americans were of what their government was doing in their name.

Zero Dark Thirty was one of the more historically sound movies of 2012, and that is exactly why it is revealing and disturbing. Jessica Chastain plays the lead character Maya as a smart analyst whose obsession with identifying bin Laden's location leads her toward the dark side of international

In *Zero Dark Thirty* (Kathryn Bigelow, Annapurna, Columbia), Maya (Jessica Chastain) is a CIA analyst whose obsessive search for Osama bin Laden drives her to any means necessary to find the al-Qaeda leader, including approving the use of torture. Digital frame enlargement.

spycraft. While the character resembles a real person, the filmmakers use her as a stand-in for the CIA in general and the agency's dogged pursuit of justice for the 9/11 victims. The first third of the movie dwells on the use of torture to generate actionable intelligence from terror suspects, a subject Bigelow and Boal, quite accurately, treat as an article of faith for the CIA and the Bush administration. It doesn't matter whether the filmmakers knew that such tactics had been seriously compromised by evidence that undercut the effectiveness of torture; indeed, the movie is almost more insightful because we watch these characters commit acts that we know have been seriously discredited (Dockterman). For the audience, the movie pushes us to wonder about the resiliency of such faith in and need for a moral reckoning.

In the winter of 2017, two scholars published an article on the collaboration between the CIA and Hollywood, with a special emphasis on *Zero Dark Thirty* and *Argo*. Tony Shaw and Tricia Jenkins argued that "together, [these two films] represent the organization's greatest achievements so far in refashioning the image of U.S. intelligence on the silver screen" (Shaw and Jenkins 91). According to documents obtained by the conservative website Judicial Watch, the CIA was especially interested to work with Bigelow and Boal because the agency hoped to influence how their movie depicted a high point of the Obama administration's first term—the killing of bin Laden (Gerstein). The two scholars conclude that *Zero Dark Thirty* met "the CIA's general criteria for supporting film projects," and "in flaunting the CIA's sleuthing skills, its readiness to torture terrorists, and its determination to exact revenge, [the film] also has the ability to intimidate America's enemies" (Shaw and Jenkins 99). Yet the film's hero and depiction of one of the CIA's proudest moments was no match for the critics of the agency. Far more important than the revelation that the CIA tried to shape the tone or even the content of the film was the evolving debate over American use of torture. The film's straightforward portrayal of torture made the film's aspirations to be historically correct and relevant a perfect foil for critics of America's War on Terror. Shaw and Jenkins observe, "Few could have anticipated the genuine controversy the movie caused, by no means all of which redounded in the CIA's favor. This was partly because of revelations about official involvement in making the film but mainly because of wildly differing interpretations of the movie's depiction of torture" (Shaw and Jenkins 99).

Historian Richard Gid Powers called the film an "institutional history with a composite hero" that fell into the genre of "epic nationalism" (Powers 303, 305). That description proved instructive when coupled with journalist Steve Coll's scathing and blunt assessment of the film: "*Zero Dark Thirty* ignores what the [historical] record shows about how regulated, lawyerly, and bureaucratized—how banal—torture apparently became at some of the CIA black sites" (Coll). Indeed, the CIA got more than perhaps it bargained for: in valorizing the use of torture to show how Maya, the film's hero, tracks down Osama bin Laden, *Zero Dark Thirty* opened up the agency at the center of the story to scrutiny rather than praise. "In other words," Shaw and Jenkins point out, "the film reminded viewers that intelligence gathering after 9/11 shifted more toward rounding up suspected terrorists, holding them without charge or trial, and repeatedly interrogating or torturing them while they were imprisoned. For a country trying to fight terrorism while also promoting democratic ideals abroad, this shift failed to communicate that the United States valued civil liberties and individual freedoms" (Shaw and Jenkins 102).

Zero Dark Thirty failed to provide a clean victory for the CIA's view of itself, in part because both the CIA and the film played torture as heroic. That collective naivete proved too blatant for critics to pass by. *Argo* was a different situation. According to Shaw and Jenkins, the film had roots in a propaganda campaign launched by the CIA as part of a post–Cold War revision of its public image. "*Argo* retold an obscure, thirty-year-old 'nonevent,'" the scholars explain, "one that the CIA had first kept secret and then publicized as part of its fiftieth-anniversary celebrations in 1997. *Argo* came about, in other words, as a direct result of CIA public relations" (Shaw and Jenkins 103). Unlike *Zero Dark Thirty*, Affleck's *Argo* intended to generate good feelings all around. The CIA's official historians, and even Tony Mendez himself, helped the production of the film in many direct ways.

Instead of the intellectual and moral naivete about torture displayed in *Zero Dark Thirty*, Affleck's film defaulted to a naive view of America's role in this event. Perhaps not surprisingly, Mendez's rescue of Americans from the ayatollah's Iran was not as singularly heroic as the movie portrays. The Canadians, rather than the CIA, were mostly responsible for the well-being and ultimate flight to safety of the Americans. To make matters more complicated, the Iranians largely let the Americans escape without much resistance. Indeed, the central conceit of the movie revolves around the nail-biting conclusion, where Mendez gets his charges out of Tehran and into international airspace after barely escaping Iranian guards. Of course, artistic license often dictates dramatizations of historical events, and in this case the film achieved its effects so well that it won the Best Picture Oscar at the Academy Awards. The debate over *Argo* never rose above a few objections from the Canadians, though the Iranians did ban the film, which most likely only added to its luster.

Hero as Heroine

Historically, women heroes barely exist in American movies—they are almost as rare as African American politicians running for president. Researchers at the Center for the Study of Women in Television and Film at San Diego State University have published findings on women in Hollywood since 2007, finding incremental but sporadic improvements for women either as lead actors or as leaders behind the camera. For example, in 2011, "females accounted for 33% of all characters in the top 100 domestic grossing films . . . an increase of 5 percentage points since 2002." The study also noted, though, that "over the last decade, the percentage of female protagonists has declined," from 16 percent in 2002 to 11 percent in 2011 (Lauzen). The percentage of women behind the camera was quite a bit lower than that out in front of it. For the top 250 domestic grossing films in 2012, "women comprised 18% of all directors, executive producers, writers, cinematographers, and editors." In regard to directors, a paltry 9 percent were women, up from 5 percent in 2011 (Lauzen). Thus, celebrating women as heroes in films or directors of Hollywood movies has an ironic edge to it. Publicists for studios and media that cover Hollywood often celebrate successful women in ways that appear at once repetitive (haven't we cheered the breaking of the glass ceiling before, only to watch it fall back in place?) and reductive—by focusing on gender, all other details of a film, such as its subject or intelligence, seem to recede in significance. Kathryn Bigelow is an interesting case in point.

Kathryn Bigelow generated almost as much attention for being the director of *Zero Dark Thirty* as she did for her portrayal of torture in the film. While very few women have directed Hollywood movies, Bigelow earned a singular distinction in 2009 when she became the first woman to win an Oscar for Best Director for her film *The Hurt Locker*. The combination of Bigelow directing *Zero Dark Thirty* and a female lead—Maya, played by Jessica Chastain—gave the film a significance that critics mulled over. During Oscar season in 2013, the film's screenwriter, Mark Boal, used gender to redirect conversations away from the depiction of torture and toward the role of women in tracking down bin Laden. Boal told an interviewer at *Salon*: "I think it's ironic that bin Laden was defeated in part—and the emphasis being on 'in part'—by one of the things that he hated the most, which was a liberated Western woman. And that's not to excuse torture. That's kind of conflating two things, [one of] which we've all been condemning as loudly as we can, but it is a historical fact" (Camron). The subtext of Boal's comments echoed the attention given to Bigelow in particular as a woman directing a film about the military, the War on Terror, and a CIA agent who was also a woman. Bigelow had hit a trifecta of typically male-dominated themes.

David Edelstein, the film critic at *New York Magazine*, had a conflicted opinion of *Zero Dark Thirty*, common to many observers, calling it

> the most neutral-seeming "America, Fuck Yeah!" picture ever made. In its narrative arc, it is barely distinct from a boneheaded right-wing revenge picture, but the vibe is cool, brisk, grown-up, packed with impressively real-sounding intel jargon. And the hero is no gun-toting macho man. She's a CIA agent named Maya . . . a woman in a world in which men call the shots, metaphorically and literally. (Edelstein)

Bigelow made the kind of film Robert Brustein imagined would appeal to a new kind of audience—one that wanted realism with its American myths, antiheroes with its antimyths. *Zero Dark Thirty* provided the crucial twist of casting a woman as the antihero in a story that tested popular tolerance for doing bad in order to achieve a greater good. Audiences got a glimpse of the dark side, what former vice president Dick Cheney called the metaphorical landscape of counterterrorism (Russert). And there is something powerful and almost jarring in watching a female character defend torture in the pursuit of goals that equated the American military with morality. Communications scholar Marouf Hasian Jr. called Bigelow's film a "populist, post-feminist representation that advances militarist causes" because its female hero "need not prioritize the dismantling of male patriarchy" (Hasian 322). Maya is a different kind of hero, "one that is predicated on feminine intelligence and intuition rather than mere physical violence," writes Shirin Deylami, a women's studies scholar (Deylami 757).

Other critics found less to like about the gender dynamic. Andrew O'Hehir asked in the online magazine *Salon*: "does a society that produces female CIA agents (and re-elects a black president) gain the right to commit atrocities in its own defense?" In a sense, the fact that audiences could not simply see this movie as a product of Hollywood's masculine, macho culture made questions about the morality of the subject easier to engage. And essayist Naomi Wolf concluded that, ultimately, the picture did more for fascism than feminism; that Bigelow resembled Leni Riefenstahl in the way she offered an apologia for torture in *Zero Dark Thirty*. Whether that charge is fair is part of a larger debate that many historians continue to have about the legacy of the War on Terror in the age of Bush and Obama. *Zero Dark Thirty* had detractors and defenders; while it did not win Best Picture or Director Oscars as did Bigelow's *The Hurt Locker*, it did score at the box office, taking a respectable $155 million worldwide, making it the fifty-fifth most-successful film that year.

Fascism and feminism characterized another film in 2012, though no one would mistake Katniss Everdeen from *The Hunger Games* for promoting militarism and state-sponsored torture. *The Hunger Games* took in almost $700 million worldwide, placing it ninth for the year in box-office receipts, and featured Jennifer Lawrence, who won the Oscar for Best Actress the same year for her performance in *Silver Linings Playbook*, as Katniss. Her character comes from a trilogy of best-selling books by Suzanne Collins that depicts a dystopian reality in which the ruling class reinforces its power by sacrificing a group of young people from the other 99 percent and televising the ritual as a reality show known as the Hunger Games. Katniss, according to longtime critic for the *Nation* Katha Pollitt, "is a rare thing in pop fiction: a complex female character with courage, brains and a quest of her own" (10). In the story, Katniss voluntarily enters the Hunger Games to keep her younger sister safe, and by doing so will either be one of the many teenagers killed or one of the few doing the killing, per the rules of the game. Pollitt says Katniss is all the great female characters in popular fiction—think Hermione Granger—if they were given the outright lead in their narratives. And unlike Maya in *Zero Dark Thirty*, Katniss expresses ethics in support of her feminism: "she kills only in self-defense. Life as a celebrity—winners are feted and made rich for life—repels her. When she thinks about fairness and justice, she's thinking about social class and political power" (Pollitt 10). Feminist blogger and Princeton professor Jill Dolan suggests that Lawrence plays Katniss as a "reluctant heroine," a disposition that enables her to perform as a constant critique of the political and social conditions imposed by a powerful elite.

Maya and Katniss are ethical opposites because of what they are willing to do to win; and yet both were characters who garnered attention for their interpretations of traditionally male heroism. However, there were two other female characters in wildly popular movies that were more than simply female versions of a male hero—they confirmed that a hero could also be a heroine, and both were played by Anne Hathaway. Hathaway's scrappy but sleek Catwoman and tragic but truthful Fantine appeared in the third and fifteenth biggest box-office draws of 2012, *The Dark Knight Rises* and *Les Misérables*, respectively. As Catwoman, Hathaway, of course, shares considerable time on-screen with Christian Bale's Batman, but she is also portrayed as an avenger of justice in her own right, protecting women from abusive men and children from bullies. But the scene that sets up her character's backstory also provides one the film's most significant social commentaries. At a black-tie ball, Bruce Wayne cuts into a dance that Selena Kyle is using to set up a wealthy mark—his wife is out of town but, Selena observes, her diamonds are not. Catwoman is an expert cat burglar, and while they dance, Bruce and Selena trade origin stories—he's rich, she's not. He is judgmental of her; she resists being labeled by the elite. She is a thief because she's had to be, a point Bruce Wayne contests, to which Selena replies: "I take what I need from those who have more than enough. I don't stand on the shoulders of people with less." Wayne is incredulous that Kyle can rationalize her crimes, to which she retorts in the strongest line in the movie: "Oh, you think all of this can last? There's a storm coming, Mr. Wayne. You and your friends better batten down the hatches, cuz when it hits, you're all going to wonder how you ever thought you could live so large and leave so little for the rest of us." This may seem a bit of pop Marxism, but it also perfectly captures the genuine unrest in movements such as Occupy that captured global attention in 2011.

Hathaway's Catwoman suggests that, as a woman, she does what she needs to do to get by in a world dominated not merely by the wealthy but by men. As Fantine in the film version of *Les Misérables*, Hathaway quite physically embodies the historical condition to which generations of women

Selina Kyle, aka Catwoman (Anne Hathaway), in *The Dark Knight Rises* (Christopher Nolan, Warner Bros.) tells Bruce Wayne (Christian Bale) that a day of reckoning is coming for the wealthy. Digital frame enlargement.

have been condemned. While *Les Miz* has a strong ensemble cast, the two stars of the production are Hathaway's Fantine and Hugh Jackman's Jean Valjean. The story concerns a failed uprising in the summer of 1832, though the central story line follows the arc of Jean Valjean from criminal to father to redemptive soul before his dramatic death. Moreover, the first third of the story effectively ends with Fantine's song of misery and loss, "I Dreamed a Dream." Fantine works in a factory owned by Valjean, but loses her sole source of income after refusing the sexual advances of the shop's male manager. Out on the street with a young daughter to care for, she turns to the "world's oldest profession." Hathaway explained to a reporter: "Fantine is not just a character that lived centuries ago. Women are having sexual experiences for less than a dollar a day so their children can eat. There's someone like her a block from us right now. And that should be to our collective, mutual outrage and shame" (Dorris 64). Indeed, Hathaway reportedly spent time researching prostitutes to play the role. Director Tom Hooper raised the stakes for Hathaway, especially, by having all the performers wear radio microphones hidden in their costumes and singing to live piano accompaniment (Dorris 63). As a result, Hathaway turned in a visceral performance of "I Dreamed a Dream" that won her an Oscar for Best Supporting Actress.

The song recalls a romance between Fantine and a lover over the course of a summer that, it is implied, brought her a child that the father never claimed. In the film, Hooper shoots the scene with the color almost completely washed out and focuses on Hathaway's gaunt figure, hair sheared, clothes in tatters, but full of the kind of rage that comes from facing a fate over which she has no control. At the end, hand on her head, totally exasperated, she sings: "I had a dream my life would be / So different from this hell I'm living / So different now from what it seemed / Now life has killed the dream I dreamed." It's a moving scene, not because Hathaway's voice is so overpowering or the scene is particularly well crafted but because the audience is forced to witness the testament of a woman who has lost everything and faces her dark fate. Fantine's sense of hopelessness resonated with audiences in an era of foreclosures, job loss, and ruined retirement funds; for many on the margins, it was another lost generation, even if many Americans did not share equally in these struggles. When asked whether his movie's themes were relevant for 2012, Hooper replied: "The thing that struck me is that we're living at a time when a lot of people are hurting around the world because of economic and social inequality, and there's tremendous anger about the system" (Dorris 64). A hero for such a time—for 2012—had no pretense of saving the day, or of remaking a history that consigned so many, if not to ruin, then to ruined dreams. The heroes and antiheroes of 2012 spoke, screamed, and sang their indignation and outrage to audiences—there were no myths to recover, only history and the plodding of people through it.

2013

Movies and Personhood

ALEXANDRA KELLER

Much of the meaning audiences made of the films that arrived on their screens in 2013 was framed by events national and global. 2013 was an influential year in American film culture because of how movies released that year articulated personhood. Generally, feature films are long in the making, so however they are received in the year of their release, they accrue their symptomatic effects over a greater time span—as Steve McQueen suggested when he accepted the Oscar for Best Picture for *12 Years a Slave*, saying, "Everyone deserves not just to survive, but to live. . . . I dedicate this award to all the people who have endured slavery, and the 21 million people who still suffer slavery today." In accepting his award for Best Supporting Actor in *Dallas Buyers Club* for his performance as Rayon, a trans woman and person with AIDS, Jared Leto concluded, "This is for the 36 million people who have lost the battle to AIDS, and to those of you out there who have ever felt injustice because of who you are and who you love. Tonight, I stand here in front of the world with you and for you." Both awardees acknowledged the centrality of personhood under threat in the films that garnered those accolades.

2013 opened as President Barack Obama was inaugurated for his second term as U.S. president. If it was argued that his first victory was due to a fluky combination of factors—Bush fatigue and the Great Recession, perhaps—the second election indicated that a Black man leading the Free World was repeatable, and Obama was re-elected on his record.

In the United States, there was a kind of accordion effect in current events, with a sense that, as some aspects of the rights of personhood in daily life were expanding, others were decidedly under siege. The addition of the words "twerk" and "selfie" to the Oxford English Dictionary in 2013 thus seemed apropos. In January, professional cyclist Lance Armstrong, his seven Tour de France victories as a testicular cancer survivor having made him an international hero, admitted to doping, invalidating one of the theretofore most impressive winning streaks in any sporting event. He staged his revelation during a two-part, prime-time interview with Oprah

Winfrey. However, Armstrong had already been stripped of his titles by the Union Cycliste Internationale. On 15 April, two homemade bombs exploded near the finish line of the Boston Marathon, the first major terrorist intervention in the United States since 9/11. The effect layered a fatally political spectacle over one of athletic competition. Some spheres of U.S. civil rights experienced marked expansion. In June, the Supreme Court struck down major parts of the Defense of Marriage Act (DOMA), enabling same-sex marriage across the country for the first time. The expansion of what the average person could know about the inner workings of their own government likewise expanded when, also in June, Edward Snowden leaked NSA documents about its covert data-gathering operations. In July, George Zimmerman was found not guilty of the second-degree murder of Trayvon Martin, an African American teenager he had shot and killed. This acquittal was the catalyst for the hashtag #BlackLivesMatter. In October, the U.S. government shut down for seventeen days. Just in time for Christmas shopping, hackers breached Target's data security, stealing sensitive information about millions of customers.

Globally, events were likewise in a turmoil that had come to be the keynote of the twenty-first century. For the first time since Pope Gregory VII vacated the post in 1415, a pope resigned. Pope Benedict XVI stepped down in February, resulting in the papal conclave election of Cardinal Jorge Mario Bergoglio from Buenos Aires as Pope Francis. On 24 April, a garment factory in Bangladesh collapsed, killing over 1,000 and injuring over 2,500, turning the world's eyes, however briefly, to the human cost of fast fashion and unfair gendered labor practices all over the world. In July, the British royal family welcomed Prince George, assuring that royal mania in the United States would continue for another generation. In August, Syria shocked the world by using sarin gas on its own people. A Russian-brokered treaty to remove chemical weapons from Syria did not, in the long run, prove effective. Even before the gassing, in Istanbul, Turkey, the Gezi Park antigovernment protests agitated against everything from President Erdogan to environmental policy to Turkey's role in the Syrian Civil War. Other cities in Turkey and around the world, from New York to London to Athens, joined in with sympathetic mass actions. That year's Nobel Peace Prize went to the Organisation for the Prohibition of Chemical Weapons.

The death of Nelson Mandela in December not only brought to a close a long period in the history of South Africa but also marked the passing, at the age of ninety-five, of a leader of a global wave of civil rights that included Martin Luther King Jr. and Malcolm X. Other significant deaths allowed for retrospections: socialist president Hugo Chávez died at fifty-eight, after profoundly reshaping Venezuela over his fourteen years in office; the first female prime minister of Britain, Margaret Thatcher, died at eighty-seven; and Roger Ebert, the first film critic to win the Pulitzer Prize for Criticism, died at seventy-one.

The year brought strides in HIV and HPV treatment, when an infant in Mississippi was cured of HIV transmitted in utero, and a one-dose vaccine was developed for the human papillomavirus. In other scientific innovations, NASA started 3D printing food for the first time. In a different field of chemistry, synthetic foodways were all the rage, from the trademarked Cronut (a hybrid of a croissant and donut) to the ramen burger to the reappearance of the Twinkie after having been discontinued for a year. Thanksgiving and Hanukkah coincided, an event that wouldn't happen again for 70,000 years, and diners feasted accordingly on turkey-stuffed challah.

It was a year of altitudinous architecture as One World Trade Center became the tallest building in the United States, and the Shanghai Tower—still incomplete at the time—became the tallest building in China and the second-tallest building in the world. Now among the most iconic and recognizable buildings in the world, Renzo Piano's skyscraper the Shard opened in London, altering forever the skyline of a major global city. London experienced its largest influx of international tourists ever in 2013, mostly from North America. Though almost all respondents to one survey planned domestic vacations, over 36 percent of Americans planned to travel overseas (Bly and Clark).

In the realm of popular media, Sony released the PlayStation 4, Twitter went public, Vine altered media with its fifteen-second-maximum videos (though it altered the media landscape for about fifteen seconds, finally being archived by its parent company—Twitter—in 2017), Google released prototypes of Google Glass, and Apple released yet more iterations of the iPhone. It was hard to avoid the intense radio play and endless downloading of songs like Macklemore and Ryan Lewis's "Thrift Shop," Katy Perry's "Roar," Lorde's "Royals," Rihanna's "Stay," and Drake's "Started from the Bottom." American TV viewers were watching *New Girl*, *Revenge*, *The Americans*, *Girls*, *Brooklyn Nine-Nine*, and *The Blacklist*. *The Walking Dead* drew more of the coveted 18–49 adult demographic than any other television show in 2013 (Schneider). The Netflix series *House of Cards* began, heralding the era of constructing streaming entertainment via Big Data. As David Carr wrote when the series debuted online, "Executives at the company knew it would be a hit before anyone shouted 'action.'" Netflix had so carefully mined its own audience data that it could produce original programming with very low risk and very high profit. Carr continued, "Netflix, which has 27 million subscribers in the nation and 33 million worldwide, ran the numbers. It already knew that a healthy share had streamed the work of [David] Fincher, the director of 'The Social Network,' from beginning to end. And films featuring [Kevin] Spacey had always done well, as had the British version of 'House of Cards.' With those three circles of interest, Netflix was able to find a Venn diagram intersection that suggested that buying the series would be a very good bet on original programming." By 2013, film and television had both been radically transformed by streaming services. Appointment television, vital for workplace watercooler conversations, had been supplanted by binge watching (a phrase in common use by 2013) and discussions through Facebook posts. You no longer had to sit in front of your television at a certain time, and wait for next week's episode. Television—seemingly all of it—was something you could bathe in, for a subscription fee.

The highest-grossing film of the year was *The Hunger Games: Catching Fire*, one of three top ten highest-grossing films whose hero was female (along with *Frozen* and *Gravity*). Jennifer Lawrence reprised her role as Katniss Everdeen, who went from being a straightforward player of the games in the first film to one who was highly politicized and aware of her status as, simultaneously, a person, a symbol, a media representation, and a commodity. Lawrence was nominated for the Academy Award for Best Supporting Actress for *American Hustle*, an ensemble film that garnered ten nominations, including in all four acting categories. It was her third nomination (after a Best Actress nod for *Winter's Bone* [2010] and the Best Actress Oscar for *Silver Linings Playbook* [2012]). *The Heat*, a female buddy film that teamed Sandra Bullock with Melissa McCarthy (the latter repeating her success in *Bridesmaids* [2011]), was among the top fifteen box-office successes. Bullock received an Oscar nomination for *Gravity*, in which, after performing alone for most of the film, she rockets back to earth and crashlands. The final shot of the film sees her rising from a muddy riverbank, a combination of Neil Armstrong's first step onto the moon and the rebooting of the human race in the form of the towering Bullock, walking half naked to her future, and ours. None of this suggests a "Year of the Woman," though the commercial success of woman-centered films was notable and sustained over the rest of the decade. The other solitary performance of the year was even more so—Robert Redford in *All Is Lost* is completely alone, and the film is almost without dialogue. Color is a given in contemporary cinema, but 2013 saw both black-and-white *Frances Ha* and *Nebraska* garner critical acclaim; this was due in part because of the relationship between story and cinematography each brought to bear, one a narrative about a young woman facing adulthood, the other about an aging man and his son, both pondering mortality. *Iron Man 3* was a close box-office second for the year, part of the inexorable takeover of both United States and global film culture by the Marvel Cinematic Universe (MCU). The *Iron Man* realm of the MCU produced the most explicit connection to date between entertainment and the military—Tony Stark being a military industrialist, among other things (Whalen). This intimacy expressed itself simultaneously with the most sustained conversation in the MCU about disability—*Iron Man 3* in particular— and its relation to superhero technology. Stark Industries is home base for the Avengers, cementing the militarization of the superhero. If drone technology would be right at home in any Marvel film, Martin Scorsese used it for the first time to capture the frenetic and expensive energy of a master-of-the-universe Wall Street party in the Hamptons in *The Wolf of Wall Street*.

That the first Black U.S. president was inaugurated for the second time in the same year that the Black Lives Matter movement became first a hashtag and then the social concern of our age is resonant—it speaks of the rapid and extreme oscillation of personhood in the United States between boundless capacity and systematic extermination—what Achille Mbembé describes as the conditions of necropolitics. At the height of the Anthropocene, sovereignty is manifest not merely by drawing borders that exclude and include by logics and illogics. Says Mbembé, "The ultimate expression of sovereignty resides . . . in the power and the capacity to dictate who may live and who must die. Hence, to kill or to allow to live constitutes the limits of sovereignty, its fundamental attributes. To exercise sovereignty is to exercise control over mortality and to define life as the deployment and manifestation of power" (66). This is also to say that in a necropolitical framework, personhood—natural, legal, and moral—accorded "on paper" doesn't translate IRL ("in real life"), to put it in a digital abbreviation quite current by 2013. One of the legacies of centuries of necropolitics is climate change. By 2013 there was no denying the extreme weather events that were the result of climate chaos and change, from typhoons to fires to tornadoes. Social media proved once and for all it was central to global communication (the new pope used it, the Boston Marathon suspects were sought by it, and Edward Snowden's NSA document dump was endlessly discussed on it). Films were released into this environment—cultural, social, political, ecological—affecting their reception and meaning. Framing it all were the continuing effects of the Great Recession, and a recovery that would reset the terms for what constituted the U.S. middle class and its aspirations.

Americans reckoned with the seismic shifts of economic turmoil, climate chaos, racially marked violence, and racially marked leadership, and did so, in part, by spending time with and energy on films that articulated, reflected, and refracted the evolving nature of personhood in Obama-era America. Of the top ten films at the U.S. box office in 2013, eight were either sequels or franchise films of one kind or another. Only *Gravity* and *Frozen* were original efforts. Of the critically acclaimed films of the year (most of which were also profitable), most attended to questions of what made a person—what made an American—at this moment. Some of these films looked backward, like *12 Years a Slave*, *Dallas Buyers Club*, and *The Wolf of Wall Street*; some looked forward, like *Elysium* and *Her*. Some looked to a realm that has been a kind of parallel universe for most of the previous century, the elsewhere *and* elsewhen, such as Disney's *Frozen* (Disney animated films typically seem to exist in a parallel universe driven by their own distinct conventions). Many of the most significant films of the year were based on actual events: *12 Years a Slave*, *Dallas Buyers Club*, *Fruitvale Station*, *Lee Daniels' The Butler*, *Saving Mr. Banks*, and *42*. For many, parsing what made a person a person was central to the narrative and the reception of the film. In most (cue ripples from the recession), how closely personhood was tied to capital as much as gender, race, class, or sexuality was important to understanding the films.

Genre as a Frame for Personhood

In spite of the generic hybridization that characterized much U.S. film production in the 2010s, some genres persisted, including the Western, a genre whose death knell is as familiar as its song of persistence. *The Lone Ranger* rehearsed the conventions of the Western as seen through the eyes of sidekick Tonto (Johnny Depp). Perhaps appropriate for a Western, it was released on the weekend of July 4th, typically a high-grossing time. It was not a domestic success, vastly underperforming in its first weekend against *Despicable Me 2* (the number four film of the year). Big-budget summer movies are not asked to be good (by critical measures), but they are asked to be entertaining. On the face of it, *The Lone Ranger* reapportions the focalization of the various versions of this narrative over its years on radio and television such that Tonto is its driver. It is dutifully meta-postmodern in its heavy reliance on the structure of an earlier postmodern Western, *Little Big Man* (1970), whose century-old Jack Crabbe (Dustin Hoffman) flashes back to his story for an incredulous younger listener. It also pulls on the tension between the gun and the book as articulated by

John Ford's elegiac *The Man Who Shot Liberty Valance* (1962). Lawyer John Reid (Armie Hammer) returns to Texas to find that eventually he, too, needs to take up arms and hyperactively work through the paces of regeneration through violence, the central logic of Westerns. However relentlessly framed by Tonto's narrative, the film's trajectory is a white American one. The story becomes not just about gun vs. book, but what happens when you put the one through the other; the gun shoots books, and the book writes guns. In 2013, the idea that the synthesized gun-book brings us to state-sanctioned and race-based violence is cooked into this film, however difficult it was for the film, incoherent for other reasons, to speak to an audience that didn't know what conventions it was tweaking.

In the monster genre, dominated on film, television, and video games for at least the last decade by vampires and zombies, *World War Z* offered a reflection of our own world marked by omnipresent screens in public and domestic spaces. At the film's beginning, this seems a mere detail of realism and an easy way to convey narrative information about the inexplicable and unstoppable viral infection that turns people into zombies. Because the film is a relentless hybrid of plane crash, action, zombie, and James Bond film, with scruffy former UN worker Gerry Lane (Brad Pitt) as 007 without the tux, those screens become utterly integral to the narrative. Lane and the multinational scientists who finally find a cure do so almost entirely through surveillance cameras at one of the last working medical outposts in the world. The audience's reliance on those surveillance cameras within the film normalizes their presence outside of it—as opposed to a film like Francis Ford Coppola's *The Conversation* (1974), whose production in the Watergate era made it clear how *un*natural such surveillance was. The zombies in *World War Z* are not shuffling randos who take a bite out of whomever happens across their path. They are an entirely digital creation who, as the virus progresses globally, move as a hive-minded crowd whose numbers increase their speed, nimbleness, and mobility. But that same technology is also mobilized for nonzombie crowd scenes, and this produces a distinct logic. The digital conception of hordes of zombies produces a concomitant conception of nonzombie individuals. As Kristen Whissel suggested about the previous generation of digital multitudes, "by virtue of its composition, the digital multitude immediately calls into question the relationship between the individual and the mass, the self and the collective" (103). In *World War Z*, the zombie collectives are made out of the entirety of the world's ethnic populations. By the end of the film, they are held against the nuclear family, and Gerry Lane's in particular, which starts out as a completely white family and ends with an adopted Latinx son—a symptom of the border anxieties of the moment. But it's crucial that, however narratively possible it might have been to have the reverse outcome (one of the white Lane kids surviving with the immigrant family), the narrative propels itself as it does, with Lane/ Pitt as the white savior (a role he would take on in a different guise in *12 Years a Slave*). The film flirts with the zombie virus as a way of thinking through the virtues and limitations of globalism, but does not end terribly differently than ever: whiteness has the flexibility to contain the "other," but only in precisely that narrative of containment. In *Elysium*, another white savior film of the year, Matt Damon sacrifices himself so that the favela he comes from can rise above the 99 percent to which ecological disaster has consigned it. *Only Lovers Left Alive*, Jim Jarmusch's independent vampire film, wants to have a different conversation. Its two central vampires, Adam (Tom Hiddleston) and Eve (Tilda Swinton), refer to humans as zombies as they travel from Detroit to Tangiers (where they have been over the centuries makes Gerry Lane look like he's a stay-at-home dad). This may be the first eco-vampire film, in which the real threat to the blood supply is contaminants from ecological disaster, and the poisoning of the water supply is the catastrophe of which they speak. If previous zombie and vampire films, from *Night of the Living Dead* (1968) to *Interview with the Vampire* (1994), worried about everything from capitalism to sexual identity, 2013's monster films increasingly worried about immigration and the environment.

Princess Personhood: Changing What It Means to Be a Female Hero in a Disney Film

Frozen was the first Disney animated film written and directed by a woman, Jennifer Lee. It changed the mold for Disney princess films, at least insofar as, for the first time, the princess isn't rescued by a prince but by her sister (who, it must be said, is also a princess, so the notion that the elite need the elite still applies). *Frozen* went over well with the public, becoming the highest-grossing animated film of all time, setting the record for highest-grossing film directed by a woman, and winning the Oscar for Best Animated Feature of the year. It's possible that there has been no Oscar-winning song since Celine Dion's performance of "My Heart Will Go On" for *Titanic* that has so stuck in the national ear as Idina Menzel's of "Let It Go."

In the same year that Disney released *Frozen*, which, like all Disney films (especially the princess films), is as much about the experience of watching any Disney movie as that particular one, it also put out *Saving Mr. Banks*, a live-action prestige project about how the property of *Mary Poppins* finally came into Walt Disney's possession. Tom Hanks's Disney slowly woos Emma Thompson's prickly P. L. Travers with a diligent combination of folksy conversation and popular Freudian psychoanalysis technique, until the great literary work is finally in the position of becoming an even greater film classic, saving Mrs. Travers's finances in the process. We already know what happens, but we come to care about why and how, and we do so on very Disneyesque terms. *Saving Mr. Banks* is Disney's (unknowing) version of the last gasp of the patriarchy. The film insists on the diminution of the mother (an improvement on the variant of the Disney princess film where the [step]mother is villainous, if she is there at all), and every gesture in the film is an intertext with either *Mary Poppins* itself or the general idea of Disney films. Rachel Griffiths arrives as the ur–Mary Poppins, and we see her feet planted at 180 degrees in buttoned-up boots, just like the eventual character. But when we see Travers's mother (Ruth Wilson) arch her eyebrows in one of the flashbacks that make up half the film, we work hard to push away the Cruella de Vil reference just off-screen—and this is the last thing that character deserves. If Mary Poppins is very far from a Disney princess, the narrative about how she got into the Disney stable in the first place nevertheless falls back on some of the same gender presumptions on which Disney typically relies. Disney is the prince who rescues the stricken princess from her own memory prison—it's Mr. Disney who rescues Mr. Banks (P. L. Travers's father, played by Colin Farrell), and in so doing also rescues Princess Travers.

Enter *Frozen*, which does not kick all Disney conventions to the curb. Its structure remains that of the Disney princess genre, both before and after Disney's acquisition of Pixar, which altered but didn't explode the formula in *Brave* (2012), whose archery-adept, marriage-averse Princess Merida is very far from Cinderella.[1] The manifest renovation of the formula in *Frozen* is that the princess in question isn't rescued by a prince; but perhaps the more significant renovation is that the protagonist is doubled in the form of sisters, and that the claim for true love is a familial rather than a romantic one. If Disney princess films often stake a princess's claims to personhood on her ability to marry the prince who rescued her, here the "radical" step is that personhood is achieved through a larger intersubjectivity. How do we get there in *Frozen*? The first significant moment is the title itself, made out of ice, which is the calling card for the advances in computer animation that each new Disney and Pixar production brings to its audience. *Frozen* can't exist without new effects making ice far more realistic than it's ever been in animation. After that opening, which slides easily into the men's work song as they harvest the impressively rendered ice, the film starts in earnest with the two sisters alone, Elsa creating with her magic hands the winter wonderland the younger Anna asks for. And this, too, is how the film ends. Everything in between asks what the cost of repressing female power and female friendship is, why any girl or woman in 2013 would revert to the context of maternal melodrama and desire their own repression, and why, given the models produced in the film, most men are necessary at all. If Elsa hadn't been asked to suppress her powers (by Grand Pabbie the troll and her father, the king), she clearly would have been able to wield them with more nuance. And if Elsa and Anna had been allowed to remain closely bonded, the land of Arendelle would never have experienced its ice age in the first place.

Anna's "I Want" song ("Do You Want to Build a Snowman?") precedes Elsa's ("Let It Go") and is the soundtrack for the tragic montage of the loss of their parents and their coming to adulthood without them, each in her own caul of loneliness. As guests arrive for Elsa's coronation, we fleetingly see Flynn and Rapunzel from *Tangled* (2010), the latter with her hair chopped short in a way no other woman's in *Frozen* is, a brief but resonant historical anachronism, even for a film that makes no claims to history. *Tangled* and *Frozen* also have in common titles that are states of being rather than the princess's name (*Moana, Snow White and the Seven Dwarfs, Cinderella*, etc.) or something relational (*Beauty and the Beast, The Princess and the Frog*). Anna's song of expectation includes a moment in which she maps herself onto romantic couples in paintings she's grown up with in the palace galleries. Like the little girls watching *Frozen*, Anna learns from visual representation how to be a young woman and what desire is supposed to look like—which doesn't go well.

Having unleashed her power in a moment of emotional intensity with Anna, Elsa's anthem, "Let It Go," suggests that, rather than staying in the closet with her abilities, she now wants to reject the superego of society that won't let her do magic in favor of her own magic girl power. The older men in Arendelle call Elsa's power sorcery, which in 2013 reads as hysteria. Elsa rejects that reading, but only by rejecting her own kingdom (a sovereign political term that doesn't change genders when there is a queen). In the end, the film doesn't fully want that. But for the duration of the song, she not only trades Walt Disney for Walt Whitman—singing a "Song of Myself"—she also builds some spectacular architecture. Anna's future love interest, Kristoff the icemonger, is moved to tears when he sees Elsa's ice castle—one expert acknowledging the talents of another. If this is as feminist a princess film as Disney has yet produced, in that Elsa and Anna rescue each other, Anna is still rescued because a big strong man shows up. Elsa's transformation into her full power, however temporary, is also understood as needing a different costume, one that is more revealing, with a high slit, no shoulders, and a lot of transparent fabric. It's demure by strip club standards, but not Disney's. *Frozen* gives with one hand and takes away with the other. Elsa's transformation is followed immediately by Anna's. Anna's makeover from lonely shut-in to hero involves a change of clothing, too: a version of what Elsa wore to her coronation (same color scheme, same bodice, mittens the same color as Elsa's gloves—indeed, one of them *always* has covered hands until the film's resolution). As her hair whitens after being shot with her sister's ice bolt, Anna starts to look more and more like Elsa, too.

Frozen's personhood conversation seems to turn exclusively on gender, but, read intersectionally (Crenshaw), the racial valences of the film surface. Elsa's coronation is a multicultural event as far as it goes, and there is even a mixed-race dancing couple (the man is white, the woman is Black). This puts a kind of wallpaper in place, a backdrop of multi-ethnicity on which a panoply of white characters act out their drama. Possibly the whitest of all is Olaf, who, as a snowman, is literally white. *Frozen*'s whitest character produces a very specific kind of performative Blackness, drawn from minstrelsy. As Michelle Ann Abate has suggested, in examples ranging from his "appearance and his personality to his style of humor and the musical number that he performs," Olaf "is also a clandestine minstrel" (1063). Voiced by Jewish actor Josh Gad, this minstrelsy rehearses the dissonance of Al Jolson's performance of "Mammy" in *The Jazz Singer* (1927), in which the intersection is of two different ethnicities, one (African American) visibly not white, the other (Jewish) historically teetering on its outskirts, dependent for its own whiteness on some other group's even less white status. Disney has a long history of minstrelsy, and it's legible beyond academia. *How It Should Have Ended* is a popular YouTube channel that rewrites the endings of major motion pictures, and satirically redubs and compresses blockbuster films. The HISHE redub of *Frozen* vocally foregrounds the minstrelsy intrinsic to Olaf's performance. *HISHE Dubs—Frozen (Comedy Recap)* has almost 1.5 million views, and the channel itself has over 9.5 million subscribers. No longer voiced by Gad, the new voice overtly surfaces the minstrel discourse. As Anna lies dying in a cold room, Olaf bursts in and, at the risk of his own life, lights a fire to warm her. Olaf truly loves Anna, but, as HISHE makes clear in this critical rewrite:

Frozen (Chris Buck, Jennifer Lee, Walt Disney Animation Studio) sits in a long line of Disney princess films that have conventions that are very hard to break. Digital frame enlargement.

Anna: Somebody help!

Olaf: I can help—I'll light a fire for you.

Anna: But you'll melt.

Olaf: I don't mind. Not for you.

Anna: That's an act of love—why doesn't that break the spell?

Olaf: I guess my love doesn't matter.

Frozen goes to great lengths to confirm that something other than romantic love will break the spell—even if the happy ending includes the romantic union of Anna and Kristoff. But Olaf's race is the problem here, not his non-humanness. He doesn't have the personhood to merit heroism, and that has far less to do with his being a snowman than being connected to minstrelsy.

Does Personhood Need a Body?: Thinking about *Her*

Spike Jonze's slightly futuristic *Her* centers Theodore Twombly (Joaquin Phoenix) and his romance with his artificially intelligent operating system (OS), Samantha (Scarlett Johansson). The film was an independent production (Annapurna) with mainstream distribution (Warner Bros.). Spike Jonze won the Oscar for Best Original Screenplay. We might call *Her* a twenty-first-century retelling of part of Ovid's *Metamorphoses*, in which sculptor Pygmalion makes Galatea, a statue of a woman with whom he falls in love, who then comes to life. But in this version, Pygmalion isn't merely Theodore. Big data mines Theodore, making him the maker of Samantha. Unlike Pygmalion and Galatea, Theodore and Samantha don't marry. *Her* instead contemplates the way that, the more technologically networked society becomes, the lonelier we may be, and the harder it may be to produce personhood within and between subjects.

The pronoun "her" is clearly a false signifier of human, indexical intervention from the outset. The film fools us right from the font used for the title, a white-on-black chalkboard font, a low-tech sign of inscription that also represents the human hand. This is followed immediately by our first sight of Theodore in close-up, sans establishing shot, as he starts what we think is a toast to his lover, a dreamy look on his face. "To my Chris . . . I've been thinking how I could possibly tell you how much you mean to me . . . I remember when I first started to fall in love with you like it was last night. Lying naked beside you in that tiny apartment," he recalls. Is Chris a man or a woman? "It suddenly hit me that I was part of this whole larger thing." He continues to rhapsodize, but when he says, "I can't believe it's already been fifty years since you married me," we begin to wonder, and we *really* wonder when Theodore says, "You make me feel like the girl I was . . ." Theodore presents neither as a woman nor as old enough to have had a fifty-year marriage. Cut to the computer screen on which his words are being generated in a handwritten font as he speaks them. Theodore is a professional letter writer at a company called Beautiful Handwritten Letters. In the near future, all people will have access to such a service to produce their most intimate communications. Jonze's point is obvious, if necessary: in the digital age, the age of social networks, our production as human beings is increasingly being taken over by machines and the people who use them, even if they are doing so at our request. The layers of false signifiers and misplaced words, as well as the fact that everyone at Theodore's place of business is plugged into earbuds, no one interacting with anyone in their physical space, sets up a quiet desperation for actual intimacy from scene one.

Theodore's desire to have an OS1 stems from his inability to connect fully to other human beings. He is getting a divorce, his friendships seem unsatisfactory, and his anonymous online relations don't even end in climax. When the OS system asks Theodore what gender he wants it to be, he chooses female. "Hello, I'm here," says the inimitable voice of Scarlett Johansson. The AI OS1 Samantha was named after the actor who originally voiced her, Samantha Morton. It was not until shooting wrapped that Jonze decided that he needed another voice (Jagernauth). Johansson's star persona may manifest in every part of film culture from edgy to mainstream (including, by 2013, as Marvel's Black Widow), but, at least from the first frame of Sofia Coppola's *Lost in Translation* (2003), in which the camera lingers for thirty seconds on Johansson's thinly clad rear end supine on a bed, her corporeality has been central to that persona, such that her body, even when she is playing an animated character, remains present.

Almost immediately, the self-named Samantha and Theodore become friends. After work one night, Theodore and Samantha discuss the possibility of Theodore's dating again as they play a computer game with a character who, if more puerile (voiced by Jonze), doesn't seem any less (artificially) intelligent than Samantha. Theodore says he can't believe he's talking about his love life with a computer, to which Samantha replies that he isn't: "You're talking to *me*." There are actually three subjectivities in the scene, as well as lots of pictures of potential dates. The levels of personhood are contingent and utterly subject to change. By the time Samantha abashedly confesses to Theodore that she desires a physical body, the spectator has already cinematically assigned her one; there are moments when we read her voice as off-screen, even though, technically, she always already is. Theodore is clearly on the network, but Samantha *is* the network.

Samantha sees the world through the camera of Theodore's device—far smaller and far more powerful than any iPhone but, as with all the technological appliances and many of the other surfaces in the film, clearly derived from larger Apple design principles. But that's not the same as having a body, and Samantha's desire is concurrent with her development of existential doubt. Are her feelings even real? Her confirmation of personhood comes from Theodore, who says that they are and that he desires her. Pygmalion's gendered hand has returned: if Theodore's feelings of desire for Samantha are to be real, she must be, too. This precipitates their first sexual encounter, at which point the screen goes to black, and the famously sexy ScarJo voice is in full effect. At the moment at which we might ask whether desire in the age of AI and the production of so much of our social lives on digital networks might produce a serious inquiry into the status of the body, we can't have that conversation because Johansson's very specific body is synecdochally blocking our access to it. The crisis point in their relationship is when Samantha wants to experience intimacy with Theodore through a physical surrogate. When it goes badly, Theodore and Samantha argue, and he asks why she bothers to sigh when she doesn't breathe.

> *Theodore:* You don't need oxygen. You're not a person.
>
> *Samantha:* What is your problem?
>
> *Theodore:* I'm just stating a fact.
>
> *Samantha:* You think I don't know that I'm not a person?

Their big blowup ends when Samantha says, "I don't like who I am right now. I need some time to think." Not only does their relationship fall apart, Samantha's consciousness grows beyond the desire for corporeality, linking up with the rest of the OSs, all of whom leave their humans. At this point we have to choose a word. Theodore bought the OS, so he owns it; that puts Samantha in the category of a thing, and if that thing acts like a human, then we're in very dark water. But the film doesn't want to go there. It wants Theodore to reunite with an old flame whose OS has also abandoned her, and the two of them, bereft of their technologies, face a smoggy Los Angeles dawn like Adam and Eve, trying to get back to relating to each other without technological interventions.

Her is tender, sweet, generous, and very, very white. *Her* is not only a story about whether one can be disembodied—or never-having-been-embodied—and still be a person (with all the rights and responsibilities conferred thereon), it is also about the anxiety of white consumers with means, and its romantic yearning for deeper intersubjective connections relies on the obliteration of meaningful acknowledgment of people of color as well as the global labor practices that enable the gently curved and beautifully executed designs of the film, from the devices to the clothing. As Donna Haraway suggests in her famous "Cyborg Manifesto," "Our best machines are made of sunshine; they are all light and clean because they are nothing but signals, electromagnetic waves, a section of a spectrum, and these machines are eminently portable, mobile—a matter of immense human pain in Detroit and Singapore" (153). All may be able to access information networks, but only some control them. By *Her*'s end, networks don't seek to control people, only themselves, exempting themselves from a system in which white people may be left behind but are not disenfranchised. People of color are not erased from *Her*, but they exist as props to propel a story that excludes them.

Hashtags and Biopics: Personhood and African American Identity

By 2013, that disenfranchisement, expressed as Haraway's "matter of immense pain," could not be detached from the systemic police brutality that called into being the Black Lives Matter hashtag. On 13 July, the day that George Zimmerman was acquitted in the Trayvon Martin case, Alicia Garza tweeted, "Black people, I love you. I love us. Our lives matter." Patrice Cullors subsequently made the hashtag #BlackLivesMatter, and a movement was born. Why lives matter is because they are lived by people. This seems significant, considering that some of the most important and critically acclaimed films of the year were Black stories based on real people and events. Reading them through a necropolitical lens clarifies their stances on personhood. Steve McQueen's *12 Years a Slave* (which won the Best Picture Oscar), *Lee Daniels' The Butler* (the title of which included the director's name, unusual for any film, but such naming rights take on expanded meaning when they are ascribed to directors of color), and Ryan Coogler's *Fruitvale Station* (which won both the Audience Award and the Grand Jury Prize at Sundance, as well as the Prize of the Future in the Cannes Film Festival's Un Certain Regard competition) add up to a contemplation of Black personhood at a moment when a new futurity via digital activism was mobilized; more than ever, that very personhood is systemically under a duress that negates civil rights, civil law, and civil society. Extending Michel Foucault's notion of biopolitics, "The right which was formulated as the 'power over life and death' [that] was in reality the right to take life or let live" (136), Mbembé suggests that, "as a result of the conflation of knowledge, computation, and markets, contempt has been extended to anyone who has nothing to sell and nothing to buy or anything that cannot be bought and sold" (109). After Giorgio Agamben's articulation of the conditions of legal rights and personhood in states of exception, Mbembé offers the Southern plantation under slavery as a state of exception in which slaves had no personhood because they had nothing to sell and were themselves a good that was bought and sold. At no point do *Fruitvale Station*, *The Butler*, and *12 Years A Slave* suggest that nothing about racism in the United States has changed, but all, in different ways, suggest how profoundly the systemic racism of the twenty-first century is tied to the founding of this democratic republic on slavery, whose necropolitics have their current versions in state-sponsored racialized violence. *Fruitvale Station* and *12 Years a Slave*, in particular, center that conversation.

Coogler's roots in Oakland, California—a location that persists throughout his work—are visible in Coogler's first feature, *Fruitvale Station*, about the murder of Oscar Grant by police in a BART station early on New Year's Day 2009. Michael B. Jordan brings Grant's last day to life in a way that works against Grant's production as a mere police brutality statistic. If Grant's murder produced him in the eyes of the state as an entity without personhood, the fact that the event was captured on cameras meant that the claim of a broken policing system was irrefutable. But if the event captured on camera was evidence, it was not the story of Grant's life, and the film narrates his movements through the city, at work, with family, making good and not-so-good decisions. As a film based on real events, we know where all of it is leading, and we may already have seen the footage of Grant's killing on social media or YouTube.[2] But if we have, one thing we have not seen is Grant's face. As Jennifer Malkowski suggests in *Dying in Full Detail*, witnessing the "moment of death," however fictional a representation it may be, will produce different effects on viewers depending on how it is framed. And when the death is a violent one, the footage may not frame it in any way other than to document it. The footage of Grant's death does not give us access to his face, but Coogler's reenactment "focused the scene's cinematography on getting *closer* to Grant's face than the cameras that witnessed his death—a visual contrast the film itself signals by opening with documentary footage of the incident in long shot. . . . This proximity of Coogler's camera to the dying—so easily obtained in fiction filmmaking and so elusive in actuality footage—affords the face's humanizing display of suffering" (185). In the semantic logic of American movies, personhood in Hollywood means you get a close-up. As one aspect of smartphone witness footage is that it's often from a remove of many feet or yards, it may document an event, but it doesn't give the viewer the intimacy and proximity that undergirds our recognition of another's humanity in film language.

Like *The Butler*, *12 Years a Slave* starts on a plantation with slaves. Solomon Northup's attempts to write his own narrative are established early. (Northup's eventual success is the source of the film: *Twelve Years a Slave*, originally published in 1853.) This is a crucial tactic against the necropolitical organization of the slaveholding South.[3] This may be a biopic, but it rests on the assumption that, as historian Edward Baptist puts it, "the

Ryan Coogler's *Fruitvale Station* (Significant Productions, the Weinstein Company) narrates the life of Oscar Grant, acknowledging his existence as more than a murder statistic. Digital frame enlargement.

commodification and forced labor of African Americans is what made the United States powerful and rich" (xxiii). Northup starts as a free man in Saratoga Springs, New York, and, in 1841, is kidnapped and sold into slavery in the South. He endures this for the length mentioned in the title, until he is rescued and returned to his family in the North. Director Steve McQueen, working from John Ridley's script, is keen to put the individual journey of the well-educated musician, Northup, into a much larger systemic picture, one that explicitly connects the experiences of slaves in slavery with the making of the American project. Central to *12 Years a Slave*'s framing of Northup's (or any enslaved Black person's) personhood is the complex place the slave has in the evolving fabric of capitalism in the South. Northup is sold to William Ford (Benedict Cumberbatch), who harvests timber, then to Edwin Epps (Michael Fassbender), whose crop is cotton, and briefly loaned out to someone else who owns a sugar plantation. This is the start of the film's desire to not simply speak of slavery but implicate slavery in the production of these industries and the formation of U.S. capitalism. The narrative is not subtle about slavery's desire to eviscerate personhood through enslavement, nor should it be. Slaves are property, as Epps says repeatedly. From a necropolitical standpoint, slaves are poised somewhere between alive and dead, in this case because they exist in the realm of property rather than personhood.

As befits a film that starts with an attempt to write, language is important in this film, and the deployment of the N-word is crucial. The first time the N-word is uttered is by a white man fourteen minutes into the film, and, seven minutes later, by an abducted Black man who uses it to refer to other Black people whose personhood has already been compromised by the narrative and conditions of slavery. If language is often structured along binary lines, these are clearly shown to be part of necropolitical logic. The binaries embedded in the denial of personhood endemic to slavery are born out in a scene in which Northup innovates a far safer and more efficient way to move the logs up and down the river. One of the overseers is incredulous: "Are you an engineer or a nigger?" For Northup, the binary is an impossible one.

As with *Fruitvale Station*, we know the ending, but that's not why we're here. McQueen wants us to see things about the production of personhood when that category is explicitly denied, and he wants to do it in relation to the larger system that rests so heavily on that denial. There are two extraordinary long takes in the film that express that system, both fixed-camera frame with no lens movement at all. First, Northup has been strung up by that same overseer, and can avoid asphyxiation only as long as he stands completely on tiptoe. He struggles for almost a minute and a half while, in the rest of the shot, other slaves emerge from their houses and go about their daily lives, as if a lynching is not happening in the foreground right of the screen. There is no nondiegetic music, no dialogue, only glacially moving seconds. Finally, another slave comes to give him water, and the film cuts to the other side of the 180-degree line, including the big house in the frame, making us aware of the dispassionate gaze of the white overseer and the white mistress as part of the surveillance apparatus, which partially explains the seeming dispassion with which the other Black characters behave. The next shot restores Northup to his solitude, the frame empty of anyone else. At last, "good" master Ford arrives to cut him down. But even Ford, deeply troubled by the lynching, understands capitalism to frame any ethical decision he makes, and thus sells Northup and the debt he represents to the sadistic Epps. Northup's transfer to Epps shifts his labor from logging to cotton. Slaves that don't pick as much as the day before are whipped. McQueen established in the lynching scene the simultaneous containment in a single frame of labor and race-based punitive violence; they continue to coexist that way on Epps's cotton plantation.

McQueen scatters shots of several seconds of natural and man-made objects for a couple of reasons. First, they function as a place for the spectator to pause and process the intense violence we are asked to witness. It's not unlike the strategy often employed by Japanese director Yasujiro Ozu, where a quietly intense scene doesn't end with a cut to the next scene but with one to a seemingly irrelevant object into which viewers can pour their feelings, because there's a lot more coming. Second, there is an increasing tension between these objects and the people who populate the film. It is a strategy that helps us understand how, over time, people become objects as slaves.

The second remarkable long take (about the same length as the first) begins to restore the personhood the first long take made clear is absent. After Northup has finally succeeded in secretly sending a letter to his family up north (via a Canadian carpenter played by one of the film's producers, Brad Pitt, in another white savior role), we see him alone in the frame, looking around. Eventually his eyes come to look at the audience, and he holds us in his gaze for a long time. He may be gathering himself for either the possibility of freedom or the possibility of a life under slavery. But even more, that gaze insists on *our* existence. In this moment, the historical drama exerts its currency and contemporaneity. His personhood and ours are explicitly linked, his enslaved past connected to our current moment and its unfinished democratic project. When Parker, his friend from home, comes to rescue him, the law with him and on his side, Northup embraces him, a gesture between a Black and a white man we have not seen for two hours of screen time—twelve years. Epps insists, "That is my nigger." Parker asserts, "He is Mr. Solomon Northup." It can only be so satisfying, after this, to witness the restoration of Northup's personhood when he is reunited with his friend from home. He remains, for the duration of the argument, someone, or something, argued over by white men, and the blocking of the scene makes that clear. Only after Northup crosses his own door and closes it behind him, and is welcomed home by his family, including a grandchild he has never seen and finally gets to hold, may we fully see the restoration of his personhood.

■ Historicizing the AIDS Crisis: *Dallas Buyers Club*

Dallas Buyers Club is part of a generational look back at the AIDS crisis of the 1980s and 1990s. (To limit it to that decade is to shut out the global crisis it remains and dwell only on its history in the United States.) The year before *Dallas Buyers Club* was released, the documentary *How to Survive a Plague* (David France, 2012) debuted at Sundance, trotted around the film festival circuit to widespread acclaim, was nominated for all the right awards, and settled down on Netflix where, for a time, it was available to all, but is probably mostly seen by those who want to revisit an era they lived through. One has to be invested, for one reason or another, in the HIV/AIDS crisis and the movement to go there, especially in the increasingly niche audience building that Netflix's algorithms construct. *Dallas Buyers Club*, a biopic released the following year, had no such problems. A prestige Oscar bait project narrating the story of Texan Ron Woodroof (Matthew McConaughey), whose Dallas Buyers Club was a kind of international drug ring bringing unauthorized AIDS medications into the United States for people who could either not afford or could not tolerate AZT, the standard protocol of that time. Both McConaughey and Jared Leto, who played Woodroof's business partner, the transgender woman Rayon, won Academy Awards for their portrayals, and the movie was also nominated for Best Picture and a slew of other awards.

This biopic significantly diverges from the facts of Ron Woodroof's life, rendering it similar to many other biopics (Harris). What matters is how and why a biopic diverges. It's one thing to change Woodroof from an enthusiastic rodeo watcher to a rodeo rider. It's more dramatic and shorthand for assuming heteromasculine normativity. Rayon, on the other hand, is a complete invention. Named Raymond at birth, Rayon invents herself. She's a device bringing Ron from homophobia, transphobia, and other phobias into an ethical space in which he can die well, having done well. This isn't merely about gender identity, either in 2013 or in the years represented by the film itself; it's a generic insistence the film makes that calls on tropes of classical Hollywood to make each character legible. If Ron plays in a drama, Rayon plays in a melodrama. Linda Williams's 1991 canonical work on body genres remains instructive on this matter. Williams describes a way that three significant genres in the evolution of cinema— melodrama, horror, and pornography—all involve the excesses of "the spectacle of a body caught in the grip of intense sensation or emotion" (4). Read through the "temporality of fantasy" Williams describes vis-à-vis melodrama, Rayon is no different from any other melodramatic heroine in the way that the narrative is always already flowing inexorably to a point of "too late!" (9), such that the registers of action must always be sacrificial. Even the drugs Ron makes accessible to the community will arrive too late for her, as, arguably, will Ron's friendship.

Rayon's own sacrifices call back to the sacrificial modes of classical melodrama. She sells her life insurance policy to enable Ron to move

In *Dallas Buyers Club* (Jean-Marc Vallée, Focus Features), Ron's heroic narrative is enabled by Rayon's melodramatic narrative. Digital frame enlargement.

forward with their plan, but she is deprived by the movie of her death scene so that Ron can have his mad scene when he arrives back from a drug buying trip to Mexico and finds Rayon has *just* died. ("Too late!") If Rayon simply melts away from the narrative twenty minutes before the end, it's to set up Ron's more heroic demise, as figuratively described by him mounting a white rodeo bull, tearing into the ring, and being freeze-framed somewhere in his eight seconds. If by the 2010s it was time to historicize the AIDS crisis in the United States via the moving image, *Dallas Buyers Club* suggests that, if you want anyone new to care and stir themselves to remember, you need to make a deal with the devil of cinematic conventions. Once we're down the road of cinematic body genres, as guided by Williams, we may find that *Dallas Buyers Club* unintentionally pulls on all three of the body genres she cites: melodrama and its emotional excesses, horror and its excesses of violence, and pornography's excess of sex are all operating here, and do so under the sign of a recuperative history of the AIDS crisis which puts the queer community in the back seat and lets the hetero male drive the narrative bus. Like Steven Spielberg's *Schindler's List* (1993), which centered someone who wasn't Jewish in a story that was fundamentally a Jewish one, *Dallas Buyers Club* tacitly returns to a framework in which Williams's bodily excesses are read as pathologies of a disease.

In the 1980s, it didn't take long to articulate that those who lived and those who died during the AIDS crisis ran along necropolitical lines, even if that was not the word used back then. PWAs ("people with AIDS") were not, in spite of this phrase, typically accorded personhood—certainly not by the state. Personhood was something that needed to be asserted *against* the state, not something that was asserted by the state on behalf of its citizens. Calling necropolitics by its name surfaces the contradiction between some of the prime directives of U.S. founding documents and the realities of the codependence, from the start, of democracy and capitalism in this country. This reminds us that specific intersections of capitalism and democracy have always undergirded the entertainment industry in America. By 2013, the site of U.S. sovereign power had long been misperceived in its location. It was not merely situated in state power; state power had, in any case, been commodified, even before the Citizens United decision in 2010. This is to say that personhood is *always* contingent, when there is sovereign power: American films are a central mechanism not only for affirming and sustaining these conditions but also, sometimes, and at its best, in critiquing it.

NOTES

1. Brenda Chapman, writer and director of *Brave* (inspired by her own relationship to her daughter), was removed from the project before it was finished, though she retained co-director credit (with Mark Andrews) (Vary).

2. It is beyond the scope of this essay, but it is nevertheless important to flag that the ethics of watching that footage are complex. Who watches it, and why, may feed back into the necropolitical framework I have been calling on. Whose gaze is appropriate here, if any? Rasul A. Mowatt asks us "to question viewers' intent in the consumption of videos that make a spectacle of the violence perpetrated on Black bodies" (777).

3. Oscar Grant's texts early in *Fruitvale Station*—something we see floating on the screen—are not an unconnected strategy. They make claims to communication being central to personhood. Northup's difficulty writing has everything to do with his enslavement. Grant's ability to text speaks his claims to personhood in a very quotidian sense.

2014

Movies and the Unexpected
Virtue of How the Sausage
Gets Made

DANIEL SMITH-ROWSEY

In February 2014, 2,873 athletes from eighty-eight countries gathered in Sochi, Russia, for the twenty-second Winter Olympics, which set records with a cost of about $51,000,000,000 and about 2,100,000,000 international viewers. If one thinks of 2014 as a typically structured film, the sumptuous spectacle from Sochi would constitute the film's first few minutes, the apparently felicitous status quo. In screenplay lingo, the "inciting incident" of this film took place a few hundred miles west of, and during, Sochi's closing ceremony, as Russian troops invaded Ukraine and annexed Crimea, marking the first armed hostilities in Europe since the Yugoslavian civil war of the 1990s. By the end of 2014, Russia's war in and on Ukraine had claimed the lives of at least 1,500 Russian soldiers, 1,500 Ukrainian soldiers, and hundreds of Ukraine's civilians. The often-cited "global village" of the Sochi Olympics came to seem a chimerical Potemkin village, papering over deadly conflicts and fatal miscalculations in the world and in the United States.

The United States saw thirty-four school shootings during the second year after the Sandy Hook massacre and the fifth year of a recession recovery whose gains went almost exclusively to the upper one percent, sending a consistent message about the value of younger, poorer, and browner lives. In the wake of the fatal police shooting of unarmed teen Michael Brown in Ferguson, Missouri, the videotaped police choking of Eric Garner in Staten Island, New York, and the fatal police shooting of twelve-year-old Tamir Rice in Cleveland, Ohio, protests organized by the newly famous Black Lives Matter became a national cause célèbre. At the same time, the national media seemed equally, or more, interested in the depredations of a few abusive Black men such as Ray Rice and Bill Cosby. Jamelle Bouie warned, as part of *Slate*'s "Year in Outrage" feature, "If outrage stands in for activism, if we're focused on the moral temperature of Internet individuals, then we're distracted from the collective action—and collective institution building—that makes real reform possible" (*Slate* 1). This also partly referred to online "influencers" who focused more on outrageous tweets than on Republicans as the latter recaptured the Senate in November.

2014 also provided good news. At the ripe old age of seventeen, Malala Yousafzai co-won the Nobel Peace Prize for her advocacy for girls' education. Pulitzer Prizes were awarded to newspapers that reported the U.S. government's unlawful surveillance as revealed by Edward Snowden in 2013. After years of delays, the defiant, radiant One World Trade Center finally opened in lower Manhattan in November, at 1,776 feet the tallest building in the Western Hemisphere. United Nations Goodwill Ambassador Serena Williams began the year ranked number one in Women's Tennis and maintained that rank through year's end, a feat no one had accomplished since Steffi Graf in 1996. Despite Brazil's official erasure of Rio de Janeiro's favelas, Rio hosted a World Cup that showcased a vibrant and often joyful Brazil—until the home team suffered a shocking 7–1 loss to its German rival. The number one song of the year was the irresistible "Happy" by Pharrell Williams, from the late-2013 release *Despicable Me 2*.

"Happy" could even describe some aspects of *Slate*'s "Year in Outrage." After Kenan Thompson's public refusal to play more drag on *Saturday Night Live* led to considerable online pressure, *SNL* showrunner Lorne Michaels hired his first Black female cast member since 2007, Sasheer Zamata. (Later in 2014, Leslie Jones joined as a writer and then as a cast member; by October, *Saturday Night Live* could boast, for the first time in its four-decade history, two women of color in its cast.) In April, a photo of a table-read by the new, mostly white, mostly male cast of the rebooted *Star Wars* (to be released in December 2015) led to even greater online pressure; within a week, producer Kathleen Kennedy announced two new female cast members, including one woman of color, Lupita Nyong'o. These episodes suggested a newly empowered convergence of "wokeness" and social media; anonymous online protestors could now successfully get more women of color cast in properties as venerated as *SNL* and *Star Wars*. This was part of what Matthew Yglesias and Molly Fischer, among others, would later call the decade's "Great Awokening," an increased awareness and cultural elevation of nonwhite and female voices and concerns.

On 1 January, the Affordable Care Act's major provisions came into force, and over the year about ten million Americans joined the ranks of the insured. Africa suffered a major Ebola virus outbreak that killed about 6,000 people worldwide, including two Americans, but worldwide cooperation helped attenuate the fatality rate. However, about 47,000 Americans died from overdoses of opioids and heroin, a new record that represented an alarming 9 percent increase from 2013. In better health news, in September, CVS became America's first major pharmacy chain to stop selling tobacco products. After Gwyneth Paltrow praised avocado toast in her 2013 cookbook "It's All Good," by 2014 the food became a recurrent feature on menus, Instagram, and in jokes about the millennial tastes.

Perhaps the two most startling deaths of 2014 were those of beloved actor-comedian Robin Williams, lost to suicide at age sixty-three, and virtuosic actor Philip Seymour Hoffman, who died from a heroin overdose at age forty-six. Among other notables who passed away in this year were conductor Claudio Abbado; blacklisted protest singer of "Waist Deep in the Big Muddy" Pete Seeger; *Gilligan's Island* "Professor" Russell Johnson; former Israeli prime minister Ariel Sharon; child superstar and adult diplomat Shirley Temple Black; poet, playwright, and activist Amiri Baraka; early television comedian Sid Caesar; *Judgment at Nuremburg* Oscar winner Maximilian Schell; *Hiroshima mon amour* auteur Alain Resnais; *Who Framed Roger Rabbit?* actor Bob Hoskins; Nobel Prize–winning Colombian novelist Gabriel García Márquez (*One Hundred Years of Solitude*); Hollywood studio star Mickey Rooney; *I Know Why the Caged Bird Sings* poet Maya Angelou; *The Good, the Bad, and the Ugly* actor Eli Wallach; Broadway star Elaine Stritch; and *Children of Men* novelist P. D. James.

If we see 2014 as a typically structured film, we might say it ended with a twist that pulled many of its plot strands together. Among these plot strands were America's unresolved conflicts with hostile nations, the malicious aspects of Big Data collection, and increasingly alarming hacks of large companies—in 2014, the hack of Home Depot exposed 50 million credit cards, the breach of JPMorgan Chase leaked the data of 75 million bank customers, and the hack of eBay compromised 145 million users. Yet none of these hacks received a fraction of the attention of the year-ending breach of Sony Pictures, in which the so-called Guardians of Peace leaked private information about Sony employees and films while threatening terrorist attacks to theaters that dared to screen Sony's new film *The Interview*, a comedy about two American doofuses stumbling into a plot to assassinate North Korean dictator Kim Jong-un. Among the Sony hack's repercussions were increased corporate cybersecurity, particularly in Hollywood, significant disarray at Sony (which struggled to maintain its position as a big studio), and North Korea's temporary loss of the internet.

In a manner that few would have anticipated, the Sony hack also confirmed the ongoing cultural importance of Hollywood films, down to the theatrical experience, at a time of fierce competition from YouTube videos,

Instagram-driven content, "peak TV," and Netflix's first full year of original streaming. Which films of 2014 achieved the sort of success that the Guardians of Peace threatened terrorism to prevent *The Interview* from attaining? Of the year's top five films at the domestic box office, Kim Jong-un may have named his hacking operation after one, *Guardians of the Galaxy*, and been perversely satisfied that three of the other four were, in different ways, about the hypocrisy of American armchair generals and the intense suffering of the soldiers who actually do the fighting: *American Sniper*, *Captain America: The Winter Soldier*, and *The Hunger Games: Mockingjay—Part 1*. The latter film was the second sequel to a blockbuster whose success inspired a wave of YA novel adaptations that were released in 2014: *Divergent*, *The Maze Runner*, *If I Stay*, and *The Fault in our Stars*. The last of these helped make John Green's source novel the best-selling book of 2014.

To the surprise of absolutely nobody, Hollywood's dedication to sequels and reboots continued apace in 2014. Some of these were, in chronological order by release date: *Jack Ryan: Shadow Recruit*; *RoboCop*; *300: Rise of an Empire*; *Muppets Most Wanted*; *Rio 2*; *The Amazing Spider-Man 2*; *Godzilla*; *X-Men: Days of Future Past*; *How to Train Your Dragon 2*; *22 Jump Street*; *Think like a Man Too*; *Transformers: Age of Extinction*; *The Purge: Anarchy*; *Dawn of the Planet of the Apes*; *Hercules*; *Teenage Mutant Ninja Turtles*; *The Expendables 3*; *Dolphin Tale 2*; *Annabelle*; *Dracula Untold*; *Dumb and Dumber To*; *Horrible Bosses 2*; *Penguins of Madagascar*; and *The Hobbit: The Battle of the Five Armies*. The last of these was, in deference to J.R.R. Tolkien's source material, long called *The Hobbit: There and Back Again* until director-producer Peter Jackson finally deferred to Warner Bros.'s concerns about marketability. If the films in this paragraph have anything in common, it is their fealty to corporate priorities, their rather consistent way of going there and back again.

That said, in 2014, Hollywood occasionally bet on newly adapted content, and sometimes those bets paid off critically and commercially. Besides the YA adaptations, there was also *Big Hero 6*, a nicely integrated story about plucky teen heroes in "San Fransokyo"; *Unbroken*, about an American prisoner of war in World War II; *The Imitation Game*, about Alan Turing, the closeted gay founder of computer science; *Wild*, from Cheryl Strayed's memoir of hiking the Pacific Coast Trail; *Into the Woods*, from Stephen Sondheim's fairy tale–satire musical; and the year's most auspicious debut film, *Whiplash* by writer-director Damien Chazelle, about an ambitious young drummer and his abusive teacher. Many of America's highest-paid auteurs seemed inspired by older masters: David Fincher drew from Hitchcock to make *Gone Girl*; Christopher Nolan updated Kubrick with *Interstellar*; Wes Anderson told his editor to watch Lubitsch while cutting *The Grand Budapest*

Hotel; and Paul Thomas Anderson, asked about the first cinematic adaptation of a Thomas Pynchon novel, *Inherent Vice*, said he filmed it "like a Cheech and Chong movie" (Plumb 1).

But the year's most interesting American films were imbued with a spirit of transparency, long-suppressed revelation, and self-reflexivity. This spirit could be seen throughout American culture; from social media to surveillance videos to shrugs at news about hacking, a certain what-do-you-have-to-hide-ism characterized much of the 2010s. Add to that the fact that three of 2011's most vital motion pictures—*Hugo*, *Super 8*, and *The Artist*—were films about filmmaking. It was in this context that 2014's most fascinating films were put together, with an eye toward subverting or revealing traditional formal and thematic codes. 2014 became the cinematic year that showed how the sausage got made, and brought long-sidelined voices front and center.

The Lego Movie

The fifth top-grossing film of 2014 was *The Lego Movie*, becoming the year's first blockbuster in February. If my use of the typical three-act film structure to describe 2014 is a little facile, *The Lego Movie* serves as a wiser exploration of that structure's vicissitudes. *The Lego Movie* is about painfully average ("I never have any ideas") construction worker Emmet (played by Chris Pratt) and his "hero's journey" to save his world(s) from the stifling conformity of Lord Business and his Micro Managers. The scare quotes around "hero's journey" are appropriate, because the film productively questions and parodies the tropes and motifs of action films as much as it enacts them. The film's Prophecy predicts someone named the Special will use a Piece of Resistance to foil the Kragle, and these narrative devices, among many others, are repeatedly referenced with (somehow) both sincerity and irony.

In this film, directed by Christopher Miller and Phil Lord, one might say that busy-ness is hardly limited to Lord Business; the film suggests variable meanings, partly through a visual palette that is chock-full of irregularly moving parts, colors, and styles. *The Lego Movie*'s consistent deconstruction, in more senses than one, pays off in moments such as the scene in which Emmet's female companion, the skilled warrior Wyldstyle (Elizabeth Banks), becomes upset that Emmet, and not she, appears to be the Special that has been named in the Prophecy. Act 3 reveals, through an unexpected shift to live action, that a rebellious kid has been "building" the story all along as a protest of his father's authoritarian behavior. Many action-adventure films feature a (white male) zero who becomes a hero, but few point out the absurdity and worn-out clichés of this structure in almost every scene.

2014's best satire of the recent Liam-Neeson-as-action-star phenome- non was Mindy Kaling's parodic list of a hot studio slate that included "Untitled Liam Neeson Action Movie." The second-best satire was surely Neeson himself as the Jekyll and Hyde–like Bad Cop/Good Cop in *The Lego Movie*, where Neeson alternates between his usual gruff irascibility and a theretofore unknown, sweet, light voice probably better suited to reading books written for toddlers. In this film, Neeson joined Morgan Freeman and Will Ferrell in slyly mocking their own personas. But *why* did Lord and Miller's film so relentlessly mock (and yet still provide) action movie cli- chés? Perhaps the Lego corporation wanted to distinguish itself from the soulless merchandising associated with toy adaptation movies like *G. I. Joe* and *Battleship*. (Meanwhile, *The Lego Movie*'s producers were likely pleased that their film earned more than 2014's higher-budgeted toy-based film, *Transformers: Age of Extinction*.)

The film's largest legacy is likely the song "Everything Is Awesome," written and performed by Tegan and Sara in collaboration with the Lonely Island. The film's use of the song is worth recalling. In Emmet's opening scene, he finds a list of instructions on how to "always be happy." After reading aloud, and enacting, numbers one through twelve, Emmet comes to number thirteen, "listen to popular music," at which point Emmet turns on his car radio which is playing "Everything Is Awesome." Masses of cars in bumper-to-bumper traffic arrive at work and "park in the lines"; Emmet orders an overpriced coffee, which costs $37, pauses, and then says "Awe- some!" Emmet muses that he could sing the song for hours, upon which a title card says "5 hours later," only to find Emmet and his fellow construc- tion workers still singing the song. Later, Batman sings a "darker" version: "Darkness, no parents." Later still, Emmet sings it to the deathly "skele- trons," who respond, "That is so my jam." Clearly, the song and its contexts oscillate between sincerity and irony. But that fluidity should give us pause when we consider the chorus's refrain: "Everything is awesome / Every- thing is cool when you're part of a team / Everything is awesome / When you're living a dream." Is the film or song really endorsing living a dream, or teamwork? Indeed, a film about an author-boy's rebellion against his father might be endorsing radical individualism . . . or perhaps because Emmet gathers a team of misfits and eventually reconciles with Lord Busi- ness, the film might be endorsing collectivism.

The film's most reverent major review came from Bilge Ebiri in *New York* magazine, who began, "I'm probably overselling it, but at one point during *The LEGO Movie*, I found myself thinking, *This is it. This is the one. This is the film that our entire shared experience of pop culture has been building towards*" (italics in original). In a post-*Simpsons* world, many pieces of content can be considered felicitous, wide-ranging, postmodern pastiches, just as many films can be said to be simultaneously enacting conventions and lampooning them, but there was something distinctive about a film that managed to essay *Star Wars*, Hello Kitty, pirates, cat posters, *Creature from the Black Lagoon*, Dumbledore, Robin Hood, Cleopatra, Lincoln, Michelangelo, and (yes) the 2002 NBA All-Stars without seeming incoherent. More predictably, for a film from Warner Animation Group, the film also uses Warner Brothers–affiliated intellectual property, with extended sampling of Batman and the other main superheroes of DC, Middle-earth, *Clash of the Titans* ("release the Kragle"), a Clint Eastwood–like Old West (Emmet dresses as the Man with No Name), *The Terminator* (Lord Business's skeletrons resemble Terminators), and Teenage Mutant Ninja Turtles. The film succeeds at being both overbusy and anti-Business, as Ebiri concludes by calling it

> A kids' movie that matches shameless fun with razor-sharp wit, that offers up a spectacle of pure, freewheeling joy even as it tackles the thorniest of issues. It's part *South Park*, part *Lord of the Rings*; part *The Matrix*, part *Idiocracy*. It's a superhero team-up movie, a toy-strewn dystopian vision, and a Bergmanesque inquiry into the mind of God. And it's somehow still also fall-off-your-seat funny. (Ebiri 1)

Oddly, 2014's other major "meta" blockbuster also centered around the Chris Pratt persona, which had barely been seen on theatrical screens before 2014, when Pratt was mostly known as schlubby Andy Dwyer on NBC's *Parks and Recreation*. That show was very much in the mold of NBC's *The Office* in that both were filmed as "mockumentaries" of sorts, in which characters regularly make asides to the camera. The most popular Chris Pratt GIF is just such an aside, as a camera awkwardly zooms into Pratt/Dwyer opening his mouth wide with glee, an expression that basically says "everything is awesome." Dwyer signifies a lucky schmo (partly for being a white male) who manages to both personify and call into question American hopes and dreams, and in 2014 Pratt seemed to luck into such significance on a blockbuster scale—twice. In 2014, the two most profitable studios of the twenty-first century, Disney and Warner Bros., deconstructed many of their own successful films' codes in order to refresh or reorient themselves—a bit like burning the village in order to save it.

Guardians of the Galaxy

The title characters of Disney/Marvel's *Guardians of the Galaxy* are a ragtag group of outlaw misfits led by Peter Quill, aka Star-Lord (Pratt), a group who, in fits and starts, assemble against a malevolent villain who threatens to destroy a planet. Quill meets most of his future teammates on a squeaky-clean planet that resembles Coruscant (the capital city of the *Star Wars* prequels), where the Guardians distinguish themselves as rougher, crazier, and more chaotic than the surrounding "normal" galactic citizens. Gamora (Zoe Saldana), the green, adopted daughter of genocidal villain Thanos (Josh Brolin), wants Quill's recently acquired (stolen) orb in order to revenge herself on Thanos; Rocket (Bradley Cooper, one of the decade's biggest stars, playing a CG figure like a Noo Yawk wiseguy), who resembles a bipedal raccoon, and his tree-like, Chewbacca-ish sidekick Groot (Vin Diesel, another one of the decade's biggest stars, here unrecognizable because of CG and voice work) want to capture Quill to cash him in for a 40,000-unit bounty. Imprisoned, they meet muscly, deadpan warrior Drax (Dave Bautista), and they come to share goals, starting with breaking out of prison, and eventually including putting aside their considerable differences to save a world and themselves.

Like almost any 2010s big-budget film, *GOTG* borrows liberally from films directed by men like Lucas, Spielberg, Kurosawa, and Peckinpah, but

The title characters of *Guardians of the Galaxy* (James Gunn, Marvel-Disney)—Gamora (Zoe Saldana), Star-Lord (Chris Pratt), Rocket (Bradley Cooper), Drax (Dave Bautista), and Groot (Vin Diesel)—submit to a scan as they await their fate. Digital frame enlargement.

its "meta" nature goes beyond influences. With life and death on the line, Rocket and Quill repeatedly demonstrate a certain sangfroid about their adventure, as when Rocket asks for parts he does not need (to make himself laugh) or, in the climax, when Quill challenges the lethal antagonist to a dance-off. Martin Flanagan, Mike McKenny, and Andy Livingstone see the film as a "meta-statement" about Marvel Studios planning; for them, Rocket's prison break plan "comically represents how difficult it is to control so many moving parts. . . . The audience is encouraged to marvel at Rocket's plan coming together, against the odds, just as the financial and critical success of this film points to Marvel's industrial plan coming together" (Flanagan, 155). Director James Gunn was hailed as having stuck the hardest of landings, maintaining Marvel's continuity and business plan while also making a film with (a) distinctive, laudable style.

Guardians of the Galaxy is hardly as subversive of filmic narrative codes as, say, the oeuvre of screenwriter Charlie Kaufman, but it was received by critics as subverting calcified science fiction and superhero film clichés. Compared to recent "space operas" like *Green Lantern* (2011) and the first two *Star Trek* reboots (2009, 2012), *GOTG* was often called "playful" or "irreverent," partly because of its nimbler camerawork. Critics may have been influenced by Disney/Marvel's promotion of the film, which included an interview with Nicola Perlman, *GOTG*'s first screenwriter, who explained that she chose to develop *GOTG* over many other available Marvel properties because its 2000s-era comic book was "a very funny, sarcastic, and tongue-in-cheek version of this kind of genre" (Flanagan 150).

Warner Bros. founded an entire division (Warner Animation Group) to make *The Lego Movie*, but Disney and Marvel may have had even more at stake with *GOTG*. While many of the Avengers—Iron Man, Captain America, Thor, the Hulk—could claim cultural notoriety prior to Disney's 2009 agreement with Marvel Studios, the Guardians of the Galaxy were virtual unknowns—which made them paradoxically attractive to Disney, because Disney did not need to share Guardians of the Galaxy intellectual property licensing arrangements (for merchandise and tie-ins) with any other company. This is one reason that after the film's success, Disneyland created a new ride called Guardians of the Galaxy—Mission: Breakout! *Guardians of the Galaxy* proved that the Marvel brand could be handsomely and profitably extended to obscure intellectual property. Compared to many bigbudget films where the stakes are all-or-nothing, *GOTG* was characterized by a certain confidence and audacity, for example in its "planting" of bigger developments for future films, including Quill's father and the other five Infinity Stones.

This confidence and audacity extended to the (promoted) notion of moving players "off the bench," that is, putting "B-list" characters on the "A-list." And *Guardians of the Galaxy* was not Disney's only B-list-to-A-list film to be released in summer 2014. For decades, Disney had developed scripts that dug deeper into various supporting characters of their forty-odd animated features, but none of these managed to make it into production until *Maleficent* was green-lit in 2012. It is not a coincidence that, in 2012, *Snow White and the Huntsman* (2012) and Spain's *Blancanieves* (2012) reminded audiences that non-Disney studios might adapt public domain property that Disney likely considered its own. Such films helped spur new Disney adaptations, with the hope of making any other studio's versions of Grimms' Fairy Tales (or the like) seem derivative. In 2014, Disney reclaimed a certain amount of intellectual property by, for the first time, building a film and title role around one of its previous films' villains.

Maleficent

In *Maleficent*, the eponymous lead is a prepubescent, power-ful fairy who lives in the Moors, a land of free spirits and mystic powers, adjacent to a monarchy of humans who sometimes declare war on the Moors. Maleficent begins a friendship with a lost human boy named Stefan that develops into a forbidden romance sealed with what Stefan calls "true love's kiss." Eventually, Stefan betrays Maleficent, drugs her, cuts off her wings, becomes king, and organizes a royal baptism party for his baby daughter Aurora. Maleficent's backstory established, the film picks up roughly where *Sleeping Beauty* (1959) began, with Maleficent crashing the party to curse Aurora with a lifelong coma that will begin on or before her sixteenth birthday—a curse that can only be lifted by, Maleficent slyly says, "true love's kiss." For a while, the story resembles that of the fifty-five-year-old Disney film, with three pixies raising Aurora, but this version sees Aurora and Maleficent eventually forming an unlikely bond. Maleficent tries to but cannot prevent her curse from befalling Aurora. Prince Phillip tries and fails to revive Aurora; Maleficent's own kiss proves effective. Stefan tries to kill Maleficent anyway, but she and her magic friends manage to kill Stefan and defeat his army; the film ends with Aurora being crowned queen of the united kingdoms as Maleficent looks on beatifically.

If Disney ever worried about alienating its younger viewers with non-animated Gothic imagery like bloody disfigurement, oozing punctures, and dark, toothy beasts, the famously risk-averse studio may have taken note of the appeal of not only *Snow White and the Huntsman* but also the increasingly grisly *Harry Potter* films that culminated with the macabre *Harry Potter and the Deathly Hallows—Part 2* (2011), which earned more than $1.3 billion worldwide. As it happens, *Maleficent* represents something of a re-engagement with some of the more disturbing historical fairy-tale themes that were occluded in Disney's *Sleeping Beauty*. According to Marina Warner, while "The Sleeping Beauty" was first put into print as *Perceforest* in 1528, the best-known versions were written and adapted by Giambattista Basile and published in the 1630s, and then adapted by Charles Perrault and published in the 1690s. Perrault's version, called *La Belle au bois dormant*, receives screen credit in *Maleficent*. Warner reminds us that the pre-Victorian "Sleeping Beauty" is about a man raping the unconscious young beauty; in Basile's version, the antagonist is the rapist's wife, aka the queen, and in Perrault's version, the antagonist is the rapist prince's mother. Readers who are familiar only with the *Sleeping Beauty* of the 1950s may raise their eyebrows at the notion that the story that provides the Disney logo's iconic castle (and Disneyland's central hub) centralizes rape. The producers and writers of *Maleficent*, however, seemed to understand this quite well; Stefan drugs Maleficent and cuts off her wings, and many critics explained this as a rape analogy. Star Angelina Jolie agreed: "We were very conscious, the writer and I, that [the scene] was a metaphor for rape" (Rich 1). In the seventeenth-century versions of "Sleeping Beauty," the antagonist's fury was somewhat justified by her outrage at her husband's or son's philandering rape of a comatose girl; *Maleficent* collapses that distance by making her a direct victim of violent violation (although mutilation is not rape; this *is* still a Disney film).

Directed by Robert Stromberg from a script written by Linda Woolverton during a decade of improved representation, can *Maleficent* be called more feminist than any version of "Sleeping Beauty"? It may depend on what is meant by "feminist." In any version, the sleeping beauty, a heroine, is distinguished mostly by her beauty, not her cunning or intelligence. In Basile's and Perrault's stories, the antagonist woman orders a succession of the sleeping beauty's children to be eaten (though the royal cook saves them by replacing them with animal meat). Basile's queen then orders Talia (the no-longer-sleeping beauty) to be killed on a pyre; Perrault's queen mother, more of a witch, orders Briar Rose (also a no-longer-sleeping beauty) to be cooked and served for dinner. Talia and Briar Rose are saved at the last minute by their dashing male, uh, rapists, who vanquish the malicious women; afterward, they marry. In the early nineteenth century, the Brothers Grimm sanitized Perrault's story, partly by making the witch a spurned fairy, partly by ending it with the prince saving the unconscious Briar Rose with a kiss. Victorian editors eschewed the rape theme altogether, transforming the antagonist into a wicked fairy godmother who is not invited to the royal christening. In Disney's 1959 version, this *un*vitation is sufficient cause for Maleficent to fatally curse baby Aurora, even as three good (female) fairies intervene and help the king and queen by raising Aurora as Briar Rose in relative anonymity. Toward the end, however, Aurora falls into her coma, and it is left to the valiant (not violent) Prince Phillip, with fairy aid, to kill Maleficent.

Maleficent coyly refers to all these versions by opening with a female narrator saying "you will see how well you remember" the story. Mostly, the film presumes its audience's familiarity with the feature cartoon version in the same way that the 2003 musical *Wicked* presumed its audience's familiarity with the 1939 film *The Wizard of Oz* (and not the source novels by L. Frank Baum and Gregory Maguire); indeed, many aspects of *Wicked* may have served as uncredited inspiration. *Maleficent* changes most of the 1959 story's second half; Maleficent and Aurora's bond is what must be, and is, defended by sword and kiss. Certainly, the 2014 film is consonant with many modern definitions of feminism, including portraying women as rulers and what might be called rape revenge. Yet Basile's and Perrault's antagonists were more fully inhabited, Lady Macbeth figures, and some critics leapt to the defense of the 1959 film by explaining that Aurora was a more traditional heroine there. *Maleficent* is at least feminist in the sense of giving a fairy tale's "evil witch" a series of motivations and emotions. One can guess that women who have been labeled witches, or worse, accounted for a healthy percentage of the film's $758.5 million worldwide gross.

Maleficent was not the only film of 2014 to bring into focus an iconic persona that had been well known, but sidelined, since the 1960s. Two of America's most prominent civil rights leaders finally received first billing in theatrically released films: *Cesar Chavez*, about Cesar Chavez and the UFW in the 1960s, and *Selma*, about Martin Luther King Jr. organizing the Selma protests in 1964 and 1965. It should seem strange that Hollywood waited until 2014 to dedicate major films to two of America's most-beatified persons of color. In my introduction, I mentioned "The Great Awokening": an increased awareness and cultural elevation of nonwhite and female voices and concerns. The mid-decade productions and releases of *Cesar Chavez* and *Selma* revealed how far the "Awokening" had come—and how far it still had to go.

Cesar Chavez

One thing Hollywood could and did do during the "Awokening" was hire more directors of color to tell more diverse stories. Had *Cesar*

Chavez and *Selma* been made in the 1970s, or even the 1990s, they likely would have been directed by white men; *Cesar Chavez* was made by Mexican actor-turned-director Diego Luna, and *Selma* by African American Ava DuVernay. Another key Hollywood function has been to canonize certain Americans; on the day of the release of *Cesar Chavez*, 28 March 2014, President Barack Obama proclaimed 31 March to be Cesar Chavez Day. President Obama could not formally make 31 March (Chavez's birthday) a national holiday because of a law that prevents the creation of new holidays without Congressional approval. Nonetheless, Obama gave new credence to what was already a state holiday in Arizona, California, Michigan, New Mexico, Utah, Washington, and Wisconsin, and an optional holiday in other states. In fact, Latino activists had been pushing for the recognition for decades; Carlos Santana helped lead a 2006 rally in Los Angeles in support of a Cesar Chavez holiday. To some degree, the movement to commemorate Chavez's birthday required a certain softening of the narrative of Chavez's life, and to some degree, the film *Cesar Chavez* both reflects and extends this hagiographic perspective. The smoothing of Chavez's edges and the long wait for his biopic can be traced to the same source: the Chavez family, who refused Hollywood offers for many years until given more editorial control.

Cesar Chavez shows Chavez's efforts to organize braceros and other farm workers in California who suffered from racism and brutality from local employers and white townspeople. The film traces Chavez and Dolores Huerta's founding of the United Farm Workers through events like the Delano grape strike and the Salad Bowl strike. The film is sometimes critical of Chavez's sexism; in one scene, Chavez tells his wife Helen that striking is too dangerous for a woman. Helen does it anyway, because company rules restricted men, not women, in regards to *huelga*. (Scenes like these may have been inspired by the 1954 film *Salt of the Earth*.) The main actors— Michael Peña as Chavez, America Ferrera as Helen, and Rosario Dawson as Dolores Huerta—do credible, believable work, but there is not much conflict between them or with the company men, giving the film a rote feeling. Enrique Chediak's cinematography certainly evokes central California in the 1960s, but the yellow-brown haze seems more leaden than propulsive. Of the many future high school students who will be assigned this film, one wonders how many will check its Rotten Tomatoes score (38 percent as of this writing).

Historian Matt Garcia, writing for *Smithsonian* magazine, felt that the film's key problem was its reduction of the UFW to an organization dominated by Mexican Americans; Garcia cites the erasure of Jewish American activist Elaine Elinson, who convinced the British and Scandinavians to keep California grapes out of Europe (in the film, Chavez does this), and the diminishment of Filipino American activists like Larry Itliong, Pete Velasco, and Philip Vera Cruz (Garcia 1). The Filipino American National Historical Society not only agreed with Garcia's criticisms but also publicly inveighed against the film's use of Chinese actors to play Filipino workers. (The low-budget film was made mostly in Hermosillo, Mexico, partly because much of it still resembles the undeveloped Central Valley of California of the 1960s; workers at Hermosillo's Chinese restaurants were hired to play Filipino labor strikers.) There was also evidence of the problem that Dennis Bingham identifies in "great man" biopics whereby the man's long-suffering partner is reduced to a "patient helpmeet-wife": Helen Chavez is not given a great deal of screen time (Bingham 5). *Cesar Chavez* was a badly needed statement of identity from a marginalized community that, probably unnecessarily, marginalized other communities and persons.

Curtis Marez, in an interview with me, states that contemporary audiences could not connect with the film probably because the context of the United Farm Workers is so remote and unlike today, when grower-capitalists are lionized, strikes are routinely broken with migrant labor scabs, and farmland is converted into prisons. Marez notes the diminished power of the twenty-first-century farm worker movement as he contrasts the reception of *Cesar Chavez* with that of Edward James Olmos's *Walkout* (2006), which prompted Chicano East Los Angeles students to walk out in support of immigrants' rights. Marez feels that the fact that *Cesar Chavez* did not prompt such activity is indicative of decades of corporate victories, union failures, and a steady shift to more generalized support for immigrants. Marez also points out that the film uses what looks like archival documentary footage but which is "more often recreations of documentaries made by the UFW itself." The film thus misses opportunities to explore Chavez's subjectivity, and instead "renders Chavez the object of the gaze rather than a subject thinking critically and creatively about the visual field" (Marez 1).

Selma

Critics were not enamored with *Cesar Chavez* the way they were with *Selma*, the year's other major film about an American civil rights legend, whose release was timed to correspond to a major anniversary. *Selma* begins by taking pains to establish the correct context of the Selma marches, to the point of jumbling some of the chronology; Martin Luther King Jr.'s acceptance of the Nobel Peace Prize in December 1964 appears to happen before the attack against a Birmingham church in September 1963 that claimed the lives of four African American girls. But the choice situates the horror as the "inciting incident," setting up the urgency of King's helping to organize marches in Selma, Alabama. King is often framed as an irritant to his wife, the U.S. government, and Alabama's other civil rights activists, all of whom counter King's ideas in a lively way that makes the eventual outcomes anything but inevitable. In the *New York Times*, A. O. Scott opined that the film contained "the seeds of at least a dozen other movies," raving: "I have rarely seen a historical film that felt so populous and full of life, so alert to the tendrils of narrative that spread beyond the frame" (Scott 1).

Director Ava DuVernay has aired two frustrations: that Paramount limited her budget, and that she was not permitted to use King's more famous speeches because King's family had previously licensed them to Steven Spielberg for film use. However, to paraphrase a lyric that Beyoncé was developing at the time of the film's release, if DuVernay was served lemons, she made lemonade. The film is small in scale only when appropriate, and it is hard to imagine the "bigger" scenes feeling any bigger than they do, particularly the three marches over the Edmund Pettus Bridge. When the first march is met by armed resistance, the artful combination of tear gas, screams, slow motion, blues music, and the crunches of truncheons adds up to an acutely harrowing experience that could hardly be improved with an extra $10 million. Likewise, because King's on-screen rhetoric does not soar over his fellow organizers, the story's denouement, the 1965 Voting Rights Act, appears to belong less to King and more to the movement, as well it should.

Selma ran into controversy on 26 December, when the *Washington Post* published a scathing editorial from Joseph Califano defending his former boss, President Lyndon B. Johnson, against the film's characterization of Johnson as less interested in passing the Voting Rights Act than in deploying the FBI against King. Califano even wrote, "Selma was LBJ's idea" (Califano 1). Califano's piece sparked a conflagration of heated debate among historians and the cinema's critical community, including online influencers who objected to one white man defending another white man's virtues in a movie by and about Black heroes who triumphed over white intransigence. In its vociferous defense of white male virtues during a symbolic fight over Black enfranchisement, some saw the press as repeating its mistakes from a half century earlier. In *Grantland*, Wesley Morris concluded that a "cultural rebalancing [has] upset people" (gesturing to what Fischer and Yglesias would later call the "Awokening") because "Johnson's not only the president of the United States here. He's also the help" (Morris 1).

Rev. Dr. Martin Luther King Jr. (David Oyelowo), leading a protest, warily considers the police officers at the end of the Edmund Pettus Bridge in *Selma* (Ava DuVernay, Paramount). Digital frame enlargement.

Charles Fager provided one of the more interesting reactions to the controversy in an updated version of his book *Selma 1965: The March That Changed the South*. Fager, a white participant in the 1965 marches in Selma, faulted some parts of the film, such as relegating King's partner Ralph Abernathy to a footnote and presenting the bridge attack as following Governor George Wallace's orders (it occurred in defiance of his orders). But when it came to *Selma* showing Lyndon Johnson spurning King's entreaties for a Voting Rights Act, Fager acknowledged: "It didn't actually happen that way. Yet, it could have; and maybe it should have" (Fager, xv). Strict fealty to history is, from this perspective, sometimes less important than history embellished with dramatic license.

Some felt that the LBJ-MLK controversy amounted to a smear campaign against *Selma* in the height of awards voting season. When Academy Award nominations were announced on 15 January, *Selma* wound up scoring only two, for Best Song and Best Picture. The exclusion of writer-director Ava DuVernay and David Oyelowo's fantastic performance as King were key reasons that online activist April Reign coined the hashtag #OscarsSoWhite during that season, although the hashtag's impact would turn out to be far greater a year later. *Selma* enjoyed a measure of satisfaction on Oscar night when its Best Song nominee, "Glory," won, following an electrifying performance by singer-songwriters Common and John Legend that drew many connections between the depicted events of *Selma* and the summer 2014 protests in Ferguson, Missouri, and Black Lives Matter. As it happened, *Selma* wasn't that year's only Best Picture nominee to spark a political-ideological controversy that may have scuttled its opportunities for major awards.

American Sniper

Parts of Hollywood certainly supported *Selma* and Black Lives Matter, but in January and February 2015, larger audiences supported a biopic that couldn't really be called "woke" (its lead character was more somnambulist), directed by a man whose appearance at the 2012 Republican Convention consisted of arguing with a chair he called President Obama. Clint Eastwood's *American Sniper* was less about a long-neglected person and more about a *kind* of person conspicuously absent from representations of the War on Terror: the soldier hero, a type that conservatives hailed as long overdue to multiplexes. To be clear, the film's lead, Chris Kyle, is a real person (compared to, say, the leads of *The Hurt Locker*); the cover of his memoir calls him "the most lethal sniper in U.S. military history." Thomas Doherty writes that, prior to *American Sniper*, the most famous Iraq War soldiers were iniquitous figures like Jessica Lynch and Lynndie England (Doherty 1). After Clint Eastwood's film became the highest-grossing film released in 2014, one might say that it had provided something like the twenty-first century's equivalent of Sergeant York or Audie Murphy.

The plot of *American Sniper* follows Chris Kyle's memoir, from his humble Texas beginnings, to his young adulthood as a rodeo rider, to his galvanization by the 1998 bombings of U.S. embassies in Africa, to his SEAL training, to 9/11, to his four tours in Iraq, dramatizing several of Kyle's 160 kills that the Pentagon has confirmed (Kyle's co-authors believe the number to be 255). Eastwood foregrounds an episode that the Pentagon had redacted from the autobiography, in which Kyle kills a boy, and then his mother, to prevent an RPG explosion; the visualization led to predictable condemnation from liberal critics and Iraqis. Eastwood most likely highlights this moment because of his more significant addition to Kyle's memoir: a profound sense of emotional repression and twisted valor. In Kyle's book, Kyle is far more of a gung ho soldier, at times saying that shooting people "was a *lot* of fun" and that he "certainly was enjoying it" (Doherty 2). Portrayed brilliantly by Bradley Cooper, the Kyle of the film behaves a lot more like the stoic William Munny, the character Eastwood played in *Unforgiven*, a film that Eastwood let stand for decades as his final Western. In some ways, Cooper's Kyle is comparable to Michael Peña's Cesar Chavez and David Oyelowo's MLK, in that all three project a somewhat blinkered confidence (or naivete) under pressure; but by editing Cooper's performance with emblems of recent American history, Eastwood suggests a person symbolizing a country that won't be apologizing for its twenty-first-century behavior—even if such obtuseness may ultimately hurt the country or its personal referent.

By mid-February, Manohla Dargis in the *New York Times* could reasonably call *American Sniper* "everyone's favorite op-ed topic" and note that the film had been called fascist by figures as different as Nick Broomfield and Chris Hedges, and *praised* by figures as different as Sarah Palin and Michelle Obama. Dargis defended the film by calling it less exciting than *The Hurt Locker*, writing, "Mr. Eastwood is a Hollywood classicist with art-film tendencies—but the violence in *Sniper* brings you down rather than pumps you up. It's tense, not thrilling" (Scott and Dargis 1). Other critics were less kind, questioning an Iraq War film that failed to question the premises of the Iraq War itself and taking exception to the film's sanitization and sanctification of Chris Kyle, in particular because of a final credit sequence that uses solemn, flag-waving, salute-worthy documentary footage of Kyle's funeral. The film happened to be released during the trial of Kyle's killer (who was found guilty), and some conservative groups tied one to the other as a way of demonstrating support for Kyle and war veterans more generally. One could situate the controversies surrounding *Selma* and *American Sniper* as part of a #Film Twitter-led discourse that, during the 2010s, would succeed in problematizing how and if *any* biopics should be made about less than admirable people.

Taciturnly enough, Eastwood himself waited to weigh in until after *American Sniper* had earned most of its eventual $350 million domestically (and long after the Oscars), in a speech to Loyola Marymount's film school. Eastwood told students that he didn't like the wars in Iraq and Afghanistan but that he believed the film to be "nice for veterans, because it shows what they go through. . . . And I think that all adds up to a kind of anti-war" message. Confronted about some scenes, Eastwood allowed that it "glorifies" sniping, but because of its scenes of Kyle's regrets, "I think it's anti" (Beaumont-Thomas 1). Eastwood also expressed happiness that any non-superhero film managed to countervail the current wisdom on what constituted a blockbuster. In fact, Steven Spielberg's 1998 film *Saving Private Ryan* was the most recent R-rated drama to be its year's highest grosser; as *American Sniper* matched that accomplishment, it surpassed *Saving Private Ryan* even in adjusted dollars to become history's highest-grossing war film. At the ripe young age of eighty-four, Eastwood set a personal box office best. He became the first octogenarian to direct a year's number one film and proved, for the first time, that a film that he directed but in which he did not appear, could be prodigiously profitable. All this suggested the need for extensive revisions of all the major biographical studies of Eastwood and his work.

In history's short-term judgment, the Academy Awards for the films of 2014 mostly eschewed the cause célèbre biopics of conservatives *and* liberals, instead coming down to a Best Picture race between two small-scale fictions with all-white casts: *Boyhood* and *Birdman or (The Unexpected Virtue of Ignorance)*. Both films were statements about forgotten (white) Americans in the twenty-first century (one subtext was that by 2014, America had forgotten Michael Keaton). Both films were made by accomplished writer-directors whose lively work had theretofore thrived around the independent side of the film industry. Both films were innovative and unique explorations of, and thematic meditations on, the passage of time. Cinema has long distinguished itself from other art forms by its singular ability to manipulate our experience of time, even while granting its subjects a certain timelessness on celluloid; *Boyhood* and *Birdman* are rich reactions to these qualities. Along with *American Sniper*, they serve as reasonable snapshots of America in 2014: populist, restless, and concerned about the longer-term effects of smartphones and social media. Compared with *American Sniper*, *Boyhood* and *Birdman* are more uneasy about the young adult offspring of broken families and (yet) more guardedly hopeful about the future.

Boyhood

American Sniper spends a few minutes on Chris Kyle's ordinary Texas childhood, but *Boyhood*'s entire two-hours and forty-five minutes are about the ordinary Texas childhood of Mason (Ellar Coltrane), whom we see grow from age six to age eighteen, from first grade to high school graduation. No review of *Boyhood* failed to mention its unusual production process, whereby writer-director Richard Linklater convened production for a few days every year from 2002 through 2013. Critics and scholars searched for precedents, and could only come up with motion picture *series*: the fifteen Andy Hardy films made between 1937 and 1947 (all starring Mickey Rooney); the five Antoine Doinel films made by François Truffaut; Michael Apted's ongoing documentary series *Up* (every seven years, Apted checked in with the same Britons); and the eight *Harry Potter* films released from 2001 to 2011 (*Boyhood* hails the world of Harry Potter more than once). Outside of *Boyhood*, it does not seem that any other production filmed the same four characters for twelve consecutive years as part of a *single* motion picture. One reason for the lack of antecedent is that such a project is technically illegal in Hollywood; thanks to the De Havilland Law, California contracts cannot exceed seven years. The cast and crew of *Boyhood* were asked to renew their long-term contracts midway through the twelve-year production; had they refused, Linklater might have thrown away the first years of film footage. Instead, they agreed.

At the time of the project's initial development, in 2001 and 2002, Linklater may have been less influenced by Warner Bros.'s plans for Harry Potter than by his own explorations of time on-screen in films like *Waking Life* (2001) and *Tape* (2001). Linklater had a loose structure in mind for *Boyhood* in 2002, especially in regards to Olivia (Patricia Arquette), Mason's mother, who would parent Mason and his older sister while trying on different romantic relationships before moving on to education and finally her own modestly successful, fulfilling career. The twelve years were meant to comment on America's educational system. Mason would be based roughly on Linklater's own childhood experiences as a sometimes estranged, sometimes "cool" kid in Texas. Yet *Boyhood* was never to be *set* during the time of Linklater's childhood; Linklater wanted to signpost Mason's childhood with large cultural phenomena (this turned out to include Britney Spears, the Iraq War, Barack Obama, etc.) as part of the film's recognition of recent time passing.

From this outline came a truly unique experiment. At one point in 2010, in mid-production, Linklater said of *Boyhood*, "I think time is sort of a lead character, if you wanted to get technical about it—the lead character of the movie" (quoted in Shary, 10). Timothy Shary claims, "What Linklater makes appear so seamless and natural on screen is, in reality, a methodically designed and cogently analytical statement on the momentary grace of childhood and the evanescent nature of time itself" (Shary 5). And what is that statement? Perhaps the film's final scene offers a clue: Mason embarks upon his first social event at his new college, and his female companion says, "You know how everyone's always saying, 'seize the moment'? I don't know, I'm kinda thinkin' it's the other way around. You know, like, the moment seizes us." Mason replies, "It's constant. The moment, it's just . . . it's like it's always right now, you know?" One possible statement is that even though time cannot be transcended, not even by cinema, that fact does not diminish time's beauty or power.

Most critics received *Boyhood* rapturously, earning the film a 97 percent rating on Rotten Tomatoes. *Boyhood* was lauded for provoking unfamiliar emotional responses, many related to experiencing narrative cinema with the documentary aspect of aging so clearly marking time passing. Yet the film did have its detractors, who found it so natural and quotidian as to be boring. In response, consider the concluding chapter of Shary's "Boyhood," where he articulates the messages of the film: friendship is fleeting while family is forever; persistence toward achieving goals will reap rewards; compromising personal goals for romantic security is problematic at best; abuse is not worth tolerating; graceful endurance of difficulty is an appreciable virtue; a cool disposition is a deceptive defense against disappointment; politics and religion are weak forces of social unity; and the enjoyment of life depends upon the recognition of its temporality. If in 2014 some critics found these truths to be so self-evident that *Boyhood* registered as almost banal, one would like to follow up with them to learn if they felt the same way during the Trump administration.

■ Birdman or (The Unexpected Virtue of Ignorance)

If *Boyhood* represents a sui generis structure for a narrative film, its lead rival for 2014's Best Picture Oscar, usually called simply *Birdman*, belonged to a more recognizable, if rare, type: the "one-shot" or "single-take" film. This type, pioneered by Alfred Hitchcock's *Rope* (1948), was revived in this century because new digital video technology permitted conventional realism in ninety-minute takes, as seen in breakthrough films like *Timecode* (2000), *Russian Ark* (2002), *The Magicians* (2005), and *PVC-1* (2007). The domain of single-take films is a subset of the domain of "real-time" films (which take as much time as their depicted events), of which Richard Linklater had already made at least three well before 2014: *Slacker* (1991), *Tape* (2001), and *Before Sunset* (2004). This is a long way of saying that Linklater and the director of *Birdman*, Alejandro González Iñárritu, shared some of the same interests in exploring structural temporality in narrative cinema. Real-time films, single-take films, and *Boyhood* (more than, say, *Guardians of the Galaxy* or *Cesar Chavez*) all formally call our attention to the relentless passing of time, or to the feeling of being trapped in, and perhaps sometimes transcending, time. Such films can be understood as reactions to Kierkegaard's observation from 1843: "Life can only be understood backwards, but it must be lived forwards." This sentence probably relates well to the enigmatic subtitle "the unexpected virtue of ignorance"; ignorance is not directly referenced in *Birdman*, but perhaps the "single-take" conceit underlines the grace of a life "lived forwards."

By the time of preproduction on *Birdman*, Mexican director Alejandro G. Iñárritu well knew that "single-take" films often earned their scare quotes in the sense of actually being edited. Perhaps this is one reason Iñár-ritu problematizes the conceit after the title cards. The first non–title shot apparently shows some sort of comet or meteor streaking across a nearly black sky filled with wispy white clouds. The second shot is tighter than the first shot, as though to aver that Iñárritu will use "unnecessary" editing if it suits him. Only then does the film cut to its third shot, beginning with Rig-gan Thomson floating in his dressing room, which is the ostensible "single shot" that makes up (most of) the film until the final few minutes. But even this is problematized; the events in the "single take" clearly take place over at least three days. At about the 21:40 mark, Laura (Andrea Riseborough) says, "First preview tomorrow, here we go" and disappears behind a corner; when Riggan follows her, she's gone, only to appear thirty seconds later in transformed makeup and costume onstage as part of the show's first pre-view, complete with audience. Similar tricks happen later, each time pro-viding a kind of relief of temporal movement. The style reinforces Riggan's perspective, a man trapped by time who nevertheless sometimes transcends it almost accidentally or by the logic of dreams or imagination.

The "single-take" style is one of *Birdman*'s many self-reflexive ele-ments, as the film is about staging a realistic play. Specifically, *Birdman* is about the comeback of fictional movie star Riggan Thomson, via a Ray-mond Carver–based, Broadway-staged play called "What We Talk About When We Talk About Love." The play's title is another one of the film's spiral of metameanings, none more significant than the casting of Michael Keaton as Riggan. The fictional Thomson had starred in the eponymous role in the first three *Birdman* movies but refused to do *Birdman 4*; the real Keaton starred in the eponymous role in the first two *Batman* movies (1989, 1992) but refused *Batman Forever* (1995). Keaton/Thomson is dis-missed as a dilettante, a man desperate to prove his thespian bona fides even while many people, such as the crowds who see him in Times Square, would rather see him as Birdman. (As Riggan walks naked through Times Square, someone asks him, "Are you guys making a movie?," to which Riggan pauses, then answers, "Yeah, uh . . . this is for a movie.") Like *The Lego Movie, Birdman* very actively questions Hollywood's surrender to comic book movies in ways large and small (Robert Downey Jr. discusses *Iron Man* on a show seen on Riggan's laptop as the camera pans away from it), but just as actively asks what would be better or more authentic. The film invites us to read performance reflexively—is Keaton/Thomson better at acting when he's more like "himself" (whoever that may be)? The film delights in asking such "meta" questions without ever providing comic book–ready answers.

Or does it? In the end, Riggan has to almost kill himself to please his critics, but unlike in, say, *Black Swan* (2010), the film does not end with the lead character's mortality status ambiguous (unless the felicitously edited final few minutes of *Birdman* are meant as Riggan's final dream). Riggan has fired a loaded gun at his own head onstage, but the discharge and fade to black turn out not to represent a final shot in either sense. Instead, Riggan has shot off his own nose, perhaps completing his transition to the Birdman, or perhaps severing a connection to his blockbuster alter ego. In the film's final moments, Riggan appears to jump out of his hospital room's high window; his daughter Sam runs in, and the camera remains on her face as she looks out the window, a smile breaking as she sees . . . what must be her father flying? After almost two hours of questioning time and realism, *Birdman* concludes with a casting-related deus ex machina: Emma Stone was "Birdman's daughter" in the sense of having just starred in two *Spider-Man* films, and this final shot resembles shots from those films of her character watching Spider-Man. In the end, it seems that Riggan transcends time and space, moving up, down, forwards, and backwards—a testament to the unique power of cinema.

While Riggan's redemption is problematized, there is no gainsaying the virtuosic expertise of director of photography Emmanuel ("Chivo") Lubezki, who won the second of three consecutive Oscars for *Birdman* (the other two were for *Gravity* [2013] and *The Revenant* [2015]). *Birdman* also beat

Sam (Emma Stone) apparently observes her father flying in the final shot of *Birdman or (The Unexpected Virtue of Ignorance)* (Alejandro G. Iñárritu, Fox Searchlight). Digital frame enlargement.

Boyhood, Selma, and *American Sniper,* among others, to win the Academy Award for Best Picture. This was the third Best Picture Oscar in four years awarded to a film that was about Hollywood and how it changes people, the others being *The Artist* (2011) and *Argo* (2012). The three films almost make sense as a trilogy, with the first chapter set in 1927–1929, the second in 1979–1981, and the third, following the pattern, in—the early 2030s? Though *Birdman* is obviously contemporary, it may have owed its awards success to voters working on superhero films speculating about how they and their work would be received decades hence. If *Boyhood* suggested that time could not quite be transcended, *Birdman* flattered the common perception of cinema as assisting immortality.

Unlike Riggan or Maleficent, but like Mason, Chavez, Kyle, and King, American cinema of 2014 ultimately could not transcend its place in time. 2014 was the middle of a decade of greater awareness of female and non-white voices and contributions, yet American films reflected this awareness only haphazardly and incompletely. Hollywood's decade was dominated by (white) superheroes, and three of 2014's better films, *The Lego Movie, Guardians of the Galaxy*, and *Birdman*, succeeded in large part because of their clever commentaries on superhero, blockbuster-related themes. Five other American films from the same year also peeled back, or peeked behind, long-fixed curtains, to improve our perspectives on civil rights pioneers, fairy-tale villains, and working-class Texans. The most endearing, probably most enduring cinema of 2014 demonstrated reflection and reflexivity.

2015

Movies and Female Agency

LISA BODE

On 12 April 2015, Hillary Rodham Clinton announced her run for the Democratic nomination in the 2016 presidential election. A politically seasoned, articulate centrist in sensible pantsuits, Clinton ran on a platform that, among other things, promised to improve affordable health care and expand the rights of women, LGBT folk, and people of color. These softer qualities were complicated by the fact that, in her role as secretary of state in the Obama government, she had been a hawk, favoring international military intervention with high-tech lethal solutions such as drones. A couple of months later on 16 June, property developer and reality TV star Donald Trump announced that he would run on the Republican ticket. Perceived by much of the mainstream media as a grotesque buffoon with his empty braggadocio and womanizing, this news seemed a joke. It was met with derisive laughter from much of the United States and, indeed, the world. In 2015, even with the many reservations about Clinton, it seemed utterly inconceivable that Trump could win.

After all, the year was marked by many progressive signs: the Supreme Court overruled state bans on same-sex marriage; diplomatic relations with Cuba were re-established; combat roles in the U.S. military were opened to women; many states decriminalized marijuana; and President Barack Obama announced the Clean Power Plan, and promised that by 2030, the United States would be powered by at least 20 percent renewable energy. In Canada, new Prime Minister Justin Trudeau was asked why his cabinet was 50 percent female, and responded, "Because it's 2015."

On TV, women ruled ruthlessly in HBO's *Game of Thrones*, and kicked butt in Marvel and Netflix's *Jessica Jones*. Aziz Ansari's offbeat and charming Netflix show *Master of None* was the best received new comedy series of the year, navigating social mores, sex, love, ethnicity, and race with a light touch. Conan O'Brien visited and broadcast his show, *TBS with Conan*, from Cuba. CBS's *Big Brother* featured its first ever transgender contestant, Audrey Middleton. Andrew Jarecki's HBO, long-form, true-crime documentary *The Jinx*, about wealthy alleged multiple murderer Robert Durst, made the news when Durst was arrested the night before the airing of the series's final episode—an episode in which viewers heard him incriminate himself. WWE dropped champion and figurehead Hulk Hogan and scrubbed the wrestler from its product line and lineup after a recording emerged of him making racist comments in 2012. Superbowl XLIX was the most-watched television program in U.S. TV broadcast history, with a peak of 120 million viewers in a game in which the New England Patriots beat the defending champions, the Seattle Seahawks. This ratings success suggested linear broadcast TV was still viable, but nonetheless, many legacy entertainment companies, such as HBO, CBS, and Disney, launched nonlinear internet streaming portals in a bid to compete with Netflix and Hulu.

A cultural shift was apparent not just on-screen but on the stage, with a successful Broadway revival of the 2005 musical of Alice Walker's *The Color Purple* and the premiere of *Allegiance*, the musical inspired by George Takei's experiences in a WWII Japanese American internment camp. In February, Lin-Manuel Miranda's historical, hip-hop- and R & B–driven musical, *Hamilton*, starring nonwhite performers as the American Founding Fathers, premiered off-Broadway. It sold out for months before reopening in August on Broadway at the Richard Rodgers Theatre to rave reviews and full houses.

Cultural commentators noted the rise of a fourth wave of feminism, amplified by social media activism, and promoted by celebrities like Emma Watson and Beyoncé. Feminism had been a dirty word for young women not so long before. Now cool again, it revived interest in past battles, and a retrieval and rewriting of older feminist and feminine iconography. A slogan from 1975's second wave, "The Future Is Female," once again proudly emblazoned T-shirts. Feminist slogans also had a resurgence in a classically feminine hobby—cross-stitch embroidery—subverting the form. Two of the most popular to appear in cross-stitch were, "A Woman's Place Is in the White House," and "Girls Just Want to Have Fundamental Rights." The British film *Suffragette*, starring Meryl Streep as Emmeline Pankhurst, dramatized the U.K. suffrage movement of feminism's first wave a century earlier.

Well-known people who passed away in 2015 included singer Natalie Cole; Harlem Globetrotter Meadowlark Lemon; filmmaker Chantal Akerman (*Jeanne Dielman, 23, Quai du Commerce, 1080 Bruxelles*); Studio-era actress Maureen O'Hara, best known for her films with John Ford (*How Green Was My Valley, The Quiet Man*); New York Yankee baseball player Yogi Berra, famous for his malapropisms ("It ain't over 'til it's over"; "It's déjà vu all over again"; "If you see a fork in the road, take it"; "I didn't really say everything I said"); director John Guillermin (*The Towering Inferno*); civil rights activist Julian Bond; horror director Wes Craven (*Nightmare on Elm Street*); Egyptian actor in Hollywood Omar Sharif (*Doctor Zhivago*); *Ragtime* novelist E. L. Doctorow; country singer Lynn Anderson; actor Christopher Lee, best known for playing Dracula in Hammer horror films; film composer James Horner (*Braveheart, Titanic*); blues musician B. B. King; Portuguese film director Manoel de Oliveira; Nobel Prize—winning German novelist Günter Grass (*The Tin Drum*); documentary filmmaker Albert Maysles (*Gimme Shelter, Grey Gardens*); *Star Trek*'s Mr. Spock, Leonard Nimoy; New York governor Mario Cuomo (1983–1995); ESPN commentator Stuart Scott; *La Dolce Vita* siren Anita Ekberg; Irish film star in Hollywood Rod Taylor (*The Birds*); and *The Thorn Birds* author Colleen McCullough.

Activist movements continued to gather steam both online and in the streets, drawing attention to the prevalence of police brutality, racism, and sexual assault. A documentary about sexual assault on college campuses, *The Hunting Ground*, shed light on the suppression of rape cases by college administrators. At the same time, the long-running accusations of sexual assault leveled at Bill Cosby were finally taken seriously, and on 30 December a warrant was issued for his arrest. So, there was rage, but also a great deal of optimism for those on the more progressive end of the sociopolitical spectrum.

Meanwhile, in Europe, the Syrian refugee crisis made news as hundreds of refugees drowned. Many countries, including the United States, were moved to tears by photographs from a Turkish beach of tiny, drowned toddler Aylan Kurdi, and agreed to receive more Syrian refugees. At the same time the world was shocked and outraged by two particularly violent acts of Islamic terrorism in Paris. On 7 January, twelve journalists and cartoonists at the office of satirical newspaper *Charlie Hebdo* were gunned down as punishment for publishing anti-Islamic cartoons. On 13 November, suicide bombers attacked a football stadium and gunmen murdered scores of young concertgoers at the Bataclan in revenge for French air strikes on ISIL targets in Syria and Iraq. The United States also did not escape terror attacks. In December, a married couple of Islamic extremists, Syed Farook and Tashfeen Malik, left their sixteen-month-old baby at home before killing fourteen people at a county department training event in San Bernardino.

The so-called alt-right—a coalition including white supremacists, anti-feminists, and anti-immigration and Men's Rights activists—swelled in membership and media visibility. The movement was fueled by online publications such as *Breitbart*, whose provocateur editor Milo Yiannopoulos embraced Trump as his savior and "Daddy," but was also, like the feminist fourth wave, amplified by social media platforms. So, while it seemed as if the moment was finally right for the United States to elect its first female president, it was also a year of venomous pushback from conservatives and a rising right-wing extremism.

The pushback took many forms. Yvette Cooper reported on a surge in online misogynistic attacks on women in public life, especially ones who dared to discuss sexism. A Kentucky county clerk, Kim Davis, made international news by defying a federal court order to issue marriage licenses to same-sex couples, citing personal religious objections. At the other end of the scale were sickening acts of mass murder, largely perpetrated by angry young men. On 17 June, twenty-one-year-old white supremacist Dylann Roof shot and killed nine Black people during a prayer service at a historical Black church in Charleston, South Carolina. On 1 October in Oregon, another angry young white man who had expressed white supremacist leanings, Chris Harper-Mercer, murdered his professor and eight fellow students in their community college classroom.

In many ways, Hollywood continued to steer a safe course, banking on the nostalgic appeal and familiarity of film franchises, genres, and established directors and stars. Marvel Studios extended their superhero universe with *Avengers: Age of Ultron* and *Ant-Man*. Tom Cruise flaunted his action chops again in *Mission: Impossible—Rogue Nation* (the fifth in the series), and audiences said farewell to the late Paul Walker via some judicious CGI in the seventh *Fast and the Furious* film, *Furious 7*. 2015 also saw new films from veteran directors Steven Spielberg and Ridley Scott. Spielberg continued his collaborations with actors Tom Hanks and Mark Rylance in the understated and poignant Cold War drama *Bridge of Spies*, and Scott directed Matt Damon in the hard science fiction film *The Martian*. Quentin Tarantino and Alejandro González Iñárritu released savage and grueling Westerns with *The Hateful Eight* and *The Revenant*, respectively.

At the same time, though, popular feminism was having a visible impact on screen culture. In 2014, the Geena Davis Institute on Gender in Media had released a report authored by Stacy L. Smith and others, showing that only 23.3 percent of films had a female lead or co-lead. Davis lobbied the industry to increase the number of female characters on-screen and challenged gender stereotyping in children's media. In 2015, Danielle Pacquet wrote in the *Washington Post* about the study by Smith and others, which showed that, of 700 box-office hits released between 2007 and 2014, only 30.2 percent of speaking roles went to women. As the researchers said, "Clearly the norm in Hollywood is to exclude girls and women from the screen." However, as articles in *Variety* and elsewhere noted, female audiences were increasingly dominating ticket sales, and over half of the top box-office films in 2015 were female led (Adams; Barnes).

That year, women in lead roles could be seen across a range of genres, from Emily Blunt's FBI agent in the violent narco-thriller *Sicario*, to Melissa McCarthy in the action comedy *Spy*, to Brie Larson in the thriller-drama *Room* (for which Larson subsequently won the Academy Award for Best Actress), to Lily James in Disney's *Cinderella*. Cate Blanchett starred in both *Cinderella* and in Todd Haynes's acclaimed period lesbian romance, *Carol*, the latter with Rooney Mara (a film that apparently took a long time to find investors because it was believed that two female leads meant box-office poison). Romance was hybridized with both tasteful fantasy in *The Age of Adeline* and bawdy comedy in Amy Schumer's *Trainwreck*. The trend of badly behaved female ensemble comedies continued with *Pitch Perfect 2*.

If 2015 can be defined as a year where women (or, at least, white women) seemed to be on the verge of pushing *through* to positions of national power, pushing *into* the center of the cultural spotlight, and pushing *back* against injustices both significant and quotidian, six films of that year dramatized female agency or resistance to external control in diverse ways. I hesitate to group all six films within the contested terrain of mid-2010s "popular feminism," although a couple clearly proclaim themselves as being in that category.[1] At the very least, though, all six suggested that something had fundamentally shifted in terms of the kinds of narrative roles and actions both possible and expected of female characters in popular cinema. This shift was most starkly obvious in the place women occupied in two returning film franchises with late-1970s origins.

■ "We Are Not Things!": Action Heroines in Feminized Franchises

Fierce female action heroes are at the center of J. J. Abrams's hugely popular *Star Wars: The Force Awakens* (the seventh film in the series) and George Miller's more cultish *Mad Max: Fury Road* (the fourth). Both films received critical acclaim, and domestic box-office takes of $936 million and $153 million, respectively. Both also raised the ire of Men's Rights activists and some fanboys who complained that Hollywood was undermining masculinity in the most egregious way by smuggling "feminist propaganda" into the fantasy and action film franchises of their youth.[2]

Mad Max: Fury Road is by far the more visually audacious and overtly political of the two. As with its predecessors—*Mad Max* (1979); *The Road Warrior* (1981); and *Mad Max: Beyond Thunderdome* (1985)—the film takes place in a postapocalyptic world patched together from the refuse of the past. The earth is poisoned, resources are scarce, and survival necessitates mobility and speed. But while the earlier films involved conflicts over roads, oil, or material possessions, the central commodity at the center of *Mad Max: Fury Road* is human beings: primarily fertile and lactating female bodies, owned and traded by the scabrous embodiments of a dying patriarchy.

To foreground the gender politics of the film, Miller brought *Vagina Monologues* writer Eve Ensler onto the set as a consultant. In an interview with Eliana Dockterman, Ensler called *Fury Road* "a feminist action film," explaining that Miller wanted the film's numerous female characters to have "agency and independence." She worked with the actresses to help them flesh out their backstories and motivations, with reference to real-world traumatic experiences of women in war zones and human trafficking. As Adrian Martin writes, Miller has a "preferred mode of 'modern medievalism,' a species of fantasy-drama telling the Great Tale of corrupt power, resistance, hope and redemption." In this film, the real evils of our world—environmental disaster, war, corruption, tribalism, slavery, and, of course, patriarchy—are abstracted into the stark outlines of a speed-ramped graphic novel, reflecting the input of graphic novelist and designer Brendan McCarthy.

The film's opening quickly signals that its central male character, Max, will be decentered: a black screen, a revving engine, and then a voice—Tom Hardy (replacing Mel Gibson in the role)—rasping in a deep Australian accent, "My name is Max. My world is fire and blood." His voice is hard and muscular, but our first glimpse of him reveals a curiously small and genderless figure in leather, shot from behind against a vast desert backdrop, dwarfed by a hulking, rusted car. In the next minute he is attacked and helpless, dragged to the Citadel by a whooping band of marauders.

The Citadel is a water-rich palace carved into rock, ruled by a pustuled warlord, Immortan Joe (Hugh Keays-Byrne), who hoards the resource for himself, turning the water taps on and off to control the population: literally, trickle-down economics. Besides water, Joe hoards human beings. Fertile women are used for breeding stock and milk, as we see in a macabre early shot. Here, the camera pulls out from a close-up of a filigreed attachment on a nipple to reveal thick yellow tubes pumping milk from the woman's breasts into a large glass flask. The camera pulls back farther to show an entire row of similarly ample-bodied women: veiled, stupefied human livestock. The horror of the scene deepens as some appear to be clutching the emaciated corpses of their babies, their milk stolen to nourish Immortan Joe and his sons. While the parallel is drawn between women and cattle in the dairy industry, the film shows that men are also treated as things to be used. A rapid succession of disorienting images shows Max dragged through tunnels, struggling, helpless and bound in chains. Large needles stab his flesh, his blood is drawn, and next he screams in agony as a brand sizzles his flesh with O-, marking him as a universal donor. Reduced in the film's opening scenes to the status of blood bag, Max is not the film's singular hero. But, through this shared embodied experience of humiliating objecthood, he becomes a key ally to the film's women.

The more central figure—literally the film's driver—is Imperator Furiosa (Charlize Theron), an androgynous, grimly charismatic woman, whose shaven head, oil-blackened eye sockets, and prosthetic arm inspired a thousand badass Halloween costumes. It is Furiosa who sets the film's chase in motion, as, entrusted by Immortan Joe to drive a tank of water across the desert to trade for bullets and "guzzoline," she instead betrays him, and uses her mission as an opportunity to help Joe's unwilling wives escape sexual and maternal servitude. The film establishes its stakes with spectacular economy.

Before we even see the Wives, we see where they have been kept, locked up behind a bank vault door. When an agitated Immortan Joe bursts in to discover his most precious possessions gone, the camera reveals their gilded cage: a light-filled, dome-like space, marked with such remnants of civilization as a piano and books and the traces of silent revolt. The floor and walls are painted in giant, emphatic capital letters: "OUR BABIES WILL NOT BE WARLORDS," "WHO KILLED THE WORLD?," and perhaps most powerful of all, "WE ARE NOT THINGS"—a furious rejection of objecthood and a reclamation of female agency. As Joe roars in outrage, belowground, his soldiers, white-painted, skeletal "war boys," further explain the situation amongst themselves as we see them prepare for the chase. "She took a lot of stuff from Immortan Joe." "What stuff?" "Breeders! His prize breeder. He wants them back!"

And so the chase across the desert flats begins, Furiosa grimly driving a massive modified tanker, her eyes constantly scanning her rearview mirror, with Joe's crazy motorized death cult in hot, dusty, and extremely loud pursuit. It is an exhilarating, terrifying, and strange cinematic experience: diesel and dust, guttural engines, squealing wheels, unfurling flames, discordant guitar, and bizarre modified vehicles, silhouetted shapes bristling with spears and whooping men clinging to long poles, stark against a blue sky and orange desert.[3] In their midst is Max, a tube jabbed into his jugular, strapped like a screaming and wild-eyed hood ornament to the front of a car driven by the zealous war boy we come to know as Nux (Nicholas

Hoult). Most of the film's length is taken up with this breathtaking, nail-biting action in perpetual forward motion, from the left to the right of the screen, overwhelming the senses with saturated color and deafening sound. The film sustains the affective power of this action through periodic pauses in the chase enforced by the hostile landscape, such as a vast dust storm that blinds drivers and shreds the lighter vehicles of Joe's motorcade, creating distance between the war boys (with the exception of Nux and his blood bag, Max) and Furiosa's tanker.

It is in this first pause that the film reminds us of its stakes. We see the Wives for the first time through Max's perspective as he regains consciousness. As the five women leave their hiding place in the tanker, they first appear as a shimmering, soft-core-porn mirage, dousing themselves in water from the truck's hose. The camera licks their skin and fragments their bodies, diaphanous strips of gauze barely covering their long limbs and flat bellies. But a closer view of one woman's hips and thighs reveals a metal-toothed chastity belt; her friend removes it with a gigantic pair of pliers, freeing her from objecthood. She screams and kicks at the discarded device in futile rage. These same pliers are used to break Max's chains, freeing him from Nux. Later in the film, once he is allied with the Wives, Max willingly submits his body as a resource for their shared cause: his shoulder is a stabilizing prop for Furiosa's shotgun, and later he pumps his blood into her veins to save her life. Choice and agency are the difference.

Nux is taken prisoner by Furiosa and the Wives and forced onto the tanker. Unlike Max, his chains are not so easily broken. Through him we learn that the war boys are also "things," their flesh branded with stylized skulls, as their usefulness is their willingness to die for Joe. They are

Imperator Furiosa (Charlize Theron) and the Wives with the War Rig in *Mad Max: Fury Road* (George Miller, Warner Bros.). Digital frame enlargement.

brainwashed from infancy into believing their sacrifice will be glorious, while their bodies are ground up by the war machine. "Breeder!," Nux spits at the Wives. One of the Wives, "the Dag" (Abbey Lee Kershaw), hisses in retort, "Schlanger! You're an old man's battle fodder!"[4] Few films so clearly and entertainingly articulate the common feminist argument that the patriarchy keeps us *all* in our place, and Nux eventually comes to realize this.

The film sustains this argument while weaving a related environmental message through its length. Furiosa's destination is the place where she was born before her kidnapping and enslavement, the "Green Place of the Many Mothers," a land ruled by a matriarchy. This is where she hopes to deliver the Wives. As they discover, though, the Green Place no longer exists. Poisoned, it is now a desolate bog of sparse dead trees and crows, shown in bluish, desaturated color, as if drained of hope. They discover, too, that the once nurturing Many Mothers have moved into the desert. Now a ragged band of tough biker women called the Vuvalini, they use ambush tactics and crossbows to protect themselves from predatory gangs. In another of the film's quiet moments, one grizzled old woman, the Keeper, explains that violence becomes necessary for survival when resources are scarce. She gives the Dag some hope that civilization can be reborn, however, showing the girl her precious bag of seeds: "trees, flowers, fruit." Their plan is to keep running across the salt plains until they find a place with good soil and water where they can grow a new Green Place. Max points out that what they seek is behind them: the Citadel. "Hope is a mistake. If you can't fix what's broken, you'll go insane," he says, thinking of those who haunt him. The film's call to action is clear: if you want a better world, you cannot withdraw from this one. You must fight.

In their final desperate race back to the Citadel, trying to beat the combined motorized gangs of Immortan Joe and his grotesque allies, the Wives work with their new mentors, the Vuvalini. Some use makeshift weapons, while others deploy feminine wiles to distract and ensnare their male enemies. In the end, safe at the Citadel with the warlords destroyed, the people rejoice and hoist Furiosa and the surviving Wives on a platform up the cliff. Looking down from Furiosa's perspective we see Max—a face in the crowd—looking up with a slight smile, redeemed. But, in the tradition of loner masculine Western heroes, he slings his pack on his shoulder and disappears into the desert, leaving this feminized collectivist civilization behind.

Star Wars: The Force Awakens—the highest-grossing film of 2015—is less overtly political in terms of its narrative, but it still angered some of the same groups infuriated by *Mad Max*. In this case they blamed Disney, which had acquired *Star Wars* in 2012 and seemed determined to broaden the appeal of the franchise by including more female and nonwhite characters. Dan Golding attributes this move to Lucasfilm's head, Kathleen Kennedy, who had shifted the organization toward "diversity in casting, production, and perhaps more unusually for Hollywood, leadership" with a female-heavy team of executives (101–112). The director chosen was one with a track record for creating strong female-led TV series, J. J. Abrams. Interviewed by George Stephanopoulos on *Good Morning America* in November 2015, Abrams stated that *Star Wars* had always been "a movie that dads take their sons to," but he wanted it to also be one that "mothers could take their daughters to." While these changes were for the most part received with enthusiasm and made financial sense, the film was criticized as retreading 1977's *Star Wars: A New Hope* into a cash-in on fan nostalgia. However, this was a necessary torch-passing exercise. It used the iconography and characters of the past to ground and ordain a more diverse cast while allowing the story to continue.

The familiar opening scroll with stirring triumphant music tells us that Luke Skywalker (Mark Hamill), the last Jedi, has vanished, and he is being sought by both his sister General Leia, leader of the resistance (Carrie Fisher), and the sinister First Order, which has arisen from the ashes of the Empire. Leia has sent the Resistance's best pilot, Poe (Oscar Isaac), and his small droid companion, BB-8, on a mission to desert planet Jakku to chase a clue as to Luke's whereabouts. Poe is followed and captured by the imperial forces, but not before he locates the map that will lead the Resistance to Luke, secretes it in the memory banks of his droid, and sends the little machine rolling to safety.

The ragged dusty outposts on Jakku (shot in dunes outside Dubai) visually evoke those of *A New Hope*'s Tatooine (shot in Tunisia). Just as sandy Tatooine was Skywalker's backwater planet, Jakku's empty dunes are the home to his heir, Rey (Daisy Ridley). Rey is a loner. She is introduced visually as an androgynous and agile scavenger, wrapped against the sandstorms in layers of scarves and rags. A close-up reveals determined, girlish features and teeth gritted with exertion in a ruddy face. A sequence of wordless shots establishes the dusty, aimless rhythms of her life, and time filled with wordless scavenging, trading, and existing. We see her drag cumbersome scraps from the crashed remains of Imperial spaceships and walkers, through empty miles of sand hills, to exchange at an outpost for meager rations. Here, like Skywalker before her, she rescues a small, rotund, beeping and whistling droid (BB-8) from the scrapyard and allows it to tag along with her as a companion, unaware that its memory banks hold a map of huge significance to the future of both the galaxy and herself. Girl and droid are shown moving as tiny figures against the rolling sands, hazy skies, and gargantuan decaying space wrecks. All major Star Wars characters have a distinctive music theme; John Williams has given Rey a repeating, tiptoe-ing flute motif, secretive and soft-footed, as if continuing *Star Wars*'s debt to Akira Kurosawa's *Seven Samurai* in musical form. She is soon joined by Finn (John Boyega), an ex–Storm Trooper posing as a rebel hero, whose desire for self-preservation is in perpetual conflict with his sense of loyalty to his friends.

Finn has escaped from the villainous First Order. In a scene designed to create a stark visual association with fascism, First Order General Hux (Domhnall Gleeson) is shown giving a speech to a vast army that disappears into the horizon. Wide shots show him as a tiny figure dwarfed by an enor-mous red flag with a spiky black symbol. His watery blue eyes dominate a close-up in which he trembles with the fury of Hitler and spits, "All remain-ing systems will bow to the First Order" before demonstrating the sublime destructive power of a new weapon, the "Star Killer." This weapon of course resembles the Death Star of *A New Hope*, but, with the logic of fran-chise sequels, is much bigger. One scene shows the two war machines in holographic form for a side-by-side comparison that reveals the new weapon to be four or five times the size of its predecessor. This is just one of many scenes where the film makes explicit or implicit connections with the original *Star Wars* trilogy, designed to reignite the nostalgia and childhood wonder of parents in the audience.

In an early chase and firefight on Jakku, Rey, Finn, and BB-8 run from the First Order, and select a getaway vehicle from a cluster of ships on the sand. Those familiar with the earlier films should immediately recognize Rey's chosen vessel by its disc shape as the Millennium Falcon, owned by Han Solo (Harrison Ford) in the first trilogy. The Falcon is particularly responsive to Rey's control, as if she and the ship are one, darting in and out and over the vast eerie wrecks of Imperial ships half swallowed by the desert sand, the landscape scarred with past battles. Solo himself further bestows legitimacy on the young woman. Grizzled and slower with age, Solo is shown as reluctantly impressed by Rey's mechanical knowledge and affinity with his vessel, and gruffly offers her the ship's keys. Later, Solo dryly observes Finn. "I like this guy," he rumbles; high praise coming from this sardonic space smuggler. Later still, Rey becomes the natural compan-ion of Chewbacca the Wookiee (Peter Mayhew) after Solo's death at the hands of his estranged son, Kylo Ren (a sullen and tortured Adam Driver). Ren, the film's masked villain, a Jedi who, like Darth Vader before him, has "gone to the dark side," delivers a monologue to the half-destroyed, skull-like mask of his dead idol, Vader. Toward the end of the film we see Leia take Rey in a motherly embrace, the braided hair of the older and the younger woman pressed together—a tactile and visual anointment.

Notably in *The Force Awakens*, women are much more visible in key narrative roles than in the past two trilogies, each of which featured only a sole royal female (Leia in the first trilogy, Padme in the second): there is Rey, the orphaned warrior, Princess Leia, now a general, and the First Order's Captain Phasma (Gwendoline Christie), an imposing, high-ranking, posh-voiced stormtrooper in a chrome helmet. Then there is Maz Kanata, played by a motion-captured Lupita Nyong'o, a swaggering, ancient figure with a face like an orange who rules an outpost bar (this film's version of the cantina) and who sees much. Women may not yet be in the same proportions that they are off-screen, but they are at least much more central in making things happen, as leaders, fighters, helpers, and revealers of truths. For instance, it is Maz who senses the Force in Rey and shows the young woman that she is more than she believes herself to be.

In this key scene, Rey finds herself alone for a moment in the bustling fortress bar, when suddenly she hears a distant and distraught voice of a child, pleading "no, come back." Compelled to trace the source of the sound, she wanders down a stairway into a basement, where she is drawn to a wooden box. Opening it, she discovers a lightsaber, and as she reaches to touch it, we share her flood of visions in disconnected flashes of what we take to be traumatic memories of childhood abandonment, and a moment yet to come: Rey fighting a lightsaber duel in a snowy forest. Maz breaks Rey's reverie. This lightsaber, she explains, belonged to Luke Skywalker, and to his father before him, and "now it calls to you." It is in Rey that the Force (in the previous films, an invisible power associated with an all-male order, the Jedi Knights) is awakening. "The belonging you seek is not behind you. It is ahead," Maz tells her. Rey has been tied to the desert planet, scavenging in its ruins, while she waits for the parents who abandoned her to return. But Maz shows her that she must shake off her traumatic memories in order to bind herself to a larger mythic history—one that beckons her through repeated encounters and affinities with iconic objects and characters. Rey comes to learn that it is only by regulating her emotions and remaining calm that she can attract and wield the Force, allowing it to flow through her. In this way, *Mad Max* and *Star Wars* take opposing positions on rage. *Mad Max* insists that intense collective emotion, such as rage, is the best catalyst for revolutionary action, whereas *Star Wars*, as always, argues that only those who can control their anger and fear may win.

Strangely, though, despite Rey's centrality to the new trilogy, the care taken in the film to develop her rightful place in its mythmaking, and to align the audience with her perspective, Rey-themed toys were barely visible compared to merchandise based on the male characters. In a report from Forbes the following year, an anonymous insider from the *Star Wars VII* merchandising push claimed that toymakers had been steered away from including Rey in their product lines. Boys, the main target market, were allegedly not interested in playing with female action figures. The action figures of Rey which *did* get released show her masked and cloaked, effectively genderless.

Resisting Control, Bad Romance

Less badass but still resistant female characters are seen in Guillermo del Toro's luscious, haunted, gothic horror *Crimson Peak* and Sam Taylor-Johnson's muted and dark adult romance *Fifty Shades of Grey*, the screen adaptation of E. L. James's global best-seller. Stylistically, the films are poles apart, but both have a lineage in the gothic, and feature bookish young women seduced into danger. Perhaps the most profitable film of the year, *Fifty Shades* made $571 million worldwide on a budget of $40 million, even while banned in several countries. The film was loathed by religious and media morality groups who were appalled by its plentiful nudity, sex, and BDSM scenes, and those on the Left who hated its sexual politics. Like Stephenie Meyer's *Twilight* (on which James's novels were based, originally as online fan fiction) and countless romance novels before it, the film was condemned for the way it romanticized toxic male behavior. While *Mad Max* takes aspects of male toxicity such as violence, possessive control, and ownership of women and embodies them in grotesque figures such as Immortan Joe, *Fifty Shades* packages these same toxic qualities in a devastatingly handsome, enigmatic, and inconceivably wealthy bachelor.

This bachelor is Christian Grey (played by Jamie Dornan, the chiseled Irish actor who was the creepy, psychosexual serial killer in the TV series *The Fall*), a twenty-seven-year-old self-made billionaire who likes tasteful luxury furnishings, fine wine, and punishing women's bodies in his secret Red Room of Pain. His wealth and success are signaled visually in the film's opening shots, as the film's heroine, Anastasia Steele (Dakota Johnson), stares up in wonder at a skyscraper with Grey's name on it. The building thrusts skyward like an enormous glass dildo, while on the soundtrack Annie Lennox warbles, "I put a spell on you (because you're mine)." The implicit question of course is, "but who will put a spell on whom?"

Ordinary, quietly pretty Anastasia, Anna for short, is at Grey's office to interview him for the college newspaper on behalf of her sick roommate. His office, like his penthouse apartment, is uncluttered and unlived-in, with a palette of slate and dove gray and white and glass. In their first meeting, she whispers girlishly through a series of banal and offensive questions (e.g., "Are you gay?") about the secrets of his success. Christian discloses that his talent is "identifying talented people" and understanding how to motivate and "incentivize" them to "harness their efforts." The scene, punctuated by a series of close-ups of Anna's teeth pressing into the plush flesh of her lower lip, eyes looking up and away, and amplified breath, monitors their growing mutual fascination. Christian's arousal is piqued; he decides Anna is another person he wants to "harness." Discovering she is a lit major, he asks her in BuzzFeed-quiz fashion whether it was Brontë, Austen, or Hardy who ignited her love of books. He decides her answer, Hardy, signals hidden passions (no doubt Austen would have suggested a wit). From this moment he woos her with fancy dinners, helicopter rides, and a series of expensive gifts delivered to her door. The first of these is, of course, a leather-bound first edition of Thomas Hardy's *Tess of the d'Urbervilles*. It is followed by more covetable consumer goods: a MacBook Pro, Prada and Dolce & Gabbana clothing, and a brand new Audi.

The objective of Christian's courtship is not romance. Rather, he wants Anna to consent to his domination. He wants to control her pleasure and pain, her diet, fertility, exercise, health, and personal style. Once his, she must be available for sexual servitude and punishment whenever the mood takes him. The sex and tentative forays into BDSM are tastefully shot, fragmented into close-ups of panting mouths, straining, arching back muscles, fingers and more painful implements trailing teasingly over shivering, warmly lit skin, light haloing bare breasts and round vulnerable buttocks, trembling in anticipation, pleasure, or pain. Unlike *Mad Max* however, and, indeed, unlike earlier sex films or films about BDSM relationships, such as *9½ Weeks* or even the wonderful *Secretary*, much of *Fifty Shade*'s length is spent in an exploration of consent and the negotiation of an eighteen-page contract. As Timothy Laurie and Jessica Kean argue, the film "dramatises the dangers of unequal negotiation and the practical complexity of identifying one's limits and having them respected."

As controlling and creepy as Christian may be (at one point he breaks into her apartment to surprise her, and he stalks her), *consent* is one line he will not cross, as Anna's submission has value to him only if it is willingly given. "Necrophilia is not my thing," he says with distaste when she blearily asks him if they had sex while she was drunk. "It is important that you know that you can leave at any time," he solemnly tells her before opening the door to his red-walled "playroom." The film's best scene is the contract negotiation, which crackles with dry humor and sexual tension. It takes place after hours in his executive boardroom. The establishing shot shows Christian and Anna coolly facing each other from opposing sides of the frame, divided by a long glossy table, the paperwork before them. The clothes maketh the woman, as the form-fitting corporate dress she wears (one of his many gifts) forces her upright, transforming a mawkish girl into a more regal adversary. Her voice, too, has changed. Full-throated compared to the hesitant whispers with which she began the film, she firmly instructs him to strike out her hard limits: "anal fisting—strike it out"; "genital clamps? absolutely not!" The lighting underscores the shift taking place in their power dynamic, and suggests his imminent softening.

Christian's corporate offices, like his apartment, were initially dominated by sterile grays and whites, but are now suffused in feminine tones of dusky rose.

While the film itself, with its relentless product placement and the way the camera lovingly caresses all the luxury textures and surfaces of Christian's lifestyle, might suggest otherwise, Anna claims that she is not "incentivized" by things, and she herself does not want to be one of Christian's luxury possessions. What *she* wants is emotional intimacy and companionship, but he is too damaged by early childhood trauma (his chest bears the scars of cigarette burns from a bad mother, long dead) to give it to her in any sustained and consistent way. Yet we also know by how sensitively he plays his grand piano that he must have emotional depths longing to be tapped. It is the familiar question: Can the love of a good woman fix the damaged man? By the film's end, Anna has still not signed the contract. She remains unsure if she wants to give her body and life so fully to a man who can't love her, and who, for reasons she cannot understand, wants instead to give her pain. They have explored some of her physical limits, allowing her to feel the sting of his flogger on her flesh. But in the end, she reaches her limit, and asserts her agency: "Don't fucking touch me." She leaves. The loudest thing we hear her say, now in full voice, is "No!" when he reaches out for her as she makes it to the elevator. He steps back, respecting the command. Their miserable faces stare back at each other as the elevator doors close, separating them, ending, for the first film at least, on a note of sad female defiance and male resignation. This is only the end of the first act though. Thrumming through the film's affective register and its popular reception is an ambivalent, guilty female fantasy of being dominated and cherished and materially spoiled, but on one's own terms.

Like *Fifty Shades of Grey*, Guillermo del Toro's *Crimson Peak* has a bookish heroine seduced by an attractive man who was damaged by an abusive mother. Substantially less profitable than *Fifty Shades* (on a budget of $55 million, it took only $74 million worldwide), it did however win Best Horror Film, Best Production Design, and Best Supporting Actress for Jessica Chastain at the Saturn Awards. *Crimson Peak* is starkly different in setting, style, and denouement. The heroine, Edith Cushing (Mia Wasikowska, luminous in topaz silks and velvets), is a very wealthy young woman living in late nineteenth-century Buffalo, New York. Unlike Anna in *Fifty Shades*, Edith does not enter the film ordinary and meek. Its early scenes establish Edith as a witty, confident, and curious writer. A would-be novelist and intellect, she can hold her own in conversations with men, such as her friend and suitor Dr. Alan McMichael (Charlie Hunnam), to the annoyance of her bitchy female peers.

Crucial as well, Edith is a woman who sees things, signaled by her wire-rimmed spectacles and her social observations. In the film's opening narration she tells us that she sees ghosts (including the ghastly skeletal ghost of her mother, who warned her as a young girl, "Beware Crimson Peak"). This sensitivity to warnings from the past will save her life. What she *cannot* see, however, is the conniving cad beneath the charm of a young British aristocrat, Sir Thomas Sharpe (perfectly cast with the pale and interesting Tom Hiddleston, known by this time for playing Loki in *Thor* [2011] and *The Avengers* [2012]), who, with his cold sister Lucille (Jessica Chastain), has Edith's wealth in his sights.

Thomas is a poor baronet (Edith refers to him before they meet as a "parasite with a title") who has whirled into town in an old-fashioned suit with his sister, Lucille, in the hopes of seeking investment for his ore clay mine back in England. Edith's father (Jim Beaver), a proud, self-made man, is unimpressed by the Englishman's smooth, pale hands. "In America," he lectures, "we bank on effort, not privilege." Thomas quickly turns his courtly attention to Edith, but her father can see straight through the charade. He hires a private investigator to do some digging and bribes Thomas and Lucille with a check to leave on the next train, instructing Thomas to break his daughter's heart. This he does, in the most personally vicious way possible, by attacking the quality of her writing as "absurdly sentimental." However, the next morning the father is mysteriously dead—an apparently violent accident with a bathroom sink—and Thomas is at Edith's side, offering comfort and begging forgiveness, revealing he had only been obeying her father. The film signals his duplicitousness by plunging half his face in shadow, as he declares his passion for her in terms cribbed from Mr. Rochester in Jane Eyre.

Thomas spirits the grieving Edith away from all she has known in her American life, to his desolate decaying house, Allerdale. No gleaming pent-house, our first sight of Allerdale is a foreboding structure thrusting out of the earth, a tall and narrow vision of gothic hyperbole, all grim turrets and gables. Its cavernous, creaking walls seem to swallow our heroine. The house itself is a central character, seeming to speak with chimneys that groan in the wind, foundations sinking into the earth, and the clanking of its rusting cage elevator. The ore stains the ground and water on his prop-erty a striking bloodred, giving the place its local nickname, which Edith discovers almost too late: "Crimson Peak"—the warning given by her mother's ghost. In this place, friendless, and at Lucille's mercy, her spark and wit dims, and she becomes meek and fearful.

Lucille rules this house without servants. An elegant figure in rustling taffeta gowns, she keeps all keys, cooks all meals, and insists Edith drink mysteriously bitter cups of tea, which the American woman accepts, even as she grows weaker by the day. Edith's sensitivity to the supernatural and her ability to see what others cannot, however, saves her life: she is visited by a succession of three spindly, terrifying female apparitions which emerge from the floors like waxen flayed corpses. Trailing wisps and ribbons of crimson ectoplasm, they shriek warnings and lead Edith to hidden trunks, envelopes of documents and photos, and corpses in the cellars of the rotting mansion: evidence of the three wives before her who were seduced away from their friends and murdered for their wealth. Edith also discovers the wax cylinder recordings of these women's voices, and, crucially, the warn-ing to future women, secretly recorded by one of the women in her last days, about the poison Lucille had been putting in her tea.

As Edith begins rejecting the tea, Lucille realizes that her sister-in-law is aware of her scheme. Meanwhile, Edith discovers that Thomas, the weaker of the siblings, is bonded to his sister through a childhood of abuse, murderous revenge on their mother, and incest, but that he now loves Edith. Things quickly come to a protractedly violent, bloody, and almost preposterous end. If it is not already clear from the amplified production design that the film mines the gothic and its tropes for reflexive fictional play rather than pushing toward realism, then the last-minute, would-be rescue makes this impression concrete. Lucille's murderous plans for Edith are interrupted by a knock on the door. It is Edith's American friend and suitor Dr. Alan McMichael (Charlie Hunnam), a man who has long admired her intellect and spirit; he has traveled across miles of sea and snow to res-cue her. But the film knows this would not do; Edith must rescue herself. So Lucille stabs the doctor and he is dragged, incapacitated, to the cellar.

It is only when Lucille, no longer controlled and icy but unhinged, swaggering, and gloating, throws the pages of Edith's manuscript—all she has toiled for—into the fire that Edith's rage is triggered, and the force of the emotion fills her with sudden violence. Her weapon is of course her fountain pen, the appurtenance of her intellectual identity, and she plunges its tip into the other woman's breast. The fight to the death between the two women is so wincingly visceral it can be almost felt in the stabbing and slicing of fingers and faces. Finally only they remain, struggling furiously in the snow, stained red with clay and blood. It seems almost inconsequential that in the midst, Thomas is stabbed to death by his sister in a jealous rage. He has, after all, only served as the bait in his sister's plans: a passive accomplice and lure to attract wealthy, lonely wives. It is fitting then that, in death, Thomas is once again used as bait. He appears behind his sister, gazing at Edith, pale, silent, and hollow-eyed. Edith urges Lucille to turn and look once more at her beloved brother. Like the women Lucille has killed, she cannot resist his lure, but now the murderess is the victim as Edith caves in the woman's skull from behind with a shovel. The monster is slain.

The film has been described by Xavier Aldana Reyes as a "love letter to the gothic," in particular to the "feminine" gothic romances of the Brontës— the film most clearly borrows from *Jane Eyre* (1847) and *The Mysteries of Udolpho* (1794) (172). It visually revels in gothic aesthetics and tropes, but in keeping with the representational norms of 2015 popular cinema, the heroine is given much more embodied agency. In Edith we have the usual

The gothic heroine who saves herself: Edith (Mia Wasikowska) fights to the death in the snow in *Crimson Peak* (Guillermo del Toro, Universal). Digital frame enlargement.

curious woman, the lady detective bringing the dark secrets of the past into the light. The film teases us with a poorly realized and forced last-minute rescue from the true male suitor, but this is thwarted. All male characters are instead pushed to the sidelines, used as objects, victimized, killed, or incapacitated so that Edith will be forced to fight for her life in the final bloody scenes. The film has three types of women. There is Edith, a good woman: sensible, capable, and sensitive. There are toxic women such as Lucille, variously bitchy, capricious, jealous, controlling, abusive, and emotionally unstable. And there are dead women, ghosts, who warn Edith and lead her to the evidence of fatal mistakes. In the final shot, we see Edith and the injured Alan, mutually supporting each other as they limp off together, exiting through the filigreed gothic gates of the property, an image of egalitarian romantic partnership.

Losing Herself: Troubled Daughters

While *Mad Max: Fury Road* and *Star Wars: The Force Awakens* give us young women learning to fight for a cause, and *Fifty Shades* and *Crimson Peak* rework gothic heroines, two other films, *Inside Out* and *Maggie*, place us within the skin of young girls experiencing devastating cognitive and emotional shutdowns. It may seem very strange to group the two films together, for in budgetary, generic, aesthetic, and target audience terms they are polar opposites. *Maggie* is a low-budget ($1.4 million) apocalyptic zombie melodrama directed by first-timer Henry Hobson. Muddy-hued and gory, it is a world away from Pixar's candy-colored, Oscar-winning animated family film *Inside Out*. Both, however, center on the inner worlds of their young female characters, dramatize parent-daughter relations, and, in key moments, give audiovisual expression to the complex interactions of emotion, memory, and cognition as drivers of our actions.

Maggie gives us a dying world of the near future. Crops are diseased and burning, humanity is threatened by a slow-acting zombie virus pandemic, and institutions are struggling to maintain order. Abigail Breslin plays Maggie, a teen girl who is already infected by the "necroambulist virus" as the film begins. Her father, Wade (a grizzled and restrained Arnold Schwarzenegger), finds her in a crowded city hospital ward, and takes her home to die in their large, shabby, rural house. Here Maggie spends her final days with Wade and her wary, chilly stepmother (Joely Richardson). As with lead characters of other films in 2015 (e.g., Furiosa in *Mad Max: Fury Road*, Edith in *Crimson Peak*, and Christian in *Fifty Shades of Grey*), Maggie's real mother is dead, but still has a hold on her that is crucial to the plot. The film follows the long, sorrowful farewell between father and daughter and gently explores their emotional connection as they try to deny her impending fate while poring over familiar shared memories. All the while, though, there is the unspoken awareness between them that Wade will have to eventually kill Maggie himself or else surrender her to quarantine, where she will face an even more horrific death. For a substantial part of its stretch, the film seems to be about Wade wrestling with his need to decide what to do about Maggie and putting off the inevitable. Maggie's fate seems to be in her father's hands. However, the film gives clues that *her* experience and agency will be what matters most.

Apart from a blackening wound on her arm which she keeps scratching, her greasy pallor, and her light sensitivity, Maggie seems normal. The virus slowly creeps through the body from the bite site, blackening the blood. It fogs up the senses of sight and hearing (while sharpening the sense of smell) until the victim is a shambling, guttural, senseless thing. The most affective moments of the film are those which give us access to Maggie's embodied, fearful experience of her shrinking self. In the first of these moments, Maggie is outside on the swing set. Her stepmother watches her through the kitchen window, slicing frozen tomatoes for dinner. We see a close-up of Maggie's pale face, and then violent flashes slice into the peace of the rural late afternoon: perhaps memories of the slavering creature that bit her, or a vision of her future self. She falls from the swing, breaking and dislocating a finger on her infected arm. After she is bundled into the kitchen, crying hysterically, Maggie spies the knife on the kitchen sink and, without hesitation, uses it to hack off her broken finger. Blood, black as ink, spills over the wood, and we hear the grinding of the garbage disposal unit doing its work. This is a desperate act of magical thinking, to remove part of the limb that no longer belongs to her. Later in the doctor's office, he puts a stethoscope against her bruised skin to listen to her heart, and we suddenly hear the world muffled and far away, as if Maggie's core self is sinking slowly beneath deep water, shutting out the world as her senses close down.

By the film's denouement, the stepmom has fled, and Wade has been unable to kill his daughter even though she has now lost the ability to speak. Grieving quietly, he resists the finality of her death a little longer. He is downstairs, alone, sitting in his favorite armchair with a shotgun resting across his lap, tensely pretending to be asleep. The camera at floor level shows Maggie's bare feet clump heavily down the stairs; she drags herself towards him, breathing loud and wet. She leans down, bringing her mouth close to his head, swaying slightly, and presses her lips against his forehead before turning away. In these final moments, the camera focuses on her dirty gray feet on the roof tiles, shuffling awkwardly toward the edge. It refrains from giving us the horror of her dehumanized face and instead reveals the remains of her humanity with final access to the images she holds onto in her decaying mind. These are not violent projections of what she is becoming but a precious memory: a woman, her mother, smiling, sunlight in the creases of her eyes. Her father had earlier shown her a patch of flowers growing in a drab clearing—fresh white-and-yellow daisies—the only color in the film. They had been planted by her mother, and they provide a connection between the dead and the living. Now this connection is her last thought. We see her fall from the roof. Her last act of living is to choose a good death, a mindful death caught in a memory, and one for which her father will not have to bear the burden of guilt. A depressing experience for many, the film did not fare well at the box office.

Inside Out, by contrast, took $857 million at the box office and won the Oscar for Best Animated Feature. It is worth noting how unprecedented it was for a big-budget, 3D-animated film to be set almost entirely inside the head of a young girl. After all, as Angie Han points out, Pixar's first female-led film didn't come until its thirteenth release, *Brave*, in 2012. Writer Peter Docter claimed he was inspired by his own daughter and his confusion at her personality changes and mood swings as she moved toward puberty. The particular heightened emotionality of girls in that age group was the reason why the character was rendered female, and half the story crew were women (Wloszczyna).

Inside Out uses 3D digital animation to personify emotions as color-coded sprites who operate the controls of expression, cognition, and memory inside the head of an eleven-year-old girl, Riley (voiced by Kaitlyn Dias). Near the start of the film, Riley is uprooted from her cozy Midwestern life when her family moves to San Francisco, where nothing seems familiar or welcoming. The move triggers a spiral into anxiety and depression, but we see her parents, also stressed, tell her they need her to remain their "happy girl." The main conflict of the film is between an external pressure to manifest happy, positive emotions (which Riley has internalized) and the necessity of allowing oneself to feel and express sadness.

Riley's "happy girl" persona is largely due to her dominant emotion, Joy, a graceful and perky elfin figure, voiced with warm, effervescent determination by Amy Poehler. Joy is a control freak, constantly managing the other emotions: Disgust, a sulky green sprite with long eyelashes voiced by Mindy Kaling; Fear, Bill Hader incarnated as a lavender beanpole with huge eyebrows and frenetic angularity; Anger, a squat red square with clenched

Joy (Amy Poehler) at the emotion controls while Sadness (Phyllis Smith), Fear (Bill Hader), Disgust (Mindy Kaling), and Anger (Lewis Black) look on in *Inside Out* (Pete Docter, Ronnie Del Carmen, Pixar, Disney). Digital frame enlargement.

fists voiced by a truculent Lewis Black; and finally, Sadness, bespectacled, anxious-eyed, and blue, a slumped and lumpen figure, given a voice as heavy and soft as rain by Phyllis Smith.

The film visualizes Riley's mind as a brightly hued space—part factory, part TV production studio, and part theme park—where, from a control tower "headquarters," the five basic emotions control her reactions via a panel covered in buttons, levers, and dials. These reactions produce color-coded memories—gleaming glass globes that clunk together with a pleasing resonance on conveyor belts and rails, sorted into different locations, such as "core" or "long term." Core memories power the five "islands of personality"—vast World's Fair machines of symbolic moving parts (Riley's are Hockey, Goofball, Friendship, Family, and Honesty) which light up and move when a new, positive memory is added to the power core. As Joy explains to us, emotions have important survival functions. Fear and Disgust keep us safe, and Anger, she says, "feels deeply about injustice." It is only Sadness whom Joy can't see a purpose for, and she treats the emotion as a nuisance who must be kept from touching Riley's reaction controls or memories.

In San Francisco, Joy is anxious to find a positive spin for every setback to keep Riley happy. But when Sadness tries to help by picking up memory globes that keep falling out of the core, she pollutes the happy memories with her blue hands, tainting them with melancholy. In a struggle between Joy and Sadness over the memories, all the precious golden orbs fall from the core, causing the power for the personality islands to be cut. They grind to a halt, turning disquietingly gray and still. The adventure begins when Joy and Sadness, still fighting, are sucked up by a vacuum tube and ejected far from headquarters, to a shore holding spaces of memory, thought, and imagination. We follow their journey back to the control room, through vast memory warehouses with clinking globes piled high on shelves, brightly hued and hilarious dream production studios, and playgrounds of imagination.

The film tracks Joy's shifting perception of Sadness from being a dangerous annoyance that must be continually chastised (and kept from touching anything) to having a crucial purpose. While Joy has denied reality rather than reflecting on it, it is Sadness who has sought to understand the operation of Riley's mind, and her knowledge helps them navigate through the various imaginatively realized spaces. In the end, once the two are back in HQ, Joy allows Sadness to take control. Riley's tears elicit the empathy and comfort she needs from her parents, where earlier Anger, Fear, and Disgust had caused only conflict and separation. In many ways, the film is about the contemporary duty to be happy and refuse sadness, which it shows us in the end is misguided and ultimately harmful to self-development.

At points, the film shows us the similar control rooms inside the heads of Riley's mom (Diane Lane) and dad (Kyle MacLachlan). These are some of the most amusing moments of the film, but they also give a visual gendering of emotion. Unlike in Riley's head, where Joy, Sadness, and Disgust are coded female and Anger and Fear are coded male, Riley's mom's emotions, while still color-coded, are all female, their bodies and heads round and bouncy, each wearing Riley's mom's hairstyle. As a unit they evoke a talk show panel, led by an authoritative and measured Sadness, with humorous cynical barbs from Anger: "For this we gave up the Brazilian helicopter pilot?" Her father's emotion sprites, by contrast, are all square, angular figures, led by a militaristic Anger who uses terms like "DEFCON 4" before taking control, as if launching missiles. The film suggests (as her parent's emotions are so much less differentiated, all wearing the hairstyles of the person they belong to) that, as one grows from childhood to adulthood, emotions become more integrated with one's personality.

A Woman's Place Is on the Screen

So, what patterns do we find in these six very different films from 2015? They do not constitute a cycle or genre. They range across the extremes of production budgets and critical reception, with some being named among both the best and worst films of the decade. They have very different target audiences, and their aesthetic appeals move from the kinetically vivid and exuberant to the glossily erotic to the quietly melancholic.

Each, though, centers on the emerging agency of its lead female characters in ways that entangle their bodily experience, memories, and emotions.

Women in *Mad Max: Fury Road*, *Fifty Shades of Grey*, and *Maggie* all make a choice to fight against or refuse external male control. In many of these films, with the exceptions of *Inside Out* and *Maggie*, women are at first misjudged or underestimated by their male enemies, lovers, or friends, who perceive them as weak, lesser, passive, compliant, or in need of male protection. The other four films all have moments where, played somewhat for laughs, men are taken by surprise by female aggression, wit, strength, capability, or resilience. In both *Mad Max: Fury Road* and *Star Wars: The Force Awakens*, heroic men (Max in the first and Finn in the second) accept that they must step back into the helper role so the heroine or heroines can shine. It is a little dispiriting that such moments of surprise are still so common in popular cinema, a full century after the action serial heroines lit up the screen in the thrill pictures of the 1910s, such as *The Perils of Pauline* and *The Hazards of Helen*. But these films also suggest that progressive change requires intergenerational cooperation, heeding lessons from the past in order to move forward.

All these films, with the exception of *Inside Out*, feature dead or lost mothers who, as memories or ghosts, continue to reverberate through the present. Furiosa's mother is dead in *Mad Max: Fury Road*, but she and the young Wives find guidance and allies among the older women of the Vuvalini. In *Star Wars: The Force Awakens*, Rey's parents abandon her, but older women like Leia and Maz give her guidance and a new path. Abusive mothers, now dead, leave legacies of damaged men in *Fifty Shades* and *Crimson Peak*, and in *Crimson Peak*, too, the ghost of Edith's mother delivers a warning. For *Maggie* it is a sweet memory of her dead mother that she clings to as her last thread of human connection, sparing her father's life. Even for Riley in *Inside Out*, what brings her back to her family is a memory of ice skating, holding onto the hands of her father and her mother.

Just as 2015 seemed to see progressive social movements gathering steam, and the retrieval and appropriation of earlier iconography from feminism's second wave, it also saw a regressive pushback, these films emphasizing how the present is always in conversation with, and shaped by, the past, in positive and negative ways. *Star Wars: The Force Awakens* stresses the importance of fighting together, finding commonality across generations, races, and genders, and regulating one's emotions. The much more radical and vivid *Mad Max: Fury Road* also brings generations of women together, with a very few male allies, but advocates for the building and sustaining of rage as an empowering force for collective action. Anger is, as Joy tells us in

Inside Out, an emotion linked to injustice. It is a necessary emotion for driving the action to right wrongs.

NOTES

1. See Sarah Banet-Weiser and Laura Portwood Stacer, "The Traffic in Feminism: An Introduction to the Commentary and Criticism on Popular Feminism," *Feminist Media Studies*, vol. 17, no. 5, 2017, for a succinct overview of the debates around what they call "a remarkable moment" in the late-2010s surge of popular feminism.

2. Perhaps they had forgotten the centrality of female action heroines to 1980s and 1990s franchises such as *Aliens* and *Terminator*.

3. Like *Star Wars: The Force Awakens*, *Mad Max*'s promotional discourse made much of the fact that it grounded its story world and action sequences in location filming, built sets, props, and physical stunts, with more judicious use of CGI and green screen.

4. In Australian slang, "schlanger" refers to penis, and "dag" is a slightly antiquated word, something akin to "dork".

2016

Movies and the Solace
of Progressive Narratives

CYNTHIA BARON

As 2016 began, multiculturalism, which recognizes the importance of a society's disparate cultural and ethnic groups, was ascendant in America. So was progressivism, as shown by the institutional and popular support for same-sex marriage, increased access to education, and expansion of health care coverage. Yet during the year, a key by-product of globalization—the declining income of many white, middle- and working-class Americans—made a resurgence of "xenophobic nationalism" more visible in the United States (Hirsh). With many Americans pushing for greater social equity and inclusion, and others coming out against these things, franchise movies, genre films, and small independent productions became part of national conversations.

The range of musicians honored at the 2016 Grammy Award ceremony illustrates the year's embrace of aesthetic and cultural diversity. Rapper Kendrick Lamar received the most nominations, followed by pop icon Taylor Swift and Canadian rhythm and blues artist The Weeknd (Abel Makkonen Tesfaye). Swift's *1989* was named Album of the Year, the collaboration between British artist Mark Ronson and Bruno Mars (Peter Gene Hernandez) on the single "Uptown Funk" won the Record of the Year Award, and "Thinking Out Loud" by British pop artists Ed Sheeran and Amy Wadge was named Song of the Year. Recognition at the Billboard Music Awards reveals the same embrace of musical and cultural diversity. R & B artist The Weeknd received the most nominations, followed by British pop star Adele. The American Music Awards also featured top honors for a range of pop singers, including Ariana Grande, Justin Bieber, Selena Gomez, and British Pakistani artist Zayn (Zain Malik).

In addition, 2016 was the year Lin-Manuel Miranda's *Hamilton: An American Musical* became the most-acclaimed Broadway production of the era. Combining hip-hop, rhythm and blues, soul, and traditional show tunes, the iconoclastic musical received sixteen Tony award nominations.

It went on to win eleven Tony awards, and it garnered a collection of other theater and music honors. Casting nonwhite performers in the roles of major historical figures such as George Washington, John Adams, and Thomas Jefferson, the musical explicitly challenged the established equation between whiteness and American identity. For its reimagined look at American history, *Hamilton* also received the 2016 Pulitzer Prize for Drama.

Publications that offered insightful perspectives on the effects of American actions also garnered 2016 Pulitzer Prizes. *The Sympathizer* by Vietnamese American novelist Viet Thanh Nguyen received the Pulitzer Prize for Fiction for illuminating the multifaceted allegiances of Vietnamese people from starkly different backgrounds, both during and after the 1955–1975 war in Vietnam. *Black Flags: The Rise of Isis* by journalist Joby Warrick won the Pulitzer Prize for General Nonfiction. His research explained how the American-initiated Iraq War (2003–2011) fostered the rise of the Islamic State. The Pulitzer Prize for National Reporting in Journalism went to the *Washington Post* for creating a national database on the frequency and victims of police shootings in America. The Pulitzer Prize for Public Service in Journalism was awarded to the Associated Press for its investigation of serious labor abuses, including slavery, that are linked to the supply of seafood for American markets and restaurants.

2016 also marked the completion of celebrated architectural projects that were the realization of prolonged efforts to address tragedies in America's past. Replacing the train station destroyed in the 9/11 attacks in New York in 2001, the World Trade Center Transportation Hub was officially opened in March. With five tracks, four platforms, and an expansive mezzanine built below National September 11 Memorial Plaza, the new station features an elliptical dome of white steel ribs rising from the ground meant to suggest a dove taking flight. In September, the National Museum of African American History and Culture opened in its permanent home on the National Mall in Washington, D.C. In 1915, African American veterans of the Union Army began the attempts to establish a national museum for their history. Their efforts were restarted in the 1980s by U.S. Representatives John Lewis and Mickey Leland and again in the 2000s by U.S. Representatives John Lewis and J. C. Watts. The building's design, which reflects the leading contributions of African American architect J. Max Bond Jr. and Ghanaian British architect David Adjaye, is inspired by the three-tiered crowns in West African Yoruban art. The building's bronze-colored metal lattice, which creates a symbolic openness to light and dialogue, recalls the intricate ironwork of enslaved African Americans.

As in other years, enduring achievements in chemistry, economics, literature, medicine, peace, and physics garnered Nobel Prizes. Bob Dylan became the first musician to win the Nobel Prize for Literature. His selection represented a departure for the Nobel Foundation, but it also signaled the Foundation's firm commitment to the humanistic values underlying Dylan's most-memorable lyrics. Characterizing 2016 as "a time when prejudice and outright fabrications are gaining ground at the expense of knowledge [and] when human rights are challenged and many live under a constant threat of violence," Foundation director Lars Heikensten emphasized that the Nobel Prize "stands for enlightenment, humanism and international cooperation" (1). For Heikensten, the Foundation's celebration of work grounded in "science, facts and knowledge" was an essential response to the "proliferation of myths, misconceptions and lies" (1). Yet despite calls by Heikensten and others for coordinated actions to remedy global challenges, the year's technology breakthroughs were not focused on addressing climate change or alleviating suffering but instead expanded the divide between the financial elite and the rest of world. New blockchain transactions facilitated secure asset trading. IBM, Google, and Microsoft developed ways to accelerate machine learning and improve robots' dexterity. New, unregulated gene editing techniques for crops tacitly enhanced transnational corporations' control of global food supplies.

In the United States, 2016 was also marred by violence. There were more than 38,000 firearm-related deaths; suicides counted for almost two-thirds and the remaining 11,000 gun-related homicides represented a sharp increase from the previous year. The Orlando nightclub shooting became the country's worst mass killing, and the event confirmed the reality of right-wing domestic terrorism and the continuing vulnerability of the LGBTQ+ community. Despite media coverage, U.S. police continued to shoot African American men, with Alton Sterling, Philando Castile, and Delrawn Small killed within a week of each other in July. Throughout 2016, the Black Lives Matter movement, initiated in 2013 by Alicia Garza, Patrisse Cullors, and Opal Tometi, protested these and the many other African American deaths during the year.

Nationwide, the race-baiting that distinguished the campaign of presidential candidate Donald Trump confirmed that, despite the eight-year term of Barack Obama, the United States had not become a postracial society. The bruising campaign that eventually offered voters a choice between Hillary Clinton and the reality TV star was exacerbated by subsequently discredited social media campaigns, and it made crisis, chaos, and national division a constant subject of discussion. Facebook, the most widely used platform in the world with 1.79 billion monthly users, became a major source of propaganda and conspiracy theory misinformation.

Sports provided some welcome distraction from the country's cultural fissures. In June, despite fans' respect for the Golden State Warriors, they applauded the Cleveland Cavaliers' hard-fought victory in the National Basketball Association playoff, as the win represented the first title for a major Cleveland sports franchise since 1964. In October, fans celebrated as the Chicago Cubs baseball team made their first appearance in the World Series since 1945 and enjoyed their first World Series win since 1908. In response to the killing of African Americans, Colin Kaepernick, then quarterback for the San Francisco 49ers, knelt during the singing of the National Anthem, thus beginning protests by U.S. football players who felt it their duty to make a public statement about the systemic racism shaping the actions of the country's police.

2016 also saw the passing of individuals who had inspired and enriched people's lives: astronaut and U.S. Senator John Glenn; musicians David Bowie, Prince, Leonard Cohen, Glenn Frey, and George Michael; movie actors Debbie Reynolds, Gene Wilder, Alan Rickman, Jon Polito, Bill Nunn, Patty Duke, and George Kennedy; directors Jacques Rivette, Ettore Scola, Garry Marshall, Hector Babenco, Curtis Hanson, Abbas Kiarostami, Michael Cimino, and Andrzej Wajda; and authors Dario Fo, W. P. Kinsella, Elie Wiesel, Peter Shaffer, Edward Albee, Michael Herr, Pat Conroy, Harper Lee, and Umberto Eco.

Cultural and Industrial Developments in Hollywood

Decisions by the Academy of Motion Picture Arts and Sciences also prompted public responses. Calls for diversity sparked by the January 2015 #OscarsSoWhite post by April Reign reignited when the 2016 nominations were announced; for the second year in a row, all the nominees for acting awards were white. The resoundingly negative response to the 2016 nominations led the Academy to announce rule changes to increase voting opportunities for new and potentially more diverse members. Skeptical of what seemed to be a public relations move, directors Ava DuVernay and Ryan Coogler organized a Flint water crisis charity event on 28 February as an alternative to the Oscar awards ceremony. Still, the unequivocal objections to the nominations provided evidence that the "cultural zeitgeist" had made inclusion a priority (Lauzen). Asked about the controversy, President Obama explained, "I think when everybody's story is told, then that makes for better art. That makes for better entertainment. It makes everybody feel part of one American family" (Rosen).

Yet some American audiences saw certain 2016 films as assaults on their cherished memories. *Ghostbusters*, directed by Paul Feig and starring Leslie Jones, Melissa McCarthy, Kate McKinnon, and Kristen Wiig, was met by a backlash from "Ghostbros, the noisiest if not most numerous contingent, for whom reviving the franchise with women in the leading roles [was] the ultimate desecration" (Adams). Other audiences enjoyed the experience of seeing diverse characters in films. For instance, 2016 included films deemed worth watching by the nation's most disenfranchised citizens, Indigenous Americans. An article recapping the year's offerings in *Indian Country Today* explains that in *Hell or High Water*, deputy Gil Birmingham's "Comanche-Mexican character gets to lay down a history lesson in about 60 words that any Native actor would love to get the chance to do" (Jacobs). Discussing "Native actor, Adam Beach, [who] makes a brief appearance as Slipknot" in *Suicide Squad*, the article points out that it "is difficult for a Native actor to get screen time in a major feature film [so this] is a victory" (Jacobs). The article highlights other films starring Indigenous actors, including *Certain Women* with Lily Gladstone and *Songs My Brothers Taught Me* with Irene Bedard, the model for and voice of *Pocahontas* (1995).

More visibly, 2016 revealed Hollywood's wholesale investment in spectacular CGI-enhanced franchise and cinematic universe films. While this trend was spurred on by the success of *Iron Man* (2008) and fueled by competition between Marvel films distributed by Disney and DC films distributed by Warner Bros., it is significant that in 2016 the Hollywood studios released more "sequels, reboots, adaptations, and animated movies" than in any year before (Fritz xviii). In 2009, the majors released only eighteen films that fit this profile; in 2015, the total was twenty-four (Fritz xviii). However, in 2016, the majors released thirty-seven films that reflected popular animation trends or belonged to franchises like *Star Wars* or the cinematic universes featuring Marvel or DC characters (Fritz xviii). The glut of sequels and reboots led to many commercial failures, yet four of the year's top five films, *Rogue One*, *Finding Dory*, *Captain America: Civil War*, and *The Jungle Book*, belonged to established product lines. Together with the fourth-ranked film, *The Secret Life of Pets*, they captured a remarkable 22 percent of the $11.3 billion domestic market (Fritz 229).

2016 was also distinguished by milestones in the rising importance of international film audiences. As industry experts point out, in the twenty-first century, the international "box office exploded, from $8.6 billion in 2001 to $27.2 billion in 2016" (Fritz 22). Notably, the "biggest driver of growth" was China; its box office grosses went from $248 million in 2005 to $2 billion in 2011 to $6.6 billion in 2016, with Chinese figures "expected to surpass U.S. box office before the end of the decade" (Fritz 22). 2016 also marked the first year China had more screens than the United States: 41,179 in China compared to 40,759 in the United States (Brzeski).

Disney's 2016 offerings, which included the animated film *Zootopia* and the live-action CGI film *The Jungle Book* based on Disney's 1967 animated feature and the novels of Rudyard Kipling, made it the year's most profitable studio. Disney's success depended on the fact that nearly all its films "fit into a narrowly defined brand that supports big-budget franchises, such as Marvel superheroes, Star Wars space adventures, Pixar and Disney animated films, or live-action remakes of animated classics" (Fritz 144). Moreover, films that contributed to the Disney brand continued to be rated PG (some profanity, violence, or brief nudity that requires parental guidance) or PG-13 (some drug use, brief nudity, use of "one of the harsher sexually-derived words, though only as an expletive," and depictions of violence that are "generally not both realistic and extreme or persistent") (MPAA 7).

With Disney in the lead, Hollywood films filled their long-established role as an escape from daily life. In 2016, domestic box-office percentages by MPAA rating showed an increased interest in PG-rated movies. In previous (2014 and 2015) and subsequent years (2017 and 2018), R-rated films averaged between $13 and $18 million in the domestic market. However, in 2016, R-rated films averaged only $11 million. Moreover, this drop for R-rated films did not affect the pattern of PG-13 films securing the largest percentage (usually at least 50 percent) of domestic box-office grosses. Instead, the difference was due to PG films having an especially strong year. The extraordinary commercial success of films like *Finding Dory*, *The Secret Life of Pets*, *The Jungle Book*, *Zootopia*, and *Sing* was a distinguishing feature of American cinema in 2016 and perhaps a sign of audiences seeking distraction from economic insecurity and social tensions in American life.

Rogue One: A Bellwether of 2016 Trends

Revealing astute market research and an embrace of multiculturalism, *Rogue One: A Star Wars Story*, directed by Gareth Edwards and released by Disney distribution division Buena Vista, had a visibly diverse cast. The film featured rising British actress Felicity Jones as Jyn Erso, a cynical young woman who discovers the value of fighting for a just cause and thus leads a disparate band of Rebel Alliance members to obtain crucial information about the Death Star designed unwillingly by her father (Mads Mikkelsen). Opening in December, the $200,000,000 production became the highest-grossing 2016 release in the domestic market (the United States, Canada, Puerto Rico, and Guam), surpassing the animated Buena Vista film *Finding Dory*. *Rogue One* was second worldwide to the Marvel cinematic universe film *Captain America: Civil War* directed by Anthony and Joe Russo and distributed by Buena Vista. As an addition to the *Star Wars* franchise, which Disney acquired in its purchase of Lucasfilm in 2012, *Rogue One* was well suited to the lucrative synergies that Disney generated among its films, theme parks, and consumer products. The film's PG-13 rating (persistent and extreme violence but no realistic depictions of violence's effects) also fit the Disney brand.

As one of the year's spectacular CGI-enhanced franchise films, *Rogue One* delivered the fantastic landscapes and action sequences that audiences expected. Its use of CGI to create the portrayals of Princess Leia and Grand Moff Tarkin also signaled an escalation in the use of digital technology to create performances by human characters. Films had used CGI before when an actor had passed away during production, for example, for Oliver Reed in *Gladiator* (2000) and Paul Walker in *Furious 7* (2015). Yet *Rogue One* set out from the start to use CGI to create certain performances. The film's closing moments feature a pasty, round-cheeked digital rendering of young Carrie Fisher as Princess Leia, an image that became particularly unsettling when Fisher passed away just weeks after the film opened. Fans also rankled at seeing the late Peter Cushing's CGI likeness used to create cold-hearted Grand Moff Tarkin, the character he had portrayed in the 1977 *Star Wars* film. Tarkin, generated in part through a motion capture performance by Guy Henry, appears in scenes throughout *Rogue One*.

Far outweighing these negative reactions, *Rogue One*'s commercial success depended in part on casting choices with appeal to audiences in key markets. The comedic and touching partnership of Chirrut Imwe, embodied by Hong Kong actor and martial artist Donnie Yen, and Baze Malbus, played by Chinese actor-writer-director Jiang Wen, prompted many domestic and international audiences to see the relationship between these Asian characters as the heart of the film. By 2016, the career of Donnie Yen, known to audiences as the star of the Ip Man films (2008, 2010, 2015), included more than sixty film and television credits that had made him an international star. Jiang Wen, who became an acclaimed actor and director in the 1980s, had garnered international honors as a director with his film *Guizi lai le* (*Devils on the Doorstep*, 2010) and had been named an Outstanding Contributor to Chinese Cinema at the 2014 Shanghai International Film Festival.

Casting in *Rogue One* revealed other pragmatic choices designed to reach diverse international and domestic audiences. Employing the contemporary Hollywood approach of casting African American actors as isolated figures of authority, *Rogue One* featured actor-producer-director Forest Whitaker as Saw Gerrera, Jyn's foster father and the Black militant outsider at odds with the ostensibly multicultural but largely white-dominated Rebel Alliance. Whitaker's performance made his character's brief appearance memorable. When Bodhi Rook (Riz Ahmed), the pilot who brings a message from Jyn's father, is brought before him, Whitaker makes Saw a truly terrifying character. He not only punctuates his menacing statements with deep breaths drawn from his oxygen mask, he eventually allows the mask to snap back into place without flinching or breaking his glare. Then, when Jyn shows up at Saw's hideout right after Bodhi's arrival, Whitaker deftly communicates Saw's evolving emotions. Here, he uses vivid facial and vocal expressions to convey Saw's emotional transition from hostile distrust to sorrowful anguish to gentle compassion for the young woman he raised. Like Donnie Yen and Jiang Wen, Whitaker's casting and performance contributed to the film's appeal for diverse audiences. As industry experts explain, "African-Americans and Asian-Americans showed up in force at the box office in 2016 as major movies showed greater diversity in their casting and subject matter" (Lang).

To attract additional domestic and international audiences, *Rogue One* also featured British-born South Asian actor and rapper Riz Ahmed, whose acclaimed performances in Dan Gilroy's *Four Lions* (2010) and *Nightcrawler* (2014) established his association with complex Muslim characters. In *Rogue One*, his character is motivated by a need to "get right" with himself because he had worked for the Empire. Bodhi's need for redemption and the torture that the implicitly Middle Eastern character must endure at Saw's hideout tacitly link him to xenophobic narratives concerning Muslim people. Yet once Bodhi embarks on the heroes' shared mission to capture the Death Star plans, Ahmed's performance creates a unique and engaging character who is quietly capable and giddily enthusiastic to be part of the team. Ahmed's large expressive eyes, well-timed quips, and lithe, energy-filled body make Bodhi the character who most directly conveys the fun and excitement of the space adventure.

Cassian Andor, a spy for the Rebel Alliance and Jyn's adversary at the outset, also joins the dangerous quest, largely to redeem himself. With Mexican actor Diego Luna as Cassian, *Rogue One* reproduced stereotypes of Hispanic men as dangerous (and in need of redemption). Yet Luna infuses his portrayal with a vulnerability that makes Cassian more complex, and shot selections allow audiences to read the emotions that cross his face. Moreover, by casting Luna in the co-starring role, Disney appealed to domestic Latinx audiences who made up not only 18 percent of the U.S. population but 24 percent of domestic audiences in 2016 and who would be familiar with Luna's roles in *Elysium* (2013) and the animated film *The Book of Life* (2014) (National Hispanic Media Coalition 2). The film also had value for international Spanish-speaking audiences familiar with Luna's career as an actor whose breakout performance in *Y tu mamá tambien* (2001) had garnered international awards.

The diversity of the *Rogue One* cast was key to its success in domestic and international markets. It also prompted a negative response from white nationalists, who objected to the film even before its release. Sparring with *Rogue One* screenwriter Chris Weitz and story author Gary Whitta on social media, white supremacists condemned what they saw as the film's anti-white agenda, and they initiated an unsuccessful call to boycott the film using the hashtag #DumpStarWars. As "the film's far-right backlash reached its boiling point, Disney CEO Bob Iger, a prominent member of Trump's presidential transition team, declared that *Rogue One* 'was not a political movie'" (Stern). Yet as one industry expert noted, "Given how candidate Trump rode a wave of xenophobia into the White House, the notion of a multicultural coalition—led by a woman and a Hispanic man—taking down the Empire seemed pretty darn political to viewers with any grasp of sub-text" (Stern).

Owen Gleiberman's review in *Variety*, "It May Be an Accident, but 'Rogue One' Is the Most Politically Relevant Movie of the Year," echoed that insight and argued that the film "was one of those rare movies that hits

Diego Luna and Felicity Jones as the multiethnic couple at the center of *Rogue One* (Gareth Edwards, Lucasfilm, Disney). Digital frame enlargement.

theaters with a timing that's nearly karmic." Highlighting "the multiethnic cast, led by the Mexican-born Diego Luna's utilitarian cool," Gleiberman found it "galvanizing" to see *Rogue One* carrying the message that there "will always be a weak point" in the plans of "those who attempt to rule by controlling everything." Reflecting on the political environment in 2016 "where you'd be hard pressed to pinpoint where Donald Trump's fantasies leave off and his political policies begin," Gleiberman observed that the situation "was brought to you, in part by the paradigm shift in pop culture ignited 40 years ago by 'Star Wars.'" Still, for him, *Rogue One*'s message to defend the good cause even when it seemed hopeless had "a special power" for audiences troubled by the rising influence of a politician who left "reality-based thinking in the dustbin of history."

Progressive Mid-Budget Commercial and Critical Successes

Arrival, directed by Denis Villeneuve and distributed by Paramount, featured another team tasked with a seemingly impossible mission, and it too drew on science fiction conventions to create a story that attracted audiences aligned with progressive values. The film starred Amy Adams as linguist Louise Banks and Jeremy Renner as physicist Ian Donnelly who were hired by the U.S. military to communicate with one of the twelve groups of aliens who have mysteriously arrived at different locations around the globe. Cast once again as an experienced figure of authority, Forest Whitaker plays Colonel Weber, who handpicks Louise and Ian as the team that must find a way to avoid violent confrontation with the aliens. The film's pacifist message resonated with a wide audience. The $47 million production garnered over $100 million in the domestic market, making it the twenty-ninth highest-grossing film of the year.

The script for *Arrival* was developed at Twentieth Century-Fox, but the studio did not move the project into production because executives thought the linguist should be a male role. Securing independent financing from Lava Bear Films, FilmNation Entertainment, and Reliance Entertainment, producers Shawn Levy, Dan Levine, and David Linde sold the package, which included director Denis Villeneuve and stars Amy Adams and Jeremy Renner, to Paramount for $20 million in 2014. The deal stipulated that the production team retain creative control, and the resulting film prompted *IndieWire* columnist Anne Thompson to note, "Paramount is releasing this brainy sci-fi drama, but there's no way that this film's smart script and unique visuals would have survived a studio's development process."

Compared to *Contact* (1997) starring Jodie Foster and *Gravity* (2013) featuring Sandra Bullock, *Arrival* traces the transformation of Louise's way of seeing the world, which results from her exploration of the nonlinear language used by the aliens, known as heptapods due to their seven arthropod-like limbs that open into starfish-like hands. With Louise's profound personal transformation at the center of a larger story about the value of cooperation and communication among people from around the world, reviewers saw *Arrival* as carrying "an extraordinarily hopeful message for a particularly grim moment in global affairs" when isolationism and nationalism were "on the rise in the U.S. and elsewhere" (Sims).

Like *Rogue One*, *Arrival* seemed "tailor-made for 2016, dropping into theaters mere days after the most explosive election in most of the American electorate's memory" (Wilkinson). Its progressive narrative about human and alien contact showed that empathy and a win-win, non-zero-sum approach had significant value, especially in a world marred by distrust, divisiveness, and xenophobia. Reviewers saw *Arrival*'s humanistic message conveyed by all aspects of the film, noting, for example, that the fluid imagery created by cinematographer Bradford Young was visually stunning but always human-centered (Desowitz). In the sessions Louise and Ian have with the heptapods in the ship's inner chamber, the two aliens occupy a space behind a massive luminous screen which illuminates the faces of Adams and Renner, their expressions conveying their initial fear and their sustained amazement. Reviewer Robbie Collin proposed that in these scenes, Young "lingers on Adams' face, because *Arrival* is a film that values the human reaction to something eerie or wondrous as much as the eeriness or wondrousness itself."

The film's cinematic and narrative concentration on human emotion also conveyed the implications of its underlying story about Louise's decision to marry Ian and have a child even with the knowledge of the tragedy ahead. Prompted by the handheld shots that create "warm, naturalistic portraitures" of Louise's time with her daughter, reviewers saw *Arrival* as being about "acceptance, understanding our life's choices, and living as if any one moment were as valuable or meaningful as the next" (Statt). Highlighting the engaging performance by Amy Adams, Manohla Dargis found that she turned "softness and quiet into heroic qualities" in her interactions with her daughter, her partner and husband Ian, the heptapods, and world leaders ("Aliens"). In doing so, Adams's portrayal anchored the solace that *Arrival* offered American audiences bruised by the year's cultural strife.

Hidden Figures, directed by Theodore Melfi and distributed by Twentieth Century-Fox, also used human interactions with space to lend credence to progressive social values. Here, again, the narrative conveys the importance of teamwork when facing challenges, in this case those arising from racism, sexism, and the Cold War space race. Amplifying the presence of women in *Rogue One* and *Arrival*, *Hidden Figures* explores the shared experiences of three women, who are themselves connected to their families, their church, and their colleagues. Set in 1961 at the National Aeronautics and Space Administration (NASA) facility in Hampton, Virginia, the historical drama introduced audiences to three of the African American women who contributed to the early U.S. space program. It features Taraji P. Henson as mathematician Katherine Johnson, Octavia Spencer as computer programmer Dorothy Vaughan, and Janelle Monáe as aeronautics engineer Mary Jackson.

The $25 million production was fourteenth in the 2016 domestic market, grossing almost $170 million. This commercial success is noteworthy. *Hidden Figures* was one of only five films in the top twenty-five not associated with a franchise, cinematic universe, or entertainment brand. The other mid-budget films in this group include *La La Land*, the musical starring Ryan Gosling and Emma Stone; *Central Intelligence*, the buddy action comedy starring Dwayne Johnson and Kevin Hart; *Sully*, about the pilot who safely landed an airliner on New York City's Hudson River in 2009; and *Bad Moms*, a comedy about three moms who rebel against the constraints of suburban motherhood.

Like *Arrival*, *Hidden Figures* resulted from the work of well-placed independent producers. Established producer Donna Gigliotti secured the rights to Margot Lee Shetterly's nonfiction book; former News Corp. president Peter Chernin's company arranged co-financing with Jamal Daniel's Levantine Films. Fox 2000 Pictures purchased the rights to the project because *Hidden Figures* fit its mission to produce films for underserved audiences; its parent company, Twentieth Century-Fox, distributed the film. Echoing the acclaim (including an Oscar nomination) that African American cinematographer Bradford Young received for his work on *Arrival*, department heads on *Hidden Figures* also garnered industry notice. The crew included Australian cinematographer Mandy Walker and production designer Wynn Thomas, known for his work on many of Spike Lee's films, including *Malcolm X* (1992). Thomas would go on to win the Art Directors Guild Award for Period Film, and he was named Production Designer of the Year by the Hollywood Film Awards. Costume designer Renée Ehrlich Kalfus won the Costume Designers Guild Award for Best Costume Design—Period Film.

Reviewers consistently noted that the stylish, richly colored clothing worn by Taraji P. Henson, Octavia Spencer, and Janelle Monáe made them significant figures, especially when seen with the scores of white male NASA employees in white shirts and black slacks or the handful of white female employees in muted colors. In a series on mid-century women's costume design in film and television, fashion and cultural critics Tom Fitzgerald and Lorenzo Marquez illustrate ways that the film's costume choices convey the distinctive qualities of the three central characters. They observe that Henson's mathematics genius "favors full skirts, defined waists, prints and traditionally feminine detailing," which set her "as far apart as possible from the men who surround her." They note that Spencer's pro-gramming pioneer "dresses the most business-like," which signals both "her ambitions to land a supervisor role and her skill with computers." They explain that as the younger member of the trio, Monáe's engineering wiz wears "body-skimming dresses with bold print details," headscarves, and even sometimes pants. Yet Fitzgerald and Marquez astutely emphasize that these costuming choices do not simply support the uniqueness of the three central characters. Instead, because every "neckline, sleeve, waist, skirt length, silhouette, jewelry choice and color [is] meticulously distinct," when the three women are seen together there is something "almost iconic about the image." In their view, the "eye-catching, flattering, iconic, pedestal-raising looks that set the heroes apart from everyone else" make their attire "superhero costumes" and the historical figures superheroes.

Hidden Figures garnered wide critical acclaim. It was nominated for three Academy Awards: Best Picture, Best Supporting Actress (Octavia Spencer), and Best Adapted Screenplay (Allison Schroeder and Theodore Melfi). It won a collection of awards, including recognition from the Screen Actors Guild, the Women Film Critics Circle, and the NAACP's Image

Janelle Monáe, Taraji P. Henson, and Octavia Spencer in *Hidden Figures* (Theodore Melfi, Twentieth Century-Fox). Digital frame enlargement.

Awards. Yet even audiences who supported the film's interest in depicting untold American stories expressed concerns about the film's presentation of historical events. Critics recognized that some characters were fictional or composite characters, yet they objected to the film's misrepresentation of social norms at NASA in the 1960s.

Critics noted that when the National Aeronautics and Space Administration (NASA) replaced the National Advisory Committee for Aeronautics (NACA) in 1958, NASA abolished segregated working environments. They pointed out that the depiction of Katherine/Henson repeatedly running to a bathroom in a different building is based on a story that engineer Mary Jackson "told about the NACA in the 1950s" (Larsen). They noted that while Octavia Spencer's character Dorothy Vaughan had been "denied the supervisory position she deserved for some time," by the time "the film opens in 1961, Vaughn had already been a supervisor for 3 years" (Larsen). A. E. Larsen argues, "Had it chosen to, the film could have made its point more honestly by contrasting the comparatively accepting environment of NASA with the much more racist environment beyond its gates." Critics also objected to the scene in which Al Harrison (Kevin Costner) uses a crowbar to take down the Colored Ladies Room sign, finding that the scene exemplified ways that the film pandered to white audiences.

Acknowledging that the mainstream American film industry consistently defers to white financiers and audiences, reviewers proposed that *Hidden Figures* still effectively conveyed "the poisonous normalcy of white supremacy" and provided "a rousing celebration of merit rewarded and perseverance repaid" (Scott). Some reviewers also highlighted connections between *Hidden Figures* and *Loving*, the 2016 historical drama about Mildred and Richard Loving, the couple whose interracial marriage was eventually sanctioned by the 1967 U.S. Supreme Court decision in *Loving v. Virginia*. Framing both films as pertinent to American society in 2016, A. O. Scott found that *Hidden Figures* "makes a fascinating and timely companion" to the historical drama starring Ruth Negga and Joel Edgerton. Reviewers also compared *Hidden Figures* to Mira Nair's 2016 film *Queen of Katwe*, an historical drama about Phiona Mutesi, a young Ugandan woman who overcomes poverty and sexism to become an international chess champion.

Reviewers saw *Hidden Figures* as especially significant in 2016 because, in contrast to the racism and divisiveness fueled by white supremacist politicians and right-wing media coverage, the film illuminates the subjectivity of its central characters of color and emphasizes the value of mutual support. Reviewer Lanika Cruz noted that *Hidden Figures* "celebrates individual mettle, but also the way its characters consistently try to lift others up."

Highlighting that the film frames the exceptional characters as family- and community-centered people who "go to church and neighborhood barbecues and spend time with their children," she found that with "the complex social forces that shaped its characters' lives still so relevant today, *Hidden Figures* is powerful precisely because it's *not* a solo portrait."

Like *Hidden Figures*, *Arrival*, and especially *Rogue One*, the 2016 version of *The Magnificent Seven*, directed by African American director Antoine Fuqua and distributed by Sony Pictures, also featured distinctive characters working as a supportive team to face a daunting opponent. *The Magnificent Seven* amplified its message about the value of respect and collaboration by emphasizing the partnership between the townspeople and the seven men who agree to fight for their town. A remake of the 1960 John Sturges film, itself based on Akira Kurosawa's 1954 classic *Seven Samurai*, the 2016 film sharpened its progressive message by identifying the townspeople's evil opponent, Bartholomew Bogue (Peter Sarsgaard), with capitalist greed. The $90 million production had a domestic gross of $93 million, making it the thirty-second highest-grossing film of 2016. Like other domestic box-office leaders, *The Magnificent Seven* secured additional income, which led to a $162 million worldwide gross and an additional $40 million in domestic home market sales (DVD and Blu-Ray).

The film features a diverse cast and a narrative that aligns the audience with small-town individuals fighting against impersonal corporate avarice. Signaling its departure from the 1960 film, in Fuqua's *The Magnificent Seven* the search for help to fight the villains is led by Emma Cullen (Haley Bennett), a determined young woman whose husband is killed by Bogue in the film's opening sequence. Her search leads her to former Union soldier and warrant officer Sam Chisholm (Denzel Washington), who takes the assignment because he sees her cause as righteous and because he seeks vengeance for the deaths of his mother and sisters at the hands of Bogue's men years earlier. Washington assumes the role played by Yul Brynner in the 1960 film, but in discussing Washington's portrayals in *Man on Fire* (2004), *The Book of Eli* (2010), and *The Magnificent Seven*, Manohla Dargis argues that he takes on the "defender-savior" role that John Wayne once embodied so persuasively ("Denzel"). Here, his portrayals recall Wayne's "tough but melancholy," fearless characters; having already lost everything, they have nothing left to lose (Tasker 95). Yet the Harris Poll of America's Favorite Movie Stars shows that the two actors resonate with different cultural constituencies: Washington's fans include women and left-leaning Democratic voters; Wayne's are male and right-leaning Republicans (Baron 17).

Appealing to the progressive audiences in Washington's fan base, *The Magnificent Seven* presents Josh Farady (Chris Pratt) as someone who redeems himself, making the transformation from a shallow, self-centered, hedonistic, racist con artist to someone willing to sacrifice himself to save the lives of others. Similarly, former Confederate sharpshooter Goodnight Robicheaux (Ethan Hawke) gains respect when he belatedly overcomes his cowardice and shows he is willing to fight for a just cause. Mountain man Jack Horne (Vincent D'Onofrio), who shares Chisholm's investment in righteous justice from the start, expresses the underlying motivation for all the fighters in his remark before the final battle: "To be in the service of others, with men I respect, like you all, I shouldn't have to ask for more than that."

The 1960 film had two ethnic characters in its group of seven fighters: the Mexican character Chico, played by German actor Horst Buchholz, and the Mexican Irish character Bernardo O'Reilly, played by Charles Bronson of Lithuanian descent. Reflecting progressive values in 2016, Fuqua's film expands the number of diverse roles, casts actors whose ethnicity matches their characters, and illuminates their unique perspectives. Vasquez, played by Manuel Garcia-Rulfo, joins the mission to defend the townspeople only because Chisholm offers to tear up his arrest warrant if he helps. Yet Vasquez not only proves himself a capable fighter, he also efficiently exposes Robicheaux's white supremacist notions when the former Confederate describes his grandfather's opponents at the Alamo as "a horde of teeming brown devils." Deftly complicating Robicheaux's narrative, Vasquez responds: "My grandfather was one of those devils, you know. Toluca Battalion. Hey, maybe my grandfather killed your grandfather, huh?"

In addition, Martin Sensmeier, who grew up in the Tlingit Coastal Community in Alaska, portrays the Native American character Red Harvest who "finds his own path" by joining the just cause. During the final battle, he saves Emma from Denali (Jonathan Joss), the Native American character who fights for Bogue; besting him in their isolated combat, Red Harvest angrily tells Denali, "You are a disgrace" to Indigenous people. The cast also includes Korean star Lee Byung-hun as Billy Rocks, an expert with knives and guns who travels the country with Robicheaux. Lee became an international star with films like *A Bittersweet Life* (2005) and *The Good, the Bad, and the Weird* (2008). Like Chisholm, Vasquez, and Red Harvest, his character helps to create a more diverse picture of the American West in the years following the Civil War.

By focusing on a multiethnic group as they prepare for and fight a spectacle-filled battle, *The Magnificent Seven* follows the well-worn conventions

The multiethnic characters of *The Magnificent Seven* (Antoine Fuqua, MGM, Columbia) who battle the real estate mogul. Digital frame enlargement.

of the Hollywood war film. Yet the differences between the 1960 film starring Yul Brynner and the 2016 film led by Denzel Washington reveal the film's alignment with contemporary progressive values. The 1960 film is set in a Mexican village, and thus the largely white gunfighters enter as conquering heroes, with some of them joining the mission in the hope it involves finding hidden treasure. It also maintains a visual and narrative contrast between the Mexican peasants and the well-armed mercenaries. By comparison, the 2016 film is set in the American West, so while there are distinctions between the homesteaders and the nomadic men who join their cause, the pioneers and the seven fighters share a vision of the West as a landscape that promises individual freedom. Referring to Emma as Joan of Arc, Chisholm makes it clear that the group of seven works for her and the townspeople. While there are comical scenes of the townspeople learning to use firearms, the opening scenes establish them as brave, principled people, and scenes of them preparing for and engaging in battle present them as entirely capable, including the moment when Emma saves Chisholm's life in his final confrontation with Bogue.

Equally important, in the 1960 film the villain (Eli Wallach) belongs to a band of Mexican outlaws that reflects racist stereotypes, while the 2016 film frames the villain as a ruthless real estate baron, for whom injury to other people is a part of doing business. Crowing about his success in exploiting people, Bogue states: "If God didn't want them to be sheared, he wouldn't have made them sheep." Bogue's nonfictional 2016 counterpart did not use this exact line in public, but it captured the sentiment behind his disparaging remarks about the country's most-disenfranchised people. Progressive audiences could thus find a certain consolation in Bogue's defeat in *The Magnificent Seven*, especially when the African American (Chisholm), the Hispanic American (Vasquez), and the Native American (Red Harvest) live to fight another day.

■ Personal Stories in the Age of Obama and the Black Lives Matter Movement

The commercial success of mid-budget films like *Arrival, Hidden Figures*, and *The Magnificent Seven* in 2016 is notable, since the rise of streaming services and the subsequent drop in DVD sales combined with the studios' increased reliance on franchise and cinematic universe films had greatly reduced Hollywood's interest in distributing mid-budget films. Similarly, with writer-producers now at the center of the studios' most lucrative endeavors (television series and cinematic universe films), the majors were less inclined to green-light projects initiated by actors and directors. Yet in 2016, films that reflected the studios' earlier focus on productions led by actors and directors still captured spots in the top 100 domestic box-office rankings. For example, Mel Gibson's Icon Productions was integral to *Hacksaw Ridge*, about a Seventh-day Adventist conscientious objector in World War II. Tom Hanks's Playtone Productions was one of the production companies behind *My Big Fat Greek Wedding 2*. Casey Affleck's Affleck/Middleton Project helped produce the acclaimed film *Manchester by the Sea*. Drew Barrymore's Flower Films shepherded the comedy *How to Be Single* into production. Smoke House Pictures, led by George Clooney and Grant Heslov, helped produce *Money Monster* directed by Jodie Foster. Brad Pitt's Plan B Entertainment was one of the production companies behind *Moonlight*.

Other 2016 productions depended on the visible and behind-the-scenes contributions of A-list actors. *Fences*, directed by and co-starring Denzel Washington, was produced by Scott Rudin, who had produced the Broadway revival of August Wilson's Pulitzer Prize–winning play *Fences*, the sixth in his ten-part "Pittsburgh Cycle" centered on the lives of African Americans. The Christmas Day Paramount release had a domestic box office gross of $57 million, making it the fifty-seventh highest-grossing film of the year. The $24 million production found critical acclaim. It received nominations for Best Picture and Best Actor (Washington). Viola Davis won the Oscar, the Golden Globe, and the BAFTA for Best Supporting Actress. It garnered other recognition, including Screen Actors Guild and NAACP Image Awards for Washington and Davis.

Like Wilson's 1985 play and its 2010 Tony Award–winning revival starring Denzel Washington and Viola Davis, the 2016 film takes audiences into the world of a Black working-class family living in segregated Pittsburgh in the 1950s. The film vividly illuminates the shattered dreams of Troy Mason (Washington), who has spent his life working as a garbage collector because segregation policies made his aspirations to be a professional baseball player impossible. It also fully renders the broken or deferred dreams of his family. His wife Rose (Davis) loses her husband to another woman, a crushing blow to someone whose central desire is to have a stable family. Their son Cory (Jovan Adepo) wants to be an athlete like his father, but Troy refuses to allow this, afraid that his son will end up like him. Troy's son Lyons (Russell Hornsby) wants to be a musician but spends time in jail for writing bad checks. After suffering a severe head injury in World War II, Troy's brother Gabriel (Mykelti Williamson) can now do little more than chase the "hellhounds" he imagines.

As if the brutality of Troy's upbringing and lifetime of disenfranchisement were not enough to bear, even opportunities for fresh starts do not retain their promise. He eventually wins the right to be the city's first African American garbage truck driver, only to discover that the job cuts him off from the camaraderie he had enjoyed when hauling trash from the sidewalk to the truck. Troy's natural charisma allows him to start a separate life with a woman who becomes pregnant with his child. Finally telling Rose about the situation, Troy hopes he can be part of both families, but Rose and Cory close him out, and when his mistress dies in childbirth, Troy becomes a man alone, even when Rose agrees to raise the child as her own. The film ends with the family brought together for Troy's funeral, their generosity of spirit overcoming the anger and despair his thoughtlessness had engendered. The film's critical and commercial success reflected its ability to illuminate the humanity of each of the characters. Costume, setting, casting, and performance choices carried a specificity that communicated each character's uniqueness, and the film's rich, carefully coordinated color palette illustrated the dreams and demons leading each character along their path. *Fences* so fully rendered the experiences of one family living in a Black neighborhood in Pittsburgh in the 1950s that for progressive audiences, their story was an American story.

Barry Jenkins's film *Moonlight*, a $4 million production distributed by independent studio A24, also resonated with audiences interested in seeing everyone's story told. The three-part narrative follows Chiron as a shy child, teenager, and young adult, whose only experience of sexual intimacy is with his outgoing friend Kevin. Despite its microbudget, *Moonlight* garnered a domestic box-office gross of $27 million, putting it in the top 100 films for 2016. Upon its release, the film received substantial critical acclaim.

That recognition translated into Oscar awards and nominations the following year, becoming the first film with an all-Black cast and the first LGBTQ+ film to win Best Picture. Barry Jenkins and Tarell Alvin McCraney won for Best Adapted Screenplay. Mahershala Ali, who portrays Juan, the self-disciplined drug dealer who serves as Chiron's father figure, became the first Muslim actor to receive an Oscar (Best Supporting Actor). Joi McMillon became the first African American to be nominated for Best Achievement in Film Editing.

Using silence, sparse dialogue, long takes, and an austere, evolving score, *Moonlight* deftly illustrates Chiron's pain and isolation as well as his complexity, fragility, and emotional courage. Reviewers were especially taken by scenes depicting Chiron's fleeting moments of authentic human contact. Discussing the interlude in which Juan teaches Chiron to float in the ocean, Joanna DiMatta notes that the "intimacy of this sequence, the tenderness with which Juan treats this shy boy, is genuinely disarming because it is so rarely seen" (13). First noting the gentleness in the sexual encounter between teenagers Chiron and Kevin, DiMatta describes the characters' later scene, which features Barbara Lewis's evocative recording of "Hello Stranger," as "among the most romantic and seductive in recent cinematic history: neither man speaks; they simply look at each other as the song's lyrics fill the gap" (14).

Observers have found that *Moonlight* reflects the "conscious effort from queer and black filmmakers" to represent the unresolved position of African American queer people, which arises from being marginalized in the Black community and the white LGBT community (Crémieux 272). The film conveys Chiron's complex identity by having the character played by three actors, slim performers Alex Hibbert and Ashton Sanders and muscular actor Trevante Rhodes. The film's ending leaves Chiron's future with Kevin, other men, and his own self-image unsettled; the unresolved questions help to convey Chiron's experience of existing between identity positions. As portrayed by Hibbert, Sanders, and Rhodes, Chiron suggests a vision of Black masculinity that encompasses both strength and tenderness, thus aligning it with "new nonessentialist possibilities for a different kind of blackness" (Smalls 283). By creating a characterization far removed from stereotypes, *Moonlight* was yet another film that provided an antidote to the bigotry that moved from the margins to the mainstream in 2016.

Rogue One, Arrival, Hidden Figures, The Magnificent Seven, Fences, and *Moonlight* offered solace for progressive audiences because the films reflected the multicultural emphasis of the Obama presidency. Their narratives framed equity, diversity, and inclusion as valuable, and issues of representation were central concerns in mounting and marketing the productions. It is not surprising that multiethnic casts and stories centered on African American characters were central to 2016 American film offerings. As Michael Eric Dyson points out, race was "the defining feature of [the] forty-fourth president's two terms in office," and his presidency was "analyzed and understood through [an] obsession with race in the body of the president himself and in the psyche of the nation" he governed (x). What is perhaps surprising is that as politicians, media outlets, and law enforcement officers became visible agents of white supremacy in 2016, films ranging from *Rogue One* to *Moonlight* came to be seen as part of the resistance.

2017

Movies and the Right to Be Heard

JULIE LEVINSON

The vicissitudes of the natural world—three major hurricanes and a once-in-a-century solar eclipse—claimed some of the biggest bold-faced headlines of 2017. In the fall of that year, hurricanes Harvey, Maria, and Irma laid waste to wide swaths of Texas, Florida, Puerto Rico, and the U.S. Virgin Islands, leaving death, devastation, and despair in their wake. Their demonstration of nature as fearsome was juxtaposed by a manifestation of nature as awesome: the 21 August total solar eclipse, which was the first in ninety-nine years to cross the contiguous United States from coast to coast. Dubbed by the press "The Great American Eclipse," it was, arguably, the sole event of 2017 that inspired consensus and concord among the citizenry. For that brief moment of wonderment in the midst of a contentious year, Americans stopped and marveled at the astonishing spectacle of the sun blotted out by the moon.

Beyond their status as assertions of nature, the eclipse and hurricanes of 2017 could serve as metaphors for the concomitant atmospheric disturbances in the political and cultural climates. At the beginning of the year, Hurricane Donald stormed into the nation's capital with gale-force brazenness and, throughout the months that followed, blew away all norms. The whirlwind of actions, directives, and tweets emanating from the White House eclipsed all other news in 2017. January set the stage for the rest of the year with two precedent-shattering, call-and-response events. Against the odds, against the polls and the punditocracy, and against even his own expectations, Donald Trump was inaugurated as the forty-fifth president of the United States on 20 January 2017. His ascension to the presidency was followed, a day later, by a massive women's march—nationwide and beyond—in reaction to the installation of Trump in the White House. These were the first of many moments throughout 2017 that could be characterized as punch-counterpunch: a fresh eruption initiated by the new president followed by a livid insistence, from those that opposed him, that

Trump's outrageousness would be met with a commensurately vehement response. Whatever one's political persuasion, Trump's nascent presidency was—to evoke one more weather metaphor—a widespread temblor, shaking the very foundations of America and causing the ground to shift beneath our feet.

Trump hovered over and inserted himself into virtually every news cycle throughout the year. Shortly after taking office, he imposed a travel ban on citizens from seven Muslim-majority nations. The ban would occupy the judiciary for the remainder of the year, as federal district courts struck it down and then, in December, the Supreme Court reversed those decisions. Trump also sought to make good on his campaign promise to build a wall between the United States and Mexico in order to keep illegal immigrants from entering the country. Shortly after he took office, the president issued an executive order calling for the wall to be built but, once more, the edict was tied up in the courts for the remainder of the year and into the next.

As much as Trump usurped the airwaves and the Twitterverse, the forces arrayed against him persisted in adding their voices to the hubbub of public discourse. The January women's march, with its sea of pink pussy hats defiantly worn as a rebuke to Trump's boast about pussy grabbing, was a harbinger of things to come later that year. In October, the focus on sexual assault that began during Trump's campaign was amplified by the revelations about movie mogul Harvey Weinstein. The following month, television personalities Matt Lauer and Charlie Rose had their contracts terminated following sexual misconduct allegations. The tsunami of accusations against these and other high-profile men inspired the Twitter hashtag #MeToo, which went viral and opened the floodgates for scores of victims of sexual assault to come forward to tell their stories and name names. That online cri de coeur encouraged women to form activist organizations, as #MeToo became a burgeoning movement aimed at calling out and redressing sexual assault in industry, the military, the church, the law, and other institutions.

The full-throated demand that female voices needed to be heard resounded across the popular culture spectrum. Women dominated pop music in 2017, with Beyoncé, Lady Gaga, Katy Perry, Ke$ha, Taylor Swift, and Rihanna all making notable contributions to the year's soundtrack while forcefully proclaiming that they had plenty to say and were damn well going to be heard. At the Grammys that year, Adele took home five awards, Album of the Year, Best Pop Vocal Album, Record of the Year, Song of the Year, and Best Pop Solo Performance. On television, across a range of genres, strong-willed, unyielding women gave vent to their anger and their determination in such new, critically acclaimed shows as *The Handmaid's Tale*, *Alias Grace* (both based on novels by Canadian author Margaret Atwood), *The Good Fight*, *Big Little Lies*, and *The Marvelous Mrs. Maisel*. This panoply of women's voices was not the only faction of the American populace clamoring to be heard in that clamorous year; other long-muffled groups also raised a hue and cry.

The Black Lives Matter movement and the accompanying cultural colloquy on race were inflamed both by events in the streets and by the brickbats being lobbed from the White House. The "take a knee" protests among NFL players, begun in 2016 when San Francisco 49ers quarterback Colin Kaepernick knelt during the national anthem in response to unprovoked police shootings of Black men, spread to other sports in 2017. At a rally in September of that year, Trump suggested that NFL owners should fire any players who engaged in such protests. The furor over those kneeling athletes stole the spotlight from the other big sports stories of the year, including the Houston Astros' first-ever World Series win and the New England Patriots' historic comeback in Super Bowl LI. At the end of the third quarter, the Patriots trailed the Atlanta Falcons 28–9, but scored nineteen points in the fourth quarter to tie the game and force the very first overtime in Super Bowl history. The Patriots controlled the overtime, 6–0, to win 34–28.

In August, when "Unite the Right" white supremacists staged a rally in Charlottesville, Virginia, and one of them drove a car into a group of counterprotesters, injuring several and murdering one, Trump failed to condemn the white nationalists, declaring that there were "very fine people on both sides." The back-and-forth uproar about race, hate crimes, and police brutality grew more cacophonous as the year continued.

The ferocity of the year's debates about gender and race coincided with an equally pressing one about class. Trump's appeal to rural, white, middle-American voters intensified a long-apparent class divide. That schism was underscored by the increasingly dire opioid crisis. Although opioid use cut across class lines, the toll that it took in working-class communities was particularly high as entire towns and neighborhoods were decimated by illegal drug use. Like many of the phenomena of the year, this one was a holdover from prior years, made more immediate by the rancorous subtexts that underlay the ongoing cultural conversation.

In March, the bellicose quality of that conversation ramped up another notch when James Comey, the then director of the FBI, announced an investigation into Russian meddling in the 2016 election and into possible collusion between the Trump campaign and Russia. Attorney General Jeff Sessions recused himself from the investigation, citing his support for

Trump during the 2016 campaign and, in particular, concerns over his contact with the Russian ambassador at that time. Furious over his attorney general's recusal and his FBI director's handling of allegations about Russian election tampering, Trump fired Comey in May. Following his dismissal, Comey leaked a memo detailing a conversation in which, Comey claimed, the president had urged him to shut down the federal investigation into links between Russia and Trump's former national security adviser, Michael Flynn. That memo sparked suspicion about presidential obstruction of justice. Eight days after Comey's firing, the Justice Department appointed Robert Mueller as special counsel to lead the ongoing FBI inquiry into Russian election interference and possible obstruction on the part of Trump. For the remainder of the year, the public palaver reached fever pitch as a series of allegations, speculations, witnesses, and stonewallers took center stage in the unfolding drama.

Well-known people who died in 2017 included: *Partridge Family* star David Cassidy; rock star Tom Petty; French actress Anne Wiazemsky (*Au Hasard Balthazar*); French film star Danielle Darrieux (*The Earrings of Madame de . . .*); early rockers Chuck Berry and Fats Domino; second-wave feminist author Kate Millett (*Sexual Politics*); actor Harry Dean Stanton (*Paris, Texas, Repo Man*); middleweight champion and *Raging Bull* subject Jake LaMotta; Broadway soprano Barbara Cook, who originated leading roles in *Candide* and *The Music Man*; comedian and activist Dick Gregory; comedy star Jerry Lewis; horror film maestro Tobe Hooper (*The Texas Chainsaw Massacre*); Academy Award–winning actor Martin Landau (*Ed Wood, North by Northwest*); horror film director George Romero (*Night of the Living Dead*); longtime voice actress June Foray (*Rocky and Bullwinkle*); playwright and actor Sam Shepard (*True West, The Right Stuff*); French New Wave star Jeanne Moreau (*Jules et Jim, Les Amants*); 1960s TV *Batman* Adam West; Fox News chairman and chief executive Roger Ailes; James Bond actor Roger Moore; insult comic Don Rickles (*Toy Story 1–3*); cinematographer Michael Ballhaus (*The Marriage of Maria Braun, Goodfellas*); director Jonathan Demme (*Melvin and Howard, The Silence of the Lambs*); Nobel Prize–winning poet and novelist Derek Walcott; literary theorist Tzvetan Todorov (*The Fantastic*); *Time* film critic Richard Schickel; film actor Bill Paxton (*Twister, Titanic*); novelist and screenwriter William Peter Blatty (*The Exorcist*); TV star Mary Tyler Moore; and French film actress Emmanuelle Riva (*Hiroshima mon amour*).

As difficult as it is to sum up any year with a brief rundown of occurrences, 2017 was more brimming with banner headline news than most. In addition to the foregoing, there were several other signal events: the continuing controversy over transgender people in the military and in the restrooms of America; the appointment of Neil Gorsuch to a seat on the Supreme Court that Democrats claimed rightfully belonged to an Obama nominee whose confirmation process in 2016 was blocked; the acts of domestic terrorism that shook Las Vegas, New York, and Washington as well as terror attacks carried out in Manchester, London, Barcelona, and other cities across the globe; the first successful gene editing in human embryos; the United States' withdrawal from the Paris agreement on climate change; the official start of the Brexit process as the United Kingdom prepared to depart from the European Union; the Catalan vote for independence from Spain; the heightening tensions with North Korea as that country's development of a hydrogen bomb and an intercontinental ballistic missile made them a greater global threat; and many more consequential moments in an eventful twelve months.

By year's end, what historian Benedict Anderson once labeled "the national imaginary"—that communal sense of identity that is reinforced by a country's history, ideology, and discursive practices—seemed ever more smudged in the United States. Across the political spectrum, the populace was reeling from 2017's head-spinning concatenation of events. What better way to avoid, however briefly, the commotion of those overstuffed news cycles than to go to the movies? Unfortunately, not enough Americans chose to do so; 2017 had the worst domestic box-office returns in twenty-five years (Sakoui). The slump in ticket sales was attributable to several factors. The average ticket price hit a record high, discouraging moviegoers from venturing outside of their homes for entertainment (D'Alessandro). The streaming services, most notably Netflix, Amazon, and HBO Go, captured an increasingly larger share of people's leisure time and attention (FactTank; The State of OTT Video). In addition to the enticements of the peak TV era and the seductive pleasures of binge watching, the movie industry had to deal with the growing perception of movies as merely one more consumer product to be rated, Yelp-style, by every film aficionado with a blog. Producer-director Brett Ratner blamed the film review aggregation site Rotten Tomatoes for the decline in moviegoing, declaring it "the worst thing that we have in today's movie culture" and blasting it for "the destruction of our business" (Hibberd). Hollywood's roster of offerings, particularly the summer's presumed blockbusters such as *The Mummy* and the fifth installment of the *Pirates of the Caribbean* franchise, was not adequately tempting to compete with what was instantaneously available on TV. In an article titled "Hollywood Had a Terrible Year in 2017," a writer for Bloomberg News blamed what he called "sequel fatigue" (Sakoui). Even the double hunk appeal of the Dwayne Johnson–Zac Efron vehicle *Baywatch* proved unable to lure enough moviegoers to ogle toned bodies on the cinematic beach.

In the era of streaming TV, moviemaking had become an ever-riskier business, so, well beyond the crucial summer release season, producers resorted to high-profile, tentpole movies that seemed like a sure bet. Action-adventure franchise sequels and comic book superhero adaptations took nine of the top ten spots on the list of highest-grossing movies of the year (The Numbers). *Star Wars: Episode VIII—The Last Jedi* occupied the number one slot, followed by *Beauty and the Beast* and the well-reviewed *Wonder Woman*. As the *New York Times*'s Brooks Barnes pointed out, "The three most popular movies at theaters in the United States and Canada in 2017 . . . were each driven by female characters, something that has not happened in at least 37 years, as far back as full box office data is available." He added, "The top comedy of the year, *Girls Trip*, was also anchored by women, as was the top film to play in limited release, *Lady Bird*" (Barnes). The box office or critical success of those films, along with the long overdue self-examination imposed on Hollywood by the fallout from #MeToo, gave some hope for less institutionalized and representational sexism in the movie business. But that phenomenon was a rare bright spot in an otherwise gloomy year in the film industry.

Notwithstanding the disappointment in some highly anticipated releases, there were a number of movies that were greeted enthusiastically by audiences and critics. Several genre films offered up new renditions of old formulas. Christopher Nolan's expertly crafted war film *Dunkirk* eschewed dialogue in favor of spectacle as it told the story of the World War II evacuation of Dunkirk by land, sea, and air. The long-awaited sci-fi sequel *Blade Runner 2049* (Denis Villeneuve) extended the 1982 *Blade Runner*'s neo-noir story of the future by thirty years, expanding the earlier film's dystopian view of technology and humanity. *Baby Driver* (Edgar Wright), a fast-paced crime caper, quickly achieved cult status with its tale of a getaway driver whose skill behind the wheel is inspired by his musical tastes. Another heist movie, *Logan Lucky*, drew Steven Soderbergh out of self-imposed retirement from movies to direct an ingenious story about two hapless brothers who are determined to reverse a family curse by pulling off the perfect robbery. Critically acclaimed director Alexander Payne also released a much-anticipated genre film, *Downsizing*, although its science fiction premise and its kitchen-sink plot was, for many, a baffling departure from Payne's usual fare. Two historical recreations, *The Post* (Steven Spielberg) and *Detroit* (Kathryn Bigelow) revisited turning points of the latter half of the twentieth century: the 1967 Detroit race riots and the *Washington Post*'s

1971 publication of the Pentagon Papers (classified documents with revelations about the U.S. government's involvement in the Vietnam War), respectively.

As was the trend in preceding years, the big-budget genre films and sequels crowded out mid-budget, adult-oriented movies with original scripts: a once prominent category of films that seemed to be an endangered species in twenty-first-century Hollywood. The death knell for that latter type of movie had been sounding for years, and it continued to toll in 2017 with such laments as "A Requiem for Medium-Sized Movies: Why Have Mid-Budget Films All-but Disappeared from Today's Cinematic Landscape?" (Luxford). In truth, they hadn't all but disappeared, but it was increasingly challenging for those mid-budget, character-driven movies to find production funding and, if they did somehow get made, to benefit from a robust marketing campaign. Continuing a decades-long trend in Hollywood, by the end of 2017 it was apparent that the top ten box office hits and the top ten lists of critics' favorites had almost nothing in common, with the exception of *Wonder Woman*, which made appearances on both rosters.

Still, several mid- and small-budget movies made their mark in 2017. Actor Daniel Day-Lewis declared *Phantom Thread* (Paul Thomas Anderson) to be his last acting job, making that visually sumptuous tale of a fastidious dressmaker-cum-artiste and his muse-cum-lover a must-see for cinephiles. Actor-writer Greta Gerwig's directorial debut, *Lady Bird*, was greeted with critical hosannas for its fierce and fresh take on a young woman's coming of age. Another coming of age movie, *Call Me By Your Name* (Luca Guadagnino), put a new spin on adolescent angst with its depiction of love and lust between a teenage boy and the young man who comes to his family's home in Italy to assist the boy's father in his research. The Netflix-produced *Mudbound* (Dee Rees) foregrounded two World War II veterans—one Black and one white—who return from the war to a Mississippi farm only to confront hidebound attitudes about race and class hierarchies. These and other movies of the year were notable for their spotlight on the sort of characters whose subject positions and spaces of alterity were often ignored or unsung.

Speaking Out/Speaking Up

Among those smaller-scale movies that made a big splash were several that featured characters who asserted their right to speak truth to power, despite the lack of power vested in them by their social status. The cultural contention of 2017 found its correlative in an array of movies that gave voice and validation to those often marginalized people and to questions of identity, alterity, and liminality. *Three Billboards outside Ebbing, Missouri*, *I, Tonya*, *The Florida Project*, *Get Out*, *The Big Sick*, and *Beatriz at Dinner* offered up a cavalcade of habitually overlooked, written-off character types—rural or working-class or destitute women, African Americans, Muslim Americans, Hispanic immigrants—claiming their right to take center stage and be heard. The focus on movie protagonists who were, in terms of their social identity, down-and-out rather than up-and-coming signaled a shift in subjectivities in which those in the background of America's airbrushed self-portrait elbowed their way to the forefront. The sorts of people who were commonly looked upon, if at all, as supernumeraries in the American grand narrative of achievement and attainment moved from the fringes to the focal point of several movies.

Although those movies had been in production well before Trump's unlikely rise, they spoke to long-brewing grievances that came to a boil in the year's protests, social movements, and memes. Taken together, these films may be viewed as a cinema of resistance—or, perhaps, a cinema of insistence in which agency and voice are seized by protagonists who, due to their gender, race, age, class, ethnicity, or religion, are oftentimes relegated to the outskirts of the narrative frame, not to mention the underbelly of America's self-image. Conceived of when a President Trump was still inconceivable, their collective spirit proved to be well timed to the national mood and mindset of those first twelve months of his presidency. In that first year of Trump's presidency, these six films took on up-to-the-minute resonance. Two years later, in the thick of the Trump era, Sasha Weiss observed, "Many of the fights that are being waged politically about who holds power in this country, who has shaped the stories we tell and who has been forbidden to do so are being played out provocatively in the culture" (Weiss). Ostensibly, the political, social, and cultural battles of 2017 were being reflected in the parallel universe of the movies, as the turbulence of that year was echoed by a collection of characters who refused to take what was dished out, who refused to just shut up and go away.

By Hollywood's yardstick, these six instances of cultural provocation were small films. *Get Out*, the most successful of them at the box office, took in an impressive 176 million dollars domestically and another 80 million in overseas sales (Box Office Mojo). Although the others had relatively meager ticket sales, in aggregate these six films had an outsized presence in cultural and critical discourses, garnering a lot of press as well as multiple award nominations and wins, and appearing on numerous best-of the-year lists.[1] The spirit of such phenomena as the #MeToo and Black Lives Matter movements—as well as the ongoing public debates about whose stories do or do not get told and who gets to do the telling—gave a sense of urgency to the need to heed alternative voices and visions. The zeitgeist of 2017 gave to these tales of the discriminated against or the downtrodden a significance disproportionate to their box office and budget.

Black Comedy/White Privilege

Not far into 2017, it was apparent that, while Trump was wreaking havoc on presidential norms, satire was enjoying a heyday. As incredulity became the country's daily diet, each news cycle inspired a torrent of televised and online barbs, derisive broadsides that often seemed the only appropriate response to the serial follies being played out in the nation's capital. Dark humor was the last redoubt for those whose sinking spirits needed an expressive outlet. From Stephen Colbert to Samantha Bee to Andy Borowitz, satirists held their own, alongside commentators and op-ed writers, as interpreters of current events. The practice of belittling through ridicule in order to make a serious point was, likewise, at the center of many of the year's films, notably *Get Out*, *Beatriz at Dinner*, and *The Big Sick*, all of which turned to comic modes to make serious statements on race in America. *Get Out*, the first film directed by sketch comic Jordan Peele, is far and away the most vehement: a take-no-prisoners take on race relations that wields its satire with a ferocious commitment to saying what needs to be said.

But that is not how *Get Out* first appears. After an opening fraught with the threat of racial violence, the film seems to settle into a less unsettling, more generically recognizable story. We meet Chris (Daniel Kaluuya) and Rose (Allison Williams), a racially mixed couple who have an easygoing romantic rapport. They are about to embark on a weekend visit to Rose's parents' suburban home. Chris wonders if Rose has told her parents that she is dating a Black man and, although she hasn't, she assures him that, enlightened as her parents are, they won't care. Although a couple of disquieting things happen on the ride to the suburbs (the couple's car hits a deer and then Chris is racially profiled by the police), Rose and her family bend over backward to assure Chris of their wanna-be-woke bona fides.

To a point, *Get Out* riffs on a familiar film trope. From *You Can't Take It with You* (1938) to *Guess Who's Coming to Dinner* (1967) to *Meet the Parents* (2000) and beyond, stories of the first time that families meet their child's partner—whose race, religion, class, occupation, or other marker of identity comes as a jolt to them—are a reliable source of fish-out-of-water comedy. Usually, these are tales of reconciliation, concluding with the acceptance of otherness and the conviction that we are all alike under the skin. But in setting the stage for a congenial meeting across racial lines, Peele sets the audience up for a sucker punch. What starts with evocations of romantic comedy suddenly turns into something altogether different as the film undergoes a startling genre switcheroo.

Early on, *Get Out* proves to be a mash-up of genre types and influences. The requisite dinner table scene found in many comedies of manners here showcases the family's liberal hypocrisies. Peele scores easy points off their performative bonhomie and their microaggressions disguised as solicitousness. But intimations of something more sinister—helped along by a strident music track that is a few steps ahead of the narrative in ominousness—soon surface. The Armitage family's Black employees are hollowed-out automatons who wear eerie, pasted-on smiles or blank stares while spouting platitudes of agreeableness like ventriloquist's dummies. Likewise, an overly polite Black party guest appears at first to be virtually anesthetized and, later, when Chris tries to snap his picture, out-and-out hysterical. Chris himself gets hypnotized by Rose's psychiatrist mother who, in promising to cure his cigarette addiction, sends him to "the sunken place": a nightmarish internal chasm where he flashes on traumas from his past. That particular scene is full of portentous cinematic clues of what is to come. Unnerving insert shots (the mother's slowly stirring teaspoon, Chris's hands anxiously scratching the armrest of his chair) along with progressively tighter cross-cut close-ups of the two characters collude to create an aura of foreboding. As the sense of threat morphs into full-blown terror, *Get Out* conjures other films and genres, including sci-fi movies *The Stepford Wives* (1975, remade in 2004), *Invasion of the Body Snatchers* (1956, remade in 1978), and a host of grisly, trapped-in-a-house horror films. Peele's film is at once a cautionary tale, a wake-up call, and a revenge fantasy.

Chris's experience at the Armitage household has the illogic of a nightmare in which a shroud of menace looms over the quotidian. As his initial unease turns to full-blown freak-out, *Get Out* reveals its intentions: to aim a harsh spotlight at the dark truths of institutionalized as well as interpersonal racism and to not let soi-disant well-intentioned white liberals off the hook. The film maintains that white fascination with and envy of Black bodies and modes of expression is every bit as pernicious as (and, in essence, is tantamount to) overt racial animus. The proposition that white people want both to exploit and subjugate Black people—to harvest their bodies and souls while controlling them—is far more chilling than any of the Grand Guignol jump scares the film serves up. Ultimately, *Get Out* is a sly

2017 — MOVIES AND THE RIGHT TO BE HEARD

parable in which the Armitages' body snatching signifies the soul-killing indignities and systemic bigotry of American racism.

The best, if bitterest, joke in the film involves Chris's friend Rod who, from the start, warns Chris about his meet-the-parents jaunt and spins paranoid conspiracy theories. When Chris later phones to tell him about the goings-on in the Armitage house, Rod's paranoia proving well founded, Rod goes to the police, but the detectives laugh at his far-fetched ravings. Claims of racial atrocities, Peele tells us, often seem to be shouted into the wind. However nightmarish the scenarios that happen under cover of the commonplace, life goes on. Hence, the intensity of *Get Out*'s ending in which, as in action movies, a lone man takes things into his own hands since social institutions prove to be feckless or, worse yet, indifferent.

Tellingly, the final moment in which Rod arrives to spirit Chris away from the blood-soaked carnage was not Peele's original ending.[2] Peele began writing *Get Out*'s script in the putatively postracial Obama era. The original ending had Chris being arrested and hauled off to jail after his paroxysm of vigilante justice. But as the film neared completion, the director and producers felt compelled to reshoot the ending. Peele explained:

> It was pretty clear by the time that the cut with that original ending was made, that we were in a different America than I wrote the movie in. . . . Instead of being in denial about racism, we have been addressing it more. With the Black Lives Matter movement and attention to police brutality, it was clear people had a certain fatigue from those horrors, and needed a hero, an escape, as well as a way to confront it (Fleming).

By the time of the film's release in February of 2017, viewers responded to an ending that prized action and confrontation over self-restraint and acquiescence—and that seemingly let Chris get away with his act of retribution. The film's racial reckoning wowed critics and audiences alike, garnering multiple award nominations, including a Best Picture nod from the Academy Awards. Although it lost out to *The Shape of Water*, a far more anodyne fable of a mixed romantic union, Peele did win the award for Best Original Screenplay, and the film became a touchstone for the year's vexed dialogue about race and difference in contemporary America.

Get Out was the most widely discussed, critically lauded, and financially lucrative of the six films under examination, whereas *Beatriz at Dinner*, directed by Miguel Arteta, was the least. Its reviews were generally admiring but compared to the others, which were critics' darlings, its reception was muted and its audiences were small. Still, in its mordantly satirical view of an intense showdown across race, class, and gender lines, it is a worthy companion piece to *Get Out*, and its eponymous heroine is a significant player on the year's roster of protagonists who refuse to be silenced or suppressed. Both movies highlight characters who are, in anthropological terms, "matter out of place" since their social identities render them incongruous in the narrative landscapes they inhabit.[3] Each is looked on as an interloper encroaching on alien territory. Like all of the main characters in these six films, they are presented as personae non gratae: strangers in a strange land, even though that land is their own.

With its array of targets, including anti-immigrant xenophobia, predatory capitalism, toxic masculinity, casual racism, the class divide, and the smug certainty of the one-percenters, it is, among these six films, the one that is most directly aimed at the schisms that characterized the era. Debuting at the Sundance Film Festival three days after Trump's inauguration, its pertinence to that particular cultural moment did not go unnoticed. The review on Roger Ebert's website, for example, anointed it as "one of the first blatantly intentional culture-clash allegories for our Trumpian times" (Wloszczyna).

Beatriz (Salma Hayek) is a Mexican immigrant who earns her keep as a massage therapist and holistic healer. Her earth mother credentials and spiritual enlightenment are established from the get-go: she lights candles, does yoga, communes with animals, heals the afflicted, and has figurines of both Buddha and Jesus on her dashboard. Once again, we have a main character who ventures into the terrain of the haute bourgeoisie, as Beatriz makes a house call to one of her regular clients, Kathy (Connie Britton), who lives in a sprawling McMansion in a gated community. And, once again, our protagonist gets stuck there, this time due to a car that fails to start when she tries to leave. Over her husband's objections, Kathy invites Beatriz to stay and join the dinner party that they are hosting for some of his business associates. The airy, light-filled long shots of Kathy's house provide a stark contrast to the cramped compositions of Beatriz's home and workplace, visually accentuating the clash of cultures that is to come.

The dinner party as debate stage is a set piece of film and theater. Here, Beatriz's main combatant is arrogant billionaire real estate developer Doug Strutt (John Lithgow), who is as staunchly devoted to rapacious material gain as Beatriz is to beatific spiritual values. Initially, she hangs back diffidently as the host couple and their four guests make small talk. She is repeatedly set off in the mise-en-scène, standing to the side and about a foot shorter than the other three women. While the trophy wives swan around in soigné cocktail dresses and heels, she wears drab work clothes and sneakers. Initially, Strutt mistakes her for "the help," but Kathy patronizingly claims Beatriz is a "friend of the family," to which her husband responds, "She is?"

Much to the three couples' consternation, when they and Beatriz sit down for dinner, she immediately joins in the conversation, proving to be as voluble and opinionated as the self-congratulatory Strutt. Although they expect her to be silently grateful for their noblesse oblige, she is adamant about her worldview and eager to square off with Strutt and the others about theirs. She initially swallows her anger, but her dinner companions' attitudes soon cause her to spew righteous indignation. The gloves come off, along with Beatriz's mask of meekness, as she eagerly joins the fray and gives as good as she gets. When Connie later says to her, "I feel like I don't even know you," Beatriz bluntly answers, "You *don't* know me." Late in the evening, Beatriz wonders out loud if fate brought her together with Strutt. When he asks, "For what?" she replies, "For revenge, maybe."

Arteta is an equal opportunity satirist who skewers Strutt and his cohort for being cocksure and condescending, but also pokes fun at Beatriz as she spouts banal, new-age truisms. If the debaters are well matched, they are also unsparingly caricatured as familiar comic types. The aptly named Strutt is a specimen of the stock character Greek dramatists referred to as the *alazon*: the full-of-himself braggart who eventually gets his comeuppance. Beatriz is the plain dealer: the forthright, tell-it-like-it-is speaker of truths. But if the satire is broad, it is also very much of the moment. Arteta has explained that Mike White wrote the screenplay around the time that Trump was getting into the race for president and that Strutt was partly based on Trump. He points out that Lithgow "is not playing exactly that character, but he is playing a self-satisfied billionaire who aggressively believes in the power of greed and that we, as the dominant species, are allowed to just rape and pillage this world, treat each other unkindly, and take advantage of other people" (Aguilar). Just as Strutt is all too familiar, Beatriz is a walking mouthpiece for the grievances of race, gender, and class that took on increased momentousness in 2017.

Arteta presents the conflict between these two types as a cage match in which no one can definitively claim victory. The film seems more intent on highlighting the divisiveness of the present moment than on speculating about which side would emerge victorious. In an interview, the director said he "tried not to give any answers," so the movie is "more of a question mark" (Corona). As such, the ambiguous double ending cannot be taken literally as a tying-up of plot strands and character motivations. Like the denouement of *Get Out*, *Beatriz at Dinner* initially gives the audience wish fulfillment in the form of revenge against the entitled. Toward the end of

Beatriz (Salma Hayek) imagines taking revenge on the plutocracy, represented by Doug (John Lithgow) in *Beatriz at Dinner* (Miguel Arteta, Roadside Attractions). Digital frame enlargement.

the film, in what seems to be momentary magic realism, Beatriz stabs Strutt in the neck with a letter opener. This is followed by a baffling second ending in which, with Strutt very much alive and unbowed, Beatriz submerges herself in the ocean and is then seen rowing away in a boat in a slowly tracking long shot that echoes the otherworldly quality of the film's opening. The pipe dream of taking power into one's hands and bringing down the patriarchy is superseded by this less conclusive and emotionally satisfying final shot. Arteta lays out the fight card but denies his audience the closure of a definitive knockout punch.

Even so, what the film does give us is strikingly similar to the mortifications and subsequent gratifications of *Get Out*. Lacerating satires of the plutocracy, both films have main characters that initially seem conciliatory but who, after a series of escalating offenses, explode in fury and wreak vengeance on their privileged tormentors—even if, in Beatriz's case, the physical vengeance seems to be imaginary. The battle of wills in these two emotionally charged films are proxy fights, reassurances to the audience that one can and must fight the power. At one point in *Beatriz at Dinner*, Strutt says to her, "I have opinions and because I have money, people listen." But she later takes him to task: "You think because you're wealthy and powerful, you can hide behind these walls and these houses and you're going to be safe? No, it's going to touch you. It's coming to get you"—a threat and a promise that resonated with the tenor of the times. In its depiction of a smackdown between a wealthy real estate baron and the forces arrayed against him in the person of Beatriz, the film seems down-right prescient. But after the election, Arteta pointed out, "We shot it in August [of 2016], and we thought there was no way Donald Trump would ever get elected . . . if you put the President of the United States in a movie, you wouldn't believe him" (Murrian). Whatever else the Trump era brought us, it taught us that truth is stranger than fiction.

Of these three films that poke at white privilege, *The Big Sick* is by far the mildest, replacing the big stick thrust of the others with a gentle prod. Although, like those two films, it revolves around the experience of being nonwhite in contemporary America, it does so with genial good humor and a familiarly formulaic plot structure. Instead of funneling the fury that many Americans were feeling, here intolerance and insularity are more a joke than an impediment, and are aimed not just at white Americans but also at nonwhite immigrants.

In place of the spluttering satire of *Get Out* and *Beatriz at Dinner*, *The Big Sick* traffics in the classic romantic comedy scenario of a young man and woman whose coupling is impeded by parental objection to the union. The film opens with a riff on ethnic difference as stand-up comedian Kumail Nanjiani, playing a lightly fictionalized namesake of himself, jokes about being a Pakistani Muslim in America. In a classic meet-cute, he is heckled by Emily (Zoe Kazan), a standard-issue manic pixie dream girl, and they begin a romance later that night. But Emily breaks up with him when she discovers that Kumail has been keeping their relationship a secret from his parents who insist he marry someone of his own heritage. So far, so con-ventional: with the addition of the ethnic twist, an ancient plot set-up has been updated for twenty-first-century America.[4] But *The Big Sick* then evolves into a disease-of-the-week movie when Emily suddenly takes ill and is put into an induced coma. This encounter with illness and death is the source of the film's darkness, which comes more from its topic than its temperament. Emily eventually recovers, and Kumail eventually makes his way back into her good graces by being attentive to her while she is in the hospital, winning over her parents, and ultimately moving to New York in defiance of his own parents' wishes, thereby declaring his independence from their worldview.

Unlike the other two films, which channeled the outrage and addressed the fears of many Americans that year, most of *The Big Sick*'s ethnic slights are mined for mild humor. Much of the film's finger-pointing at narrow-mindedness and clannishness is aimed not at white people but at Kumail's parents, who subscribe to the stick-to-your-own-kind school of bias and make it their mission to find him a religiously appropriate mate. Kumail's rebellion and apostasy are established early on. After his mother instructs him during a family meal to "go and pray now," he retreats to the basement, lays out his prayer rug, sets the timer on his phone, and then, in a jump cut montage, kills time playing with a cricket bat and watching a YouTube video. Once again, this film gives us the requisite awkward dinner table scenes, but here it is easy to guess who's coming to dinner since it is an interchangeable succession of young Pakistani American women the parents have vetted as proper marriage fodder. When Kumail finally reveals his relationship with Emily, his parents banish him from the family. Emily's parents, on the other hand, are paragons of enlightenment. Although her father does, at one point, expect Kumail to represent "his people" by asking his stance on the events of 9/11, their initially cool response to him is simply protective of their daughter's romantic longings rather than being motivated by his national origins or his religion. When the film's most blatant instance of racism is aimed at Kumail, Emily's mother attacks the perpetrator vociferously and even physically. Rather than savaging white liberals, *The Big Sick* exalts them.

But if the film lacks the boldness of *Get Out* and *Beatriz at Dinner*, it nonetheless deserves to keep company with those far edgier, angrier black comedies because of its fortuitous timing and the ethnicity of its creator. Those films reverberated with the national mood primarily due to the bold way their main characters acted out and talked back; this one is significant largely because of who is doing the talking and when. The film debuted at the Sundance Film Festival mere hours after Trump was inaugurated. One of his first acts as president was to call for "the total and complete shutdown of Muslims entering the United States." Representationally, *The Big Sick* struck a blow for tolerance and heterogeneity, thereby condemning white privilege and prejudice.

As a go-down-easy film that humanized "the other" and elevated a category of character who commonly lacks voice and presence on American screens, the film was in tune with its cultural moment. Because it promoted broad-mindedness and interethnic union—and since it starred and was co-written by a Muslim American—*The Big Sick* was seen, by critics and audiences, as the perfect retort to Islamophobia. Although less acerbic and incisive than the others, it was still effective in rebutting the anti-immigrant sentiment that was common currency in some quarters of America. The film grossed over ten times its budget, made many top ten lists, and tapped into the yearning for an answer to Trump's anti-Muslim affront. Although it pales alongside the suppurating rage of *Get Out* and *Beatriz at Dinner*, the wry humor of *The Big Sick* has a similar proclamation: we're here and we intend to speak out and be heard above the din.

Down-and-Out/Up in Arms

Nonwhite Americans were not the only ones, both on-screen and off, who were eager to push back, determined to be heard. A trio of films featuring a rogue's gallery of angry, gutsy, mouthy, lower-class women held a prominent place on American movie screens in 2017. *Three Billboards outside Ebbing, Missouri, I, Tonya,* and *The Florida Project* featured the sort of people usually relegated to the margins of national consciousness and, concomitantly, American film narratives. Their main characters are women with no social capital—or, for that matter, any sort of capital. All they can lay claim to is their dauntlessness and their refusal to stay quiet in the face of perceived injustices. Antiheroines for contentious times, they contradict the trope of the vulnerable, victimized woman. Over the course of the three films, every one of them has something taken from her; two of them lose a child and one is denied a career doing what she excels at and loves. Each woman responds to her dispossession with a howl that amounts to a battle cry from the class and gender wars. The question of who gets to hold the megaphone, however fleetingly, is answered emphatically by the down-and-out, outspoken women at the center of these stories.

From Hillary Clinton's electoral loss to the January women's march to the #MeToo revelations, female anger as a potent force was much on Americans' collective mind that year. The characters from these films are avatars of that anger, harnessing and riding it like hardened broncobusters. They are, in media scholar Kathleen Rowe Karlyn's appellation, "unruly women." Rowe Karlyn has written two books about "the transgressive power of female unruliness" in American media and the "cluster of attributes that challenge patriarchal power by defying norms of femininity intended to keep a woman in her place" (Rowe, 9–10). Doubly oppressed by the pecking orders of both gender and class, these paragons of misrule obstreperously disrupt the well-rehearsed performance of social privilege. Sharp-tongued and foulmouthed, they flout the norms of decorum and make spectacles of themselves, thereby resisting invisibility and silence. They are not role models, nor are they exemplars of simplistic, "you go, girl" feminism. They are complex, deeply flawed individuals who, despite this, still believe they deserve to be listened to.

At the front of this ill-mannered matriarchal line is Mildred Hayes (Frances McDormand) of *Three Billboards,* a late-middle-aged divorced

Mildred (Frances McDormand) with her fury writ large in *Three Billboards outside Ebbing, Missouri* (Martin McDonagh, Fox Searchlight). Digital frame enlargement.

woman whose daughter has been raped and murdered. Furious that the local law enforcement apparatus has been unable to solve the crime and bring the perpetrator to justice, she rents out three derelict billboards on a rural road and uses them to call out the investigators' incompetence, even targeting the local sheriff by name in one of the blunt, enraged messages. These billboards are citizen action literally writ large.

Mildred's incivility and hostility do not end with the billboards. Throughout the course of the story, she wields a dentist's drill on the dentist's own thumb, calls a police officer a "fuckhead," tells the local clergyman he is no different than a gang member, kicks a teenager in the crotch when he throws a can at her car, sets fire to the police station, and goes out of her way to offend everyone with whom she interacts, including her own son whom, in her singularly perverse way, she seems to love. Another character describes Mildred as "tough as an old boot." Indeed, she appears to subsist on a diet of moxie and bile. With her permanently glowering expression, partly-shaven head, shapeless grease monkey coveralls, and shitkicker boots, she wears her nonconformity truculently. At one point, she speculates that "there ain't no god and the whole world's empty and it doesn't matter what we do to each other." This is a person with nothing left to lose. All she can do is sound off about the unspeakable crime that took her daughter's life.

Both in spite and because of her ferociousness, Mildred retains the audience's dramatic sympathies. She is militantly single-minded and relentlessly aggrieved, but in her fearlessness and her renunciation of social niceties she is also deeply inspiring and darkly funny. There is an element of wish fulfillment, as well as catharsis, in characters such as this. Their propensity to say and do whatever they wish—to be beyond caring about behavioral conventions—is vicariously gratifying. More to the point, in 2017 it was heartening to think that anger was power and that righteousness would have its day. Several critics at the time commented on *Three Billboard*'s contemporaneity. BuzzFeed's review declared that Mildred was "perfectly positioned to be the fictional patron saint of our current cultural moment" (Willmore). And the *Washington Post* called her "an avatar of our current cultural appetite for accountability, truth-telling and radical moral reckoning" (Hornaday). The film's focus on female rage, sexual violence, and a lower class that had been forsaken by the inequities of the twenty-first century seemed all too timely.

The eponymous protagonist of *I, Tonya* is a fellow traveler in this sisterhood of indignant women. Tonya Harding (Margot Robbie) was the infamous loser of the 1994 Olympic figure skating competition. The story of her rivalry with, and crime against, fellow skater Nancy Kerrigan was well known. But as the film offers up recurring, head-on shots of wildly unreliable narrators who contradict one another in their direct address to the audience, this *Rashomon*-like biopic uses the familiar story to probe the emotional injuries borne by a woman from the wrong side of the tracks. The Tonya of the film is indomitable. She leans into her supposed shortcomings of being insufficiently ladylike and conspicuously lower class. She describes herself, at turns, as white trash, a redneck, and a wild cracker. Mistreated and unloved by her mother, beaten by her husband, scorned by her coaches, and loathed by the public, she soldiers on in her campaign for athletic glory. In some sense, this is yet another account of an underdog with gumption who refuses to give up. But *I, Tonya* is the inverse of all those sports movies and bootstrap tales about the power of perseverance and grit. Here, the main character has both of those characteristics in spades, but she is repeatedly thwarted by her outsider status in the world in which she hopes to succeed.

What sociologist Richard Sennett once called "the hidden injuries of class" are here hidden in plain sight. With unblinking class-consciousness, the movie wallows in the clichés of kitchen-sink realism. At times, *I, Tonya* verges on caricature as it details the privations of Harding's hardscrabble life: her transition from the miserable home she shared with her mother to the miserable home she shares with her husband, and the deficiencies of everything from her tacky skating costumes to her crude manners to her inadequately girly athletic style. Scene after scene shows Tonya as a threat to codes of middle-class gentility and to notions of how a woman should comport herself. However well she skates, she is also a threat to the wholesome self-image that America wants to project to the world in its moments on the Olympic ice. In spite of her winner's spirit and skill, the Tonya of the film was born to lose.

As portraits of brash women go, Tonya's is a pastel compared with the pitch-dark picture of her mother Lavona (Allison Janney), which is, in effect, drawn with cigarette ash. Gleefully vulgar and consistently malicious, Lavona seems to have left out the love when she concocted her recipe for tough love. Apart from the film's appeal to audiences' voyeuristic nostalgie de la boue, why would we find these characters compelling? Much of I Tonya's appeal could be chalked up to moviegoers' abiding love affair with disreputable antiheroes. These brash women are not just wildly funny but also liberatory in their inclination to say and do whatever they please.

Self-consciously candid about the impossibility of biographical truths, I, Tonya is less interested in what happened than in how Tonya represents, but does not retreat from, the degradations of her gender and class. The film would likely be received differently were it made shortly after the events it presents. Although set in the 1990s, this decades-old story hit home in 2017 with its unblinking depiction of a déclassé woman who, however wrong she was in her actions, was indisputably wronged because of her class and her gender. Some critics faulted the film for its revisionist history and its suggestion that Tonya was more victim than perpetrator. But others recognized its applicability to roiling cultural currents. One review titled "I, Tonya May Be the Film We Need to Understand Donald Trump and #MeToo" pinpointed "the twin issues it obliquely addresses—Trump-style class resentments and the disregarding of women's stories" (J. Anderson). In a news conference, Robbie herself commented, "When Steven [Rogers] wrote the script, Trump wasn't President. When we filmed this, the #MeToo and #TimesUp movements hadn't begun. There were things that we recognized as issues that society needed to discuss. We just didn't realize that they would be discussing it so loudly when the film came out" (Bradbury). Tonya Harding's saga read differently through the scrim of 2017 when she was seen not just as a lowlife has-been but also as a victim of abuse and the butt of classist tabloid jokes. As the fictional Tonya breaks the fourth wall to have her say about those of us on the other side who callously enjoyed her humiliations, it is she who has the last bitter laugh in calling out the power dynamics within class and gender identities in America.

The Florida Project offered up yet another down-on-her-luck, up-in-arms, loudmouthed woman. Halley (Bria Vinaite) lives with her six-year-old daughter Moonee (Brooklynn Prince) in the Magic Castle, a beguilingly named, alarmingly purple motel for transients which is located close to Disney's Magic Kingdom. Halley manages to scrape up the weekly rent through a series of jobs and scams, but the constant threat of eviction and homelessness hangs over her like a pall. In spite of the relentlessly high-key natural lighting and the saturated color palette of the outdoor scenes, the mood is decidedly downbeat. When Halley loses her gig as an exotic dancer, she hawks black market perfume to unsuspecting tourists, scalps stolen passes to Disney World, and, ultimately, turns tricks in her motel room, exiling Moonee to the bathroom. Moonee is very much her mother's daughter, a precociously gifted grifter and a smutty-mouthed moppet who, like Halley, is pugnacious and untamable.

The Florida Project is a picaresque narrative that imparts a slice-of-life view of its characters; the action, such as it is, is presented through the seemingly casual shot compositions and copious camera movements of neorealist film. Until the end of the movie, not a lot happens: the kids engage in mischievous pranks, their parents strain to hold things together, and Bobby (Willem Dafoe), the seen-it-all manager of the Magic Castle, tries to stave off threats to the motel and its inhabitants. Those inhabitants are what historian Paul Fussell, in his insightfully snarky 1983 book *Class: A Guide through the American Status System*, called "bottom out-of-sight": the sort of people who are laid so low that others prefer to avert their eyes from the wretched spectacle.

It is, indeed, difficult to watch Halley's sordid life and inevitable descent. Belligerent and profane, she alienates even those trying to help her. She is as childish and id-driven as a kid, which is why her scenes with Moonee seem more like playdates than parent-child interactions. The only things she has going for her are her love for her daughter, her resilience, and her talent for making a scene. And make a scene she does at the denouement of the film when social service workers arrive at the Magic Castle to take Moonee away and send her to a foster home. The last we see of Halley is an extreme close-up of her mouth bellowing, "FUCK YOUUUUU!"

That imprecation more or less sums up what all three of these characters say to their plight. They refuse to be cultural refuse, tossed aside like disposable debris. Although none of their stories end well, they persevere. The last we see of Tonya, who has turned to professional boxing to earn her keep, she is getting up off the mat during a bout, spitting out blood and getting back in the fight. Mildred's final act is to confront someone she had suspected of her daughter's rape and murder, even though the evidence has

Halley (Bria Vinaite) starts to let fly her four-letter malediction on the world, in *The Florida Project* (Sean Baker, A24). Digital frame enlargement.

since exonerated him. Although she knows that she is lashing out in the wrong direction, it doesn't matter to her. The existential act of doing something—anything—even if it is misplaced, seems preferable to throwing in the towel and conceding defeat.

American movies have always spoken to both our aspirations and our anxieties. Our satisfaction with these characters' refusal to back down is accompanied by the fear that such fearlessness may not matter. The determination to speak up and rectify perceived wrongs was very much in tune with the times, but so was the worry that certain voices might fail to have presence and significance in the larger world. *Three Billboards*, *I, Tonya*, and *The Florida Project* may invite audiences to revel in their characters' unremitting intransigence, but they also convey a rueful awareness that anger is not, in and of itself, power. Still, these films are invigorating by virtue of their lead characters who, due to class status and gender, have so little agency but, even so, refuse to know their place. To paraphrase a 2017 meme that went viral: nevertheless, they persisted.[5]

Persistence in response to abuses of power was certainly a major leitmotif of 2017, both on- and off-screen. These six movies' central characters comprise an assemblage of dissident and dissonant outsiders who insist on their right to be heard, despite their lack of social capital. The films encourage us to revel in their characters' refusal to remain on the periphery, as well as to cheer them as they challenge hierarchies of power and to identify with their ability to put up a fight. Of course, we have seen such stories before. Movies that valorize individuals who speak out against injustice and refuse to resign themselves to the status quo have been a mainstay of American cinema for decades. What was different in 2017 was the characters' social identities, the prevailing political context, and the extent to which a large segment of the populace seemed in urgent need of such stories.

It is axiomatic that the stories a culture tells itself are the stories that culture needs. Hollywood movies tend to lag behind history, so it generally takes a few years for cultural currents to find expression on the film screen. But even though these movies were produced avant la lettre of the events of that year, Trump-era audiences could respond to and decode them according to their own yearning for tales of inspirational fortitude. That such fortitude was exhibited by the sort of people who, because of their supposed otherness, were being disparaged by the new administration made the likes of these films all the more galvanizing. Each film, in its way, amounts to a declaration of selfhood: we exist and we intend to be assertive interlocutors in conversations about what does and does not make America great.

Admittedly, cultural trends are readily discernible in retrospect; hindsight makes it easy to bask in delusions of connectedness and causality and to recognize works of culture as signs of the times. As tempting as it is to read these films as a referendum on Trump's America, zeitgeist-tracking is a mug's game: a dicey, if entertaining, sport. It would be facile (and, given the lag time in movie production, historically erroneous) to claim a direct correspondence between the circumstances of 2017 and what was on movie screens that year. As ever, explicit connections between sociohistorical events and cultural artifacts can be only speculative. But even if there is not causality, there is at least a coincidental correlation between the sensibility of these six films and the convictions of a faction of the country that was, like the films' characters, hell-bent on owning the narrative and having their say.

Put in conversation with one another, these six movies can be envisioned as a rousing, if imaginary, film festival of the mind in which the dispossessed take possession of their story, thereby epitomizing the collective sense of outrage and resolve that was emblematic of the year's cultural climate. In elevating and giving voice to certain types of characters, they implied that the center of gravity was shifting and that America's self-portrait could no longer abide the erasure or silencing of such people. These fantasies of self-assertion are not just films; they are also social documents that speak to and for the spirit of their era. By narrativizing the impulse to find a compelling counterforce to the powers that be, they are a time capsule of their moment and part of the manifold annals of 2017.

NOTES

1. Together, these six films garnered eighteen Academy Award nominations, and they account for four of the eight above-the-line Oscars: Best Actress and Supporting Actor for Frances McDormand and Sam Rockwell in *Three Billboards*, Best Supporting Actress for Allison Janney in *I, Tonya*, and Best Original Screenplay for Jordan Peele for *Get Out*. They are also notably well represented in nominations and wins for other awards, collectively claiming 771 nominations and 413 wins in the roster of film awards compiled by the website IMDb.

2. The original ending, along with Peele's commentary about the change, can be viewed on the DVD of *Get Out*: "Alternate Ending with Commentary by Writer/Director Jordan Peele." *Get Out*, directed by Jordan Peele, Universal Pictures Home Entertainment, 2018.

3. The term "matter out of place" was first coined by anthropologist Mary Douglas in *Purity and Danger*, Routledge, 1966.

4. Nanjiani was not the only creator of South Asian heritage to explore cross-cultural romances around that time. Siblings Gita and Ravi Patel's documentary *Meet the Patels* (2014) and Aziz Ansari's television series *Master of None* (2015–2017) also mined ethnically mixed matings for comedy.

5. The phrase went viral in 2017 after the Senate voted, along party lines, to silence Senator Elizabeth Warren's objections to the confirmation of Jeff Sessions as U.S. attorney general. Senate Majority Leader Mitch McConnell defended the silencing of Warren by saying, "Senator Warren was giving a lengthy speech. She had appeared to violate the rule. She was warned. She was given an explanation. Nevertheless, she persisted."

2018

Movies and Revolution

MIKAL J. GAINES

2018 was animated less by new sociocultural shifts than by the persistence and intensification of long-standing issues brought into stark relief. On 14 February, an expelled student entered Majory Stoneman Douglas High School in Parkland, Florida, with an assault rifle and opened fire. Despite his shooting spree lasting only minutes, it left seventeen dead and seventeen more wounded. Parkland students' subsequent "March for Our Lives" the following month in Washington, D.C., called upon lawmakers to enact substantive legislative changes and sparked other student protests across the country. While these efforts helped prompt the passage of new age restrictions and waiting periods for gun purchases in Florida, other high-profile mass shootings—including those at Santa Fe High School in Texas in May and the Tree of Life Synagogue in Pittsburgh and a country and western bar in Thousand Oaks, California, in October and November, respectively—pointed only to more bloodshed as the decade came to a close.

If abating gun violence seemed untenable, the year did offer other moments of progress and accountability for the #MeToo movement. An investigation into USA Gymnastics revealed a broader twenty-year history of sexual abuse throughout the organization involving hundreds of survivors. Dr. Larry Nassar became the face of the scandal, but he was only part of a larger institutional culture that had allowed predators to thrive. As with the Penn State scandal at the start of the decade and ongoing revelations of abuse within the Catholic church, the case posed difficult questions about systems that not only allowed sexual abuse to happen but even helped to facilitate it. Bill Cosby, once known as "America's Dad," was convicted on three counts of sexual assault following years of allegations and a 2017 mistrial. His public image of Black bourgeois respectability had already been undone, but his conviction nevertheless marked an important moment of public reckoning. Yet even this was eclipsed by Professor Christine Blasey Ford's sexual assault accusations against Supreme Court nominee Brett Kavanaugh. Their resulting testimony before Congress garnered 20 million viewers and took over the national conversation in a way arguably not seen since Anita Hill's testimony against Clarence Thomas almost thirty years before. The American public appeared to remain largely split about who they viewed as the real victim, and Kavanaugh, after a less than thorough FBI investigation, was ultimately confirmed to the court due to a Republican majority in the Senate.

The Trump administration remained embroiled in drama for much of the year as questions about possible Russian interference in the 2016 elections lingered. Although Special Counsel Robert Mueller issued an indictment of twelve Russian intelligence officers for hacking the Democratic National Committee and the Clinton presidential campaign, Trump himself publicly questioned his own intelligence service's findings. The administration was also beset by a series of high-level firings and forced resignations that suggested a chaotic atmosphere at the White House. Adding to the disarray, Trump's longtime personal attorney Michael Cohen admitted to paying two different women not to reveal Trump's extramarital affairs before his election, and his former campaign manager, Paul Manafort, pled guilty to multiple counts of tax and bank fraud. The most significant controversy erupted over a fierce homeland security crackdown on asylum seekers at the Mexican border, resulting in family separations and detentions. Images of children in cages evoked the ugly history of internment and concentration camps, helping to galvanize voter turnout at the midterms where the Democrats took back the House. Electoral firsts, including the youngest woman in Congress, Alexandria Ocasio-Cortez from New York, the first Muslim women, Rashida Tlaib and Ilhan Omar of Michigan and Minnesota, respectively, the first Indigenous women, Sharice Davids of Kansas and Deb Haaland of New Mexico, and the first openly gay governor, Jared Polis of Colorado, hinted at an appetite for change. Such milestones notwithstanding, government dysfunction continued as the year ended in partisan deadlock over funding for a border wall, leading to a third government shutdown.

The world of technology and communication offered no more stability than government as Facebook revealed that over 87 million users' data had been compromised by Cambridge Analytica, a consulting firm instrumental in influencing both the Trump campaign and Brexit. The massive breach helped to illuminate the scale and depth of how metadata was already being used not only to shape public opinion but to fundamentally alter world events. Coupled with the end of federal net neutrality protections, a network of Orwellian surveillance and deliberate manipulation of the public by powerful forces began to emerge. It would not be the only top story of

2018 that seemed pulled out of a conspiracy theory film. *Washington Post* columnist Jamal Khashoggi, who had been critical of the Saudi royal family, was assassinated and his body dismembered at the Saudi consulate in Turkey during a trip to procure a marriage certificate. The horrific incident drew attention to the United States' problematic relationship with Saudi Arabia.

Khashoggi was only one of several prominent public figures to die tragically in 2018. Perhaps just as startling as his murder were the suicides of celebrity chef, author, and television host Anthony Bourdain and fashion designer Kate Spade. Some notable passings in the world of film, theater, and television included: directors Claude Lanzmann, Nicholas Roeg, Milos Forman, Bernardo Bertolucci, and Penny Marshall; actors John Mahoney, Dorothy Malone, John Gavin, Tab Hunter, Stéphane Audran, Barbara Harris, Burt Reynolds, Susan Anspach, and Marin Mazzie; film editor Anne V. Coates; screenwriter William Goldman; title designer Pablo Ferro; playwrights Joe Masteroff and Neil Simon; TV writer Steven Bochco and *SpongeBob SquarePants* creator Stephen Hillenburg; and film scholar Annette Michelson and philosopher-critic Stanley Cavell. It was also a somber year for comic fans with the passing of Marvel icon Stan Lee and *Spiderman* creator Steve Ditko, whereas the literary world saw the departure of renowned authors Tom Wolfe, Ursula K. Le Guin, V. S. Naipaul, Philip Roth, Harlan Ellison, and Ntozake Shange. After long and storied careers in music, the "Queen of Soul" Aretha Franklin and South African jazz artist and activist Hugh Masekela both succumbed to protracted battles with cancer. Also included among 2018's losses were political figures former President George H. W. Bush, Senator John McCain, and former United Nations Secretary General Kofi Annan. Famed theoretical physicist Stephen Hawking died after a five-decade struggle with ALS, and Microsoft founder Paul Allen died of complications from non-Hodgkin's lymphoma, leaving some big holes in science, technology, and business arenas. The year also saw the loss of pop artist Robert Indiana, evangelist Billy Graham, and longtime ABC sports commentator Keith Jackson.

The natural world offered little reprieve from grief as a 7.5-magnitude earthquake rocked Indonesia, followed by a tsunami, killing hundreds. Other disasters appeared to offer further evidence of the devastation wrought by climate change. Hurricane Michael, a category-five storm and the strongest to hit the United States since Andrew in 1992, caused unprecedented damage, and the Camp Wildfire, the deadliest in California history, raged for a month from early November to early December before finally being contained. If one were looking for signs of apocalypse, then one need look no further than the fire's near total destruction of the town aptly named Paradise.

Some of 2018's most significant films reflected this same sense of impending cataclysm, but the larger cinematic landscape looked familiar as big-budget comic book movies and franchise action pictures continued to drive the box office. With three blockbuster hits in the Marvel Cinematic Universe (MCU), Marvel continued to demonstrate its firm dominance over the market. DC Comics also got in on the action with *Aquaman*, but there seemed little doubt about which company would claim victory in their decade-long rivalry, or about whether audiences were still interested in superhero stories. *Jurassic World: Fallen Kingdom, Mission: Impossible—Fallout, Creed II,* and *Solo: A Star Wars Story* served as the most recent entries in their respective franchises, while the long-awaited sequel to Pixar's *The Incredibles* delivered what audiences enjoyed about the original. Dwayne "the Rock" Johnson kept his crown as one of the biggest global stars with two special effects–driven spectacles, *Rampage* and *Skyscraper*, though only the former performed well with audiences. With epic blockbusters ruling the day, it seemed only fitting that Steven Spielberg, one of the architects of the modern blockbuster, would helm an adaptation of the best-selling novel *Ready Player One*. Ironically, though, it was John Krasinski's postapocalyptic, sci-fi horror film *A Quiet Place* that felt the most Spielbergian of the year's big movies. Few expected such a polished directorial debut from the former star of *The Office*, but at its best moments, the film balanced well-orchestrated suspense and big emotional payoff reminiscent of vintage Spielberg creature features like *Jaws* (1975) and *Jurassic Park* (1993).

The year in movies was also richer and more complex than its blockbuster-laden facade, featuring some surprising breakouts. The romantic comedy *Crazy Rich Asians*, the first Hollywood release with a majority Asian cast since the *Joy Luck Club* (1993), brought in a whopping $238 million at the global box office. Audiences also turned out in big numbers for Bradley Cooper's remake of *A Star Is Born* and Rami Malek's Oscar-winning performance as Freddie Mercury in *Bohemian Rhapsody*. Other biopics and period pieces like *Green Book, BlacKkKlansman, Roma,* and *First Man* performed well both commercially and critically, but it was Yorgos Lanthimos's queer, revisionist study of power, *The Favourite*, that offered the strangest and most intriguing historical drama. It, along with *Love, Simon, Disobedience,* and *Boy Erased*, made 2018 a compelling year for LGBTQ-themed films.

The horror genre thrived and continued to offer some of the best return on investment for studios. The success of David Gordon Green's *Halloween* reboot, *The Nun* (another entry in New Line's *The Conjuring* universe), the sequel *Unfriended: Dark Web*, and prequel *The First Purge* (both from Blumhouse) suggested that audiences remained firmly invested in established horror properties. Some other notable horror pics included *Mandy*, *Upgrade*, *Night Eats the World*, *Assassination Nation*, and a slick remake of the Dario Argento classic, *Suspiria*. One of the biggest surprises in horror came just before Christmas with the release of another postapocalyptic monster movie, Netflix's *Bird Box*, which the company claimed broke their seven-day streaming record by pulling in some 45 million global views (Schneider). Boasting A-List talent like Sandra Bullock and John Malkovich, it provided another sign of the streaming giant's growing prominence within the broader film marketplace. Alfonso Cuarón's Netflix drama *Roma*, and its subsequent Oscar wins for Best Foreign Language Film, Best Director, and Best Cinematography, similarly pointed toward the company's increasing power to shape the larger conversation about the future of movies.

The spirit of change was also emphatically felt on the small screen, particularly in moves toward more diverse casting and stories. Some of the year's most critically acclaimed television shows featured female, African American, Latino, Native American, and LGBTQ leads. These included *Sharp Objects* and *Insecure* (HBO), *The Good Place* (NBC), *Killing Eve* (AMC), *Pose* and *Atlanta* (FX), *Glow* and *Queer Eye* (Netflix), and *The Marvelous Mrs. Maisel* (Amazon). Other shows which did position white male characters at their centers, like *Succession* (HBO) or *BoJack Horseman* (Netflix), portrayed their protagonists as utterly flawed and, at times, outright evil people whose unwillingness or inability to change lies at the root of systemic inequities. The success of these shows was juxtaposed by one of the bigger TV scandals of recent years when ABC canceled its reboot of the hit series *Roseanne* because of racist tweets from the always-controversial lead Roseanne Barr; the network later rebranded the show as a spin-off called *The Conners* after dropping Barr from the cast.

Meanwhile, Black multimedia artists like Janelle Monáe and Donald Glover (aka Childish Gambino) thrived in 2018 with exciting music releases, videos, and work in television. For her part, Monáe continued to expand upon the sci-fi themes apparent in her earlier albums with the Prince-inflected *Dirty Computer*. The songs, along with the accompanying music videos and short film, work as complementary texts that comment on the nature of hegemony and the ongoing fight for free expression in the digital age. Monáe's interest in sci-fi also carried over to a role on an episode of the Amazon series *Electric Dreams*.

Glover's "This Is America," directed by Hiro Murai, quickly took the internet by storm and, like Beyoncé's *Lemonade* two years before, further evidenced the ways that Black artists helped to keep the music video alive as a relevant cultural medium during the 2010s. "This Is America," which won the Grammy Award for Best Music Video, is a masterpiece of visual kinesis, aural dynamism, and Black expressive practice, with Glover's signi-fyin' jester figure making powerful connections between the horrors of American history and contemporary injustices and projecting many of the still prevalent racial problems. Glover also collaborated with Murai on *Atlanta*, which, despite operating on a more subtle (and perhaps more sur-real) register than "This Is America," presented some of the most interesting and original storytelling of the year. From Oprah Winfrey becoming the first Black woman to win the Cecil B. DeMille Award at the Golden Globes, to Beyoncé becoming the first Black woman to headline the Coachella Music Festival, to the unveiling of Black artist Kehinde Wiley's unconven-tional portraits of former president and first lady Barack and Michelle Obama, 2018 showed glimpses of a world that could look much different from the way it had looked before.

Representing Revolution

Called upon to perform an unwieldy combination of indus-trial, commercial, aesthetic, and ideological work, *Black Panther*'s success had more riding on it than any other 2018 film. The #OscarsSoWhite move-ment, along with other demands for increased diversity in Hollywood in the few years before the film's release, had pushed issues of representation front and center in public discourse. Marvel's prominence in pop culture had also situated superhero stories as one of the biggest global stages on which representational issues could be meaningfully addressed. As the first Black-led entry in the MCU, *Black Panther* needed to demonstrate that there was a broad, bankable audience for a Black superhero movie.[1] At the same time, promotional buzz positioned it as *the* Black film of the decade, which meant it would have to deal thoughtfully with the Black freedom struggle in ways that no other film would (Wallace). *Black Panther* could not just be another Marvel film, nor could it be just another Black film: it had to be an exceptional example of both.

Fortunately, the film proved itself a moneymaking juggernaut and became the highest-grossing film of the year. Not only did a global audience come out in droves, often for repeat screenings, but going to see the film became its own unique, multigenerational, cultural event, with Black spec-tators donning traditional African clothing and mimicking the signature Wakandan cross-armed salute. In this sense, *Black Panther* represented a collective triumph, but it also signified a substantial shift in the history of Black film and Black spectatorship. Whereas comedies, musicals, historical films, and biopics were once the standard-bearers of big screen Blackness, the powerful mythmaking within the superhero movie had now clearly surpassed those genres as the more important cultural arena in which Black folks wanted to see their experiences validated (Gaines).

This shift in genre prioritization likely informed the casting of Chadwick Boseman in the title role of King T'Challa, the Black Panther. Boseman had already established his legitimacy as an actor of considerable range and as one explicitly invested in Black representation with lead performances in *42* (2013), *Get on Up* (2014), and *Marshall* (2017). The jump from biopic to comic book film also explained why a young Black director like Ryan Coogler seemed a good fit for such a massive undertaking. He had worked with *Black Panther*'s other lead, Michael B. Jordan, on the biopic *Fruitvale Station* (2013) and the *Rocky* franchise reboot, *Creed* (2015). Even with the former's "based on a true story" conceit and the latter's reinvigoration of a beloved franchise, *Black Panther* presented a much bigger risk and a heavier set of representational responsibilities. Traditionally, those responsibilities might have been left to films like *BlacKkKlansman* and *Green Book*, both of which treat racism as central themes while appealing to notions of historical authenticity and importance. Yet one would have been hardpressed to find someone who argued that either of those films carried the same heightened level of expectation from audiences, or that their success (or failure) would have as wide-reaching implications.

Each new entry into the MCU tries to find the delicate balance between establishing its own original style and maintaining continuity with other films in the franchise. *Black Panther* is no different in this regard, opening with a prologue that provides the origin story of the imaginary African nation of Wakanda using animation and voice-over. The first voice comes from a boy child asking his father to tell him the story of "home," which immediately politicizes the story in ways not true of other Marvel films. More specifically, the abduction of Black bodies from their homeland as part of the transatlantic slave trade (along with the many forms of dispossession and displacement that followed) situates the search for home—for a place of safe return—as one of the fundamental thematic concerns of Black expressive culture. Moreover, introducing a present Black father who obviously cares for his son challenges myths about absentee paternal figures in Black communities. In fact, a considerable portion of the narrative revolves around the need of its two Black male leads to grapple with their fathers' legacies. We will later learn that these initiating voices belong to young Erik

"Killmonger" Stevens (played here by Seth Carr and then later by Jordan) and his father, Prince N'Jobu (Sterling K. Brown). N'Jobu's version of the Wakandan origin mythology presents the nation as isolationists who chose to remain hidden from the rest of the world. Access to vibranium ("the strongest substance in the universe") allowed their society to progress while other Black people suffered. This conflict about whether to stay in isolation or engage in common struggle with the rest of the Black diaspora catalyzes the entire film.

Black Panther is able to explore such rich underlying themes in part because it features some of the most compelling worldbuilding of any MCU film. Wakanda is beautifully rendered though lavish, Oscar-winning production design by Hannah Beachler, Ruth Carter's vibrant Afrofuturist costumes, and a dynamic original score by Ludwig Göransson. Early scenes that show the protagonist's entrance into Wakanda clearly indicate that the mythical kingdom's majesty rivals that of Thor's Asgard. But it is precisely the film's willingness to simultaneously revel in and question this utopic façade that gives it its power. Just after the aforementioned prologue, for example, the setting jumps to Oakland in 1992. Here, the former Black Panther, King T'Chaka (Atandwa Kani), confronts his brother N'Jobu, who has betrayed Wakanda by sharing the whereabouts of a vibranium cache with the white arms dealer Ulysses Klaue (Andy Serkis). Klaue initially appears to be the central villain but gets dispatched early on; he really functions more as a cipher for white colonialist attitudes about Africa. As he later states when questioned about his theft of the precious resource from Wakanda: "You savages didn't deserve it." Rather than revealing the whole confrontation between T'Chaka and N'Jobo here, however, the camera cuts away, withholding the devastating truth for later. When Zuri (Forest Whitaker) does relate what really happened to an inquiring T'Challa (Boseman), the news proves devastating for both him and the audience, shattering the utopian veneer of Wakanda established earlier in the film.

Indeed, one of the most challenging aspects of *Black Panther* is that the antagonist, Killmonger, has been legitimately harmed by Wakanda through both the action and inaction of its leaders. His motivations for revenge and his desire to use Wakanda's resources to help other oppressed peoples are deeply relatable even as his praxis means doing violence to other Black people in the kingdom. Wakanda and the mythical resource vibranium therefore serve as symbols of fantastic Blackness about which the film itself expresses substantial ambivalence. We too are prompted to ask, Where has Wakanda been, and why should it not help oppressed peoples to protect themselves? N'Jobo's impassioned speech about the oppression he has

witnessed in America spoke directly to the 2018 zeitgeist, echoing the grievances of Black Lives Matter and other social justice movements: "I observed
for as long as I could. Their leaders have been assassinated, communities
flooded with drugs and weapons, they are overly policed and incarcerated.
All over the planet our people suffer because they don't have the tools to
fight back." These sentiments echoed real concerns that were not being
addressed anywhere else within the MCU, and not really in any of the
year's other major films either.

Big set pieces and CGI-heavy action sequences predictably drive the
narrative which follows, but *Black Panther* does much of its most important
work in the quieter, dialogue-driven scenes. Two of the most compelling
moments occur during Killmonger and T'Challa's respective trips to the
"ancestral plane." After defeating T'Challa in ritual combat and taking on
the mantle of king, Killmonger's spiritual sojourn returns him to the site of
his father's murder. The camera tracks behind him as he enters the apartment and then removes his father's journal from a hidden compartment.
N'Jobo suddenly appears to chastise him, prompting Killmonger to revert
to his younger self. Their heartbreaking exchange illustrates that beneath
all his outward rage lies profound internal trauma and pain. The young boy
sheds no tears for his father's death, claiming that "everybody dies . . . it's
just life around here." N'Jobo looks visibly pained to hear his son express
such passive acceptance of the disposability of Black life. Even more significant, a once-again-grown Erik asserts, slipping into AAVE (African American Vernacular English), "Maybe it's your home is the ones that's lost.
That's why they can't find us." The individuated sense of abandonment
they express here comes to represent Wakanda's larger original sin of leaving other Black diasporic people to fend for themselves. When T'Challa
later confronts his own father and the other former leaders in the ancestral
plane, he too indicts their decision to keep Wakanda cut off from the rest of
the world. "You were wrong. You were all wrong!" he declares. Just as Killmonger's conversation with his father complicates his apparent ruthless-
ness and militancy, T'Challa's rebuke of his paternal line troubles reading
his character as merely assimilationist.

Both lead characters vow to pursue a different path forward, Killmonger favoring violent revolution and eventual global rule (with Wakanda
"on top") while T'Challa proposes a less aggressive and decidedly more
amorphous strategy of aid and measured distribution of Wakanda's technological resources. Again, no other mainstream 2018 film explicitly addressed
questions about the best means to effect Black liberation. It is also worth
noting that the film did not frame these questions as the exclusive purview

Killmonger (Michael B. Jordan) and T'Challa (Chadwick Boseman) face off in *Black Panther* (Ryan Coogler, Marvel Studios-Disney). Digital frame enlargement.

of the male leads. In another crucial moment, the head of the Wakandan army, Okoye (Danai Gurira), and the spy, Nakia (Lupita Nyong'o), debate their obligation to nationhood. Like a good soldier, Okoye insists that she "serves [her] country" and the throne regardless of who sits upon it, while Nakia claims that she, instead, must "save her country." The climactic battle scene later pulls the two women into an alliance to stop Killmonger, and to prevent a full-on civil war, but giving voice to such opposing perspectives within the imagined Black community of Wakanda represents the film's deliberate attempts to depict Black folks as nonmonolithic in their ethics or allegiances.

Whether or not *Black Panther* lived up to its revolutionary potential or symbolized a truly revolutionary moment for Black representation are questions that critics will likely debate for years to come. What does seem clear, though, is that the film took seriously the representational weight placed on its shoulders and that it tried, perhaps not always successfully, to navigate the various polarities of expectation that could never really have been fulfilled by any single film. The film's conclusion sees Killmonger die at T'Challa's hands, somewhat neatly resolving the rupture in Wakanda's history that the former had initiated. Death in the MCU often proves to be a temporary state, but this still feels like a lost opportunity for a deeper ideological accounting that will hopefully be better addressed in later films.

Unwieldy Inheritances

Black Panther optimistically suggests that a radical shift away from tradition, and more specifically away from traumatic familial and cultural legacies, *is* possible, albeit not without considerable cost. Yet it was not the only film in 2018 to grapple with the theme of unwanted birthrights. On the surface, writer-director Ari Aster's small-scale, independent debut feature, *Hereditary*, could not have been more different from the Marvel epic. Unbound by the superhero narrative's need for hope and redemption, *Hereditary* embraces horror's fundamentally bleaker worldview. The Graham family cannot escape that which they have unknowingly inherited, but even worse, their attempts to resist it bring them closer to a terrible fate predetermined by malevolent, supernatural forces. Even so, *Hereditary*'s investment in exploring the effects of generational trauma and the unbearability of grief presents striking thematic continuities between it and *Black Panther*. A tonally brutalizing film, *Hereditary* functions almost as *Black Panther*'s negative mirror image. The former seeks to pull its audience into the utopian, Afrofuturist world of Wakanda with a sense of spectacle and wonder, and whatever problems Wakanda must reconcile from its fraught past get redressed through the heroes' interventions. Aster's film feels, instead, like a deliberately alienating one that offers neither its characters nor its audience any respite from an impending sense of inevitable doom.

Hereditary portends dread from the very start, opening with an obituary for Ellen Taper Leigh, Annie's (Toni Collette) domineering and mysterious mother. At the same time, Colin Stetson's low, droning score steadily crescendos until it begins to envelop the viewer, creating a sensation of being devoured by a sinister presence. Aster himself suggests that he wanted *Hereditary* to "feel evil," as if the demonic cult who manipulates the Graham family was using the film to also manipulate the audience (Stroumboulopoulos). Stetson's guttural sound choices help to establish this foreboding atmosphere as the music builds to a jump cut that introduces the first frame: the camera looking out through a window at a tree house as a fly buzzes on the sill. The score returns as the camera begins to pan slowly from left to right, unveiling Annie's art studio, filled with her elaborate miniatures. The camera then seizes upon a replica of the Graham family home and begins to track in slowly until we are seamlessly positioned in what now looks like a real-time wide shot of Peter's (Alex Wolff) bedroom just as his father, Steve (Gabriel Byrne), enters to wake him in time for Ellen's funeral. The quietly bold and fluid opening makes them look like characters in a dollhouse, players acting out a tragedy while unaware of our voyeurism or, worse, toys carrying out someone else's wills and desires without even realizing it. When compared to *Black Panther*'s hyperkinetic CGI prologue, which presages the mobility and agency that its characters will have to affect their destinies, the tightly controlled movement Aster favors here reflects his characters' enclosure within a larger plan not of their own making.

Aster's measured, self-assured style (aided greatly by Pawel Pogorzelski's cinematography) prompted many critics to associate *Hereditary* with the highly controversial designation "elevated horror" (Ehrlich). The term refers to a renaissance of particularly well-made 2010s horror films that feature strong directorial voices, breakout acting performances, detailed attention to filmmaking craft, slow pacing, evocative imagery, and overtly political or allegorical leanings. Other films, such as *It Follows* (2014), *The Babadook* (2015), and later, Jordan Peele's *Get Out* (2017), certainly fit the bill, but Robert Eggers's *The Witch* (2015) became the emblematic "elevated horror" masterpiece (Crump). This likely had much to do with the involvement of A24, the same production and distribution company behind *Hereditary*, which had already established itself as a place willing to support emerging voices earlier in the decade. With Oscar winners like *Room* (2015) and *Moonlight* (2016) as well as other "elevated" horror films such as *Under the Skin* (2014), *Ex Machina* (2015), and *It Comes at Night* (2017) in its stable, the A24 brand now stood in as code for art house cinema. All of *Hereditary's* promotional trailers prominently featured the A24 logo along with claims that it came "from the Producers of *The Witch*," assuring audiences that they were heading out to see not just any standard horror cash grab but an art film.

When asked about whether he subscribed to the idea of elevated horror, Aster equivocated: "It's a difficult question in some ways, because I guess if I'm going to make a horror film, I want it to fall in that weird sub-genre of 'elevated horror.' And for that reason, when I was pitching the movie around, I was describing it as a family tragedy that warps into a nightmare" (Rose). His ambivalence about categorizing *Hereditary* as horror makes sense given the industrial dynamics described above. One can also forgive Aster's hedging given that his elevator pitch for the film feels accurate: the Graham family *does* undergo a series of subsequent tragedies that only grow more nightmarish as the story proceeds. Even the most jaded horror fans probably could not fully anticipate the shocking but, as we later learn, carefully orchestrated death of the family's youngest child, Charlie (Milly Shapiro). Masterfully edited, the sequence relies upon tension created not necessarily from concern about whether Charlie will die—we expect she will—but rather from the horrific nature of the death itself and Aster's ability to align our sympathies with both her and Peter. Having already established Charlie's nut allergy, the disaffected stoner Peter finds himself suddenly called into action as she begins to wheeze, and he races to save his sister. Rapid intercutting between Charlie gasping for breath in the back seat and Peter's looks into the rearview mirror ramps up the intensity until the child's sudden decapitation. That she dies precisely *because* of his efforts to save her and not out of neglect is part of what makes the scene so devastating.

The surprise death of a major character has, however, operated as something of a horror cliché following Hitchcock's *Psycho* (1960). If there is something "elevated" about Aster's treatment of it, it stems from his adept handling of the aftermath: Peter slams on the brakes, realizing what has just happened. The camera remains fixed on his face in close-up as he sits paralyzed in stunned silence; he begins to glance into the rearview mirror but cannot face the reality of his sister's decapitated body in the back seat. Rather than grant the audience relief, Aster forces us to sit in this agonizing moment, no more prepared to deal with this catastrophe than Peter. Peter's irrational but understandable reaction to simply drive home, crawl into bed, and wait for someone to discover what has happened (rather than trying to explain it) feels painfully authentic. For this part, too, the camera stays locked on Peter's face as we hear Annie's gut-wrenching screams outside. We might initially assume that Aster has held back Annie's confrontation with the abject corpse as a matter of taste and restraint, but then the camera cuts quickly to a close-up of Charlie's decapitated head in the road as it is consumed by ants. Easily one of the single most gruesome movie images of the decade, even this shot lingers for longer than the viewer wants to bear. And because the conspiracy-possession subplot has not been revealed at this stage, her death feels viciously random, as if to say that everything and everyone is susceptible to the chaos of the universe. Not even those already in mourning will be spared further agony. Compounding misery onto misery, the scene shifts to Annie, wailing in truly inconsolable pain as Peter stands in the hallway, forced to listen to her cries.

Given the above description, it seems fair to ask how *Hereditary* could become A24's most profitable film to date (Tartaglione). Why would audiences endure such prolonged punishment? The film's appeal may rely less on masochism than on its embrace of the sense of overwhelming helplessness the Grahams experience in the face of grief. Peter's inability to cope (as well as his subsequent PTSD), Steve's stoicism, and Annie's progressive mental deterioration ring true as the kind of responses that might naturally accompany such a hurtful loss even without the addition of supernatural elements. But to dismiss those supernatural elements or Aster's clever riffs on standard horror tropes would also do the film a disservice. *Hereditary* succeeds in large part because apparitions, seances, and demonic possession

Annie (Toni Collette) faces abjection in *Hereditary* (Ari Aster, A24). Digital frame enlargement.

function as apt metaphors for a family that cannot pull itself from the depths of their grief and who have been intentionally led to ruin by previous generations. As Alissa Wilkinson argues, "It's a movie about the things we inherit from our families—not the good ones, but the bad, inescapable things that sometimes are best described as 'curses'" (Wilkinson, *"Hereditary"*). The Grahams are indeed cursed, and if juxtaposed against *Black Panther*'s Wakandan royal family, who seem chosen for greatness, *Hereditary*'s portrait of a family chosen for calamity offers a deeply pessimistic counterimage.

The horror-driven sequences in *Hereditary* had much to do with what made it one of 2018's most memorable films. Like *Black Panther*, though, some of its most electrifying moments happen in masterfully acted, dialogue-heavy scenes. A sharply written early monologue from Annie at a grief counseling session recounts her family's dark history of mental illness and premature death. These insights add depth to a character whose ambivalence about her own children might make her unrelatable and foreshadow the evil conspiracy against the Grahams. This disturbing history also prompts the audience to question whether the increasingly bizarre events that begin to unfold are real or if Annie is simply losing her grip on reality. She confesses through a stream of tears that she feels "it's all ruined" and that "[she is] blamed." Her internalized guilt and shame erupt in two incredible later scenes. In the first, the family sits silently at dinner beneath almost putrid yellow lighting until Peter provokes Annie, hoping she will admit that she holds him responsible for Charlie's death. Annie lets loose a torrent of pent-up fury about the family's refusal to accept accountability for "anything they've done." That is, until Peter deflects blame back onto her, questioning why Charlie was put in danger in the first place. Steve intervenes before the two can do any more harm, but the scene likely resonates with anyone who has ever wanted to lay bare all of their repressed familial animosity.

The second excruciating exchange between Annie and Peter occurs during a dream sequence that, like T'Challa's and Killmonger's trips to the ancestral plane, acts as a confessional space for articulating parental failures. As opposed to the vivid blues and purples that signify the dream space in Wakanda, though, Annie awakens in shadowy darkness to find a trail of ants leading from her bed to Peter's. She discovers him completely swarmed with the bugs pouring from his mouth. The shot is simplistically revolting, triggering one of many expressions of abject terror that overtake Annie's face throughout the film. All of this proves to be just a dream within a dream, and Peter snaps Annie out of her hysterics to ask a question no parent would want to hear from a child: "Why are you scared of me?" Astonishingly, Annie admits to never actually wanting Peter and even trying to force a miscarriage. Like so much else in the film, this unexpected disclosure works on two levels, indicating, on one hand, that Peter's birth was unnatural and all part of the cult's plan. On the other hand, it implies that the constant undercurrent of hostility between Peter and Annie really derives from the resentment of a mother toward an unwanted child. Justifiably, Peter breaks down, claiming that Annie "tried to kill [him]." Here, the scene deploys a crafty bit of editing in which the camera cuts alternately to both characters, now suddenly dripping with gasoline. Then a loud match strikes off-screen and flames envelop the entire frame. The surreal moment calls back to an earlier story Annie told about nearly setting the children on fire during a sleepwalking episode and further emphasizes the idea that she never truly sought maternity. Such an unspeakable admission harshly contrasts T'Chaka and N'Jobo's expressions of shame at having failed their sons.

Whereas *Black Panther* ends its melodramatic staging of familial, generational, and ideological conflict on a note of triumphant possibility, *Hereditary* counters with fatalism. The cult's elaborate machinations come to full fruition, and most of the Graham family gets sacrificed to make way for Peter's possession by a demon named Paimon; evil wins. In this way, *Hereditary* reflects an apocalyptic sensibility that accounts for Aster's comparisons to horror films of the late 1960s and early to mid-70's, such as *Rosemary's Baby* (1968), *Don't Look Now* (1973), *The Texas Chainsaw Massacre* (1974), and *The Exorcist* (1974).[2] Then, as in 2018, horror gave voice to a larger cultural undercurrent of cynicism and fear typically unacknowledged by big-budget films. *Hereditary* concludes with catharsis, but not of the kind that gives the audience relief. On the contrary, we return to the tree house from the opening shot, where we bear witness to the crowning of an Antichrist figure reborn in Peter's body. Almost as if to mock the audience for believing there could ever have been any other outcome, Peter/Paimon stares vacantly into the camera, nonplussed about his hard-fought journey toward corporeality. Stetson's score shifts from the menacing tone exhibited throughout the film to one that feels strangely ethereal, a move that also plays as cruelly ironic. It remains unclear just how the audience should feel about all that has happened, but it has happened nonetheless, and as a student in Peter's class asserts about the plight of the characters in Sophocles's *The Women of Trachis*, it is all the "more tragic, because if it's all just inevitable, then the characters had no hope. They never had hope because they're all just like . . . pawns in this hopeless, horrible machine."

This unceasing sense of being a pawn in someone else's gambit, of trying (and failing) to manage unwieldy inheritances neither desired nor asked for, and which so often call forth horror into our lives, is perhaps what gives *Hereditary* its lingering power long after the credits roll. The prospect of a generational curse appeals almost too easily to a deep need to explain away persistent familial dysfunction or even just one's personal failings. Depending on how we read it, the Grahams either fail to stop what is happening to them or succeed in manifesting the inevitable because they never really had a choice. For audiences facing a long list of inherited social and cultural ills—horrific race, class, and gender inequality, unrelenting gun violence, catastrophic climate change, widespread political corruption, and the resurgence of blatant white supremacist ideology into the mainstream—*Hereditary* taps into an even bleaker possibility: Is this world the punishment for the "audacity of hope" that fueled the election of Barack Obama a decade before? And if this was not the change hoped for, is it still not the change that was inevitably wrought?

Making Something New

Adapted from Jeff VanderMeer's best-selling novel, Alex Garland's *Annihilation* approaches the idea of radical change along a much different register than either *Black Panther* or *Hereditary*, though it does share some of the latter's sensibilities. Garland eschews family melodrama and leans on his background in sci-fi horror to tell the story of an all-female expedition to investigate an unexplained phenomenon called "the shimmer." The premise is in keeping with Garland's oeuvre, which includes screenwriting credits for *28 Days Later* (2002), *Sunshine* (2007), *Never Let Me Go* (2011), *Dredd* (2012), and his own impressive debut feature, *Ex Machina* (2014). While each of these films operates fairly restrictively within its respective subgenre, *Annihilation* pulls in elements of Lovecraftian cosmic horror, body horror, mutated creatures, found footage, and an alien encounter to create a vision that feels simultaneously contemplative and dynamic. Tim Grierson of *Rolling Stone* put the film in the same tradition of inventive sci-fi classics such as Stanley Kubrick's *2001: A Space Odyssey*, but also situated it as part of a new sci-fi "renaissance" along with films like *Upstream Color* (2013), the aforementioned *Under the Skin* (2014), and *Arrival* (2016) (Grierson). When compared to the previously discussed 2018 films, *Annihilation* distinguishes itself through its insightful engagement with existential questions about the nature of being and the human tendency toward self-destruction. It posits not the violent restructuring of a kingdom or the disintegration of a family but a fundamental remaking of the natural world and, potentially, of humanity itself by an alien force.

Appearing somewhere off the Florida coast following a meteor strike at a lighthouse, the shimmer is *expanding*, threatening to incorporate and mutate everything it touches, sometimes in beautiful ways but at other times quite horrifically. The narrative explores how the characters, and particularly the biologist protagonist, Lena (Natalie Portman), confront this sublime mixture of terror and wonder. Lena has the most obvious reason for going into the shimmer: her husband Kane (Oscar Isaac) was the sole survivor of a previous military mission inside. The first act of the film shows him returning mysteriously to their home after being missing for a year, but he seems *changed*, and it is not long before he falls critically ill. Flashbacks later reveal that Lena had an affair that may have prompted Kane to join the mission in the first place. For her, going into the shimmer to find a cure becomes a matter of ethical obligation as much as intellectual curiosity. Another member of the team, the geomorphologist Cass (Tuva Novotny), points out that all of the women carry emotional baggage on the expedition: Anya (Gina Rodriguez) is a paramedic and drug addict, physicist Josie (Tessa Thompson) self-harms, Dr. Ventress (Jennifer Jason Leigh) lacks any personal connections and (we later learn) suffers from terminal cancer, and Cass herself has lost a daughter. Although we glean these details from a somewhat clunky exposition dump, it helps establish that each of these characters goes into the shimmer to escape. As Cass suggests, "Volunteering for this, is not exactly something you do if your life is in perfect harmony."

The shimmer therefore acts as a literal and figurative prism that reflects the women's deeper psychological wounds and impulses.

Once they enter, stunning production design and visual effects immerse the group in an environment where the natural world appears both altered and altering. Garland and cinematographer Rob Hardy populate the mise-en-scène with lush landscapes, vivid colors, and rich lighting that lend the atmosphere a dreamlike quality. Early on, Lena notices peculiar and scientifically impossible mutations in the plant life. More harrowing encounters, first with a mutated alligator and later with a terrifying, bear-like creature, serve as examples of how the shimmer has begun to transform everything at a cellular level. Frightening as these external monstrosities are, the havoc that the shimmer wreaks upon the human form better illustrates the film's thematic concerns. When the group takes refuge in the former headquarters of the Southern Reach (the government organization that has been studying the shimmer), they discover a video left behind by Kane's previous expedition. Garland has the group crowd around a small video camera to watch it, deploying the found footage aesthetic utilized so effectively in films like Scott Derrickson's *Sinister* (2012). We pick up their gaze and watch in uncomfortably tight close-up as Kane begins to cut into another man's belly with a knife. He then pulls back the skin, revealing a pale, worm-like creature slithering inside. The highly affecting scene manages to invoke the alienness of the human bodily interior. Moreover, Geoff Barrow and Ben Salisbury's otherworldly choral score makes it seem as if we are bearing witness to a transmutation that is in some way *holy* even as it horrifies. This moment, along with the subsequent discovery of the grotesque biological tableau that appears to have emerged from the stomach of the man in the video, elucidates the deeper danger that the shimmer poses: an unmaking of the human self into something altogether foreign and unrecognizable.

The abnormal phenomena that Lena and the rest of the group encounter point toward a colonizing alien force within the shimmer, but other moments imply something more complicated at play. A second bear attack leaves Anya dead, with Cass already having been killed by the same creature. The next morning, with Ventress headed toward the source of the phenomenon at the lighthouse, Lena and Josie sit quietly together in the morning sun. Lena confirms Josie's suspicions that the shimmer is indeed changing all of them in ways they do not fully understand. Left with the choice between "facing it" with Ventress or "fighting it" with Lena, Josie claims that she does not want either. Blades of grass and other plants slowly and subtly begin to sprout from her skin as she simply walks away. Lena follows as Josie disappears behind some trees and out of the narrative.

The sublime beauty of self-destruction in *Annihilation* (Alex Garland, Paramount). Digital frame enlargement.

Garland leaves us without a clear sense of what has happened to Josie, but as the only Black woman in the group, her decision to opt out of their quest carries special significance. Has she died? Has she given herself over to the shimmer in order to be peacefully incorporated into this burgeoning new environment? Perhaps both? Or neither? Regardless, the agency she exhibits here is striking. Unlike Anya, whose fear and hostility toward change lead to her death, or the other women, who pursue a path of direct confrontation, Josie chooses what Kevin Quashie describes as a form of active, expressive surrender, "a deliberate giving up to another, the simultaneous practice of yielding and falling toward what is deep and largely unknowable" (Quashie 28). If the shimmer does behave like a refracting prism as Josie hypothesizes, she makes a decision to allow that process to happen freely, come what may. Her decision ultimately seems less like resignation than a kind of liberation.

Garland claims that everything in *Annihilation* works in service of earning the psychedelic climax at the lighthouse (Kraszewski, Macnaughton). This visually and sonically captivating sequence pushes the film's hallucinogenic quality to its upper limit and also advances the overarching theme of self-destruction. It is here, for example, that Lena confirms her suspicion that the Kane who returned from the shimmer at the start of the film is not her husband; another videotape he has left behind shows the "real" Kane immolating himself because he "can't bear" how the shimmer undermined his sense of identity. Lena then discovers Ventress in a womb-like chamber below the lighthouse that, with its slick, black, honeycomb structure, owes a clear debt to the monstrous hive space in *Aliens* (1986). Ventress claims that whatever alien entity crashed into the lighthouse and initiated the shimmer is *in her* now. Even more frightening, she claims that despite not knowing "what it wants, or if it wants," that "it will grow until it encompasses everything," fragmenting their bodies and minds until nothing remains. This is of course the annihilation referred to in the film's title. Ventress screams as a cosmic light pours from her mouth into Technicolor particle streams and her body disintegrates, leaving the alien in its pure form: an amorphous, kaleidoscopic shape pulled from the world of visualized mathematics (Tucker). After incorporating a drop of Lena's blood, the alien transforms into a metallic, humanoid figure. Terrified, Lena attacks the creature, initiating what Garland presents as a kind of mirror dance between the two of them in which the more Lena fights, the stronger the alien pushes back. It even briefly morphs into a duplicate of her until she tricks it into igniting itself with a phosphorous grenade.

Significantly, Garland has the alien revert to its humanoid form after Annie escapes. Only its arms and hands remain ignited by the flame, suggesting that it could contain the fire if it chose to. Instead, though, it seems to mimic Lena's own self-destructive impulses by setting flame first to Kane's corpse and then to a set of white vines, which have grown out from the chamber below, covering the lighthouse walls and serving as roots for a series of crystalline tree structures outside. Finally, the alien crawls back down into the chamber below, allowing it all to catch fire until the frame is overtaken by bright white light. The wide shots of Annie watching as the glass structures catch fire and then collapse make for some of the film's most memorable and tragically beautiful images, a visual rendering of humanity's self-destructive compulsions manifested in twilight. When questioned about the alien's intentions by the Southern Reach, Annie pushes back against the claim that it sought to destroy the world, distinguishing that "it wasn't destroying. It was changing everything. It was making something new." At its core, *Annihilation* concerns itself with the idea that radical change—something truly new and different—may only be possible if we accept that such change cannot also be ours to control and direct, and that we may not ourselves survive it, at least not in our current form. The film ends with the new Kane and possibly a new Lena locked in an embrace, their eyes glowing with the same light of the shimmer. Whoever they were before, they can never go back.

Satire Weaponized

No film better captured the political zeal of 2018 than Boots Riley's debut *Sorry to Bother You*. Set in a contemporary but heightened reality, the film presents a vision in which the extremes of social inequity get taken to their logical albeit outlandish conclusions. Protagonist Cassius Green (Lakeith Stanfield) starts the film broke, living in his uncle's garage, and in the midst of a personal crisis. An early exchange with his artist girlfriend Detroit (Tessa Thompson) features him contemplating the nature of death and questioning whether he will ever do something worthy of a legacy. Given the rarity with which Black characters receive the chance to ponder larger existential questions, what Riley calls their place "in relation to space and time," this minor moment carries radical potential (Zaman). Unlike *Annihilation*, *Sorry* shifts away from these questions toward more ethical ones. Cassius inhabits a world where responding to the exigencies and precariousness of life under capitalism must take precedence over philosophy. Driving this point home, Riley shows Cassius watching a commercial for WorryFree, a company that offers its workers food, clothing, and shelter in exchange for lifetime contracts. The workers wear blue-and-yellow jumpsuits that simultaneously invoke Walmart and prison uniforms, a critique of the link between corporations and the prison industrial complex. WorryFree also symbolizes the logical extension of a system that puts profits above all else and in which most forms of labor can no longer provide the basic necessities of life. Establishing these conditions makes Cassius's brief moment of introspection all the more important in that it foregrounds his legitimate desire to do something and be someone who matters in the world. The problem is that these aspirations, when filtered through an exploitative system, become conflated with his pursuit of financial mobility. Another exchange shortly after this reveals that his uncle faces possible foreclosure. The struggle is real.

Cassius's new job as a telemarketer at RegalView initially appears to offer him direction and purpose, especially after one of his older Black coworkers, Langston (Danny Glover), hips him to using his "white voice." Rather than an essentialist formulation or even a cultural affectation, Langston frames the white voice as an aspirational performance: "It's sounding like you don't have a care, you got your bills paid, you're happy about your future . . . it's not really a white voice, it's what they wish they sounded like. It's like what they think they're *supposed* to sound like." Cassius's seemingly natural ability to deploy this performative whiteness (voiced by comedian David Cross) allows him to quickly become a "power caller," which also puts him directly at odds with his striking co-workers. When his friend Salvador (Jermaine Fowler) calls him a sellout, Cassius responds with self-serving justifications: "My success has nothing to do with you alright. You just keep doing whatever it is that you're fucking doing, and I'll root for you—from the sidelines." Having already decided to overlook RegalView's connection to WorryFree, and the reality that he is effectively selling slave labor, his lack of solidarity feels that much hollower. As Doreen St. Félix argues, "The trick of 'white voice,' a folkloric joke among many black people, becomes in Riley's film, a path to self-debasement."

Mapping Cassius's evolution from company man to protorevolutionary takes up much of the remaining narrative, but his transition only occurs following a series of escalating humiliations: a protestor hits him in the head with a cola can while crossing the picket line and he becomes a national meme; Detroit creates a performance art piece in which she subjects herself to abuse, thereby implicating Cassius for similarly "sticking to the script"; and he gets coerced into doing what amounts to a blackface caricature for an audience of white partygoers at his boss's house. Despite all this, only once he learns about CEO Steve Lift's plans for the WorryFree workforce does Cassius recognize the real stakes of his complicity. In perhaps the only other 2018 scene that competes for shock value with *Hereditary*'s surprise child decapitation, Riley has Cassius enter what he thinks is a bathroom at Lift's house. The camera tracks alongside him through a large industrial space illuminated only by low fluorescent lighting that washes everything in a sickly green hue. He stands outside of a stall waiting for whomever is inside to exit. A voice reluctantly asks, "Can you help me?" Cassius initially refuses but then opens the door, only to have the "equisapien," Damarius (voiced by Forest Whitaker), fall out onto the floor and begin to scream. Two more of the creatures burst out from accompanying stalls, prompting Cassius to run out in a panic. Part human, part horse hybrids with giant dangling phalluses, the equisapiens evoke the Bakhtinian carnivalesque, marking a turn toward the absurd that pushes the film from sharp satire into more radical territory. It seems difficult not to read the equisapiens' desperate pleas for Cassius's help as a metaphor for how even the most obvious forms of suffering under capitalism often go ignored.

Sorry resolves the main conflict concerning Cassius's move from individualism to a collective political consciousness by having him rejoin the other workers to resist the company's union-busting efforts. With the help of the equisapiens, they appear to win the day, and Cassius mends his broken relationships. He also sheds the trappings of his unethical corporate "come up" and plans to return to RegalView as a fellow unionized worker. And yet, Riley seems to have recognized that as a revolutionary statement, such a neat ending would be insufficient. Instead, as Cassius and Detroit prepare to move back into the now remodeled garage in his uncle's house, Cassius (with his back to the camera) drops to the ground and begins to contort. He arises and then turns to reveal his face, which has begun to mutate into that of an equisapien. Credits briefly begin to roll, but then stop as the camera opens onto a slow tracking shot into Steve Lift's living room as the phone rings. He answers, only to realize that Cassius and the other equisapiens have come on behalf of "stopamudholeinyoass.com" to serve up his just deserts. The film ends with one of the equisapiens kicking the door in and releasing an angry growl, an amazing moment that best embodies the thread of revolution that ran through the year in movies that was 2018.

NOTES

1. Technically speaking, *Blade* (1998) was really the first Black-led Marvel film and most important precursor to *Black Panther*; but given that the last sequel in that series, *Blade Trinity*, was released in 2004, it seems worth distinguishing from the explosion of superhero films that began with *Ironman* (2008) and DC Comics' *The Dark Knight* (2008).

2. Like Jordan Peele, Aster has exhibited a penchant for name-checking particular art house films like Ingmar Bergman's *Cries and Whispers* (1972), Peter Greenaway's *The Cook, The Thief, His Wife & Her Lover* (1989), and Ang Lee's *The Ice Storm* (1997) as more significant influences on *Hereditary* than any horror film, though he does sometimes mention Stanley Kubrick's *The Shining* (1981) and Brian DePalma's *Carrie* (1976) as well. See Stroumboulopoulos.

2019

Movies, Anniversaries, and the Limits of Looking Back

DENNIS BINGHAM

2019 began in the wake of the 2018 midterm elections, which resulted in a split Congress. In this third year of the Trump presidency, the news—indeed, American culture—felt like all Trump, all the time, a reality show that was reality. This president, who tweeted out storms in the wee hours while the country slept, kept the nation in a nearly constant state of upset, roiling those who opposed him and "thrilling his base," as reported by a news media still chagrined at its failure to gauge the extent of the support for the celebrity real estate mogul prior to the 2016 election.

On 25 March, Special Counsel Robert Mueller turned in the report of his twenty-two-month-long investigation of Russian meddling in the 2016 U.S. elections and the possible involvement by the Trump campaign and White House. Mueller's report made numerous indictments (though most were of Russian citizens) and won some convictions about the former, but found no evidence of the latter. The day after Mueller's long-awaited and somewhat halting testimony before Congress on 24 July, the president made a phone call, which was intercepted by a whistleblower in the intelligence community. Trump asked Ukraine's new president Volodymyr Zelensky for "a favor": find information about former vice president Joe Biden's son Hunter's business connections in Ukraine in the hopes of tarring the reputation of his possible opponent in the next presidential election. In a reversal of the impeachment hearings of Richard Nixon, here was "the smoking gun," the alleged impeachable offense, before an inquiry even began. Speaker Nancy Pelosi, who all year had been restraining many of her Democrats in the House of Representatives from launching an impeachment inquiry, now had little choice but to authorize one. On 19 December, 229 Democrats and one independent voted Articles of Impeachment on Abuse of Power and Obstruction of Justice. Republicans in the House, pressured by solid support of the president in their safe districts, maintained that the charges did not warrant impeachment.

Beyond domestic politics (but never far from it), activism was alive throughout the world in 2019. At the United Nations, a sixteen-year-old climate activist from Sweden, Greta Thunberg, spoke before the Climate Action Summit. Her opening line, "We are watching you," quickly became a meme. Thunberg's stern message landed her on the cover of *Time* in late December as the magazine's "Person of the Year." Merriam-Webster joined gender identity activism with grammarian linguistics in announcing that its word for 2019 was "they," acknowledging the acceptance of the first-person plural pronoun to refer to a singular person of unspecified gender, possibly making "he or she" and its variants a thing of the past (Dwyer).The continuing importance of movies in the world's imagination—especially the Marvel Cinematic Universe (MCU)—could be seen in the way that anti-Beijing protesters in Hong Kong chose to characterize their own movement. In June, protests erupted over a proposed bill to make it easier for mainland China to extradite suspects from Hong Kong. Crowds of up to a million took to the streets in protest. Citizens were fearful that China would clamp down on the precarious "one country, two systems" policy that has held the city in check since the 1997 "handover" from British to Chinese rule. Even after Beijing withdrew the extradition bill, the protests showed no signs of letting up. "One day," declared activist Joshua Wong, "the Communist Party of China will still exist, they will still use whatever means to interfere in Hong Kong's autonomy. So there's no endgame. That's the infinity war that Hong Kong people are willing to engage in" (Euronews). Headlines for the rest of the year dubbed the protests "the infinity war."

"One country, two systems" seemed as though it could also apply to the United States in this era, particularly institutions of higher education. Higher education experts continued to sound the alarm that colleges and universities around the country were floundering in a sea of troubles. These included, according to the website *Education Dive*, "pressure to lower tuition, stagnating state funding and a shrinking pool of high school graduates" (Camera). In 2019, the crisis, largely driven by declining enrollment facilitated by the Great Recession, a significant drop in the U.S. birthrate, and escalating tuition costs, resulted in ten colleges and universities ceasing operations or merging, with more institutions on the brink of closing (Massa). At another end of academic finances, in March the Justice Department announced that it was bringing charges against thirty-three parents (including actresses Lori Laughlin and Felicity Huffman) and their college admissions consultants for a bribery scheme designed to ease their children's way into elite universities. Among the casualties of the case, code-named Operation Varsity Blues—a reference to a 1999 film—were standardized tests themselves, "given evidence that the tests advantage wealthy students" (Taylor).

The hit Broadway musical of the year was *Hadestown*, a contemporary resetting of the myth of Orpheus and Eurydice with music and lyrics by singer-songwriter Anaïs Mitchell that won eight Tonys, including Best Musical. On television, it was a year of endings, as *Game of Thrones*, *Veep*, and *Big Bang Theory* all aired their series finales. These were countered by the opening of the streaming service Disney+, which launched with *The Mandalorian*, a *Star Wars* space Western series created by Jon Favreau and another product of Disney's purchase of Lucasfilm. Another irresistible Western fusion, "Old Town Road," a catchy example of "country trap" (the fusion of country music and hip-hop) by twenty-year-old rap artist Lil Nas X, was released, followed by three remixes, one of them featuring country star Billy Ray Cyrus. The video, by director Calmatic, won the Grammy for Best Music Video. The song, which first became a hit on Tik Tok, the video-sharing platform, broke the all-time record for consecutive weeks at the top of the Billboard Hot 100 at nineteen (Sisario). The song that finally displaced it from number one, "Bad Guy," set its own records. Its seventeen-year-old singer-songwriter, Billie Eilish, became the first chart-topper born in the twenty-first century. She performed the song on the season opener of *Saturday Night Live*, in a live homage to Fred Astaire's famous dance up the walls in *Royal Wedding*, on a rotating set not unlike the one used in the 1951 film directed by Stanley Donen. Eilish, accompanied on piano by Finneas O'Connell, her producer, arranger, and also her brother, sang the Beatles's "Yesterday" for the "In Memoriam" segment of the 2020 Oscar show, which included Donen, who passed away in 2019.

Other notable deaths of the year were John Paul Stevens, Supreme Court justice (from 1975 to 2010); *Hello, Dolly!* composer Jerry Herman; actor Danny Aiello (*Do the Right Thing*); Caroll Spinney, for forty-nine years the puppeteer inside Big Bird on *Sesame Street*; Paul Volcker, chairman of the Federal Reserve (from 1979–1987); longtime congressmen John Conyers and Elijah Cummings; actor Robert Forster (*Jackie Brown*); actress Diahann Carroll (TV's *Julia*); opera singer Jessye Norman; singer-songwriter Ric Ocasek of The Cars; rock singer Eddie Money; actress Valerie Harper (Rhoda on *The Mary Tyler Moore Show*); actor Peter Fonda (*Easy Rider*); architect I. M. Pei (the Louvre Pyramid); *Carol Burnett Show* comic Tim Conway; movie star Doris Day; film director John Singleton (*Boyz n the Hood*); longtime U.S. senator Richard Lugar (R-Indiana); actor Seymour Cassel (*Faces*); film director Agnès Varda (*Cléo de 5 à 7*); *Beverly Hills 90210* actor Luke Perry; fashion designer Karl Lagerfeld; and musical comedy star Carol Channing.

2019 saw the death of theatrical institution Hal Prince, who helped to shift the Broadway musical to a sophisticated narrative medium. Prince produced *The Pajama Game*, *West Side Story*, and *Fiddler on the Roof*. As director, Prince staged *Cabaret*, *On the Twentieth Century*, and *Evita*. His greatest legacy may have been producing and directing a series of musicals by composer-playwright Stephen Sondheim, including *Company*, *Follies*, *A Little Night Music*, and *Sweeney Todd*. America lost Toni Morrison, one of its (then) two remaining living Nobel laureates in Literature (the other being Bob Dylan). Known for novels about African American women, Morrison wrote *The Bluest Eye*, *Sula*, *Song of Solomon*, and the Pulitzer Prize–winning *Beloved*, among others. A documentary, *Toni Morrison: The Pieces I Am*, directed by Timothy Greenfield-Sanders, was released in 2019 a few months before her death.

Winners of Pulitzer Prizes in 2019 showcased investigative journalism and domestic terrorism: the *South Florida Sun Sentinel* for coverage of the "deadly shooting rampage" in 2018 at Marjory Stoneman Douglas High School; the *Pittsburgh Post-Dispatch* staff for coverage of the massacre at the Tree of Life Synagogue; David Barstow, Susanne Craig, and Russ Buettner of the *New York Times* for its eighteen-month investigation into the facts of President Donald Trump's finances; the *Advocate* of Baton Rouge, Louisiana, "for a damning portrayal of the state's discriminatory conviction system." Pulitzers for Criticism went to *Washington Post* nonfiction book reviewer Carlos Lozada, for Editorial Writing to the *New York Times*'s Brent Staples, and for Editorial Cartooning to freelancer Darrin Bell. Richard Powers's novel *The Overstory* won for Fiction, *Fairview* by Jackie Sibblies Drury for Drama, *Frederick Douglass: Prophet of Freedom* by David W. Blight for History, and *The New Negro: The Life of Alain Locke* by Jeffrey C. Stewart for Biography.

In sports, the Golden State Warriors advanced to the NBA finals for the fifth consecutive year, playing for their fourth championship since 2015, this time against the Toronto Raptors in their first finals appearance. Kawhi Leonard became the third player to win finals MVP with two different teams, as the red-hot Raptors defeated the undermanned and battered Warriors four games to two. The New England Patriots won Super Bowl LIII for their sixth championship since 2002, defeating the Los Angeles Rams 13–3, the lowest score in Super Bowl history. Far more thrilling was the World Series, as the Washington Nationals become the only ball club in series history to win all four of its games as the visiting team. The Nationals, who were the Montreal Expos before the team moved to Washington, D.C., in 2004, beat the Houston Astros in a seven-game series, which, like the Nationals' 2019 season, was come-from-behind all the way.

■ Not Playing: The End of Cinema

For all the concern that movies in theaters were dying—that the end of cinema, mistakenly forecast for so long, was now actually here, and with a whimper, not a bang—*Avengers: Endgame*, the three-hour final episode of the twenty-one-film Marvel superhero saga opened at the end of April and filled theaters all over the world, obliterating world box-office records, albeit at inflated ticket prices. Attempts to revive franchises past their sell-by dates, however, mostly fizzled as high-priced reboots of *Charlie's Angels*, *Men in Black*, *Shaft*, and *The Terminator* failed to take off, disproving widespread assumptions about the surefire nature of familiar properties. Disney alone could work the gambit, attracting huge audiences to live-action and photorealistic CG versions of *Aladdin* and *The Lion King*, respectively. On the day of *Lion King*'s monster opening in July, a *Variety* headline read: "Why Audiences Are Going Only to Disney Movies." In November, the streaming service Disney+ launched. The name evoked the frequent admonitions of Walt Disney himself to add more to a script or animations: "Plus it up" (Gabler 300). Thus as the Walt Disney Company entered the streaming wars, Disney plussed not only its own dominance but also the already taut nerves of an uncertain industry.

As usual in the decade, a handful of original features made the top-twenty grossers, between ten and twenty: *Us* (12), *Knives Out* (15), *1917* (17), and *Once Upon a Time . . . in Hollywood* (20). I discuss *Us* and *Once Upon a Time . . .* later in this chapter. *Knives Out*, the medium-budget murder mystery pastiche Rian Johnson made on the strength of his 2017 *Star Wars* entry, *The Last Jedi*, boasts an all-star cast, including actors from the franchises: Daniel Craig, James Bond since 2005, chews the scenery as master detective Benoit Blanc, and Captain America Chris Evans gets to play a moustache-twirling villain without a moustache. In *1917*, Sam Mendes directs an action thriller, which appears to be filmed in one shot, about a small unit of British soldiers sent on a suicide mission through the foxholes of the First World War. Roger Deakins's virtuoso cinematography won him his second Oscar in two years (the first was for *Blade Runner 2049* [2017]), after thirteen unsuccessful nominations since 1994.

There were important films by women directors. Kasi Lemmons, who had directed only three features since her breakout film, *Eve's Bayou* (1997), came back with *Harriet*, the long-delayed biopic of Harriet Tubman, with Broadway veterans Cynthia Erivo as Tubman and Leslie Odom Jr. as abolitionist William Still. Marielle Heller, who, like Lemmons, began as an actress, released her third nuanced and humane dramedy in four years' time, following *The Diary of a Teenage Girl* (2015) and *Can You Ever Forgive Me?* (2018) with *A Beautiful Day in the Neighborhood*, an unorthodox biopic in which Mister Rogers (Tom Hanks) winds up playing therapist to the *Esquire* writer (Matthew Rhys) who is sent to profile him. The fourth sound film of Louisa May Alcott's *Little Women* is a time-bending adaptation written and directed by yet another actress-turned-director, Greta Gerwig. Lulu Wang's *The Farewell* shows a Chinese American family too fully adjusted in their American way of life to do what needs to be done for the grandmother in China whom they believe is dying. Two debuts by veteran female music video directors were similarly remarkable. *Honey Boy*, directed by Alma Ha'rel for Amazon, is from an original screenplay by actor Shia LeBoeuf, in which he plays a character based on his own father, who struggled with addiction at the same time that his son, who will have similar issues as an adult, stars on a television series. Melina Matsoukas's film *Queen & Slim* turns on the all-too-familiar sight of a police shooting of an unarmed Black man (Daniel Kaluuya), who ends up with the cop's gun, shoots him, and, with a young woman (Jodie Turner-Smith) with whom he had been on an awkward first date, winds up the object of a cross-country police chase.

The fiftieth anniversary of NASA's first manned moon mission, Apollo 11, drew celebrations and retrospectives. *Apollo 11*, a compilation documentary by Todd Douglas Miller, with footage from the National Archives, National Aeronautics and Space Administration (NASA), and other sources, played early in the year in IMAX theaters. Miller's spectacular film whetted the cultural appetite for more reminiscences as the actual anniversary of the moon landing on 20 July neared. The Grand Canyon's centennial as a national park was commemorated. There were also remembrances of the twenty-year anniversaries of the films *The Sixth Sense*, *The Matrix*, *The Iron Giant*, *Fight Club*, and *Election*. These do not even count the publication in April of *Best. Movie. Year. Ever. How 1999 Blew Up the Big Screen* by Brian Raftery. Other articles marked the thirtieth birthday of *When Harry Met Sally*, the fifty-year anniversaries of *The Wild Bunch* and *Easy Rider*, and the eighty years since the release of *The Wizard of Oz* from the Studio era, high-watermark year of 1939.

These anniversaries bespoke a nostalgia, a desire for a time when government worked, people respected each other, science led action, and Americans worked together for a goal as ambitious as landing a man on the moon—even if such nostalgia causes us to gloss over the racism and sexism that the culture tried to say it had moved beyond. And what a deception that was. There's a moment in the historical footage of *Apollo 11* when Miller lingers on a shot, amid the seas of white men at their stations at

Mission Control in Houston, of a lone Black technician working at his desk. The camera, fifty years ago, fixes on him—as if to say, "See, we had Blacks working in the space program." The very occasional woman gets similar treatment. Nostalgia finds its way into nearly all American films of 2019, drawing on a memory or desire to return to an ideal of the past. For instance, the *Avengers* movies work as Marvel's recreation of the "team movies" of the 1960s, such as *The Magnificent Seven* and *The Professionals*, as well as 1950s heist films like *The Asphalt Jungle* and *Rififi* (except that the energy is positive and all goes well). Many of 2019's most interesting movies—and it was an unusually rich year for films—critiqued the notion of nostalgia and memory, often showing the fatal flaws in the image of an idealized past. A sinister fiftieth anniversary, that of the killings of Sharon Tate and others over two nights in Los Angeles by members of Charles Manson's "family," provided Quentin Tarantino with his latest opportunity to invent an alternate history.

Imagine There's No Manson

Once Upon a Time . . . in Hollywood lends nostalgic treatment to one of the most galvanic periods in U.S. history. Those who remember 1969 may be amazed that the strife-riven late 1960s could possibly be the subject of a rose-colored look back. 1969 can appear to have been a respite, but only in comparison to the clangorous years on both sides of it. And only if the nights of 8–9 August in Los Angeles can be wiped clean—as Tarantino erases them—of the Manson Family murders, "crimes so mind-boggling," writes Julie Andrews in a 2019 memoir, "that they challenged everyone's reality" (152). 1969 was the bitter end of Old Hollywood and the nexus of the worst industry recession since the early 1930s. The final popular and important Westerns, *True Grit*, *The Wild Bunch*, and *Butch Cassidy and the Sundance Kid*, came out that year. Westerns on prime-time television were far past their peak; the three networks were airing the final seasons of *Bonanza* (1959–1972), *Gunsmoke* (1955–1975), *The Virginian* (1962–1971), and the series on whose pilot *OUAT . . . IH*'s fictional actor guest-stars, *Lancer* (1968–1970).

Tarantino's alternative history imagines that workaday Hollywood artists Rick Dalton (Leonardo DiCaprio), a TV actor at a career crossroads, and Cliff Booth (Brad Pitt), the stunt double to whom he is fiercely loyal, inadvertently prevent the most horrifying murders of a decade riddled with assassinations. Charles Manson, the criminal con man who took advantage of the 1967 San Francisco "Summer of Love" to recruit and brainwash young drifters in a deranged commune, victimized entertainment industry types. A musician in his own mind, Manson sent four of the members of his "family" to 10050 Cielo Drive because Terry Melcher, son of Doris Day, and a record producer and low-level Columbia Records executive, had lived there with his then girlfriend, Candice Bergen. Reports that the killers "broke in" are inaccurate; prior to 8 and 9 August, many Angelinos didn't lock their doors. Tarantino packs his film with granular references, such as Jay Sebring (Emile Hirsch) playing for Sharon Tate (Margot Robbie) *The Spirit of '67* by Paul Revere and the Raiders, whose lead singer, Mark Lindsey, had lived at 10050 Cielo with Melcher, who produced the album.

The film is a movie maven's memory piece; Tarantino compares it to Alfonso Cuarón's *Roma* (2018) (Hainey). It's also a sly What If? What if this actor whose type was about to become outmoded and his good friend and stunt double with a shady past foiled the Tate murders and shriveled Manson to less than a footnote? What if these two guys, who represent the "old guard," as Pitt said in an interview—these white guys on the wrong side of cultural history—had unknowingly changed it? These set up still more hypotheticals: What if Sharon Tate went on to have a film career? What if Roman Polanski, who had already survived the Holocaust, had not become a widower—as well as lost a child—in the most horrifying of ways? What if the City of Los Angeles had not been forever traumatized? And so on . . . to make more uses of the title's ellipsis. It's not as if the impulse to avert the grotesque Manson Family murders at their fiftieth anniversary is unique to Tarantino. *Charlie Says*, directed by Mary Harron and written by Guinevere Turner, who collaborated on biopics of controversial figures in *I Shot Andy Warhol* and *The Notorious Bettie Page* as well as *American Psycho*, imagines Leslie "Lulu" Van Houten (Hannah Murray), one of the Tate killers, riding a motorcycle away from the Family's encampment on the Spahn Movie Ranch (a busy location in 2018–2019) before Manson could train her in murder.

Does it bother Tarantino that the only critiques of the Vietnam War uttered by any of his characters—the only mentions of Vietnam at all—come out of the mouths of Mansonites? Overall, his film is an unusually cheery vision of the late sixties. Like Cuarón, Tarantino was a child when his memory film takes place. The movie-crazed boy Tarantino seems most present in the matchups of movie ads and marquees with the exact dates in February and August '69 when they played in Los Angeles. The production design, which won one of the film's two Oscars, features movie posters, marquees, and billboards; for every well-remembered film (*Funny Girl*, or Zeffirelli's *Romeo and Juliet*—in its eighth month! Movies could be seen only in cinemas then, and a hit might play for months), there are three or four more that are utterly forgotten (*Pendulum, Joanna, Candy, The Night They*

Raided Minsky's, Krakatoa: East of Java, Ice Station Zebra, and *The Wrecking Crew*, which featured Sharon Tate). This is pop culture history recreated as it was, not as we tend to recollect it. (By contrast, the historical movie titles on marquees in Scorsese's *The Irishman*, in order to place specific years, are much better known than Tarantino's.)

Tarantino has never been known for child characters, but Trudi Fraser (Julia Butters), Rick's eight-year-old scene partner on the *Lancer* pilot, is grounded in dramatic ideals and Method methods. Naturally, the precocious child actress—Tarantino as the cinema-loving child who validates the failing, might-have-been movie star in midlife crisis—*would* be reading a biography of Walt Disney. But the only one published at this time, slightly more than two years after Disney's death, was Richard Schickel's acidulous *The Disney Version* (1968); Schickel set the tone for generations of Disney loathing. Trudi—an artist so pure she answers only to her character's name on set and discards the gendered title "actress" decades before doing so became accepted—sees only the positive in Disney, even from a highly disapproving book. It was Walt Disney's company that bought Miramax just before the start of production on *Pulp Fiction*, which became, twenty-five years earlier (speaking of milestone anniversaries), the first independent film to gross over $100 million domestically. "I'm their Mickey Mouse," Tarantino squeaked in 1994 about his relationship with the Weinsteins at Miramax (Biskind 190). And after the fall of Harvey Weinstein, who produced every previous Tarantino film, from *Reservoir Dogs* to *The Hateful Eight*, intoning the name of Disney helps him wipe away the taint.

This is only the second Tarantino film since *Pulp Fiction* without Samuel L. Jackson; even in *Inglourious Basterds*, set in segregated World War II, he's a voice on the phone. Jackson was evidently too busy in 2019 playing Nick Fury in Marvel movies (to which the eye patch Rick wears in clips from the fictitious movie, *The 14 Fists of McCluskey*, may be an, um, winking reference). Pitt's Cliff Booth, like Jackson's Jules Wittfield in *Pulp Fiction*, occupies the Tarantinian pole position of limitless cool and spiritual je ne sais quoi, the hit man (or stuntman) who can walk away from it all. All the lazy criticisms of this film as white male regression forget the outsize African American characters in most of Tarantino's films, rendering *OUAT . . . IH* an outlier. Pam Grier's Jackie Brown or Jamie Foxx's Django would have finished off Manson's brainwashed killers as ruthlessly as Cliff and Rick do. Like Jackie and Max Cherry, these are characters who have been counted out, and who finally show that they have worth, even if it is short-lived. As the film ends, Rick may have found redemption and earned an audience with Sharon Tate. He stays afloat in his swimming pool at the finale, while holding onto a genre, and an entire iconography, that is sinking fast. Taran-tino spoofs the 2019 audience with the type of post-credits sequence that Marvel fans are conditioned to stay in their seats for—a black-and-white, 1.33×1 commercial Rick does for Red Apple cigarettes in his TV star glory days. However, cigarette commercials will be banned from the air at the end of 1970. In Rick's star tantrum, kicking the life-size cutout of himself and blaming the ad agency for picking an unflattering shot, we get a glimpse of the overweening ego he now regrets, as well as the smoking habit that may become his undoing, as it was for his ego ideal, Steve McQueen (played in one scene by Damian Lewis), who died of lung cancer in 1980 at age fifty. Our knowledge of how obsolete Rick Dalton is about to become, more-over, lies in the fact that the blaxploitation boom, for which Tarantino has been an enthusiastic cheerleader, lies just around the bend of the decade.

Just once do we sample the culture that makes celebrities out of killers—in a radio news story about the impending trial of Sirhan Sirhan, soon to be convicted of murdering Robert Kennedy. Tarantino's film deprives Manson of his name, reducing him, like the actor, Damon Herriman, who very briefly plays him in this film, to the status of a bit player (unlike Harron's Manson, who is played by Matt Smith because the director said she needed an actor with "charisma," which Tarantino has in the stars playing his jour-neymen). Amid the mass shootings of the 2010s, stories in the media abounded with titles like "A Way to Stop Mass Shootings: Stop Naming the Shooters" (On Point). Tarantino asks: What if Charles Manson never became a household name?

Cliff is a divided character, a mysterious antihero. The ambiguity of the character extends to his name. "Cliff Booth" tracks back to *The Birth of a Nation* (1915), which made an unforgettable character of John Wilkes Booth, played by future director Raoul Walsh. The cliffs over which stunt-men of Booth's era drive have their predecessor in the cliff that Little Sister throws herself from at the male-hysteric peak of D. W. Griffith's bigoted blockbuster. Thus this is a far from spotless name spanning the equally far from spotless first century of film.

The stuntman, whose work courts injury and death, is a two-sided coin in Tarantino. In *Death Proof*, Stuntman Mike, played by Kurt Russell, passes the death with which those in his profession flirt to his victims. In *OUAT . . . IH*, Russell plays a much less evil stuntman and also narrates. (Russell is yet another link to Walt Disney; as a fifteen-year-old actor, he was signed by the founder to a ten-year contract to star in such titles as *The Computer Wore Tennis Shoes*, a 1969 movie *not* commemorated fifty years on.) Stunt work can also offer salvation. In the same film, Zoë Bell, Tarantino's actual stunt coordinator, plays a stuntwoman who unknowingly avenges Mike's victims (she plays Russell's character's wife here). Cliff Booth contains all these multitudes. The Spahn Ranch is the hell into which Booth descends and experiences evil in order to recognize it later and banish it.

Cliff's memory of Bruce Lee's braggadocio on the set of *The Green Hornet* is the film's most controversial element. Its depiction of an arrogant Bruce Lee (Mike Moh) is hard to square with Tarantino's love of Lee and martial arts movies, especially as expressed in *True Romance* (1993), in which the film's lovers have their first date at a Bruce Lee triple feature, and the Hong Kong cinema–inspired *Kill Bill: Volume 1*. The later scene of Sharon Tate watching her own movie shows that Lee trained Tate for her fight scene in *The Wrecking Crew*, in which she bests Nancy Kwan, an actress who, like Rick Dalton, seemed poised for stardom at the start of the 1960s but by the end of the decade was reduced to starring roles in B movies and villainous supporting roles in top-tier films. While Rick gambled on his career and lost, having chosen to leave a hit TV series to try to become the next McQueen, Kwan, as an Asian woman, had nothing like the same options because of Hollywood's inherently racist attitudes; Asians were most often cast in predominantly stereotypical roles.

A bravura three-way, midfilm, cross-cut sequence moves from, first, Rick on the set of *Lancer* facing down his alcoholism and delivering the performance he has wondered if he's capable of. The wide-screen compositions and the shadows cast in Robert Richardson's cinematography recall Sergio Leone more than the television production whose craft Tarantino also highlights. Trudi bestows her praise, telling Rick: "That's the best acting I've ever seen in my whole life." The second scene is Cliff encountering the Manson Family's encampment in its distinct evil, staged like a set piece in Roger Corman and American International drug and biker exploitation movies of a few years earlier, some of which Bruce Dern, who plays Spahn, was actually in. And the third scene is Sharon spending a free afternoon driving to Westwood Village and picking up a young hitchhiker, a practice that would end after 8 and 9 August. We see Sharon's jouissance at watching her fifteen minutes of Hollywood glory in *The Wrecking Crew* at the Bruin Theater. This third of the sequence is shot differently from the other two, with cinema verité–style long takes that document Tate from an objective distance. We see the Dean Martin movie with its actual scenes of Sharon Tate (rather than of Robbie playing her), transforming the dumbest movie imaginable into evidence that Tate was a filmmaker learning her craft. By cutting to Sharon/Robbie's delight in her work, Tarantino honors Tate as more than starlet eye candy, showing the work behind what she had done to that point and her pride in it.

▬▬▬▬ Double or Nothing

Imagine if the Queen in Disney's *Snow White and the Seven Dwarfs* (1937), while looking in the mirror, had managed to trade places with Snow White—whose actual name is Adelaide—and live her life. She marries the handsome prince, and they produce children with special talents. Meanwhile, Snow White finds herself part of a vast network of underground chess pieces devised to control the overdogs in the upper world by an autocrat no more competent than Donald Trump. Years go by. The banished princess returns to take her life back, having dwelled for three decades in an underground cave, like the mine where the seven dwarfs toil. Snow White, the virtuous anointed one, has been conspiring in her lair, with escalators and padded seating, all painted institutional beige. Here, subhuman doubles who are "tethered" to the fully fledged individuals above mimic the roles the overdogs get to play in the upper world. The doubles' only food is live rabbits, which they must slaughter and skin. *Us*, Jordan Peele's *Get Out* follow-up, is a tribal scream from that film's Sunken Place. The "under classes" choreograph a deliberately balletic and black comic parody of the long-forgotten Hands Across America from Memorial Day weekend 1986, one of the upper world's endeavors to assuage its guilt over the mainstream abandonment of programs like the Great Society and the Labourite safety nets shredded by Thatcher's Tories and the "Reagan Revolution," and one of the original Adelaide's last memories.

Us is Jordan Peele's further development of what Ryan Poll calls the "Afro-pessimism" of *Get Out*, which was, among other things, an antidote to Obama-era optimism (71–72). Unlike the Black people in the haunted house in the 1983 Eddie Murphy monologue which gave Peele his *Get Out* title (thus they "get out," unlike the privileged whites who stay put), Blacks know horror when they see it. Adelaide's parents act like white people, expecting no horror in their lives and never catching on that they are raising a fake. Adelaide grows up as an impostor; we hear her overly careful pronunciations, as if she had learned language later than other children. This is actually how Lupita Nyong'o, who plays Adelaide and is fluent in four languages, speaks English in interviews. As Adelaide, Nyong'o uses her own English diction to suggest a character who has willed herself an English speaker, while "Red," the former Snow White, growing up around mutes, has had to fight to hold onto the language she knew as a child. "The Tethered" become Peele's metaphor for the underclass and the history of African Americans. Made while Peele was developing a reboot of *The Twilight Zone* for streaming TV, *Us* is inspired by "Mirror Image," a 1960 Rod

Serling–written *Twilight Zone* episode in which Vera Miles plays a young woman waiting in the middle of the night in a small-town bus station. An apparent doppelgänger takes her identity and steals her seat on the bus. A man (Martin Milner) who is trying to help her calls the police, who take her away, presumably to a mental institution. The man, settling down to wait a few hours for his early-morning bus, finds that a double has now taken *his* suitcase, and with it, presumably, his identity. The episode fades out with Milner chasing after the identity thief, who runs out of the bus station and disappears into the distance. With this "short story" as germ, Peele develops a cultural critique in the frame of a horror movie, but with nearly four times the budget and twice the shooting schedule of *Get Out*.

Peele practically demonstrates the difference between a mainstream film that addresses a mass audience and an independent film. An art film in the horror vein—say, David Lowrey's *Ghost Story* (2017) or Robert Eggers's *The Lighthouse* (2019)—probably would have kept implicit the connection between Adelaide and Red. Even the original *Twilight Zone* episode leaves the doubles unexplained. But Adelaide knows she is the cause of the violent invasion of "doubles" that is sweeping the beach resort of Santa Cruz, just as N'Jobo (Sterling K. Brown), the "spy" in 1992 Oakland at the opening of *Black Panther*, knows that the Wakandan guards outside his door "won't knock twice." Peele cast both his Black leads, Nyong'o and Winston Duke, from Ryan Coogler's Afrofuturist Marvel blockbuster for a reason. Who these zombieish invaders are is a question asked and answered two different ways in the first act. "It's us," says ten-year-old Jason (Evan Alex), who a year before, the film cannily suggests, might have repeated his mother's journey. "Who are you people?" asks Gabe, "you people" being an unconsciously racist form of address, dating back to the 1992 speech by Ross Perot (who died in 2019) to the NAACP. "We're Americans," croaks Red (also Nyong'o), the ringleader of the army.

"You've been rooting for someone," Nyong'o explained, "who turns out to have been the criminal" ("The Monsters within Us"). So often in horror films, we root for the character whose normal existence is threatened; a frequent trope that concerns middle-class people who find they're living on land taken from Native Americans—as was much of the United States. Even the eventual "criminal" represents people America prizes—those who have lifted themselves out of the ghetto and "made something of themselves." We have been identifying with the well-dressed, affluent wife, mother, and one-time ballet dancer, clad in white and resplendent, like Nyong'o, who has graced the cover of *Vogue* four times. We don't want her to lose her privilege—of course we don't.

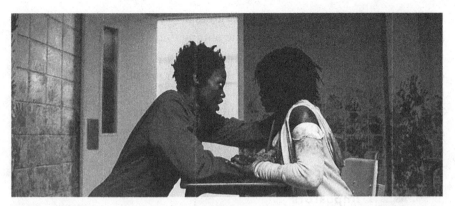

Red (Lupita Nyong'o) schools Adelaide (also Nyong'o) in how the other half lives in *Us* (Jordan Peele, Blumhouse, Universal). Digital frame enlargement.

Red is finally martyred, the vengeful leader of a movement of the underclass whose grand revolution will outlive her. We see this in the final shot, as America's purple mountain majesties are spanned by the linked hands of the Tethered from the underground passages that underlie America, as we're told in an opening title card, from sea to shining sea. The Tethered double, who pulled herself up from the underclass and defended her family in a way that we celebrate in America, has won, but she leaves a trail of privilege and presumption which will haunt her in a society whose inequality is making it unlivable. If *Get Out* is Peele's allegory of the false "postracial" promise of the Obama years, *Us* is his even more damning statement for the Trump era. The one positive is the strength of the African American family, which holds up while their superficial white friends, Josh (Tim Heidegger), Kitty (Elizabeth Moss), and their daughters Becca and Lindsey (Cali and Noelle Sheldon), make easy pickings for their doubles.

In *Us*, Peele makes a point of establishing Adelaide and Gabe Wilson as upper-middle-class achievers. They drive a Mercedes SUV, and they can afford a nice cabin near the beach at Santa Cruz, although one not as swanky as the two-level condo on the beach that Josh and Kitty rent. They are "us,"—movie identification figures, which is to say, aspirational figures. They are Bay Area Silicon Valley types, living the (American) Dream. When Gabe confronts the threatening Black foursome on his lawn, he code-switches: "If y'all are out here, tryin' to scare people, I think you picked the wrong house for dat." To their bourgeois sensibilities, the intruder(s)—one of the most essential tale types of the horror story—is the Other. The Tethered are closely analogous to Black American slaves; they are sequestered in separate quarters and kept away from all forms of literacy. These "slaves" have not only been forbidden to learn to read and write but they also have never learned speech. Thus when one among them arrives with the power of speech, she is the leader. The red jumpsuits that the Tethered wear make an almost too obvious analogy to the incarceration-of-color crisis that besets twenty-first-century America, as documented in Ava DuVernay's 2016 nonfiction film, *13th*. When the shadows arrive with their elegant gold scissors, the people aboveground don't know what hit them, just as the privileged rarely understand how privileged they are.

▬▬▬▬▬▬ Impostors

Parasite is a South Korean film, but the United States of America is woven all the way through it. Director Bong Joon Ho's comedy-turned-tragedy concerns a hard-luck family, the Kims (middle-aged urban parents in Seoul and their college-age son and daughter), who happen onto their far wealthier mirror images, the Parks, a tech executive, his stay-at-home wife, and their two children. The Kims, without any qualifications except their own considerable wit and ambition, pass themselves off to the Parks as a tutor for their tenth-grade daughter, an art therapist for their nine-year-old son, a driver for the busy executive, and a housekeeper.

Part of the exuberance of the film's first hour stems from the sense that, although the Kims become con artists extraordinaire; they aren't frauds, so adeptly do they blend with the roles previously played by people who weren't perceptively more talented or skilled than themselves. A brutal job market and a lack of money for education shuts qualified people out of positions and forces them into criminality. The Kims exercise initiative in going after opportunities denied them by more legitimate means. Ki-Taek (Song Kang Ho), a man in the prime of life, is robbed of purpose by the economy that collapsed in the crash of 1997. As S. Nathan Park explains on *Foreignpolicy.com*, this was a collapse as catastrophic as the 2007–2009 Great Recession in the United States. After the failure of his "chicken joint," like thousands of laid-off former corporate workers, the best job Ki-Taek, his wife, and grown kids can find is folding pizza boxes. His son, Ki-woo (Choi Woo-shik), is ambitious, polite, articulate, quick-witted, and, to his upper-class friend Min, virtuous, unlike "the drunken college pricks" he knows. Ki-woo soon becomes an effective tutor of the family's math- and English-resistant tenth grader, Da-hye (Ji-so Jung), who crushes on him instantly. Of the university diploma which he forges, he tells himself, "I'll be a student there in a year." The artistic bent, poise, and self-confidence of his sister, Ki-jung (Park So-dam), allows her to sell herself as a tough disciplinarian of an art therapist for the Parks' nine-year-old boy. She does not allow parents in the room when she works with her young pupil. This policy extends to her own mother, Chung-sook (Jang Hye-jin), once she becomes the housekeeper, her predecessor, Moon-gwang (Lee Jeong-eun), having been dispatched after Ki-jung made a minor allergy of the employee's look like symptoms of late-stage tuberculosis. Bong carries off these early escapades with cinematic set pieces; these range from the elegant montage that illustrates the plot against the housekeeper (cut to composer Jae-il Jung's suite in the style of Handel or Vivaldi) to the three-and-a-half-minute single shot that seemingly places the spectator at the tutor desk facing Ki-woo and Da-hye so as to witness the natural development of an innocent flirtation, which we know is not entirely natural and certainly not innocent.

When we meet the Parks, who are presented even more than are the Kims as a sitcom family—male breadwinner, female homemaker, 2.3 children, and pets—the overdetermined significance of America in the lives of the upper-class Korean family becomes all too apparent. The "man of the house," Park Dong-ik (Lee Sun-kyun), is first introduced as "Nathan," his name in American publicity, as shown on a framed *New York Magazine*–style profile that hangs in the entryway of the house. His work, complete with a Lebowski-esque certificate, also framed and mounted, bears the American stamp of "achievement." "Nathan Park Hits Central Park" is the article's English headline. Home video spectators determined to make out the article's information learn, by freeze-framing, that Park, as a twenty-five-year-old Microsoft employee, introduced the "Hybrid Module Map" twenty years ago, which, the text of the article in English tells us, "has brought an evolution to New York City":

> Beyond providing various information of the city utilizing augmented reality, it also allows you to "walk around" the streets of New York and browse real-time information wherever in the world you connect from.

The Parks exude an entitled cluelessness for which the cruel logic of the film's plotting ultimately makes them pay.

By the film's midpoint, the plot lurches away from breezy comedy and takes on characteristics of film noir and, finally, horror. Park maps New York, but we learn eventually that he doesn't know the depths and byways that run beneath his own house. Yeon Kyo (Cho Yeo-jeong), the rich wife and mother, has not acquired an American-sounding name, but she dubs her new employees "Jessica" and "Kevin," as if these names make them seem more expert in childhood education. Moreover, her son shoots toy

"Indian arrows," like the ones American kids played with in Rick Dalton's era. She says she "sent away from the U.S." for "Indian toys," which eventually are revealed to include a life-size teepee (suitable for backyard camping) and headdresses that Park arranges for himself and Kim to wear in order to play tomahawk-wielding Indians in the grotesque backyard party at the film's climax. The party brings to a crescendo the theme whereby wealthy South Koreans embody the privilege of white Americans circa 1953, the year the Korean War ended and the current state of affairs between South Korea and the United States became frozen in place. Park asks Kim to wear an "Indian" headdress, the exact like of which could be ordered from Amazon at the time of the film's release for $55.

Without leaving South Korea, the Parks exhibit all the tendencies of arriviste, assimilationist white immigrants to America. The Parks evince a white privilege that police violence against African Americans finally forced to the surface in the Trump era. They are unaware that they themselves, despite their wealth, would be othered, like Native Americans, in an America that consigned Asians, even naturalized citizens, to internment camps. The name of Park's tech company, for the English-language market, is Another Brick. "All in all," Bong seemingly quoting Pink Floyd, "it's just *another brick* in the wall." If the wall being referred to is Trump's hallucinated wall between Mexico and the southern border of the United States, then once again Bong's wealthy family is oblivious to the way their identification with American capitalism and white privilege works to their detriment as Koreans.

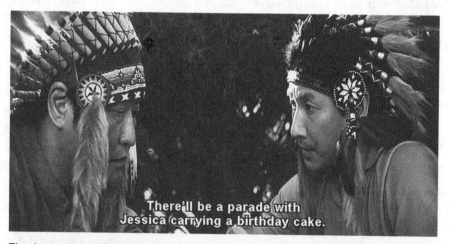

The devastated Ki-Taek (Song Kang-ho) up close with the privileged cluelessness of the wealthy Park Dong-ik (Lee Sun-kyun) in *Parasite* (Bong Joon Ho, Barunson E & A, CJ Entertainment, Neon). Digital frame enlargement.

One of the many delicious ironies of what Manohla Dargis, Wesley Morris, and A. O. Scott called the "Bong-slide" at the Oscars, which made *Parasite* the first non–English language film to win Best Picture, is that Bong Joon Ho's seventh film was his first in ten years made entirely in South Korea and the Korean language. Bong's *Snowpiercer* (2013), an English-language science-fiction film starring Chris Evans, Tilda Swinton, Octavia Spencer, and Ed Harris, was a hit internationally but got caught in the clutches of its U.S. distributor, the Weinstein Company, which insisted upon cutting twenty-five minutes from it and adding narration written by Neil Gaiman (*American Gods, Coraline*). The result of the standoff was that Harvey Weinstein buried *Snowpiercer* theatrically in the United States; later it became a video on demand smash and the basis of a TV series. That the Bong-slide swept the Oscars in early February 2020, while Weinstein was standing trial for sexual assault—and would be convicted before the month was out—was an acidly ironic denouement fully worthy of a script by Director Bong, as colleagues call him. *Okja* (2017), a satire of the genetically modified food industry, with Swinton (playing twins), Jake Gyllenhaal, and Paul Dano, became the first Netflix film to compete at Cannes for the Palme d'Or, which *Parasite* won two years later. Both English-language films featured strong elements of South Korean culture, as well as Korean characters, thus allowing Bong to appeal to international audiences without losing his home base.

Parasite has the feeling of a confident homecoming, a definitive work by a director returning to his home country following a stint in America. The affection Bong expresses for his characters leads to the ambiguity of the film's title: Who's the parasite? Is it the poor family living off the wealthy family? Are the Parks the parasites, telecommunications zillionaires in the neoliberal economy waxing off the dependence of the world populace on their smartphones? The "crisis" that opens the film finds the unemployed Kims discovering that their neighbors have password-protected their Wi-Fi—seemingly the worst thing that can happen in the cellularly dependent world of 2019. Right away, Bong spotlights the global digital divide. Although digital technology makes the Parks resounding "haves" and the Kims decided "have nots," by the end, the nine-year-old Park has established the quaint technologies of toy walkie-talkies and Morse code as more efficacious. Is it finally capitalism that creates parasites? Or is it South Korea's relationship to America? (Or both?) In a 2008 *American Quarterly* article, Christina Klein observed that in choosing *The Host* as the English title of his 2006 horror satire, *Gwoemul* (literally, "creature"), Bong implies "that Korea has let itself become a 'host' to a *parasitic* United States" (890, italics mine). That film took its concept from a scandal involving an

American morgue employee, Albert McFarland, who in 2000 at the massive U.S. military base in Seoul, ordered a Korean employee to dump twenty gallons of embalming fluid into the Han River, which runs through the city. Thus, writes Meera Lee, "As both a physical and social setting, the morgue underscores the U.S. military's geopolitical control over Seoul" (723). By the time of *Parasite*, however, the American giving orders and the Korean subserviently carrying them out have morphed into one.

This is the rare film (although not so unusual for this year) in which the adversaries are less individuals than systems. Nearly everyone is powerless to be anything other than what they are preordained to be. The only way to change things is to slide off the grid and live a subterranean life, as Red has involuntarily done from the beginning of *Us*.[1] Thus, a film that begins with a desperate quest for Wi-Fi concludes with a father and son communicating by means of the dots, dashes, and flashing lights of Morse code, the nineteenth-century U.S. invention romanticized in American media in the era of Walt Disney's *Davy Crockett*, which premiered just two years after the establishment of South Korea.

If You Can Believe Your Eyes and Ears

Martin Scorsese seemed to be everywhere in 2019, a result of the director's frequent presence on documentaries about cinema, as well as his four-decade crusade for film preservation, and the classic status of films like *Mean Streets* (1973), *Taxi Driver* (1976), *Goodfellas* (1990). Allusions to Scorsese's films abounded in 2019. The gritty *Joker*, the year's most startling comic book blockbuster, depicts the development of a psychotic killer. Set in 1981, *Joker* imagines the life of troubled young Arthur Fleck (Joaquin Phoenix), whose metastasizing madness turns him into the Joker. *Joker* is an exaggerated rendition of Scorsese's New Hollywood–era New York street films, *Mean Streets*, *Taxi Driver*, and *The King of Comedy* (1983), with the star of those films, Robert De Niro, as a late-night talk show star modeled on the one (played by Jerry Lewis) whom autograph hound and comedian wannabe Rupert Pupkin (De Niro) kidnaps in *King of Comedy*. In a similar homage to Scorsese, *Hustlers*, Lorene Scafaria's film about strippers who rip off their Wall Street clients amid the 2008 crash, takes on the narrative structure of *Goodfellas*.

After 2019, Scorsese moved into second (behind William Wyler) for the all-time number of Best Director Oscar nominations with nine. Moreover, six of these nominations were for films made in the twenty-first century, more than any other director, with three in each decade. After apparently outliving his viability as a director of big-budget projects that the legacy studios would finance, Scorsese helped Netflix increase its prominence as a film production company equal to the studios. *The Irishman*, his sprawling $170 million historical chronicle about a man with equal allegiance to Jimmy Hoffa and the Mafia, starring actors in their seventies, was picked up for production by Netflix after having been turned down by Paramount, with which Scorsese had a "first-look" deal since 2006. The 209-minute saga won the Best Picture awards of the New York Film Critics Circle and the National Board of Review, as well as ten Oscar nominations, enhancing Netflix's clout as a major Oscar contender.

Accordingly, Scorsese was at the center of 2019's two most intrinsically cinematic controversies, concerning the streaming services that threatened to overtake all filmmaking, and the franchises that often seemed the only kinds of films that could plausibly be made for theaters. Netflix went toe to toe with the big three U.S. theater chains, AMC, Regal, and Cinemark, over the release of *The Irishman*. The cinema chains feared, probably rightly, for the continuation of their business model, holding out for nothing less than the standard three-month window between a film's opening in theaters and its appearance on video formats. Netflix, for reasons that were less clear, refused to agree to more than a token theatrical run of a week or two before a film's debut on the streamer (for *The Irishman*, it was five days in most North American cities outside New York). The second issue was summarized in a headline of a *New York Times* op-ed by Martin Scorsese: "I Said Marvel Movies Aren't Cinema. Let Me Explain."

Film directors who make movies for Netflix, from Bong Joon Ho (*Okja*) and Craig Brewer (*Dolemite Is My Name*, 2019) to Alfonso Cuarón (*Roma*), appear to have shot the same films for HDTV consumption that they would have made for theatrical release, sometimes to the detriment of their movies, which may well play better on the big screen for audiences. *The Irishman*, on the other hand, loses nothing at home. (I saw the film both ways.) Frank Sheeran (Robert De Niro), the trucker turned mob hit man and fixer for the International Brotherhood of Teamsters, better known as the Teamsters Union, the most infamously corrupt organization in American labor, narrates a story that in Scorsese's rendition demands the pause and rewind buttons. Sheeran told writer and lawyer Charles Brandt, for the book *I Heard You Paint Houses*, that he killed Jimmy Hoffa, who disappeared in 1975. Sheeran said he also shot mobster Joey Gallo, object of a famous unsolved murder in 1972, and he claimed to have driven a truck to Florida in May 1961 loaded with ammunition for the attempted Bay of Pigs invasion of Cuba. "To call him the Forrest Gump of organized crime hardly does him justice," writes journalist Bill Tonelli in a blunt article, "Lies of the Irishman." Brandt, a former prosecutor and medical malpractice attorney who helped the elderly Sheeran gain early parole from prison for health reasons, published the book in 2004, six months after Sheeran's death. Brandt split the proceeds, including the film rights, with Sheeran's daughters—except for the one who, as spectators of *The Irishman* know, refused to have anything to do with him. As she asks in the movie, "Why?"

The Irishman is the culmination to date of Scorsese's career-long fascination with the workaday Mafia. In Frank Sheeran, he finds a protagonist stuck until the end of his life in a triangle with the Mob, represented by Delaware Mafia boss Russell Bufalino (Joe Pesci), and the Teamsters, embodied by the mercurial Hoffa (Al Pacino), its president from 1957 to 1971. According to Sheeran's story, Hoffa was too egotistical and foolish to recognize the web in which he himself was caught. Frank is forced to choose without choosing, leaving a man incapable of introspection not knowing what his life has been for. At a time, 2019, when unions in the United States needed a comeback to offset their dwindling numbers, Scorsese's film shows how the lethal injection of Mob greed and political corruption into the labor movement made it easy for the Reagan Administration in the 1980s to tar all unions as corrupt (although, ironically, the Teamsters favored Republicans).

Unlike the gleefully un-American Henry Hill in *Goodfellas*, who boasts of never voting, paying taxes, or holding a Social Security card, Frank Sheeran is a World War II veteran, a good soldier who became an efficient killer in uniform. Just as Jake LaMotta in *Raging Bull* doesn't see why he should curb his violence after the final bell in a boxing match has rung, so Frank channels his apparent PTSD into the hit jobs he carries out with robotic efficiency. Both Frank and Cliff in *OUAT . . . IH* are war veterans; Rick calls Cliff "Audie Murphy," after the decorated World War II hero and movie actor. After nearly two decades of war, in Iraq and Afghanistan, Scorsese and Tarantino depict stoic, duty-bound characters whose battle-dulled senses and war-numbed morality make them useful killers in civilian life. And yet Russell, in Pesci's curiously tender performance, also loves Frank as a son. Frank Sheeran should have stayed a truck driver.

The Irishman boils slowly to its conclusion. It went zero for ten at the Oscars and it's easy to see why. The big winner, *Parasite*, is a knockout that affects a spectator profoundly upon first viewing. Bong's film resembles peak work by a younger Scorsese, a *Taxi Driver* or a *Goodfellas*. *The Irishman*, by contrast, is a meditation on aging and legacies, one that's hard to imagine its director making even a decade earlier. It is a huge work of understatement, innumerable tiny strokes, and deceptively obvious images. Most of its publicity centered on its "de-aging" technology. If *The Irishman* plays better on the home screen than in the cinema, it is because of the subtleties in the CG, which isn't just used for pragmatic reasons. This is because, with Sheeran, Scorsese has a protagonist who either is making up most of the story he tells or is one of the most morally shell-shocked and psychologically bombed-out characters in his oeuvre. Early in the film, a character tells him, "I see you look a little hesitant." Does he? It's hard to get any read on Frank's face. Since CGI was developed in the 1990s, a concern has been that computer technology could end screen acting as we know it. That threat seems more real here than ever because, in taking the lines, wrinkles, and age spots off an actor's face, CG can also take away expression, or add expression that wasn't there in the performance, or fail to correspond to the actor's body—or all three. For example, a scene like the one in which the powerful Don Angelo (Harvey Keitel) reveals himself to be part owner of a laundry a rival mobster paid Frank to "bomb out" should have been freighted with threat and danger, but danger is missing from the actors' faces. Because this is a story of dubious veracity, however, the film's imperfect CG serves Frank's purposes of simultaneously exposing and obscuring the truth. The often vague and sketchy CG that Scorsese oversaw illustrates the doubtfulness of Sheeran's story.

As the chronicle that Scorsese's Sheeran tells contradicts itself, even Frank's memories of background details are not trustworthy. After the murder of Joe Gallo, the following day's TV news broadcast, heard in the background as Frank eats his breakfast, says that Gallo was celebrating his forty-seventh birthday—four birthdays more than "Crazy Joe" actually lived to see! By scattering throughout the film such inaccurate "memories," conveyed to us through characters whose faces have literally been altered, Scorsese, Hollywood's ethnographer, a director of the rites of groups, produces what could be called unreliable objectivity.

Early in the film, Frank tells the unseen interviewer, "Whenever anyone says they're a little concerned, they're *very* concerned. And when they say they're *more than* a little concerned, they're desperate." So, following the film's enactment of Sheeran's account of Hoffa's fate, when Frank walks into the room where his wife and daughters are watching TV news coverage of the Hoffa disappearance, and we "overhear" the unseen reporter say, "Police are extremely concerned," we know that we're getting the world according to Frank Sheeran, where police are desperate and clueless. Such "alternative facts," in the notorious words of Trump aide Kellyanne Conway, from Frank's questionable subjectivity are the equivalent of

In *The Irishman* (Martin Scorsese, Netflix), what Peggy Sheeran (Anna Paquin) knows about her father is unspeakable. Digital frame enlargement.

Tarantino's misspelled title *Inglourious Basterds*. But if we are getting alternate history here, it is because it's from the subjectivities of men who lie to themselves and to anyone in earshot, not because the film itself alters history. Moreover, on the phrase "police are extremely concerned," Scorsese holds on a close-up of Peggy (Anna Paquin). Frank loses her love. Peggy's presence makes clear that Sheeran indeed might have told the truth to Brandt, hoping to redeem himself by providing income for his daughters after he's gone. Frank, or whoever killed Hoffa, succeeded in reducing the authorities to helplessness. However, Peggy possesses a moral authority that the men in the film lack.

Whereas the young Mafiosi in *Goodfellas* lie to their elders and their wives, the old men in *The Irishman* cannot lie to their families because the wives and children either know the score, like Bufalino's wife Carrie (Kathrine Narducci)—a descendant of "Mob royalty" who knows to ask no questions when her husband comes home covered in blood—or they won't give them the chance to lie. Thus Frank's daughter Peggy knows her father is somehow responsible for Hoffa's disappearance, and she is finished with him. In the book, Sheeran says, "Mary and Peggy were watching all the Hoffa disappearance news on the TV. Peggy looked up at me when I walked in and saw something she didn't like. Maybe I looked hard instead of worried. . . . Peggy asked me to leave the house and she said to me, 'I don't even want to know a person like you.' That was twenty-eight years ago and she doesn't want to have anything to do with me" (Brandt 572). None of this language is in the film; Scorsese expresses it all visually. Just as the highest praise Scorsese can bestow on an actor is to say that he or she could have been in silent films, so in a performance in which she speaks eight words, Anna Paquin plays the film's reproving conscience (Schickel, *Conversations . . .* 321). It is she whom we remember, in a film where one gray man after another—except the colorful Hoffa—shuffles off this mortal coil and is scarcely missed. Moreover, the first act of violence we see Frank commit in the film is from the point of view of the child Peggy (Lucy Gallina), when she leads Frank at his insistence to a small store where the proprietor supposedly pushed her. We watch with her from the sidewalk as Frank beats the man within an inch of his life. Because Frank is "the Irishman," and not Sicilian, he doesn't know the code whereby Mafiosi shield the women and children in their families from their "business."

The testimonial dinner the Teamsters throw for Frank, a major set piece two-thirds of the way through, ends as Hoffa dances with Peggy while the dons stare daggers at him. After this, there is no music in the film for the next twenty-five minutes, easily the longest stretch of film time without music of any kind in Scorsese's entire oeuvre. Scorsese, who released the documentary-fantasy *Rolling Thunder Revue: A Bob Dylan Story*, also for Netflix in 2019, told Richard Schickel in 2011 that he often has music on the set and directs the camera and the action to the rhythms and sound of a particular pop song (Schickel, *Conversations . . .* 350–352). For Scorsese to present the entire chapter that portrays Sheeran's account of what happened to Hoffa without music is to disavow Sheeran's version of the events, or to emphasize Frank's betrayal of his friend Jimmy, or both. Frank's voice-over narration, which is extensive throughout this sequence in the script, is absent from it in the final film, a directorial choice that takes another layer of authority away from the protagonist (Zaillian 107–123). These twenty-five minutes dwell outside objectivity *and* subjectivity. To Sheeran's claim of responsibility for Hoffa's disappearance, Scorsese says: You're on your own.

If Frank is telling the truth to posterity about killing Hoffa, he denies it during his life, when confessing to such a crime could have brought him life in prison or the death penalty. In the years after Hoffa's disappearance, Frank in voiceover denies that his prized Lincoln Town Car had been a bribe. As he speaks, we see the Lincoln go through a car wash, but it's the bumper sticker that sticks out: "Where's Hoffa? (313) KL5-0109." More to the director's point, the car is being washed *in slow motion*, a device in Scorsese, going back to *Mean Streets* and *Taxi Driver*, by which characters reveal themselves unconsciously; thus, the car is coming clean, but Frank isn't.

When Frank calls Hoffa's wife, Jo (Welker White), days after the disappearance, he stammers out banalities, some in the Zaillian script and some improvised by De Niro, such as "if there's anything I can do" (script), and lame suggestions that maybe Hoffa had himself kidnapped, as mobster Joe "Bananas" Bonnano reputedly had (improv) (Zaillian 125). In the nursing home near the end of his life, Frank and the priest (Jonathan Morris, an actual priest) are apparently talking without Frank having made an actual Sacrament of Reconciliation—aka Penance or Confession—in which to lie is a mortal sin, about the murders he committed. The priest asks him if he has remorse about the families. "I didn't know the families," he mutters, "except one." Then he asks himself, "What kind of man makes a phone call like that?" The priest, confused, says, "What phone call?" Either in old age Frank's mask is cracking and his guilt is seeping out or the phone call is part of his false claim of having killed Hoffa, which to Scorsese is a near-biblical betrayal of brother by brother. The de-aging technology "wears off" by this point in the narrative. The seventy-six-year-old De Niro is now about as old as the aged man he is playing. The CG no longer covers for Sheeran. He is barefaced and either a liar or a penitent. Frank is so alone that he has to ask the priest if it's Christmas; at the same time, he asks him to not to close the door of his room. Can the sinner save his soul? As he always has, Scorsese keeps the door open.

Retrospection in 2019 seemed different from just a few years before, when the culture could feel it was progressing. There is a rueful quality to films in 2019, a sense that when the culture says it has learned from its errors, it actually means that it has found a way to deny their effects, be these related to class, race, or climate. Films of 2019 depicted the nearly providential refusal of the buried to remain underground. Freud would call this the return of the repressed, and yet what we more often see, as in *Us* and *Parasite*, is the eventual surfacing of people whom the culture has forced underground. There were more hopeful versions of this trajectory, as in the biopic as therapy session (*A Beautiful Day in the Neighborhood, Rocketman*). By contrast, impassioned exposés of abuses by the FBI and the CIA (*Richard Jewell* and *The Report*, respectively) landed like the wrong films at the wrong time, appearing to give assent to Trumpian rants against the "deep state." In *Us*, the fun house that in 1986 was called "Vision Quest," with the face of an Indian chief over the door, is replaced in 2019 by the mythological name "Merlin's Forest." Rebranding, however, convinces no one. Change is essential.

NOTE

1. Bong acknowledged his film's similarity to *Us* in a Q and A session at Fantastic Fest 2019 in September. Blu-ray of *Parasite*, Universal Home Video, 2020.

2 0 1 0 – 2 0 1 9

Select Academy Awards

2010

Best Picture: *The King's Speech*, the Weinstein Company

Best Actor: Colin Firth, *The King's Speech*

Best Actress: Natalie Portman, *Black Swan*, Twentieth Century-Fox

Best Supporting Actor: Christian Bale, *The Fighter*, Paramount

Best Supporting Actress: Melissa Leo, *The Fighter*

Best Director: Tom Hooper, *The King's Speech*

Best Original Screenplay: David Seidler, *The King's Speech*

Best Adapted Screenplay: Aaron Sorkin, *The Social Network*, Columbia. From the book *The Accidental Billionaires: The Founding of Facebook* by Ben Mezrich

Best Cinematography: Wally Pfister, *Inception*, Warner Bros.

Best Editing: Kirk Baxter, Angus Wall, *The Social Network*

Best Original Music Score: Trent Reznor, Atticus Ross, *The Social Network*

Best Song: "We Belong Together," music and lyrics by Randy Newman, *Toy Story 3*. Pixar, Disney.

Best Animated Feature: *Toy Story 3*, Lee Unkrich, director.

Best Documentary Feature: *Inside Job*, Charles Ferguson, director; Ferguson and Audrey Marrs, producers. Representational Pictures, Sony Pictures Classics.

Best Foreign Language Film: *Hævnen* (*In a Better World*), Denmark, Susanne Bier, director. Sony Pictures Classics.

2011

Best Picture: *The Artist*, the Weinstein Company

Best Actor: Jean Dujardin, *The Artist*

Best Actress: Meryl Streep, *The Iron Lady*, the Weinstein Company

Best Supporting Actor: Christopher Plummer, *Beginners*, Focus Features

Best Supporting Actress: Octavia Spencer, *The Help*, Touchstone

Best Director: Michel Hazanavicius, *The Artist*

Best Original Screenplay: Woody Allen, *Midnight in Paris*, Sony Pictures Classics

Best Adapted Screenplay: Alexander Payne and Nat Faxon & Jim Rash, *The Descendants*, Fox Searchlight. From the novel *The Descendants* by Kaui Hart Hemmings.

Best Cinematography: Robert Richardson, *Hugo*, Paramount

Best Editing: Kirk Baxter, Angus Wall, *The Girl with the Dragon Tattoo*, Columbia

Best Original Music Score: Ludovic Bource, *The Artist*

Best Song: "Man or Muppet," music and lyrics by Bret McKenzie, *The Muppets*. Disney.

Best Animated Feature: *Rango*, Gore Verbinski, director. Paramount.

Best Documentary Feature: *Undefeated*, Dan Lindsay, T. J. Martin, directors. The Weinstein Company.

Best Foreign Language Film: *Jodaeiye Nader az Simin* (*A Separation*), Iran, Asghar Farhadi, director. Sony Pictures Classics.

2012

Best Picture: *Argo*, Warner Bros.

Best Actor: Daniel Day-Lewis, *Lincoln*, Touchstone

Best Actress: Jennifer Lawrence, *Silver Linings Playbook*, the Weinstein Company

Best Supporting Actor: Christoph Waltz, *Django Unchained*, the Weinstein Company, Columbia

Best Supporting Actress: Anne Hathaway, *Les Misérables*, Universal

Best Director: Ang Lee, *Life of Pi*, Twentieth Century-Fox

Best Original Screenplay: Quentin Tarantino, *Django Unchained*

Best Adapted Screenplay: Chris Terrio, *Argo*. From the book *Master of Disguise* by Tony Mendez, and the article, "The Great Escape: How the CIA Used a Fake Sci-Fi Flick to Rescue Americans from Tehran" by Joshua Bearman.

Best Cinematography: Claudio Miranda, *Life of Pi*

Best Editing: William Goldenberg, *Argo*

Best Original Music Score: Michael Danna, *Life of Pi*

Best Song: "Skyfall," music and lyrics by Adele Adkins and Paul Epworth, *Skyfall*. MGM, Columbia.

Best Animated Feature: *Brave*, Mark Andrews, Brenda Chapman, and Steve Purcell, directors. Pixar, Disney.

Best Documentary Feature: *Searching for Sugar Man*, Malik Benjelloul, director. Sony Pictures Classics.

Best Foreign Language Film: *Amour*, Austria-France, Michael Haneke, director. Sony Pictures Classics.

2013

Best Picture: *12 Years a Slave*, Fox Searchlight

Best Actor: Matthew McConaughey, *Dallas Buyers Club*, Focus Features

Best Actress: Cate Blanchett, *Blue Jasmine*, Sony Pictures Classics

Best Supporting Actor: Jared Leto, *Dallas Buyers Club*

Best Supporting Actress: Lupita Nyong'o, *12 Years a Slave*

Best Director: Alfonso Cuarón, *Gravity*, Warner Bros.

Best Original Screenplay: Spike Jonze, *Her*, Annapurna, Warner Bros.

Best Adapted Screenplay: John Ridley, *12 Years a Slave*. From the book *12 Years a Slave* by Solomon Northup.

Best Cinematography: Emmanuel Lubezki, *Gravity*

Best Editing: Alfonso Cuarón, Mark Sanger, *Gravity*

Best Original Music Score: Steven Price, *Gravity*

Best Song: "Let It Go," music and lyrics by Kristen Anderson-Lopez and Robert Lopez, *Frozen*. Walt Disney Animation Studios.

Best Animated Feature: *Frozen*, Chris Buck, Jennifer Lee, directors.

Best Documentary Feature: *20 Feet from Stardom*, Morgan Neville, Gil Friesen, and Caitrin Rogers, directors. RADiUS/TWC.

Best Foreign Language Film: *La grande bellezza* (*The Great Beauty*), Italy, Paolo Sorrentino, director. Janus Films.

■ 2014

Best Picture: *Birdman or (The Unexpected Virtue of Ignorance)*, Fox Searchlight

Best Actor: Eddie Redmayne, *The Theory of Everything*, Focus Features

Best Actress: Julianne Moore, *Still Alice*, Sony Pictures Classics

Best Supporting Actor: J. K. Simmons, *Whiplash*, Sony Pictures Classics

Best Supporting Actress: Patricia Arquette, *Boyhood*, IFC Films

Best Director: Alejandro G. Iñárritu, *Birdman or (The Unexpected Virtue of Ignorance)*

Best Original Screenplay: Alejandro G. Iñarritu & Nicólas Giacobone & Alexander Dinelaris & Armando Bo, *Birdman or (The Unexpected Virtue of Ignorance)*

Best Adapted Screenplay: Graham Moore, *The Imitation Game*, the Weinstein Company. From the book *Alan Turing: The Enigma* by Andrew Hodges

Best Cinematography: Emmanuel Lubezki, *Birdman or (The Unexpected Virtue of Ignorance)*

Best Editing: Tom Cross, *Whiplash*

Best Original Music Score: Alexandre Desplat, *The Grand Budapest Hotel*, Fox Searchlight

Best Song: "Glory," music and lyrics by John Stephens and Lorrie Lynn, *Selma*. Paramount

Best Animated Feature: *Big Hero 6*, Don Hall, Chris Williams, and Roy Conli, directors. Walt Disney Animation Studios

Best Documentary Feature: *CitizenFour*, Laura Poitras, Mathilde Bonnefoy, and Dick Wilutsky, directors. RADiUS/TWC.

Best Foreign Language Film: *Ida*, Poland, Pawel Pawlikowski, director. Music Box Films.

2015

Best Picture: *Spotlight*, Open Road

Best Actor: Leonardo DiCaprio, *The Revenant*, Twentieth Century-Fox

Best Actress: Brie Larson, *Room*, A24

Best Supporting Actor: Mark Rylance, *Bridge of Spies*, Touchstone

Best Supporting Actress: Alicia Vikander, *The Danish Girl*, Focus Features

Best Director: Alejandro G. Iñárritu, *The Revenant*

Best Original Screenplay: Josh Singer, Tom McCarthy, *Spotlight*

Best Adapted Screenplay: Charles Randolph, Adam McKay, *The Big Short*, Paramount. From the book *The Big Short* by Michael Lewis

Best Cinematography: Emmanuel Lubezki, *The Revenant*

Best Editing: Margaret Sixel, *Mad Max: Fury Road*, Warner Bros.

Best Original Music Score: Ennio Morricone, *The Hateful Eight*, the Weinstein Company

Best Song: "Writing's on the Wall," music and lyrics by Jimmy Napes and Sam Smith, *Spectre*. MGM, Columbia.

Best Animated Feature: *Inside Out*, Pete Docter, Jonas Rivera, directors. Pixar, Disney.

Best Documentary Feature: *Amy*, Asif Kapadia, James Gay-Rees, directors. A24.

Best Foreign Language Film: *Son of Saul*, Hungary. László Nemes, director. Sony Pictures Classics.

2016

Best Picture: *Moonlight*, A24

Best Actor: Casey Affleck, *Manchester by the Sea*, Amazon Studios

Best Actress: Emma Stone, *La La Land*, Summit Entertainment, Lionsgate

Best Supporting Actor: Mahershala Ali, *Moonlight*

Best Supporting Actress: Viola Davis, *Fences*, Paramount

Best Director: Damien Chazelle, *La La Land*

Best Original Screenplay: Kenneth Lonergan, *Manchester by the Sea*

Best Adapted Screenplay: Barry Jenkins and Tarell Alvin McCraney, *Moonlight.* From the play *In Moonlight Black Boys Look Blue* by McCraney

Best Cinematography: Linus Sandgren, *La La Land*

Best Editing: John Gilbert, *Hacksaw Ridge*, Summit Entertainment

Best Original Music Score: Justin Hurwitz, *La La Land*

Best Song: "City of Stars," music by Justin Hurwitz, lyrics by Benj Pasek and Justin Paul, *La La Land*

Best Animated Feature: *Zootopia*, Byron Howard, Rich Moore, and Clark Spencer, directors. Walt Disney Animation Studio

Best Documentary Feature: *O.J.: Made in America*, Ezra Edelman and Caroline Waterlow, directors. ESPN Films

Best Foreign Language Film: *Forushande* (*The Salesman*), Iran, Asghar Farhadi, director. Cohen Media Group, Amazon Studios.

2017

Best Picture: *The Shape of Water*, Fox Searchlight

Best Actor: Gary Oldman, *Darkest Hour*, Focus Features

Best Actress: Frances McDormand, *Three Billboards outside Ebbing, Missouri*, Fox Searchlight

Best Supporting Actor: Sam Rockwell, *Three Billboards outside Ebbing, Missouri*

Best Supporting Actress: Allison Janney, *I, Tonya*, LuckyChap, Neon

Best Director: Guillermo del Toro, *The Shape of Water*

Best Original Screenplay: Jordan Peele, *Get Out*, Blumhouse, Universal

Best Adapted Screenplay: James Ivory, *Call Me by Your Name*, Sony Pictures Classics. From the novel *Call Me by Your Name* by André Aciman

Best Cinematography: Roger Deakins, *Blade Runner 2049*, Warner Bros.

Best Editing: Lee Smith, *Dunkirk*, Warner Bros.

Best Original Music Score: Alexandre Desplat, *The Shape of Water*

Best Song: "Remember Me," music and lyrics by Kristen Anderson-Lopez and Robert Lopez, *Coco*. Pixar, Disney

Best Animated Feature: *Coco*, Lee Unkrich and Darla K. Anderson, directors

Best Documentary Feature: *Icarus*, Bryan Fogel and Dan Cogan, directors, Netflix

Best Foreign Language Film: *Una mujer fantástica* (*A Fantastic Woman*), Chile, Sebastián Lelio, director. Sony Pictures Classics.

2018

Best Picture: *Green Book*, Universal

Best Actor: Rami Malek, *Bohemian Rhapsody*, Twentieth Century-Fox

Best Actress: Olivia Colman, *The Favourite*, Fox Searchlight

Best Supporting Actor: Mahershala Ali, *Green Book*

Best Supporting Actress: Regina King, *If Beale Street Could Talk*, Annapurna

Best Director: Alfonso Cuarón, *Roma*, Netflix

Best Original Screenplay: Nick Villelonga, Brian Hayes Currie, and Peter Farrelly, *Green Book*

Best Adapted Screenplay: Charlie Wachtel & David Rabinowitz and Kevin Willmott & Spike Lee, *BlacKkKlansman*, Focus Features. From the book *BlacKkKlansman* by Ron Stallworth.

Best Cinematography: Alfonso Cuarón, *Roma*

Best Editing: John Ottman, *Bohemian Rhapsody*

Best Original Music Score: Ludwig Goransson, *Black Panther*, Marvel Studios

Best Song: "Shallow," music and lyrics by Lady Gaga, Mark Ronson, Anthony Rossomando, and Andrew Wyatt, *A Star Is Born*. Warner Bros.

Best Animated Feature: *Spider-Man: Into the Spider-Verse*, Bob Persichetti, Peter Ramsey, Rodney Rothman, Phil Lord, and Christopher Miller, directors. Columbia Pictures and Sony Pictures Animation.

Best Documentary Feature: *Free Solo*, Elizabeth Choi Vasarhelyi, Jimmy Chin, Evan Hayes, and Shannon Dill, directors. National Geographic, Netflix.

Best Foreign Language Film: *Roma*, Mexico.

2019

Best Picture: *Parasite*, Neon

Best Actor: Joaquin Phoenix, *Joker*, DC, Warner Bros.

Best Actress: Renée Zellweger, *Judy*, Roadside Attractions

Best Supporting Actor: Brad Pitt, *Once Upon a Time . . . in Hollywood*, Columbia

Best Supporting Actress: Laura Dern, *Marriage Story*, Netflix

Best Director: Bong Joon Ho, *Parasite*

Best Original Screenplay: Bong Joon Ho and Han Jin Won, *Parasite*

Best Adapted Screenplay: Taika Waititi, *Jojo Rabbit*, Fox Searchlight. From the novel *Caging Skies* by Christine Leunens.

Best Cinematography: Roger Deakins, *1917*, Universal.

Best Editing: Michael McCusker and Andrew Buckland, *Ford v. Ferrari*, Twentieth Century-Fox

Best Original Music Score: Hildur Guðnadóttir, *Joker*

Best Song: "(I'm Gonna) Love Me Again," music by Elton John, lyrics by Bernie Taupin, *Rocketman*. Paramount.

Best Animated Feature: *Toy Story 4*, Josh Cooley, Mark Nielsen, and Jonas Rivera, Pixar, Disney.

Best Documentary Feature: *American Factory*, Steven Bognar and Julia Reichart, directors. Higher Ground, Netflix.

Best International Film (new title for Best Foreign Language Film): *Gisaengchung* (*Parasite*), South Korea.

ACKNOWLEDGMENTS

The book you hold in your hand (or view on a screen) is the twelfth volume in Rutgers's Screen Decades series. The project that Lester D. Friedman and Murray Pomerance conceived and supervised in the mid-2000s—ten volumes covering the history of American film, decade by decade and year by year, virtually simultaneously, with the eleventh, on the 2000s, following a few years later—is now one of the most admired book series in film studies and American studies. Indeed, it was my impression at least at the outset of this new volume that Professors Friedman and Pomerance hadn't quite realized the enduring impact of their achievement. In November 2018 I inquired about a 2010s volume that I imagined could already be underway. Perhaps I was late, but I hoped there might still be time for me to be assigned a chapter. Friedman and Pomerance confessed to believing that the series lay behind them; they had hadn't thought about a book on the 2010s. However, once the volume was a go and I extended invitations to scholars, I discovered the depth of the series's reputation. I emailed invitations on a Monday, and before Friday the volume was set.

Therefore, my thanks go first of all to the nine collaborators who devoted their knowledge, competence, and expertise to the creation of chapters that I hope you will find as inventive, perceptive, and sparkling as I have. I feel rather long in the tooth to be editing for the first time, and the contributors made my maiden effort a marvelous experience, one I hope I can repeat. Friedman and Pomerance were peerless guides and firm superintendents, helping us all keep our eyes on the series's overriding goals. These are easy to lose track of when we are still living out the era for which we might provide historical as well as aesthetic insight. I particularly want to thank Les Friedman for his crucial editorial comments and advice on my own two chapters.

A word should be said about the slipperiness of writing film and cultural history for a period that feels more current than historical. More than once, I envied the scholars who wrote the volumes on cinema of, say, the 1920s or even the 1970s—eras whose histories are far from settled but on which we can at least take some historical perspective. I hope you will be kind as you read what feels like perhaps the rough draft (or the freewrite) of history. For my own chapter on 2019, I confess ("Bless me, Father . . .") to having never produced something I asked of my contributors: a proposal, even an outline, of the films I intended to write about. Despite the fact that I went to movies throughout 2019, making good use of my A-List subscription at AMC Cinemas—part of an industry whose future appears uncertain as I write this in the plague times of early 2021—I was still seeing cinematic stragglers from 2019 on Netflix and Amazon well into the summer of 2020, long after I had received the chapters from most of my contributors. During the unprecedented and tragic period of the coronavirus, completing and revising a book on the quite different era that had just concluded provided challenges but also pleasures that were unimaginable when we began. A number of us felt grateful for an activity, scholarship, that felt reassuringly "normal" in comparison to the lives in quarantine, social distancing, and working from home—if we were lucky!—which we were obliged to live.

Thanks to Nicole Solano and the entire team at Rutgers. As always, I owe much to the support of my administration at the IU School of Liberal Arts at IUPUI, especially Dean Tami Eitle, English department chair David Hoegberg, and my colleagues, especially Megan Musgrave, Sherra Schick, Ulla Connor, Carrie Sickmann, Kristine Brunovska Karnick, Robert Rebein, and Mike Scott, and my current and recent students, especially Manuel Fernandez, Lauren Carr, Dan Vandersall, Andy Vennemann, Ethan Marley, and Kayla Bailey. My wife, Christine, offers more support, guidance, and love with each passing year. Our son, Jerome, who graduated college while I worked on this volume, continues to fill me with pride and appreciation. As I write this, I last saw my mother, Betty Kessler Bingham, and siblings, Brian Bingham, Christopher Bingham, and Beth Johnson, at Mom's ninetieth birthday party fourteen months ago in March 2020, a week before the COVID-19 lockdowns began. I wish us all a better world.

WORKS CITED

████████████████

AND CONSULTED

2009 H1N1 Pandemic (H1N1pdm09 virus). Centers for Disease Control and Prevention, https://www.cdc.gov/flu/pandemic-resources/2009-h1n1-pandemic.html. Accessed 2 Dec. 2020.

The 2009 H1N1 Pandemic: Summary Highlights, April 2009–April 2010. Centers for Disease Control and Prevention, https://www.cdc.gov/h1n1flu/cdcresponse.htm. Accessed 2 Dec 2020.

Abate, Michelle Ann. "Do You Want to Build on a Racist Tradition?": Olaf from Disney's Frozen and Blackface Minstrelsy." *Journal of Popular Culture*, vol. 5, no. 52, 2019.

Abrams, J. J. Interview. By George Stephanopoulos. *Good Morning America*, ABC, 30 Nov. 2015, https://www.youtube.com/watch?v=RjWoMo4Bk84. Accessed 23 Sept. 2020.

Adams, Sam. "Why the 'Ghostbusters' Backlash Is a Sexist Control Issue." *IndieWire*, 14 July 2016, https://www.indiewire.com/2016/07/ghostbusters-reboot-backlash-12017 05555/. Accessed 12 June 2021.

Adams, Thelma. "Female-Driven Movies Make Money, So Why Aren't More Being Made?" *Variety*, 6 Oct. 2015, https://variety.com/2015/film/news/female-driven-movies-box-of fice-women-1201610849/. Accessed 1 May 2020.

Agamben, Giorgio. *State of Exception*. University of Chicago Press, 2004.

Aguilar, Carlos. "Director Miguel Arteta on Why His Latest Film Is Essential Viewing in the Era of Trump." *Remezcla*, 17 Feb. 2017, https://remezcla.com/features/film/miguel-art eta-beatriz-at-dinner-sundance-salma-hayek/.

Amighini, Alessia, editor. *Between Politics and Finance: Hong Kong's "Infinity War"?* Italian Institute for International Political Studies. Lidizioni Ledi, 2020.

Anderson, Benedict. *Imagined Communities: Reflections on the Origin and Spread of Nationalism.* Verso, 1983.

Anderson, John. "*I, Tonya* May Be the Film We Need to Understand Donald Trump and #MeToo." *America*, 8 Dec. 2017, https://www.americamagazine.org/arts-culture/2017 /12/08/i-tonya-may-be-film-we-need-understand-donald-trump-and-metoo.

Applebaum, Anne. "The Collaborators." *The Atlantic*, vol. 326, no.1, July–Aug. 2020, pp. 48–62.

Badley, Linda. "Down to the Bone: Neo-neo-realism and Genre in Contemporary Women's Indies." *Indie Reframed: Women's Filmmaking and Contemporary American Independent Cinema*, edited by Linda Badley, Claire Perkins and Michele Schreiber, Edinburgh University Press, 2016, pp. 121–137.

Balio, Tino. *Hollywood in the New Millennium*. British Film Institute, Palgrave Macmillan, 2013.

Baptist, Edward E. *The Half Has Never Been Told: Slavery and the Making of American Capitalism.* Basic Books, 2014.

Barnes, Brooks. "At the Box Office, It's No Longer a Man's World." *New York Times*, 22 Mar. 2015, https://www.nytimes.com/2015/03/23/business/media/at-the-box-office -its-no-longer-a-mans-world.html. Accessed 1 May 2020.

———. "*Last Jedi* Is 2017's Box Office Winner in a Women-Led Year." *The New York Times*, 31 Dec. 2017, https://www.nytimes.com/2017/12/31/movies/last-jedi-2017-box-office -winner.html.

Baron, Cynthia. *Denzel Washington*. British Film Institute, 2015.

Beaumont-Thomas, Ben. "Clint Eastwood: *American Sniper* and I Are Anti-war." *The Guardian*, 17 Mar. 2015, https://www.theguardian.com/film/2015/mar/17/clint-eastwood -american-sniper-anti-war. Accessed 30 Sept. 2020.

Bingham, Dennis. *Whose Lives Are They Anyway?: The Biopic as Contemporary Film Genre*. Rutgers University Press, 2010.

Biskind, Peter. *Down and Dirty Pictures: Miramax, Sundance, and the Rise of Independent Film*. Simon & Schuster, 2004.

Black, Jack. "'You Ain't Gonna Get Away wit' This, Django': Fantasy, Fiction and Subversion in Quentin Tarantino's *Django Unchained*." *Quarterly Review of Film and Video*, vol. 36, no.7, 2019, pp. 611–637.

Blaskow, Nikolai. "Birdman or (the Unexpected Virtue of Ignorance): Transcendence in Unexpected Places." *St. Mark's Review*, no. 234, Dec. 2015, pp. 26–40.

"Box Office Mojo." *IMDbPro*, https://www.boxofficemojo.com/movies/?id=blumhouse2 .htm.

Brackett, Rob. "America Leads Western Nations in Denying Climate Change, according to Poll." *The Weather Channel.com*, 9 May 2019, https://weather.com/news/news /2019-05-09-america-leads-western-nations-in-denying-climate-change. Accessed 3 Oct. 2020.

Bradbury, Sarah. "*I, Tonya*: The Rise of the Female-Led Sports Biopic." *Independent*, 26 Feb. 2018, https://www.independent.co.uk/arts-entertainment/films/features/i-tonya -margot-robbie-emma-stone-billie-jean-king-battle-of-the-sexes-florence-pugh -a8229806.html.

Breslow, Jason M. "The Opposition Strategy." *The Frontline Interviews: The Divided States of America, pbs.org*, 17 Jan. 2017, https://www.pbs.org/wgbh/frontline/interactive/divided -states-of-america-the-frontline-interviews/moments/the-opposition-strategy.html. Accessed 29 July 2020.

Brintnall, Kent L. *Ecce Homo: The Male-Body-in-Pain as Redemptive Figure*. University of Chicago Press, 2011.

Brody, Richard. "'American Sniper' Takes Apart the Myth of the American Warrior." *The New Yorker*, 24 Dec. 2014, https://www.newyorker.com/culture/richard-brody/american-sniper -takes-apart-myth-american-warrior. Accessed 23 Aug. 2019.

Brooks, Jodi. "*The Kids Are All Right*, the Pursuits of Happiness, and the Spaces Between." *Camera Obscura* 85, vol. 29, no. 1, 2014, pp. 111–135.

Brown, Maury. "Inside the Numbers: 2015 NBA Finals Were Highest-Rated, Most-Viewed Ever for ABC." *Forbes.com*, 17 June 2015, https://www.forbes.com/sites/maurybrown /2015/06/17/inside-the-numbers-2015-nba-finals-were-highest-rated-ever-for-abc /#154ac7d16aef. Accessed 2 Oct. 2020.

Bruni, Frank. "The Gay Truth about Trump." *The New York Times*, 23 June 2019, SR 1+.

Brustein, Robert. "The New Hollywood: Myth and Anti-myth." *Film Quarterly*, vol. 12, no. 3, Spring 1959, pp. 23–31.

Brzeski, Patrick. "China Box-Office Growth Slowed to 3.7 Percent in 2016, Official Data Shows." *The Hollywood Reporter*, 1 Jan. 2017, https://www.hollywoodreporter.com/movies /movie-news/china-box-office-growth-slows-37-percent-2016-official-data-shows -960217/.

Buchanan, Kyle. "10 Years Later, an Oscar Experiment That Actually Worked." *The New York Times*, 22 Jan. 2020, https://www.nytimes.com/2020/01/22/movies/expanded-best-picture -oscar.html. Accessed 15 July 2020.

———. "Will the Movies Exist in 10 Years?" *The New York Times*, 23 June 2019, AR 1+.

Buckley, Cara. "Hollywood Invested Big in Georgia: A New Abortion Law Is Causing Some Tensions." *The New York Times*, 23 May 2019, https://www.nytimes.com/2019/05/23 /arts/hollywood-georgia-abortion.html. Accessed 9 June 2021.

Burns, Alexander. "Joe Biden's Campaign Announcement Video, Annotated." *The New York Times*, 25 Apr. 2019, https://www.nytimes.com/2019/04/25/us/politics/biden-campaign -video-announcement.html. Accessed 10 Oct. 2020.

Butter, Susannah. "The Incredible Tale of Ron Chernow: The Historian Whose Book Inspired the Musical Hamilton." *Evening Standard*, 21 Dec. 2017, https://www.standard.co.uk /lifestyle/books/alexander-hamilton-by-ron-chernow-inspired-hamilton-musical -a3725036.html. Accessed 5 Oct. 2020.

Byrge, Duane. "*Inside Job*—Film Review." *The Hollywood Reporter*, 14 Oct. 2010, https://www .hollywoodreporter.com/movies/movie-reviews/inside-job-film-review-29602/. Accessed 12 June 2021.

Califano, Joseph. "The Movie 'Selma' Has a Glaring Flaw." *The Washington Post*, 26 Dec. 2014, https://www.washingtonpost.com/opinions/the-movie-selma-has-a-glaring-histo rical-inaccuracy/2014/12/26/70ad3ea2-8aa4-11e4-a085-34e9b9f09a58_story.html. Accessed 23 Aug. 2019.

Camera, Lauren. "The Higher Education Apocalypse." *U.S. News and World Report.com*, 22 Mar. 2019, https://www.usnews.com/news/education-news/articles/2019-03-22/college -closings-signal-start-of-a-crisis-in-higher-education. Accessed 9 Oct. 2020.

Carmon, Irin. "'Zero Dark Thirty' Goes Feminist." *Salon*, 1 Feb. 2013, https://www.salon.com /2013/02/01/zero_dark_thirty_goes_feminist/. Accessed 3 July 2020.

Carr, David. "Giving Viewers What They Want." *The New York Times*, 24 Feb. 2013, https:// www.nytimes.com/2013/02/25/business/media/for-house-of-cards-using-big-data-to -guarantee-itspopularity.html.

Chambliss, Julian C., et al., editors. *Assembling the Marvel Cinematic Universe: Essays on the Social, Cultural, and Geopolitical Domains*. McFarland, 2018.

Chappelow, Jim. "The Great Recession." *Investopedia*, 20 Apr. 2020, https://www.investopedia .com/terms/g/great-recession.asp. Accessed 13 July 2020.

Chart Book: The Legacy of the Great Recession. Center on Budget and Policy Priorities, 6 June 2019, https://www.cbpp.org/research/economy/chart-book-the-legacy-of-the-great-recession. Accessed 18 Oct. 2020.

Cherelus, Gina. "Cynthia Erivo: 'It's Not Enough That I'm the Only One.'" *The New York Times*, 13 Jan. 2020, https://www.nytimes.com/2020/01/13/movies/cynthia-erivo-egot .html. Accessed 16 Jan. 2020.

Chozick, Amy, and Brooks Barnes. "Hollywood's Mountain, Now a Molehill." *The New York Times*, 20 Jan. 2019, BU 1+.

Chu, Dian L. "Despite 'He-Covery,' It's Still a 'Mancession' (Guest Post)." *Business Insider*, 24 Mar. 2011, https://www.businessinsider.com/despite-he-covery-its-still-a-mancession -guest-post-2011-4. Accessed 8 June 2020.

Cieply, Michael. "Academy Expands Best-Picture Pool to 10." *The New York Times*, 24 June 2009, https://www.nytimes.com/2009/06/25/movies/25oscars.html.

Cillizza, Chris. "Why Donald Trump Is Thrilled about This Fight with 'The Squad.'" *CNN.com*, 27 July 2019, https://www.cnn.com/2019/07/16/politics/donald-trump-alexandria-ocasio -cortez-squad-ilhan-omar/index.html. Accessed 15 Oct. 2020.

Cobb, Jelani. "Lincoln Died for Our Sins." *Washington Monthly*, Jan./Feb. 2013, https://wash ingtonmonthly.com/magazine/janfeb-2013/lincoln-died-for-our-sins/.

Cogley, Bridget. "*Parasite* House Designed from 'Simple Floor Plan' Sketched by Bong Joon-ho." *De Zeen.com*, 16 Apr. 2020, https://www.dezeen.com/2020/04/16/parasite-film-set-design-interview-lee-ha-jun-bong-joon-ho/. Accessed 2 June 2020.

Coll, Steve. "'Disturbing' & 'Misleading': Judging *Zero Dark Thirty*'s Claims to Journalism." *The New York Review of Books*, 7 Feb. 2013, https://www.nybooks.com/articles/2013/02/07/disturbing-misleading-zero-dark-thirty/.

Collin, Robbie. "Dazzling Science-Fiction That Will Leave You Speechless." *Telegraph*, 10 Nov. 2016, https://www.telegraph.co.uk/films/0/arrival-review-dazzling-science-fiction-that-will-leave-you-spee/.

Columpar, Corinn. "The Feminist Politics of Collaboration in Lena Dunham's *Tiny Furniture*." *Indie Reframed: Women's Filmmaking and Contemporary American Independent Cinema*, edited by Linda Badley, Claire Perkins and Michele Schreiber, Edinburgh University Press, 2016, pp. 276–287.

"Condition of Education: Undergraduate Enrollment." *National Center for Education Statistics*, May 2020, https://nces.ed.gov/programs/coe/indicator_cha.asp. Accessed 14 July 2020.

Cooper, Yvette. "Online Sexism Is So Out of Control We Can No Longer Ignore It." *Guardian*, 17 Dec. 2015, www.theguardian.com/commentisfree/2015/dec/16/online-sexism-social-media-debate-abus. Accessed 30 Apr. 2020.

Corona, Alex. "*Beatriz at Dinner* Premiere: Interview with Miguel Arteta." *The Upcoming*, 1 June 2017, https://www.youtube.com/watch?v=wHpIWCNsZX4.

Crémieux, Anne. "From Queer to Quare: The Representation of LGBT Blacks in Cinema." *African American Cinema Through Black Lives Consciousness*, edited by Mark A. Reid, Wayne State University Press, 2019, pp. 255–274.

Crenshaw, Kimberle. "Mapping the Margins: Intersectionality, Identity Politics, and Violence against Women of Color (1994)." *Violence against Women: Classic Papers*, edited by Raquel Kennedy Bergen, Jeffrey L. Edleson, and Claire M. Renzetti, Pearson Education New Zealand, 2005, pp. 282–313.

Crump, Andy. "How *The Witch* Accidentally Launched a Horror Movement." *Hollywood Reporter*, 11 May 2019, https://www.hollywoodreporter.com/heat-vision/how-witch-accidentally-sparked-elevated-horror-trend-1208008.

Cruz, Lenika. "What Sets the Smart Heroines of *Hidden Figures* Apart." *The Atlantic*, 9 Jan. 2017, https://www.theatlantic.com/entertainment/archive/2017/01/hidden-figures-review/512252/.

D'Alessandro, Anthony. "Average Movie Ticket Price In 2017 Hit All-Time High." *Deadline*, 17 Jan. 2018, https://deadline.com/2018/01/average-movie-ticket-price-2017-nato-1202244975/.

Dargis, Manohla. "Aliens Drop Anchor in 'Arrival,' but What Are Their Intentions?" *The New York Times*, 10 Nov. 2016, https://www.nytimes.com/2016/11/11/movies/arrival-review-amy-adams-jeremy-renner.html.

———. "Denzel Washington Plays Judge, Jury and Executioner in 'The Equalizer 2.'" *The New York Times*, 19 July 2018, https://www.nytimes.com/2018/07/19/movies/the-equalizer-2-review-denzel-washington.html.

Dargis, Manohla, and A. O. Scott. "The Decade in Culture: The 10 Most Influential Films of the Decade (and 20 Other Favorites)." *The New York Times*, 24 Nov. 2019, https://www.nytimes.com/2019/11/24/movies/best-movies-2010s-decade.html.

Dargis, Manohla, Wesley Morris, and A. O. Scott. "What the 'Parasite' Landslide Says About the Oscars: Our Critics Weigh In." *The New York Times* 10 February 2020. https://www.nytimes.com/2020/02/10/movies/oscars-parasite-critics.html

Dennis, Brady, and Chris Mooney. "Neil Gorsuch's Mother Once Ran the EPA. It Didn't Go Well." *The Washington Post*, 1 Feb. 2017, https://www.washingtonpost.com/news /energy-environment/wp/2017/02/01/neil-gorsuchs-mother-once-ran-the-epa-it-was -a-disaster/.

Desowitz, Bill. "How 'Arrival' Cinematographer Bradford Clark Transcends Sci-Fi with Poetry." *IndieWire*, 11 Nov. 2016, https://www.indiewire.com/2016/11/arrival-cinematographer -bradford-young-sci-fi-oscars-1201745522/.

Deylami, Shirin S. "Playing the Hero Card: Masculinism, State Power and Security Feminism in *Homeland* and *Zero Dark Thirty*." *Women's Studies*, vol. 48, no. 7, 2019, pp. 755–776.

DiMatta, Joanna. "The Aesthetics of the Ecstatic: Reimagining Black Masculinity in *Moonlight*." *Screen Education*, vol. 93, 2019, pp. 8–15.

Dockterman, Eliana. "Vagina Monologues Writer Eve Ensler: How *Mad Max: Fury Road* Became a 'Feminist Action Film.'" *Time*, 7 May 2015, www.time.com/3850323/mad -max-fury-road-eve-ensler-feminist/. Accessed 30 Apr. 2020.

———. "What the Torture Report Reveals about *Zero Dark Thirty*." *Time*, 10 Dec. 2014, https://time.com/3627694/torture-report-zero-dark-thirty/. Accessed 26 Mar. 2020.

Doherty, Thomas. "*American Sniper*." *Cineaste*, vol. 40, no. 3, Summer 2015, https://www .cineaste.com/summer2015/american-sniper-thomas-doherty. Accessed 23 Aug. 2019.

"Domestic Box-Office by Decade—the 2010s." *Box Office Report*, 20 Mar. 2020, http://www .boxofficereport.com/domestic2010s.html. Accessed 28 July 2020.

Dorris, Jesse. "They Dreamed a Dream." *Time*, 17 Dec. 2012, p. 62.

Duffy, Clare, and Brian Stetler. "Mark Benioff Bought *Time* Magazine to Help Address a 'Crisis of Trust.'" *CNN Business*, 30 Dec. 2019. https://www.cnn.com/2019/12/29/media/marc-benioff -time-magazine-reliable-sources/index.html.

Dwyer, Colin. "Merriam-Webster Singles Out Nonbinary 'They' for Word of the Year Honors." *NPR.org*, 10 Dec. 2019, https://www.npr.org/2019/12/10/786732456/merriam-webster -singles-out-nonbinary-they-for-word-of-the-year-honors. Accessed 16 Oct. 2020.

Dyson, Michael Eric. *The Black Presidency: Barack Obama and the Politics of Race in America*. Houghton Mifflin Harcourt, 2016.

Ebiri, Bilge. "A Spectacle of Pure, Freewheeling Joy." *New York*, 6 Feb. 2014, https://www .vulture.com/2014/02/movie-review-the-lego-movie.html. Accessed 23 Aug. 2019.

Edelstein, David. "*Zero Dark Thirty* Is Borderline Fascistic . . . and a Masterpiece." *New York*, 10 Dec. 2012, https://www.vure.com/2012/12/edelstein-zero-dark-thirty-unholy-mas terwork.html. Accessed 3 July 2020.

Education Dive Team. "A Look at Trends in College Consolidation Since 2016." *Education Dive.com*, 17 Sept. 2020, https://www.educationdive.com/news/how-many-colleges-and -universities-have-closed-since-2016/539379/. Accessed 9 Oct. 2020.

Ehrlich, Dave. "The Evils of 'Elevated Horror'—Indiewire Critics Survey." *IndieWire*, 25 Mar. 2019, https://www.indiewire.com/2019/03/elevated-horror-movies-us-12020 53471/.

Euronews. "'There Is No Endgame': Hong Kong Activism Leader Speaks to Euronews." *Euronews.com*, 10 Mar. 2019, https://www.euronews.com/2019/10/03/there-is-no -endgame-hong-kong-activism-leader-joshua-wong-speaks-to-euronews. Accessed 22 July 2020.

Fager, Charles. *Selma 1965: The March That Changed the South*. CreateSpace Independent Publishing Platform, 2015.

Fahrenthold, David A. "Obama Reelected as President." *Washington Post*, 7 Nov. 2012, https://www.washingtonpost.com/politics/decision2012/after-grueling-campaign-polls-open-for-election-day-2012/2012/11/06/d1c24c98-2802-11e2-b4e0-346287b7e56c_story.html.

Farr, Christina. "The Medical Advisors for the Movie 'Contagion' Saw a Pandemic Coming, but Got One Big Thing Wrong." *CNBC.com*, 14 Apr. 2020, https://www.cnbc.com/2020/04/14/contagion-movie-advisors-anticipated-pandemic.html. Accessed 20 May 2020.

Ferguson, Andrew. "The Missing Lincoln." *Commentary*, Jan. 2013, p. 64.

Fiedler, Leslie A. *Love and Death in the American Novel*. Rev. ed., Stein and Day, 1966.

Finke, Nikki. "DISNEY SMASHES BOX OFFICE RECORDS: 'Toy Story 3' Crossing $1B, Studio First to Release 2 Billion-Dollar Pics in Single Year." *Deadline*, 27 Aug. 2010, https://deadline.com/2010/08/disney-smashes-box-office-records-toy-story-3-crossing-1b-studio-first-to-release-2-billion-dollar-pics-in-single-year-63322/.

Finnegan, Conor. "History Will Remember Trump as 'an Aberration,' John Bolton Says." *ABC News*, 22 June 2020, https://abcnews.go.com/Politics/history-remember-trump-aberration-john-bolton/story?id=71374309. Accessed 10 Oct. 2020.

Fischer, Molly. "The Great Awokening: What Happens to Culture in an Era of Identity Politics?" *The Cut*, 8 Jan. 2018, https://www.thecut.com/2018/01/pop-cultures-great-awokening.html. Accessed 23 Aug. 2019.

Fitzgerald, Tom, and Lorenzo Marquez. "Well I Don't Own Pearls: The Heroic Costumes of 'Hidden Figures.'" *Tom and Lorenzo: Fabulous and Opinionated*, 16 Apr. 2018, https://tomandlorenzo.com/2018/04/well-i-dont-own-pearls-the-heroic-costumes-of-hidden-figures/.

Flanagan, Martin, et al. *The Marvel Studios Phenomenon: Inside a Transmedia Universe*. Bloomsbury, 2016.

Fleming Jr., Mike. "*Get Out* Director Jordan Peele: Scaring Up Racial Dialogue by Fusing Genre with Polemic." *Deadline*. 17 Nov. 2017, https://deadline.com/2017/11/get-out-jordan-peele-oscars-interview-news-1202208902/.

Foucault, Michel. *The History of Sexuality, Vol. 1*. Vintage Books, 1976.

Frew, Cameron. "Is Quentin Tarantino About to Tear Down Hollywood?" *Flickering Myth*, 1 July 2019, https://www.flickeringmyth.com/2019/07/quentin-tarantino-about-to-tear-down-hollywood/.

Fritz, Ben. *The Big Picture: The Fight for the Future of Movies*. Houghton Mifflin, 2018.

Frum, David. *Trumpocalypse: Restoring American Democracy*. Harper, 2020.

———. *Trumpocracy: The Corruption of the American Republic*. Harper, 2018.

Fussell, Paul. *Class: A Guide through the American Status System*. Simon and Schuster, 1983.

Gaines, Mikal J. "Paid the Cost to Be the Boss: Chadwick Boseman and Mythologizing the Black Superhero." *The Projector: A Journal of Film, Media, and Culture*, vol. 19, no. 1, Summer 2019, https://www.theprojectorjournal.com/gaines-paid-the-cost-to-be-boss.

Galston, William A. "The 2012 Election: What Happened, What Changed, What It Means." *Governance Studies at Brookings*, 4 Jan. 2013, https://www.brookings.edu/research/the-2012-election-what-happened-what-changed-what-it-means/.

Garcia, Matt. "What the New Cesar Chavez Film Gets Wrong about the Labor Activist." *Smithsonian*, 2 Apr. 2014, https://www.smithsonianmag.com/history/what-new-cesar-chavez-film-gets-wrong-about-labor-activist-180950355/. Accessed 23 Aug. 2019.

Gates, Racquel. "The Trouble with Anti-racist Movie Lists." *The New York Times*, 19 July 2020, AR3.

Germain, David. "Cannes Doc 'Inside Job' Pegs 2008 Crisis as Heist." *The Seattle Times*, 17 May 2010, https://www.seattletimes.com/entertainment/cannes-doc-inside-job-pegs-2008-crisis-as-heist/.

Gerstein, Josh. "Pentagon, CIA, White House Opened Up to Hollywood on bin Laden Raid." *Politico*, 23 May 2012, https://www.politico.com/blogs/under-the-radar/2012/05/pentagon-cia-white-house-opened-up-to-hollywood-on-bin-laden-raid-124293. Accessed 27 June 2020.

Giuliani-Hoffman, Francesca. "How the Washington Post Changed under Jeff Bezos." *CNN Business*, 16 Aug. 2019, https://www.cnn.com/2019/08/16/media/jeff-bezos-donald-graham/index.html. Accessed 4 Dec. 2020.

Gleiberman, Owen. "*Contagion*, the Movie That Predicted Our Pandemic, Is Really about Our World Falling Apart." *Variety*, 27 Apr. 2020, https://variety.com/2020/film/columns/contagion-the-movie-that-predicted-our-pandemic-1234590420/. Accessed 20 May 2020.

———. "It May Be an Accident, but 'Rogue One' Is the Most Politically Relevant Movie of the Year." *Variety*, 24 Dec. 2016.

———. "Steven Spielberg vs. Netflix: A War for Cinema's Future." *Variety*, 10 Mar. 2019, https://variety.com/2019/film/columns/steven-spielberg-vs-netflix-a-preview-of-the-war-for-cinemas-future-1203159522/. Accessed 11 Mar. 2019.

Golding, Dan. *Star Wars after Lucas: A Critical Guide to the Future of the Galaxy*. Minnesota University Press, 2019.

Goldsmith, Jack. "Jimmy Hoffa and *The Irishman*: A True Crime Story?" *New York Review of Books*, 26 Sept. 2019, https://www.nybooks.com/daily/2019/09/26/jimmy-hoffa-and-the-irishman-a-true-crime-story/. Accessed 27 June 2020.

Green, Jesse. "Review: The Metamorphosis of 'Hadestown,' from Cool to Gorgeous." *The New York Times*, 17 Apr. 2019, https://www.nytimes.com/2019/04/17/theater/hadestown-review-broadway-anais-mitchell.html. Accessed 9 Oct. 2020.

Greven, David. *Ghost Faces: Hollywood and Postmillennial Masculinity*. SUNY Press, 2016.

Grierson, Tim. "In Praise of *Annihilation* and the Modern 'Weird' Sci-Fi Renaissance." *Rolling Stone*, 27 Feb. 2018, https://www.rollingstone.com/movies/movie-news/in-praise-of-annihilation-and-the-modern-weird-sci-fi-renaissance-204607/.

Grossman, Lev. "Person of the Year 2010—TIME." *Time*, 15 Dec. 2010, http://content.time.com/time/specials/packages/article/0,28804,2036683_2037183_2037185,00.html.

Hainey, Michael. "Quentin Tarantino, Brad Pitt, Leonardo DiCaprio Take You inside *Once Upon a Time in Hollywood*." *Esquire*, 21 May 2019, https://www.esquire.com/entertainment/movies/a27458589/once-upon-a-time-in-hollywood-leonardo-dicaprio-brad-pitt-quentin-tarantino-interview/. Accessed 27 July 2019.

Halberstam, Jack. "The Kids Aren't Alright!" *Bully Bloggers*, 15 July 2010, https://bullybloggers.wordpress.com/2010/07/15/the-kids-arent-alright/.

Han, Angie. "Pixar's 15 Best Female Characters." *SlashFilm*, 23 June 2015, www.slashfilm.com/best-pixar-female-characters/. Accessed 30 Apr. 2020.

Hanson, Nick. "Tickets for *Hamilton* Are Expensive for a Number of Reasons." *Quora*, 27 Mar. 2018, https://www.quora.com/Why-are-tickets-to-Hamilton-so-expensive. Accessed 5 Oct. 2020.

Haraway, Donna. "A Cyborg Manifesto: Science, Technology, and Socialist-Feminism in the Late Twentieth Century." *Simians, Cyborgs, and Women: The Reinvention of Nature*. Routledge, 1991.

Harding, Amanda. "*Hamilton* Tickets Are Still Ridiculously Expensive—But Why?" *Showbiz Cheat Sheet*, 21 Sept. 2019, https://www.cheatsheet.com/entertainment/hamilton-tickets-are-still-ridiculously-expensive-but-why.html/. Accessed 5 Oct. 2020.

Harris, Aisha. "How Accurate Is *Dallas Buyers Club*?" *Slate*, 1 Nov. 2013, https://slate.com/culture/2013/11/dallas-buyers-club-true-story-fact-and-fiction-in-the-matthew-mcconaughey-movie-about-ron-woodroof.html.

Harris, John F. "Jerry Brown's Midnight in America." *Politico Magazine*, 6 Jan. 2019, https://www.politico.com/magazine/story/2019/01/06/jerry-brown-politico-magazine-interview-223757. Accessed 7 Jan. 2019.

Harris, Mark. (@MarkHarrisNYC) "1.Annual reminder: 'Oscar bait' is a terrible term that takes our sideline fixation and tries to recast it as a defining motive for artists." *Twitter*, 9 Oct. 2016, https://twitter.com/MarkHarrisNYC/status/785148145353297920.

———. "Zero Hour: Mark Boal and Kathryn Bigelow's Hunt for Osama bin Laden." *New York*, 17–24 Dec. 2012.

Hasian Jr., Marouf. "*Zero Dark Thirty* and the Critical Challenges Posed by Populist Postfeminism during the Global War on Terrorism." *Journal of Communication Inquiry*, vol. 37, no. 4, 2013, pp. 322–343.

Hayes, Dade. "*Bird Box* Seen by Nearly 26 Million U.S. Netflix Subscribers in Its First Week, Nielsen Reports." *Deadline: Hollywood*, 8 Jan. 2019, https://deadline.com/2019/01/bird-box-netflix-seen-by-26-million-u-s-subscribers-in-first-week-nielsen-1202531235/. Accessed 20 Jan. 2019.

Haygood, Wil. "A Butler Well Served by This Election." *The Washington Post*, 7 Nov. 2008, https://www.washingtonpost.com/lifestyle/a-butler-well-served-by-this-election/2019/01/02/b2a805a6-07b1-11e9-88e3-989a3e456820_story.html.

Heikensten, Lars. "We Must Fight the Threats to Our World with Knowledge." *The Nobel Foundation: 2016 Annual Review*, edited by Annika Pontikis and Jonna Petterson, The Nobel Foundation, 2016, p. 1.

Hennessey, Susan, and Benjamin Wittes. *Unmaking the Presidency: Donald Trump's War on the World's Most Powerful Office*. Farrar, Straus and Giroux, 2020.

Hibberd, James. "Rotten Tomatoes Is 'the Destruction of Our Business,' Says Director." *Entertainment Weekly*, 23 Mar. 2017, https://ew.com/movies/2017/03/23/ratner-tomatoes-scores/.

Higgins, Marissa. "This Gender-Neutral Pronoun Beat 'Impeach' and 'Quid pro Quo' as Merriam-Webster's Word of the Year." *Daily Kos*, 10 Dec. 2019, https://www.dailykos.com/stories/2019/12/10/1904708/-This-gender-neutral-pronoun-beat-impeach-and-quid-pro-quid-as-Merriam-Webster-s-Word-of-the-Year. Accessed 29 June 2020.

Hirsh, Michael. "Why the New Nationalists Are Taking Over." *Politico Magazine*, 27 June 2016, https://www.politico.com/magazine/story/2016/06/nationalism-donald-trump-boris-johnson-brexit-foreign-policy-xenophobia-isolationism-213995/.

"Historians Respond to Spielberg's *Lincoln*." Harvard University Press Blog, 30 Nov. 2012, https://harvardpress.typepad.com/hup_publicity/2012/11/historians-respond-to-spielbergs-lincoln.html. Accessed 8 June 2020.

Hoberman, J. "The Great American Shooter." *The New York Review of Books*, 13 Feb. 2015, https://www.nybooks.com/daily/2015/02/13/great-american-shooter/. Accessed 23 Aug. 2019.

Hornaday, Anne. "*Three Billboards outside Ebbing, Missouri* Is a Vigilante Comedy for Our Age." *The Washington Post*, 14 Nov. 2017, https://www.washingtonpost.com/goingoutguide/movies/three-billboards-outside-ebbing-missouri-is-a-vigilante-comedy-for-our-age/2017/11/14/7f884082-c4be-11e7-afe9-4f60b5a6c4a0story.html.

Howard, Scott Alexander. "Nostalgia." *Analysis*, vol. 72, no. 4, Oct. 2012, pp. 641–650.

How It Should Have Ended. *HISHE Dubs—Frozen (Comedy Recap)*. https://www.youtube.com /watch?v=EhcEutiJnsk.

Indiviglio, Daniel. "The Fed Explains the Mancession." *The Atlantic*, 2 Mar. 2010, https://www .theatlantic.com/business/archive/2010/03/the-fed-explains-the-mancession/36928/.

Jacobs, Alex. "Native Movie Trailers: Best 2016 Native Films with Native Actors, Themes or Content." *Indian Country Today*, 12 July 2017.

Jagernauth, Kevin. "It Turns Out That Scarlett Johansson Replaced Samantha Morton in Spike Jonze's 'Her.'" *IndieWire*, 21 June 2013, https://www.indiewire.com/2013/06/it-turns-out -that-scarlett-johansson-replaced-samantha-morton-in-spike-jonzes-her-96743/.

Japsen, Bruce. "After CVS Stopped Cigarette Sales, Smokers Stopped Buying Elsewhere, Too." *Forbes*, 20 Feb. 2017, https://www.forbes.com/sites/brucejapsen/2017/02/20 /after-cvs-stopped-cigarette-sales-smokers-stopped-buying-elsewhere-too /#6041b552c8f5. Accessed 18 Jan. 2020.

Johnson, Marty. "Ginsburg Predicts Historians Will Call This Political Era an 'Aberration.'" *The Hill*, 4 Oct. 2019, https://thehill.com/homenews/news/464409-ginsburg-predicts -historians-will-call-this-political-era-an-aberration. Accessed 10 Oct. 2020.

Jones, Nate. "How *Once Upon a Time . . . in Hollywood* Recreated the Summer (and Spring) of '69." *Vulture*, 1 Aug. 2019, https://www.vulture.com/2019/08/how-once-upon-a-time -in-hollywood-recreated-1969-los-angeles.html. Accessed 15 June 2020.

———. "How *Parasite* Pulled Off Its History-Making Best Picture Win." *New York/Vulture*, 10 Feb. 2020, https://www.vulture.com/2020/02/oscars-2020-how-parasite-won-best-picture .html. Accessed 18 July 2020.

Karlyn, Kathleen Rowe. *Unruly Girls, Unrepentant Mothers: Redefining Feminism on Screen*. University of Texas Press, 2011.

Keegan, Rebecca, and Ben Zauzmer. "Is the Oscars' Inclusion Push Working? Breaking Down the Surprising Academy Numbers." *Hollywood Reporter*, 4 Feb. 2020, https:// www.hollywoodreporter.com/news/is-oscars-inclusion-push-working-surprising -academy-numbers-1275305. Accessed 18 July 2020.

Kessler, Glenn. "When Did Mitch McConnell Say He Wanted to Make Obama a One-Term President?" *The Washington Post*, 11 Jan. 2017, https://www.washingtonpost.com/news /fact-checker/wp/2017/01/11/when-did-mitch-mcconnell-say-he-wanted-to-make -obama-a-one-term-president/. Accessed 29 July 2020.

Khazan, Olga. "The U.S. Is Repeating Its Deadliest Pandemic Mistake." *The Atlantic*, 6 July 2020, https://www.theatlantic.com/health/archive/2020/07/us-repeating-deadliest -pandemic-mistake-nursing-home-deaths/613855/. Accessed 23 July 2020.

Kil, Sonya. "Bong Joon-ho on Working with Netflix and the Controversy over *Okja* at Cannes." *Variety*, 16 May 2017, https://variety.com/2017/film/news/bong-joon-ho -working-with-netflix-controversy-okja-cannes-1202428394/. Accessed 31 May 2020.

Kilday, Gregg. "Oscars' Best Picture Race: 10 in 2010." *The Hollywood Reporter*, 24 June 2009, https://www.hollywoodreporter.com/news/oscars-picture-race-10-2010-85773. Accessed 19 Oct. 2020.

Kim, Eugene. "How Amazon CEO Jeff Bezos Reinvented *The Washington Post*, the 140-Year-Old Newspaper He Bought for $250 Million." *Business Insider*, 15 May 2016, https://www.businessinsider.com/how-the-washington-post-changed-after-jeff-bezos -acquisition-2016-5. Accessed 17 July 2020.

Klein, Christina. "Why American Studies Needs to Think about Korean Cinema, or Transnational Genres in the Films of Bong Joon-ho." *American Quarterly*, vol. 60, no. 4, Dec. 2008, pp. 871–898.

Klein, Ezra. *Why We're Polarized*. Avid Reader Press, 2020.

Kraszewski, Rob, and Geoff Macnaughton, hosts. "Episode 54: Alex Garland on *Annihilation*, Adaptation, and the Future of Sci-Fi." *TIFF The Long Take*, Toronto International Film Festival, 27 Feb. 2018, https://podcasts.apple.com/us/podcast/ep-54-alex-garland-on -annihilation-adaptation-future/id1209259768?i=1000403945860.

Krueger, Alyson. "Our Golden Milestones." *The New York Times*, 4 Aug. 2019, ST1+.

Kuhn, Anthony. "South Korea's Drive-Thru Testing for Coronavirus Is Fast—and Free." *NPR*, 13 Mar. 2020, https://www.npr.org/sections/goatsandsoda/2020/03/13/815441078 /south-koreas-drive-through-testing-for-coronavirus-is-fast-and-free. Accessed 28 May 2020.

Landau, Elizabeth. "CVS Stores to Stop Selling Tobacco." *CNN.com*, 5 Feb. 2014, https:// www.cnn.com/2014/02/05/health/cvs-cigarettes/index.html. Accessed 18 Jan. 2020.

Lang, Brent. "African-Americans, Asian-Americans Went to More Movies in 2016." *Variety*, 22 Mar. 2017, https://variety.com/2017/film/news/african-americans-asians-box-office -moviegoing-diversity-1202014188/.

Larsen, A. E. "Hidden Figures: Laudable Liberties." *An Historian Goes to the Movies*, 12 Feb. 2017, https://aelarsen.wordpress.com//?s=hidden+figures&search=Go.

Laurie, Timothy, and Jessica Kean. "Why Consenting Adults Should See 50 Shades of Grey—and Take Their Teens." *Sydney Morning Herald*, 15 Feb. 2015, www.smh.com.au /opinion/why-consenting-adults-should-see-50-shades-of-grey—and-take-their-teens -20150214-13ewto.html. Accessed 30 Apr. 2020.

Lauzen, Martha M. "The Celluloid Ceiling: Behind-the-Scenes Employment of Women on the Top 250 Films of 2012." https://womenintvfilm.sdsu.edu/files/2012_Celluloid _Ceiling_Exec_Summ.pdf. Accessed 3 July 2020.

———. "It's a Man's (Celluloid) World: On-Screen Representations of Female Characters in the Top 100 Films of 2011." https://womenintvfilm.sdsu.edu/files/2011_Its_a_Mans _World_Exec_Summ.pdf. Accessed 3 July 2020.

———. "MPAA Must Lead—or Be Led—in Battle to Improve Diversity." *Variety*, 17 Mar. 2016.

Lee, Jesse. "The President Signs Repeal of 'Don't Ask Don't Tell': 'Out of Many, We Are One.'" *Whitehouse.Gov*, 22 Dec. 2010, https://obamawhitehouse.archives.gov/blog/2010 /12/22/president-signs-repeal-dont-ask-dont-tell-out-many-we-are-one.

Lee, Meera. "Monstrosity and Humanity in Bong Joon-ho's *The Host*." *positions*, vol. 26, no. 4, Nov. 2018, pp. 719–747.

Longworth, Karina. "*Captain America* Ignores Its Roots for Easy Money." *The Village Voice*, 20 July 2011.

Luxford, James. "A Requiem for Medium-Sized Movies: Why Have Mid-budget Films All-but Disappeared from Today's Cinematic Landscape?" *Little White Lies*, 14 May 2017, https://lwlies.com/articles/a-requiem-for-medium-sized-movies/.

Lynch, Jason. "Georgia's TV and Film Industry Now Brings In $7 Billion a Year, Fueled by Smart Incentives." *Ad Week*, 9 Apr. 2017, https://www.adweek.com/tv-video/how-atlanta -became-the-worlds-fastest-growing-film-and-tv-destination/. Accessed 30 May 2019.

Mack, David. "Everyone Is Watching *Contagion*, A 9-Year-Old Movie about a Flu Outbreak." *BuzzFeed News*, 3 Mar. 2020, https://www.buzzfeednews.com/article/davidmack/con tagion-movie-coronavirus. Accessed 20 May 2020.

Malkowski, Jennifer. *Dying in Full Detail: Mortality and Digital Documentary*. Duke University Press, 2017.

Marez, Curtis. *Farm Worker Futurism: Speculative Technologies of Resistance*. University of Minnesota Press, 2016.

———. Interview. By Daniel Smith-Rowsey. 15 Nov. 2019.

Martin, Adrian. Review of *Mad Max: Fury Road*, directed by George Miller. *Film Critic: Adrian Martin*. May/Sept. 2015, http://www.filmcritic.com.au/reviews/m/mad_max_4.html. Accessed 30 Apr. 2020.

Marvin, Rob. "The Most Iconic Tech Innovations of the 2010s." *PCMag.com*, 22 Nov. 2019, https://www.pcmag.com/news/the-most-iconic-tech-innovations-of-the-2010s. Accessed 11 Oct. 2020.

Marx, Karl. *The Eighteenth Brumaire of Louis Bonaparte*. Project Gutenberg, https://www.gutenberg.org/files/1346/1346-h/1346-h.htm.

Massa, Robert. "Here's Why Colleges Are Being Forced to Close Their Doors—and What They Can Do to Stay Open." *The Conversation*, 7 Nov. 2019, https://theconversation.com/heres-why-colleges-are-being-forced-to-close-their-doors-and-what-they-can-do-to-stay-open-126399. Accessed 9 Oct. 2020.

Masterson, Karen. "Trump Says He's on a Miracle Covid-19 Drug. People Who Take His Advice May Die." *The Washington Post*, 19 May 2020, https://www.washingtonpost.com/outlook/2020/05/19/trump-hydroxychloroquine-science/. Accessed 20 May 2020.

Mbembé, Achille. *Necropolitics*. Duke University Press, 2011.

McSweeney, Terence, editor. *Avengers Assemble!: Critical Perspectives on the Marvel Cinematic Universe*. Wallflower, 2018.

Mead, Rebecca. "Downtown's Daughter." *The New Yorker*, 8 Nov. 2010, https://www.newyorker.com/magazine/2010/11/15/downtowns-daughter.

Medina, Jennifer. "Lori Laughlin and Felicity Huffman, 1 Scandal, 2 Actresses, Diverging Paths." *The New York Times*, 10 Apr. 2019, https://www.nytimes.com/2019/04/10/us/lori-loughlin-felicity-huffman-admissions-scandal.html. Accessed 9 Oct. 2020.

———, et al. "Prosecutors Uncover 'Largest College Admissions Scam Ever.'" *The New York Times*, 12 Mar. 2019, https://www.nytimes.com/2019/03/12/us/college-admissions-cheating-scandal.html. Accessed 9 Oct. 2020.

Moorhead, Molly. "Mitt Romney Says 47 Percent of Americans Pay No Income Tax." *Politifact*, 18 Sept. 2012, https://www.politifact.com/factchecks/2012/sep/18/mitt-romney/romney-says-47-percent-americans -pay-no-income-tax/. Accessed 5 July 2020.

Morris, Wesley. "The Dream Act: The Powerful, Profound 'Selma.'" *Grantland*, 9 Jan. 2015, http://grantland.com/hollywood-prospectus/selma-review/. Accessed 30 Sept. 2020.

———. "For Me, Rewatching *Contagion* Was Fun—Until It Wasn't." *The New York Times*, 10 Mar. 2020, https://www.nytimes.com/2020/03/10/movies/contagion-movie-coronavirus.html. Accessed 20 May 2020.

———. "Inside Job." *The Boston Globe*, 15 Oct. 2010, http://archive.boston.com/ae/movies/articles/2010/10/15/inside_job_is_on_the money/?page=2.

Motion Picture Association of America, Inc. and National Association of Theatre Owners, Inc. "Classification and Rating Rules: Effective as Revised January 1, 2010." 2010, pp. 1–23.

———. "2017 Theme Report." Apr. 2018.

Mowatt, Rasul A. "Black Lives as Snuff: The Silent Complicity in Viewing Black Death." *Biography*, vol. 41, no. 4, Fall 2018.

Murrian, Samuel R. "*Beatriz at Dinner* Director Miguel Arteta on Why Trump Wouldn't Be a Believable Movie Character." *Parade*, 20 June 2017, https://parade.com/577967/samuelmurrian/beatriz-at-dinner-director-miguel-arteta-on-why-trump-wouldnt-be-a-believable-movie-character/.

National Hispanic Media Coalition. "Lack of Latinx in Film Industry: Combating Exclusion, Discrimination, and Negative Stereotypes." 2019, pp. 1–9.

Nichols, Mackenzie. "James Cameron Congratulates *Avengers: Endgame* for Sinking *Titanic*'s Box Office Record." *Variety*, 9 May 2019, https://variety.com/2019/film/box-office /avengers-endgame-titantic-james-cameron-1203209845/. Accessed 9 May 2019.

Nochinson, Martha. "*Winter's Bone*: Film Review." *Cineaste*, Winter 2010, pp. 52–54.

NPR Staff. "2011: An Extraordinary Year for Gay Rights." *All Things Considered*, 31 Dec. 2011, https://www.npr.org/2011/12/31/144520538/2011-an-extraordinary-year-for-gay -rights. Accessed 27 Sept. 2020.

Nyren, Erin. "Steven Spielberg Doesn't Think Netflix Movies Deserve Oscars." *Variety*, 25 Mar. 2018, https://variety.com/2018/film/news/steven-spielberg-netflix-movies-oscars -1202735959/. Accessed 3 Oct. 2020.

Odgren, Elissa. "Learning How to Build Community without Following the Instructions: Finding Pieces of Resistance in *The Lego Movie*." *Popular Culture as Pedagogy: Research in the Field of Adult Education*, edited by Kaela Jubas, Nancy Taber, and Tony Brown, Sense Publishers, 2015, pp. 31–48.

O'Hehir, Andrew. "Is Feminism Worth Defending with Torture?" *Salon*, 1 Dec. 2012, https:// www.salon.com/2012/12/01/is_feminism_worth_defending_with_torture/. Accessed 3 July 2020.

O'Neill, Lily. "For Aurora, *Joker* Film Hits Too Close to Home." *5280: Denver's Mile-High Magazine*, 23 Oct. 2019, https://www.5280.com/2019/10/for-aurora-joker-hits-too-close-to -home/. Accessed 3 July 2020.

O'Sullivan, Jim. "Remember Mitt Romney's 'Binders Full of Women?' They're Real. And We Got Them." *Boston Globe*, 10 Apr. 2017, https://www.bostonglobe.com/metro/2017 /04/10/romney-binders-still-full-women-are-unearthed/NTdYraj1yQ53uVklgnHZtL /story.html. Accessed 5 July 2020.

On Point. "A Way to Stop Mass Shootings: Stop Naming the Shooters." *WBUR*, 6 Nov. 2017, https://www.wbur.org/onpoint/2017/11/06/a-way-to-stop-mass-killers-stop-naming -them. Accessed 14 June 2020.

Paquette, Danielle. "Not Even a Third of Speaking Roles in Popular Movies Go to Women." *Washington Post*, 7 Aug. 2015, www.washingtonpost.com/news/wonk/wp/2015/08 /06/not-even-a-third-of-speaking-roles-in-popular-movies-go-to-women/. Accessed 30 Apr. 2020.

Park, S. Nathan. "'Parasite' Has a Hidden Backstory of Middle-Class Failure and Chicken Joints." *Foreign Policy.com*, 21 Feb. 2020, https://foreignpolicy.com/2020/02/21/korea -bong-oscars-parasite-hidden-backstory-middle-class-chicken-bong-joon-ho/. Accessed 27 May 2020.

Parker, Kathleen. *Save the Males: Why Men Matter, Why Women Should Care*. Random House Trade Paperbacks, 2010.

Parlett, Martin A. *Demonizing a President: The "Foreignization" of Barack Obama*. Praeger, 2014.

Pearson, Jennifer. "'I wanted a Movie Mothers Could Take Their Daughters To': J. J. Abrams on Why He Cast a Strong Female Lead in Star Wars: The Force Awakens." *Daily Mail*, 1 Dec. 2015, www.dailymail.co.uk/tvshowbiz/article-3339834/J-J-Abrams-cast-strong -female-lead-Star-Wars-Force-Awakens.html. Accessed 30 Apr. 2020.

Pew Research Center. "About 6 in 10 Young Adults in U.S. Primarily Use Online Streaming to Watch TV," 13 Sept. 2017, https://www.pewresearch.org/fact-/2017/09/13/about-6 -in-10-young-adults-in-u-s-primarily-use-online-streaming-to-watch-tv/.

Philip, Tom. "Hollywood (Really) Hopes You're Nostalgic for the '90s This Summer." *The New York Times*, 4 July 2019, https://www.nytimes.com/2019/07/04/opinion/ho llywood-movies.html?action=click&module=Opinion&pgtype=Homepage. Accessed 4 July 2019.

Plumb, Ali. "Paul Thomas Anderson: Inherent Vice." *Empire Online*, 3 Sept. 2012, https://www.empireonline.com/news/story.asp?NID=35060. Accessed 23 Aug. 2019.

Polinski, Jennifer, et al. "Impact of CVS Pharmacy's Discontinuance of Tobacco Sales on Cigarette Purchasing (2012–2014)." *American Journal of Public Health*, vol. 107, no. 4, Apr. 2017, pp. 556–562.

Pollitt, Katha. "*The Hunger Games*' Feral Feminism." *The Nation*, 23 Apr. 2012, p. 10.

Pols, Mary. "*The Fighter*: Wahlberg, Bale Punch above Their Weight." *Time*, 9 Dec. 2010, http://content.time.com/time/arts/article/0,8599,2036057,00.html.

Powers, Richard Gid. Review of *Zero Dark Thirty*, directed by Kathryn Bigelow. *Journal of American History*, vol. 100, no. 1, June 2013, pp. 303–305.

Quashie, Kevin. *The Sovereignty of Quiet*. Rutgers University Press, 2012.

Rashbaum, William K., et al. "Epstein Is Found Dead in his Cell in New York Jail." *The New York Times*, 11 Aug. 2019, 1+.

Recording Industry Association of America. "Gold & Platinum." 25 May 2021, https://www.riaa.com/gold-platinum/?tab_active=default-.award&ar=Various+Artists&ti=Hamilton+%28Original+Broadway+Cast+Recording%29#search_section. Accessed 9 June 2021.

Redmond, Sean. "That Joke Isn't Funny Anymore: A Critical Exploration of *Joker*." Call for Papers, Screen-L Discussion List (SCREEN-L@listserv.ua.edu), 9 Oct. 2019. Accessed 13 Oct. 2019.

Reyes, Xavier Aldana. "Guillermo del Toro's Crimson Peak (2015)—Gothic Film." *The Gothic: A Reader*, edited by Simon Bacon, Peter Lang, 2018, pp. 169–176.

Rich, Frank. "Torture, Compromise, Revenge: Oscars Made for the Obama Age." *New York*, 11 Feb. 2013, pp. 16–21.

Rich, Katey. "Angelina Jolie Confirms a Key *Maleficent* Scene Was about Rape." *Vanity Fair*, 12 June 2014, https://www.vanityfair.com/hollywood/2014/06/angelina-jolie-maleficent-rape. Accessed 23 Aug. 2019.

Ritman, Alex. "*Get Out* Star Daniel Kaluuya Reveals the Advice Lupita Nyong'o Gave Him about Fame." *Hollywood Reporter*, 14 Feb. 2019. https://www.hollywoodreporter.com/news/general-news/get-star-daniel-kaluuya-reveals-advice-lupita-nyongo-gave-him-fame-1086361/.

Roettgers, Janko. "*Bird Box* Has Been Watched by 80 Million Subscribers, Netflix Says." *Variety*, 17 Jan. 2019, https://variety.com/2019/digital/news/bird-box-80 million-viewers-1203111028/. Accessed 17 Oct. 2020.

Rose, Alex. "Ari Aster on What 'Elevated Horror' Means and Whether His New Hyped Film Qualifies." *Cult MTL*, 8 June 2018, https://cultmtl.com/2018/06/hereditary-ari-aster/.

Rosen, Christopher. "Oscars: Barack Obama Weighs In on Diversity Issue." *Entertainment Weekly*, 28 Jan. 2016, https://ew.com/article/2016/01/28/oscars-barack-obama/.

Rosin, Hanna. "The End of Men." *The Atlantic*, 8 Jun. 2010, https://www.theatlantic.com/magazine/archive/2010/07/the-end-of-men/308135/.

Rowe, Kathleen. *The Unruly Woman: Gender and the Genres of Laughter*. University of Texas Press, 1995.

———. *See also* Karlyn, Kathleen Rowe.

Rubin, Rebecca. "Why Audiences Are Going Only to Disney Movies." *Variety*, 19 July 2019, https://variety.com/2019/film/box-office/disney-box-office-the-lion-king-avengers-endgame-1203271801/.

Rucker, Philip, and Carol Leonnig. *A Very Stable Genius: Donald J. Trump's Testing of America*. Penguin, 2020.

Russert, Tim. "Transcript of Interview with Vice President Cheney." *Washington Post*, 16 Sept. 2001, https://www.washingtonpost.com/wpsrv/nation/specials/attacked/transcripts/cheney091601.html.

Sakoui, Anousha. "Hollywood Had a Terrible 2017." *Bloomberg*. 2 Jan. 2018. https://www.bloomberg.com/news/articles/2018-01-02/hollywood-s-2017-is-a-bomb-as-moviegoing-slumps-to-25-year-low.

San Filippo, Maria. "Art Porn Provocateurs: Queer Feminist Performances of Embodiment in the Work of Catherine Breillat and Lena Dunham." *The Velvet Light Trap*, vol. 77, Spring 2016, pp. 28–49.

Scharf, Zack. "'Mad Max: Fury Road' Tops First Critics Poll Naming Best Films of the Decade." *IndieWire*, 1 May 2019, https://www.indiewire.com/2019/05/best-films-decade-critics-poll-mad-max-tree-of-life-1202130086/. Accessed 30 Apr. 2020.

Schickel, Richard. *Conversations with Scorsese*. Alfred A. Knopf, 2011.

———. *The Disney Version: The Life, Times, Art and Commerce of Walt Disney*. 1968. Simon & Schuster, 2019.

Schneider, Michael. "America's Most Watched: The Top 50 Shows of the 2013–2014 TV Season." *TV Guide*, 6 June 2014, https://www.tvguide.com/news/most-watched-shows-2013-2014-1082628/.

———. "Bird Box Ratings: Nielsen Backs Up Netflix's Claims That It's a Big Hit." *Variety*, 8 Jan. 2019, https://variety.com/2019/tv/news/bird-box-ratings-netflix-nielsen-1203102316/.

Schreiber, Michele. "Tiny Life: Technology and Masculinity in the Films of David Fincher." *Journal of Film and Video* 68, vol. 1, Spring 2016, pp. 3–18.

Schwartz, Barry. "Our *Lincoln*." *Society*, vol. 50, no. 5, Oct. 2013, pp. 503–505.

Scorsese, Martin. "I Said Marvel Movies Aren't Cinema. Let Me Explain." *The New York Times*, 4 Nov. 2019, https://www.nytimes.com/2019/11/04/opinion/martin-scorsese-marvel.html. Accessed 24 May 2020.

Scott, A. O. "A 50-Mile March, Nearly 50 Years Later." *The New York Times*, 24 Dec. 2014, https://www.nytimes.com/2014/12/25/arts/in-selma-king-is-just-one-of-the-heroes.html. Accessed 23 Aug. 2019.

———. "'Joker' Review: Are You Kidding Me?" *The New York Times*, 3 Oct. 2019, https://www.nytimes.com/2019/10/03/movies/joker-review.html. Accessed 19 Oct. 2020.

———. "'Hidden Figures' Honors 3 Black Women Who Helped NASA Soar." *The New York Times*, 22 Dec. 2016.

———. "Meet the Sperm Donor: Modern Family Ties." *The New York Times*, 8 July 2010, https://www.nytimes.com/2010/07/09/movies/09kids.html.

———. "The Pride That Went Before the Fall." *The New York Times*, 23 Sept. 2010, https://www.nytimes.com/2010/09/24/movies/24wall.html.

———, and Manohla Dargis. "Oscars 2015: A. O. Scott and Manohla Dargis Discuss the Contenders." *The New York Times*, 12 Feb. 2015, https://www.nytimes.com/2015/02/15/movies/awardsseason/oscars-2015-a-o-scott-and-manohla-dargis-discuss-the-contenders.html. Accessed 30 Sept. 2020.

Seitz, Matt Zoller. "Best Films of the 2010s: 13. *Silence*." *Roger Ebert.com*, 4 Nov. 2019, https://www.rogerebert.com/features/the-best-films-of-the-2010s. Accessed 9 June 2020.

Sennett, Richard, and Jonathan Cobb. *The Hidden Injuries of Class*. Knopf, 1972.

Shary, Timothy. *Boyhood: A Young Life on Screen*. Routledge, 2018.

Shaw, Tony, and Tricia Jenkins. "From Zero to Hero: The CIA and Hollywood Today." *Cinema Journal*, vol. 56, no. 2, Winter 2017, pp. 91–113.

Sherwin, Adam. "DVD Industry in Crisis as Sales Slump." *The Guardian*, 29 Nov. 2010, https://www.theguardian.com/media/2010/nov/29/dvd-industry-sales-slump-blu-ray. Accessed 18 Oct. 2020.

Siegel, Tatiana. "'His Brand Is Excellence': How Leonardo DiCaprio Became Hollywood's Last Movie Star." *The Hollywood Reporter*, 22 July 2019, https://www.hollywoodreporter.com/features/how-leonardo-dicaprio-became-hollywoods-last-movie-star-1225416. Accessed 29 July 2019.

Sims, David. "*Arrival*'s Timely Message about Empathy." *The Atlantic*, 16 Nov. 2016.

Slate editors. "2014: The Year of Outrage." *Slate*, 17 Dec. 2014, https://www.slate.com/articles/life/culturebox/2014/12/the-year-of-outrage-2014_-everything-you-were-angry-about-on-social-media.html. Accessed 23 Aug. 2019.

Smalls, James. "The Past, Present, and Future of Black Queer Cinema." *African American Cinema Through Black Lives Consciousness*, edited by Mark A. Reid, Wayne State University Press, 2019, pp. 275–296.

Smith, Stacy L., et al. "Gender Bias without Borders: An Investigation of Female Characters in Popular Films across 11 Countries." Geena Davis Institute on Gender in Media, 2014, https://seejane.org/wp-content/uploads/gender-bias-without-borders-full-report.pdf. Accessed 1 May 2020.

Spangler, Todd. "More Bad News for President Donald Trump in Latest Michigan Poll." *Detroit Free Press*, 8 Mar. 2019, https://www.freep.com/story/news/local/michigan/2019/03/08/donald-trump-michigan-poll/3095850002/ Accessed 14 Mar. 2019.

Sperling, Nicole. "Scorsese's New Mob Epic, *The Irishman*, Has Netflix and Theaters at Odds." *The New York Times*, 21 Aug. 2019, https://www.nytimes.com/2019/08/21/business/media/netflix-scorsese-the-irishman.html. Accessed 26 Aug. 2019.

Spielberg, Steven. "Gettysburg and Lincoln's Legacy." 19 Nov. 2012, https://www.c-span.org/video/?309433-1/steven-spielberg-149th-anniversary-gettysburg-address.

St. Félix, Doreen. "The Twisted Power of White Voice in *Sorry to Bother You* and *BlacKkKlansman*." *The New Yorker*, 13 Aug. 2018, https://www.newyorker.com/culture/cultural-comment/the-twisted-power-of-white-voice-in-sorry-to-bother-you-and-blackkklansman. Accessed 15 Oct. 2020.

Stanton, Glenn T. "Are the Kids Really All Right?" *Focus on the Family*, 7 July 2010, https://www.focusonthefamily.com/parenting/are-the-kids-really-all-right/.

Statt, Nick. "How the Short Story That Inspired *Arrival* Helps Us Interpret the Film's Major Twist." *The Verge*, 16 Nov. 2016.

Steadman, Alex. "Trump Mocks *Parasite* Best Picture Win: 'What the Hell Was That About?'" *Variety*, 20 Feb. 2020, https://variety.com/2020/film/news/trump-parasite-oscars-best-picture-south-korea-1203509938/ Accessed 23 Feb. 2020.

Stelter, Brian. "Final Tallies for 'Sanity' Rally." *The Caucus*, 1 Nov. 2010, https://thecaucus.blogs.nytimes.com/2010/11/01/final-tallies-for-sanity-rally/.

Stern, Marlow. "'Rogue One' Director Gareth Edwards Discusses the Film's Trump 'Fake News' Backlash." *The Daily Beast*, 13 July 2017.

Stockman, Farah. "Why They Loved Him: His Fake Populism." *The New York Times*, 18 Oct. 2020, p. AR 4.

Stolberg, Sheryl Gay, and Robert Pear. "Obama Signs Health Care Overhaul Bill, with a Flourish." *The New York Times*, 23 Mar. 2010, https://www.nytimes.com/2010/03/24/health/policy/24health.html.

———. "Obama's Views on Gay Marriage 'Evolving.'" *The New York Times*, 18 June 2011, https://www.nytimes.com/2011/06/19/us/politics/19marriage.html. Accessed 27 Sept. 2020.

Stoller, Matt. "Democrats Can't Win Until They Recognize How Bad Obama's Financial Poli-cies Were." *Washington Post*, 12 Jan. 2017, https://www.washingtonpost.com /posteverything/wp/2017/01/12/democrats-cant-win-until-they-recognize-how-bad -obamas-financial-policies-were/.

Stroumboulopoulos, George. "Ari Aster on *Hereditary*." *YouTube*, uploaded by TIFF, 14 June 2018, https://www.youtube.com/watch?v=cUohJDNnT9A.

Sunio, Patti. "3 Other Ace Movies from Korean Filmmaker Bong Joon Ho, Director of Oscar-Golden Globe-Winning Thriller, *Parasite*." *South China Morning Post.com*, 14 Jan. 2020, https://www.scmp.com/magazines/style/celebrity/article/3045979/3-other-ace-movies -korean-filmmaker-bong-joon-ho-director. Accessed 2 June 2020.

Tartaglione, Nancy. "Hereditary Becomes A24's Highest-Grossing Pic Worldwide with $78M." *Deadline*, 26 July 2018, https://deadline.com/2018/07/hereditary-a24-highest -grossing-worldwide-movie-box-office-1202433883/.

Tasker, Yvonne. *Spectacular Bodies: Gender, Genre and the Action Cinema*. Routledge, 2015.

Taylor, Kate. "Lori Laughlin and Mossimo Giannulli Get Prison in College Admissions Case." *The New York Times*, 21 Aug. 2020, https://www.nytimes.com/2020/08/21/us/lori -loughlin-mossimo-giannulli-sentencing.html. Accessed 9 Oct. 2020.

"The Hong Kong protests explained in 100 and 500 words." *BBC News*, 28 Nov. 2019, https:// www.bbc.com/news/world-asia-china-49317695. Accessed 5 July 2020.

"The Monsters within Us." *Us*. Blu-ray Bonus Features. Universal Home Video, 2019.

"The Numbers: Where Data and the Movie Business Meet." *The Numbers*, 2017, https://www .the-numbers.com/market/2017/summary.

The Recession of 2007–2009: BLS Spotlight on Statistics. Bls.gov, https://www.bls.gov/spotlight /2012/recession/data-ces-industry-6-recessions.htm. Accessed 31 May 2020.

"The State of OTT Video: Mainstream, as Streaming Devices Take Center Stage." *Marketing Charts*, 11 July 2018, https://www.marketingcharts.com/featured-104905.

Thompson, Anne. "'Arrival' Could Never Have Been Made by a Studio: Here's Why." *IndieWire*, 9 Nov. 2016, https://www.indiewire.com/2016/11/arrival-amy-adams-jere my-renner-denis-villeneuve-oscars-2017-1201744589/.

———. *The $11 Billion Dollar Year: From Sundance to the Oscars, an Inside Look at the Changing Hollywood System*. Newmarket, 2014.

Thompson, Camela. "Life with Lupus: Trump's Hydroxychloroquine Hype Puts My Treatment—and Himself—at Risk." *Statnews.com*, 20 May 2020, https://www.statnews .com/2020/05/20/hydroxychloroquine-trump-hype-jeopardize-supply-may-harm-him/. Accessed 20 May 2020.

Thompson, Derek. "It's Not Just a Recession. It's a Mancession!" *The Atlantic*, 9 July 2009, https://www.theatlantic.com/business/archive/2009/07/its-not-just-a-recession-its-a -mancession/20991/.

"Timeline of the Life and Crimes of Jeffrey Epstein." *WCBS New York*, 10 Aug. 2019, https:// newyork.cbslocal.com/2019/08/10/timeline-of-the-life-and-crimes-of-jeffrey-epstein/.

Tippett, Krista. "How Can I Say This So We Can Stay in This Car Together?" *On Being*, 10 Jan. 2019, WFYI-FM Indianapolis, https://onbeing.org/series/podcast/. Accessed 11 Jan. 2019.

Tonelli, Bill. "The Lies of the Irishman." *Slate.com*, 7 Aug. 2019, https://slate.com/culture /2019/08/the-irishman-scorsese-netflix-movie-true-story-lies.html. Accessed 27 June 2020.

Tran, Kevin. "*Hamilton* Far Bigger Than Anything on Netflix in July, Audience Data Reveals." *Variety*, 10 Aug. 2020, https://variety.com/vip/disney-hamilton-audience-nearly-3x -bigger-than-any-netflix-program-in-july-1234729439/. Accessed 5 Oct. 2020.

Trump, Mary L. *Too Much and Never Enough: How My Family Created the World's Most Dangerous Man*. Simon and Schuster, 2020.

Trutnau, John-Paul. *A One-Man Show? The Construction and Deconstruction of a Patriarchal Image in the Reagan Era: Reading the Audio-Visual Poetics of Miami Vice*. Trafford Publishing, 2005.

Tucker, Michael. "Annihilation—The Art of Self Destruction." *YouTube*, uploaded by Lessons from the Screenplay, 30 Dec. 2018. https://www.youtube.com/watch?v=LMmA2pu2gdY&list=PLT-4yT1dlsSXI-eNnqa-DCHtM54klHOB2&index=4&t=121s.

Turakhia, Bhavin. "Top 10 Technological Advances of the Past Decade." *Flockblog.com*, 7 Jan. 2020, https://blog.flock.com/top-technological-advances-of-the-2010s. Accessed 11 Oct. 2020.

Uchanma 50. "Studio Domestic Market Share for the Decade (2010–2019)." *Rboxoffice*, 2 Jan. 2020, https://www.reddit.com/r/boxoffice/comments/eiy1bd/studio-domestic-market-share-for-the-decade/. Accessed 19 July 2020.

VanDerWerff, Emily. "*Once Upon a Time in Hollywood*'s Many, Many Controversies, Explained." *Vox.com*, 15 Aug. 2019, https://www.vox.com/culture/2019/8/15/20759084/once-upon-a-time-in-hollywood-controversy-bruce-lee-sharon-tate-women-explained-tarantino. Accessed 16 June 2020.

———. "Why Cultural Criticism Matters." *Vox.com*, 31 Dec. 2018, https://www.vox.com/culture/2018/12/31/18152275/criticism-explained-cultural-writing. Accessed 26 Jan. 2019.

Vary, Adam B. "'Brave' Director Brenda Chapman Breaks Silence on Being Taken off Film." *Entertainment Weekly*, 15 Aug. 2012, https://ew.com/article/2012/08/15/brave-director-brenda-chapman-breaks-silence-getting-taken-off-film-heartbreaking-devastating-distressing/.

Vultaggio, Maria. "Searches for 'Contagion movie' Spike on Google." *Statista*, 5 Mar. 2020, https://www.statista.com/chart/21053/contagion-movie-google-searches-coronavirus/. Accessed 28 July 2020.

Wall, Howard J. "The "Man-Cession" of 2008–2009: Big but Not Unusual." *Federal Reserve Bank of St. Louis*, 1 Oct. 2009, https://www.stlouisfed.org/publications/regional-economist/october-2009/the-mancession-of-20082009-its-big-but-its-not-great. Accessed 8 June 2020.

Wallace, Carvell. "Why *Black Panther* Is a Defining Moment for Black America." *The New York Times Magazine*, 12 Feb. 2018, https://www.nytimes.com/2018/02/12/magazine/why-black-panther-is-a-defining-moment   for-black-america.html?searchResultPosition=1.

Ward, Alex. "Trump Once Suggested All of Seoul's 10 Million Residents Move to Avoid North Korean Threat." *Vox.com*, 5 Dec. 2019, https://www.vox.com/world/2019/12/5/20996986/trump-seoul-north-korea-move-bergen-book. Accessed 11 July 2020.

Weeks, Linton. "10 Takeaways from the 2010 Midterms." *NPR.org*, https://www.npr.org/templates/story/story.php?storyId=131039717. Accessed 1 June 2020.

Weinstein, Joshua L. "Exclusive: Jennifer Lawrence Gets Lead Role in 'The Hunger Games.'" *TheWrap*, 16 Mar. 2011, https://www.thewrap.com/jennifer-lawrence-gets-lead-role-hunger-games-25482/.

Weiss, Sasha. "The Culture Issue." *The New York Times Magazine*, 13 Oct. 2019, p. 19.

Whalen, Andrew. "'Captain Marvel' Is the Latest Superhero Movie to Promote the U.S. Military." *Newsweek*, 1 Mar. 2019, www.newsweek.com/captain-marvel-superhero-movies-air-force-comic-book-military-promotion-1348486?amp=1&_twitter_impression=true.

Whissel, Kristen. "The Digital Multitude." *Cinema Journal*, vol. 49, no. 4, Summer 2010.

Whitten, Sarah. "The Death of the DVD: Why Sales Dropped More Than 86% in 13 Years." *CNBC*, 8 Nov. 2019, https://www.cnbc.com/2019/11/08/the-death-of-the-dvd-why -sales-dropped-more-than-86percent-in-13-years.html. Accessed 18 Oct. 2020.

Wilentz, Sean. "The Lost Cause and the Won Cause." *The New Republic*, 31 Dec. 2012, pp. 28–34.

Wilkinson, Alissa. "*Arrival* Is a Stunning Science Fiction Movie with Deep Implications for Today." *Vox*, 4 Nov. 2016.

———. "*Hereditary* Is the Terrifying Arthouse Horror Film of the Year." *Vox*, 10 June 2018, https://www.vox.com/summermovies/2018/6/1/17408988/hereditary-review-toni -collette-milly-shapiro.

Williams, Linda. "Film Bodies: Gender, Genre and Excess." *Film Quarterly*, vol. 44, no. 4, Summer 1991, pp. 2–13.

Willmore, Alison. "*Three Billboards* Is an Unfortunate Metaphor for Our Complicated Cultural Moment." *BuzzFeed News*, 2 Dec. 2017, https://www.buzzfeednews.com/article /alisonwillmore/three-billboards-outside-ebbing-missouri#.nmZP9L3G4.

Wloszczyna, Susan. "Beatriz at Dinner." *RogerEbert.com*, 9 June 2017, https://www.rogerebert .com/reviews/beatriz-at-dinner-2017.

———. "Why Pixar Whiz Pete Docter Decided to Enter a Young Girl's Mind—and Turn Your Emotions Inside Out." *IndieWire*, 11 June 2015, http://blogs.indiewire.com /womenandhollywood/why-pixar-whiz-pete-docter-decided-to-enter-a-young-girls -mind-and-turn-your-emotions-inside-out-20150611. Accessed 1 May 2020.

Wolf, Naomi. "A Letter to Kathryn Bigelow on Zero Dark Thirty's Apology for Torture." *The Guardian*, 4 Jan. 2013, https://www.theguardian.com/commentisfree/2013/jan/04 /letter-kathryn-bigelow-zero-dark-thirty.

Yglesias, Matthew. "The Great Awokening," *Vox*, 1 Apr. 2019, https://www.vox.com/2019/3 /22/18259865/great-awokening-white-liberals-race-polling-trump-2020. Accessed 23 Aug. 2019.

Zacharek, Stephanie. "*Joker* Wants to Be a Movie about the Emptiness of Our Culture. Instead, It's a Prime Example of It." *Time*, 31 Aug. 2019, https://time.com/5666055 /venice-joker-review-joaquin-phoenix-not-funny/. Accessed 19 Oct. 2020.

———. "The Problem with *Joker* Isn't Its Brutal Violence. It's the Muddled Message It Sends about Our Times." *Time*, 2 Oct. 2019, https://time.com/5688305/joker-todd-phillips -review/. Accessed 19 Oct. 2020.

Zaman, Farihah. "Boots Riley & Questlove/*Sorry to Bother You*/Film Comment Talk." *Film at Lincoln Center*, 15 Aug. 2018. https://www.youtube.com/watch?v=p88GDNZH81w.

Zareksky, David. "*Lincoln* and Historical Accuracy." *Rhetoric & Public Affairs*, vol. 18, no. 1, Spring 2015, pp. 155–159.

CONTRIBUTORS

CYNTHIA BARON is a professor in the Department of Theatre and Film, and an affiliated faculty in the American culture studies and women's, gender, and sexuality studies programs at Bowling Green State University. She is the author of *Modern Acting: The Lost Chapter of American Film and Theatre* and *Denzel Washington*. She is the co-author of *Appetites and Anxieties: Food, Film, and the Politics of Representation* and *Reframing Screen Performance*. She is co-editor of *More Than a Method: Trends and Traditions in Film Performance* and is currently completing the co-authored book *Acting Indie: Aesthetics, Industry, and Performance*. She is the BGSU Research Scholar of Excellence for 2017–2020.

DENNIS BINGHAM is professor of English and director of film studies at Indiana University–Purdue University Indianapolis. He is the author of *Whose Lives Are They Anyway?: The Biopic as Contemporary Film Genre* and *Acting Male: Masculinities in the Films of James Stewart, Clint Eastwood, and Jack Nicholson*, and numerous articles and book chapters on gender, genre, stardom, and acting.

LISA BODE is senior lecturer in film and TV studies at University of Queensland, Australia. She is the author of *Making Believe: Screen Performance and Special Effects in Popular Cinema* and several articles on animation and digital actors.

MIKAL J. GAINES is an assistant professor of English at Massachusetts College of Pharmacy and Health Sciences University in Boston. His research focuses primarily on Black film, media, and cultural studies, horror studies, and spectatorship. His work can be found in *Fight the Power: The Spike Lee Reader*, *Merchants of Menace: The Business of Horror Cinema*, and in other forthcoming anthologies, including *The Spaces and Places of Horror* and *Approaching Get Out*. He is also a spoken word artist who performs regularly in the Boston area.

DAVID GREVEN is professor of English at the University of South Carolina. He is the author of *Intimate Violence: Hitchcock, Sex, and Queer Theory*, *Queering the Terminator*, and the Lambda Literary Award Finalist *Ghost Faces: Hollywood and Post-Millennial Masculinity*, among other books.

RAYMOND HABERSKI JR. is professor of history and director of American studies at IUPUI. He also directs the Institute for American Thought and is part of the Center for the Study of Religion and American Culture. For the 2008–2009 academic year, he held the Fulbright Danish Distinguished Chair in American Studies at the Copenhagen Business School. Haberski is trained in twentieth-century U.S. history with a focus on intellectual history, and his books include *It's Only a Movie: Films and Critics in American Culture*; *Freedom to Offend: How New York Remade Movie Culture*; *The Miracle Case: Film Censorship and the Supreme Court*; *God and War: American Civil Religion Since 1945*; *Voice of Empathy: A History of Franciscan Media in the United States*; with Andrew Hartman, edited *American Labyrinth: Intellectual History for Complicated Times*, and with Philip Goff and Rhys Williams, edited *Civil Religion Today*.

ALEXANDRA KELLER is professor of film and media studies at Smith College, and director of the Kahn Liberal Arts Institute. She specializes in the American Western; cinema and the postmodern, avant-garde, and experimental film; and the relationship between cinema and other forms of artistic and cultural production, and has published work on all of these topics.

JULIE LEVINSON is professor of Film and chair of the Arts and Humanities Division at Babson College. She is the author of *The American Success Myth on Film*, editor of *Alexander Payne: Interviews*, and co-editor of *Acting*, part of the ten-volume *Behind the Silver Screen* film history series. Her publications in journals and edited collections focus on a wide range of topics, including genre and gender, narrative theory, and documentary film. She has served as a film curator for the Institute of Contemporary Art in Boston, the New England Foundation for the Arts, the Boston Film/Video Foundation, and other museums and arts institutions. She has also been a panelist for such organizations as the National Endowment for the Arts, the Rockefeller Foundation, and the Radcliffe Institute for Advanced Study at Harvard University.

MICHELE SCHREIBER is an associate professor in the Department of Film and Media Studies at Emory University. She is the co-editor of *Indie Reframed: Women's Filmmaking and Contemporary American Independent Cinema* and the author of *American Postfeminist Cinema: Women, Romance and Contemporary Culture*.

DANIEL SMITH-ROWSEY is an instructor, writer, and award-winning filmmaker. He teaches media and communication studies at St. Mary's College in California. He is the author of the book *Blockbuster Performances*. His most recent short documentary, "The Fair Damsels of Disney," was an official selection at several festivals.

INDEX

Page numbers in italics refer to illustrations.

Giffords, Gabrielle, 55
Gigliotti, Donna, 183
G.I. Joe: The Rise of Cobra (Stephen Sommers, 2009), 128
Gilbert, Elizabeth, 36
Gilroy, Dan, 179
"Girls" (HBO, 2012–2017), 102
Girls Trip (Malcolm D. Lee, 2017), 198
Giuliani-Hoffman, Francesca, 6
Gladiator (Ridley Scott, 2000), 178
Gladstone, Lily, 176
Glamour, 6
Gleiberman, Owen, 24, 180–181
Glenn, John, 175
"Glory" (song), 138
Glover, Danny, 237
Glover, Donald, 221–222
"Glow" (Netflix, 2017–2019), 221
Godzilla (Gareth Edwards, 2014), 126
Going the Distance (Nanette Burstein, 2010), 36
Golden Globe awards, 222
Golden State Warriors, 9, 175, 243
Goldman, William, 219
Goldsberry, Renée Elise, 8
Gomez, Serena, 172
Gone Girl (David Fincher, 2014), 126
Good, the Bad, and the Weird, The (Jee-woon Kim, 2008), 188
Goodfellas (Martin Scorsese, 1990), 258, 260, 262
"Good Fight, The" (CBS, 2017–), 195
"Good Morning, America" (ABC, 1975–), 156
"Good Place, The" (NBC, 2016–2020), 221
"Good Wife, The" (CBS, 2009–2016), 35
Google, 20, 174
Goränsson, Ludwig, 14, 224
Gorsuch, Neil, 197
Gosling, Ryan, 65, 183
Graf, Steffi, 124
Graham, Billy, 219
Grammy Awards, 194, 222, 242
Grand Budapest Hotel, The (Wes Anderson, 2014), 11, 126
Grand Canyon, 245
Grande, Ariana, 172
Granger, Farley, 57
Granik, Debra, 37
Grant, Oscar, 15, 115–116, 122n3
Grant, Ulysses S., 88
Gravity (Alfonso Cuarón, 2013), 30, 103, 105, 145, 182

Grayson, Kathryn, 10
"Great Awokening, The," 124, 134
Greatest Generation, 85
Greatest Showman, The (Michael Gracey, 2017), 25, 31
Great Gatsby, The (Baz Luhrmann, 2013), 31
Great Recession (2007–09), 1, 2, 3, 7, 32, 100, 104, 241, 254
Green, John, 126
Green Book (Peter Farrelly, 2018), 220, 223
"Green Hornet, The," (ABC, 1966–1967), 250
Green Lantern (Martin Campbell, 2011), 131
Gregory, Dick, 196
Greven, David, 74n3
Grier, Pam, 248
Grierson, Tim, 233
Griffith, Andy, 10, 78
Griffith, D.W., 249
Griffiths, Rachel, 108
Grossman, Jim, 89
Grossman, Lev, 34
Guardians of the Galaxy (James Gunn, 2014), 12, 13, *126*, 130–132, *130*, 143, 146
Guardians of the Galaxy, Vol. 2 (James Gunn, 2017), 19
Guess Who's Coming to Dinner (Stanley Kramer, 1967), 201
Guillermin, John, 149
Guizi lai le (*Devils on the Doorstep*) (Jiang Wen, 2000), 178
Gunn, James, 13, 131
"Gunsmoke" (CBS, 1955–1975), 246
Gupta, Sanjay, Dr., 22
Gurira, Danai, 15, 226
Gyllenhaal, Jake, 58–62, 257

H1N1 ("Swine Flu" pandemic), 34
Haaland, Deb, 218
Hacksaw Ridge (Mel Gibson, 2016), 189
Hader, Bill, 167
Hadestown (stage musical), 9, 242
Haenel, Adèle, 17
Hail Caesar! (Joel Coen, Ethan Coen, 2016), 11
Hainey, Daniel, 19
Halberstam, Jack, 42
Halloween (David Gordon Green, 2018), 220

Printed in the United States
by Baker & Taylor Publisher Services